he pages in this book were
GHT-to-LEFT format. No a
can read the stories the wa

IGHT TO LEFT?!

aditional Japanese manga starts
the upper right-hand corner, and
oves right-to-left as it goes down
e page. Follow this guide for an
sy understanding.

r more information and sneak
eviews, visit cmxmanga.com.
ll 1-888-COMIC BOOK for
e nearest comics shop or
ad to your local book store.

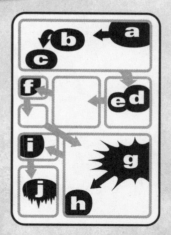

LAPISLAZULI NO OUKAN by Natsuna Kawase © 2004 by
Natsuna Kawase. All rights reserved. First published in
Japan in 2005 by HAKUSENSHA. INC., Tokyo.

THE LAPIS LAZULI CROWN Volume 2, published by
WildStorm Productions, an imprint of DC Comics. 888
Prospect St. #240. La Jolla, CA 92037. English Translation
© 2009. All Rights Reserved. English translation rights in
U.S.A. And Canada arranged with HAKUSENSHA. INC.,
through Tuttle-Mori Agency, Inc., Tokyo. CMX is a trade-
mark of DC Comics. The stories, characters, and incidents
mentioned in this magazine are entirely fictional. Printed
on recyclable paper. WildStorm does not read or accept
unsolicited submissions of ideas, stories or artwork.
Printed in Canada.

This book is manufactured at a facility holding chain-of-
custody certification. This paper is made with sustainably
managed North American fiber.

DC Comics, a Warner Bros. Entertainment Company.

Sheldon Drzka – Translation and Adaptation
MPS Ad Studio – Lettering
Larry Berry – Design
Sarah Farber – Assistant Editor
Jim Chadwick – Editor

ISBN: 978-1-4012-2121-8

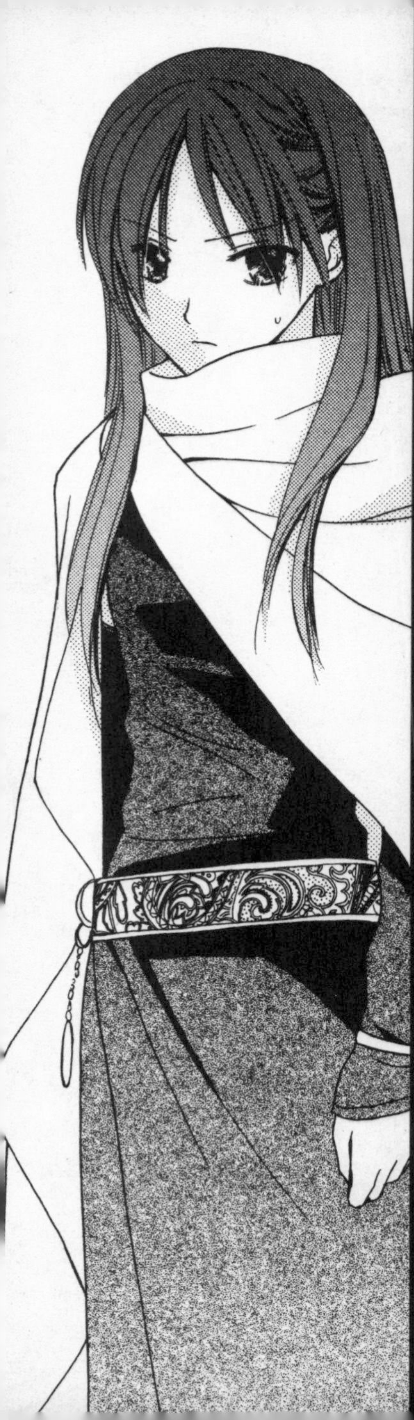

KNOW WHAT'S INSIDE

With the wide variety of manga available, CMX understands it can be confusing to determine age-appropriate material. We rate our books in four categories: EVERYONE, TEEN, TEEN + and MATURE. For the TEEN, TEEN + and MATURE categories, we include additional, specific descriptions to assist consumers in determining if the book is age appropriate. (Our MATURE books are shipped shrink-wrapped with a Parental Advisory sticker affixed to the wrapper.)

E

EVERYONE

Titles with this rating are appropriate for all age readers. They contain no offensive material. They may contain mild violence and/or some comic mischief.

T

TEEN

Titles with this rating are appropriate for a teen audience and older. They may contain some violent content, language, and/or suggestive themes.

T+

TEEN PLUS

Titles with this rating are appropriate for an audience of 16 and older. They may contain partial nudity, mild profanity and more intense violence.

M

MATURE

Titles with this rating are appropriate only for mature readers. They may contain graphic violence, nudity, sex and content suitable only for older readers.

CMX

The Palette of 12 Secret Colors

Volume 6

By Nari Kusakawa. Cello, the aspiring color wizard, is struggling to g[e]
through her final exams. It's not helping that's she's just learned that Dr. Gue[ll]
may be leaving the island for good and is keeping this information secret fro[m]
her. Having just admitted their true feelings for each other, she thought they [']
be together forever. Could the goal she's struggled so hard to achieve now [be]
slipping away from her due to a broken heart? Is there any way Dr. Guell ca[n]
be talked into staying? Find out what happens to the young couple, the[ir]
friends, and all their colorful bird partners in this final volume.

JYUNI HISOKU NO PALETTE © 2003 Nari Kusakawa/HAKUSENSHA. INC.

THE LAPIS LAZULI CROWN

Volume 2

By Natsuna Kawase

CONTENTS

3 **Chapter 4**

43 **Chapter 5**

83 **Chapter 6**

133 **Final Chapter**

183 **Author's Post
    Script**

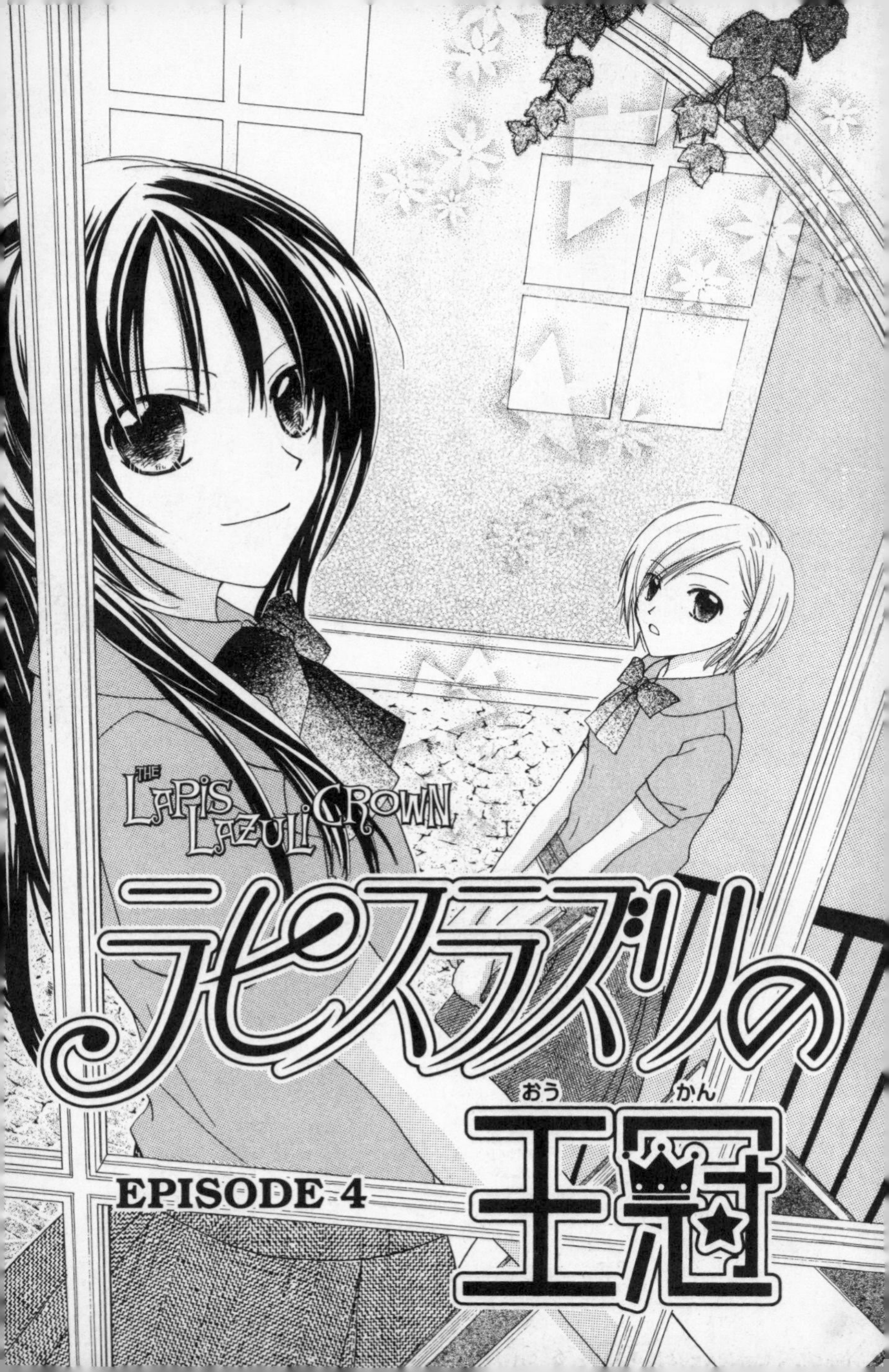
THE LAPIS LAZULI CROWN
ラピスラズリの王冠
おうかん
EPISODE 4

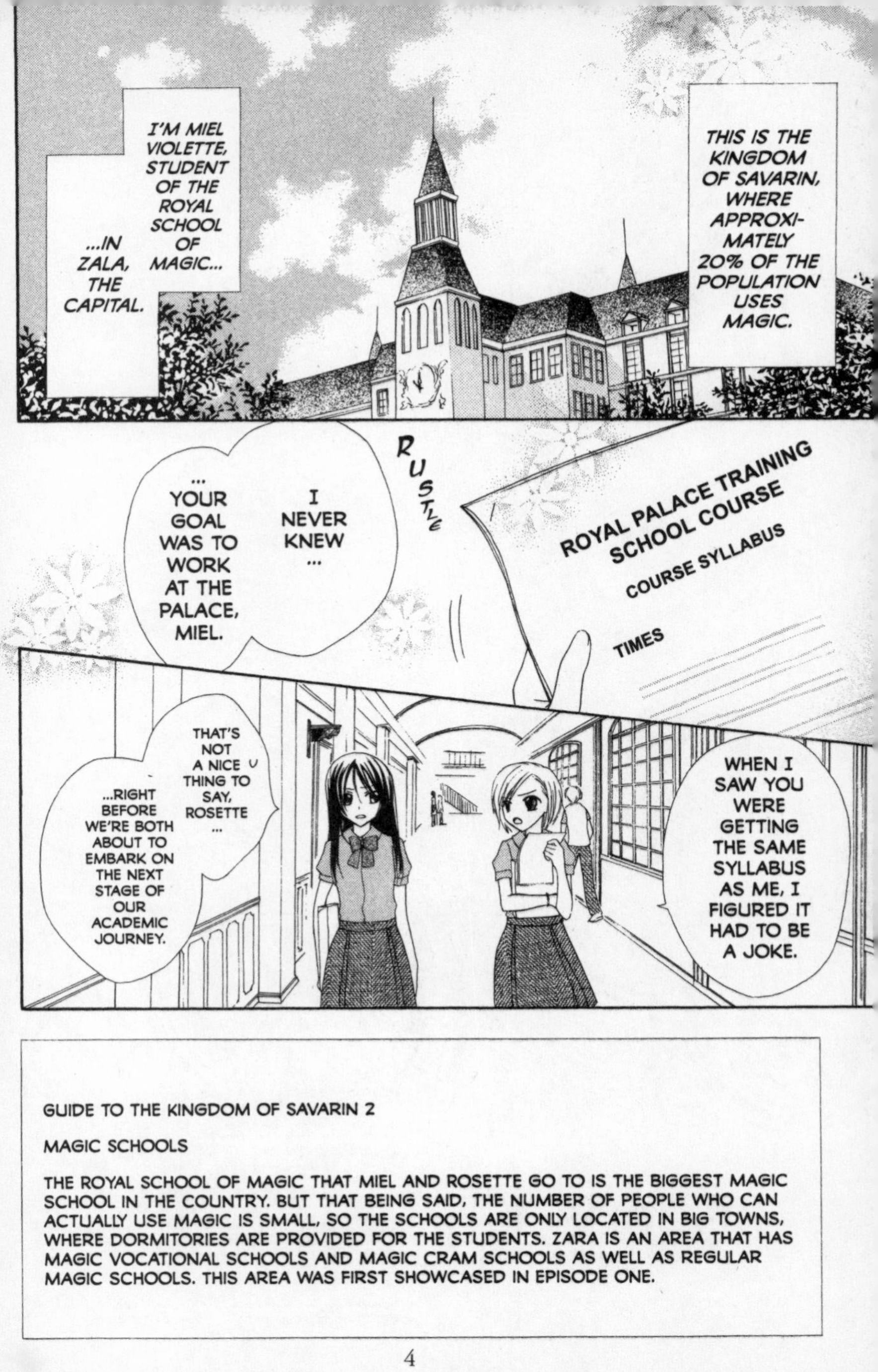
THIS IS THE KINGDOM OF SAVARIN, WHERE APPROXIMATELY 20% OF THE POPULATION USES MAGIC.
I'M MIEL VIOLETTE, STUDENT OF THE ROYAL SCHOOL OF MAGIC...
...IN ZALA, THE CAPITAL.
ROYAL PALACE TRAINING SCHOOL COURSE
COURSE SYLLABUS
TIMES
RUSTLE
I NEVER KNEW ...
... YOUR GOAL WAS TO WORK AT THE PALACE, MIEL.
WHEN I SAW YOU WERE GETTING THE SAME SYLLABUS AS ME, I FIGURED IT HAD TO BE A JOKE.
THAT'S NOT A NICE THING TO SAY, ROSETTE ...
...RIGHT BEFORE WE'RE BOTH ABOUT TO EMBARK ON THE NEXT STAGE OF OUR ACADEMIC JOURNEY.

GUIDE TO THE KINGDOM OF SAVARIN 2

MAGIC SCHOOLS

THE ROYAL SCHOOL OF MAGIC THAT MIEL AND ROSETTE GO TO IS THE BIGGEST MAGIC SCHOOL IN THE COUNTRY. BUT THAT BEING SAID, THE NUMBER OF PEOPLE WHO CAN ACTUALLY USE MAGIC IS SMALL, SO THE SCHOOLS ARE ONLY LOCATED IN BIG TOWNS, WHERE DORMITORIES ARE PROVIDED FOR THE STUDENTS. ZARA IS AN AREA THAT HAS MAGIC VOCATIONAL SCHOOLS AND MAGIC CRAM SCHOOLS AS WELL AS REGULAR MAGIC SCHOOLS. THIS AREA WAS FIRST SHOWCASED IN EPISODE ONE.

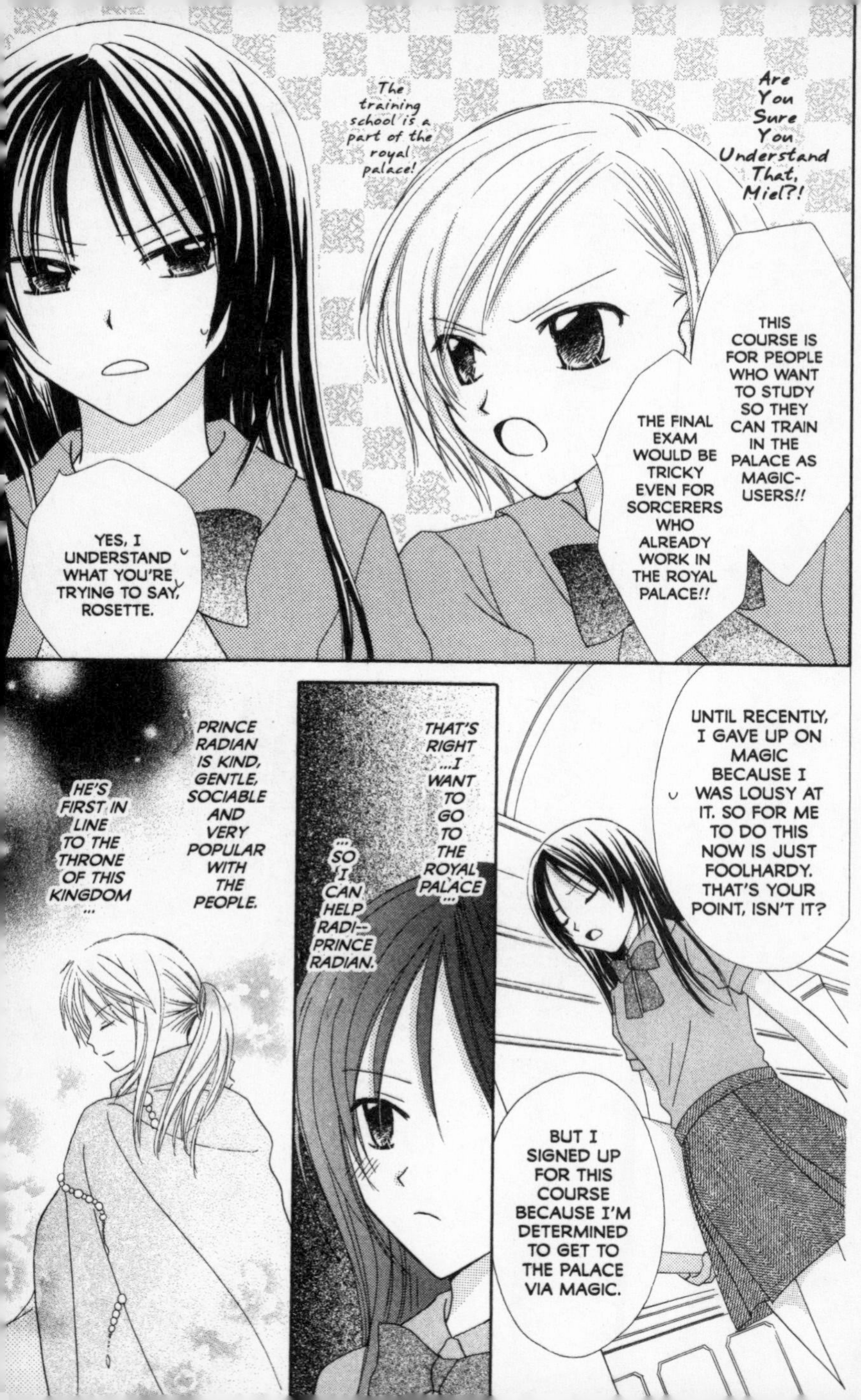
Are You Sure You Understand That, Miel?!
The training school is a part of the royal palace!
THIS COURSE IS FOR PEOPLE WHO WANT TO STUDY SO THEY CAN TRAIN IN THE PALACE AS MAGIC-USERS!!
THE FINAL EXAM WOULD BE TRICKY EVEN FOR SORCERERS WHO ALREADY WORK IN THE ROYAL PALACE!!
YES, I UNDERSTAND WHAT YOU'RE TRYING TO SAY, ROSETTE.
UNTIL RECENTLY, I GAVE UP ON MAGIC BECAUSE I WAS LOUSY AT IT. SO FOR ME TO DO THIS NOW IS JUST FOOLHARDY. THAT'S YOUR POINT, ISN'T IT?
BUT I SIGNED UP FOR THIS COURSE BECAUSE I'M DETERMINED TO GET TO THE PALACE VIA MAGIC.
THAT'S RIGHT ...I WANT TO GO TO THE ROYAL PALACE ...
... SO I CAN HELP RADI-- PRINCE RADIAN.
PRINCE RADIAN IS KIND, GENTLE, SOCIABLE AND VERY POPULAR WITH THE PEOPLE.
HE'S FIRST IN LINE TO THE THRONE OF THIS KINGDOM ...

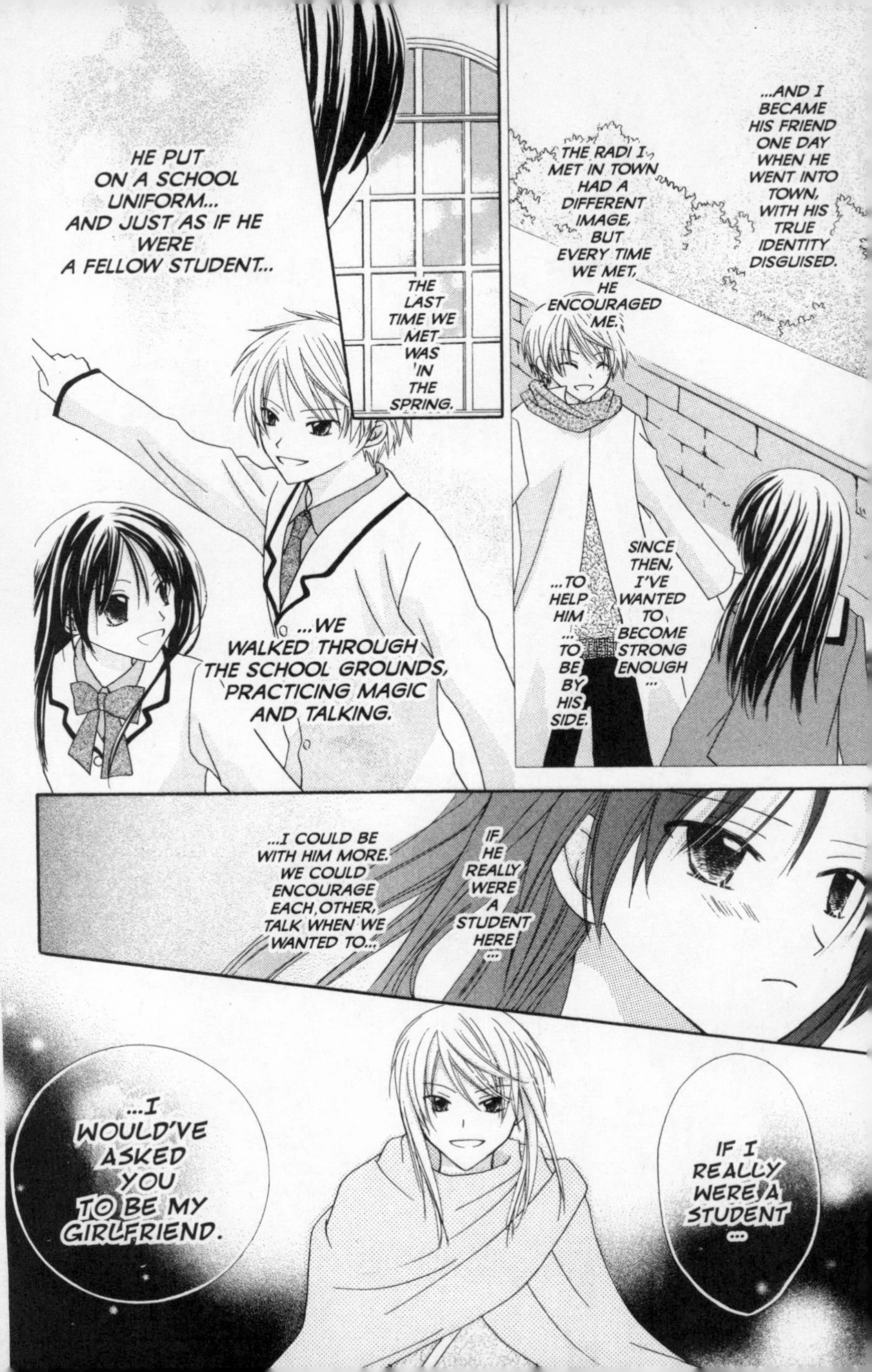
...AND I BECAME HIS FRIEND ONE DAY WHEN HE WENT INTO TOWN, WITH HIS TRUE IDENTITY DISGUISED.
THE RADI I MET IN TOWN HAD A DIFFERENT IMAGE, BUT EVERY TIME WE MET, HE ENCOURAGED ME.
SINCE THEN, I'VE WANTED TO BECOME STRONG ENOUGH...
...TO HELP HIM ... TO BE BY HIS SIDE.
THE LAST TIME WE MET WAS IN THE SPRING.
HE PUT ON A SCHOOL UNIFORM... AND JUST AS IF HE WERE A FELLOW STUDENT...
...WE WALKED THROUGH THE SCHOOL GROUNDS, PRACTICING MAGIC AND TALKING.
IF HE REALLY WERE A STUDENT HERE...
...I COULD BE WITH HIM MORE. WE COULD ENCOURAGE EACH OTHER, TALK WHEN WE WANTED TO...
IF I REALLY WERE A STUDENT...
...I WOULD'VE ASKED YOU TO BE MY GIRLFRIEND.

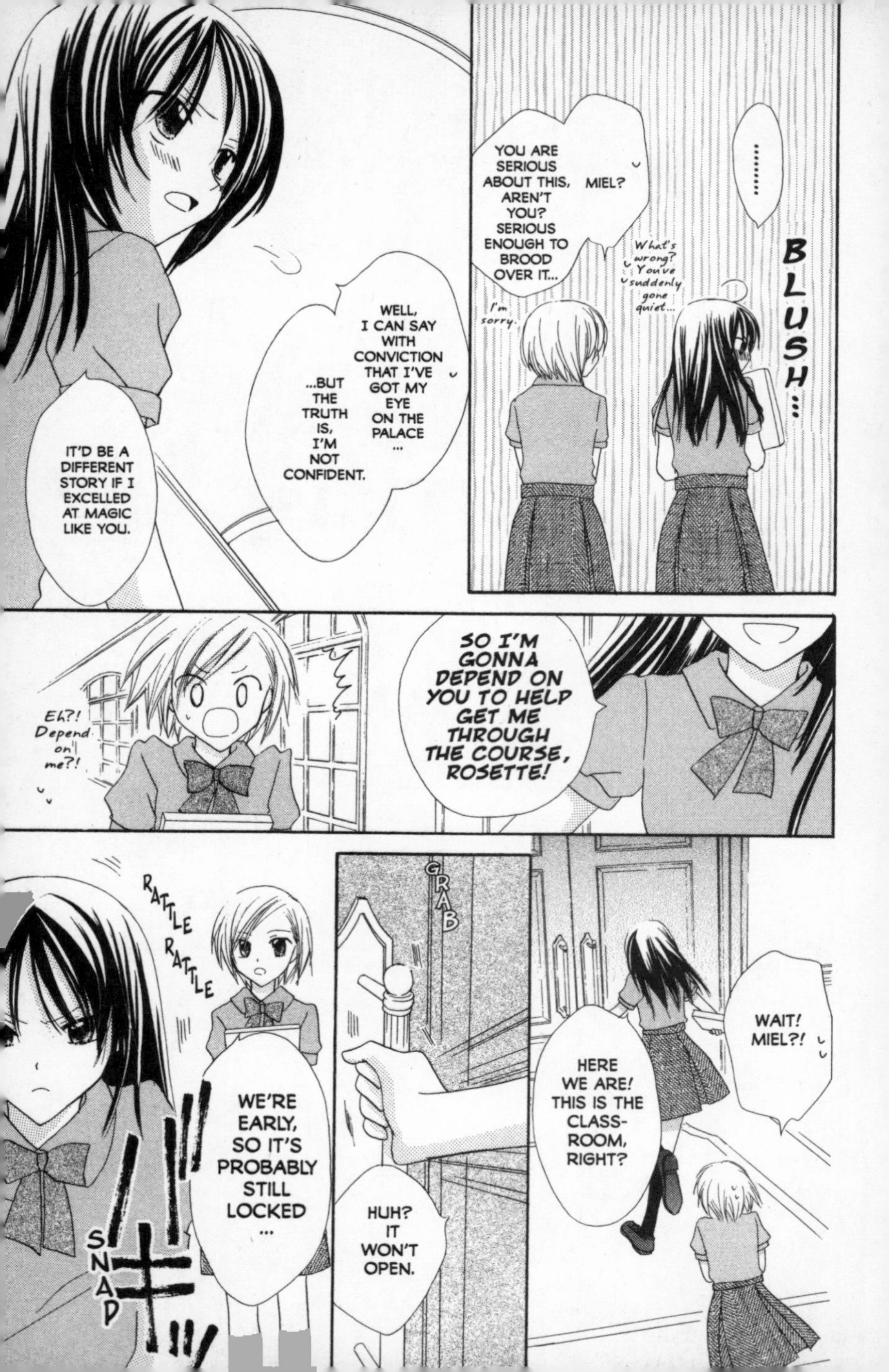
……
BLUSH…
What's wrong? You've suddenly gone quiet…
YOU ARE SERIOUS ABOUT THIS, MIEL? AREN'T YOU? SERIOUS ENOUGH TO BROOD OVER IT…
I'm sorry.
WELL, I CAN SAY WITH CONVICTION THAT I'VE GOT MY EYE ON THE PALACE …
…BUT THE TRUTH IS, I'M NOT CONFIDENT.
IT'D BE A DIFFERENT STORY IF I EXCELLED AT MAGIC LIKE YOU.
SO I'M GONNA DEPEND ON YOU TO HELP GET ME THROUGH THE COURSE, ROSETTE!
Eh?! Depend on me?!
WAIT! MIEL?!
HERE WE ARE! THIS IS THE CLASS-ROOM, RIGHT?
GRAB
HUH? IT WON'T OPEN.
RATTLE RATTLE
WE'RE EARLY, SO IT'S PROBABLY STILL LOCKED …
SNAP

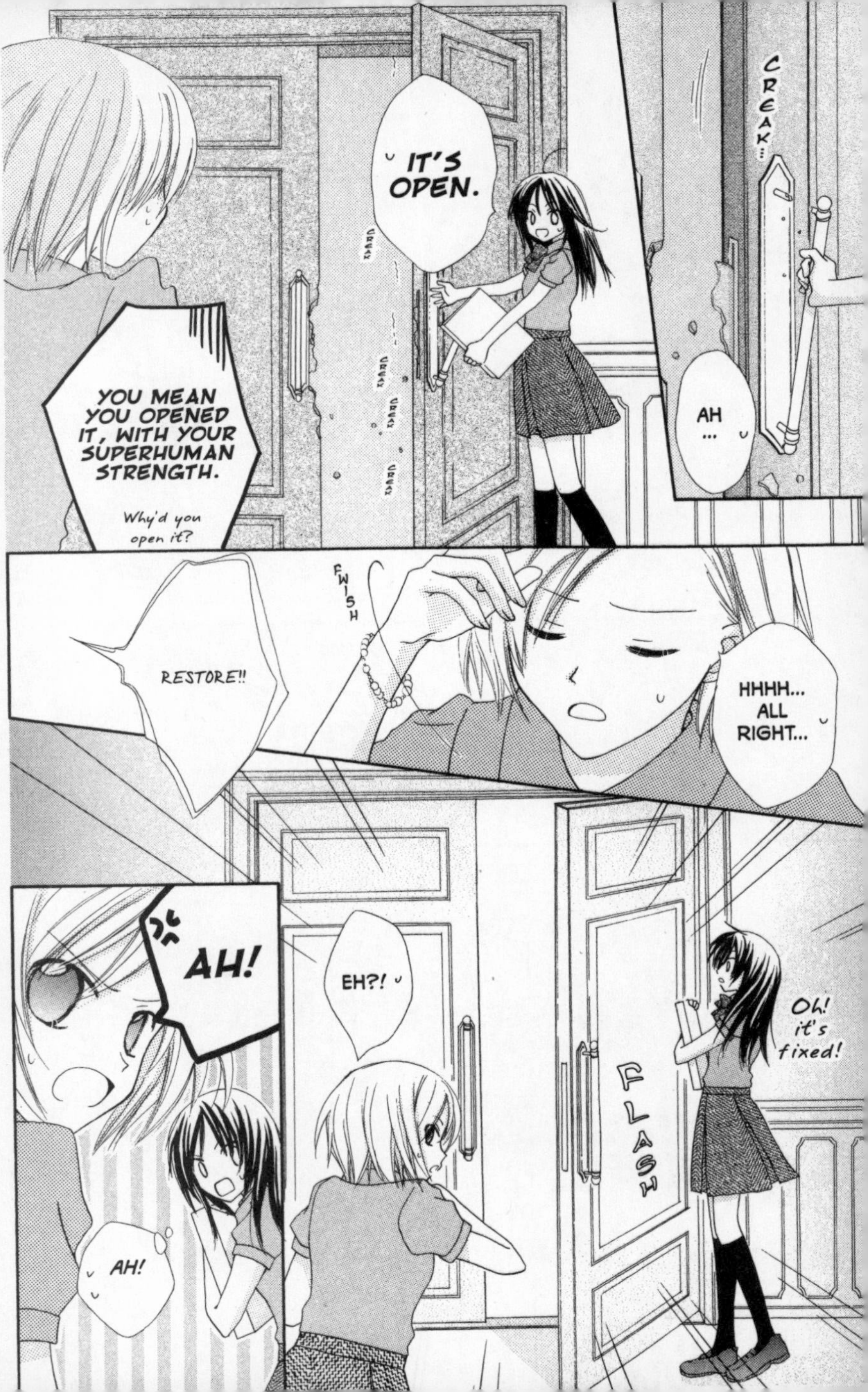
CREAK...
AH ...
IT'S OPEN.
CREAK
CREAK
CREAK
CREAK
YOU MEAN YOU OPENED IT, WITH YOUR SUPERHUMAN STRENGTH.
Why'd you open it?
HHHH... ALL RIGHT...
FWISH
RESTORE!!
Oh! it's fixed!
FLASH
EH?!
AH!
AH!

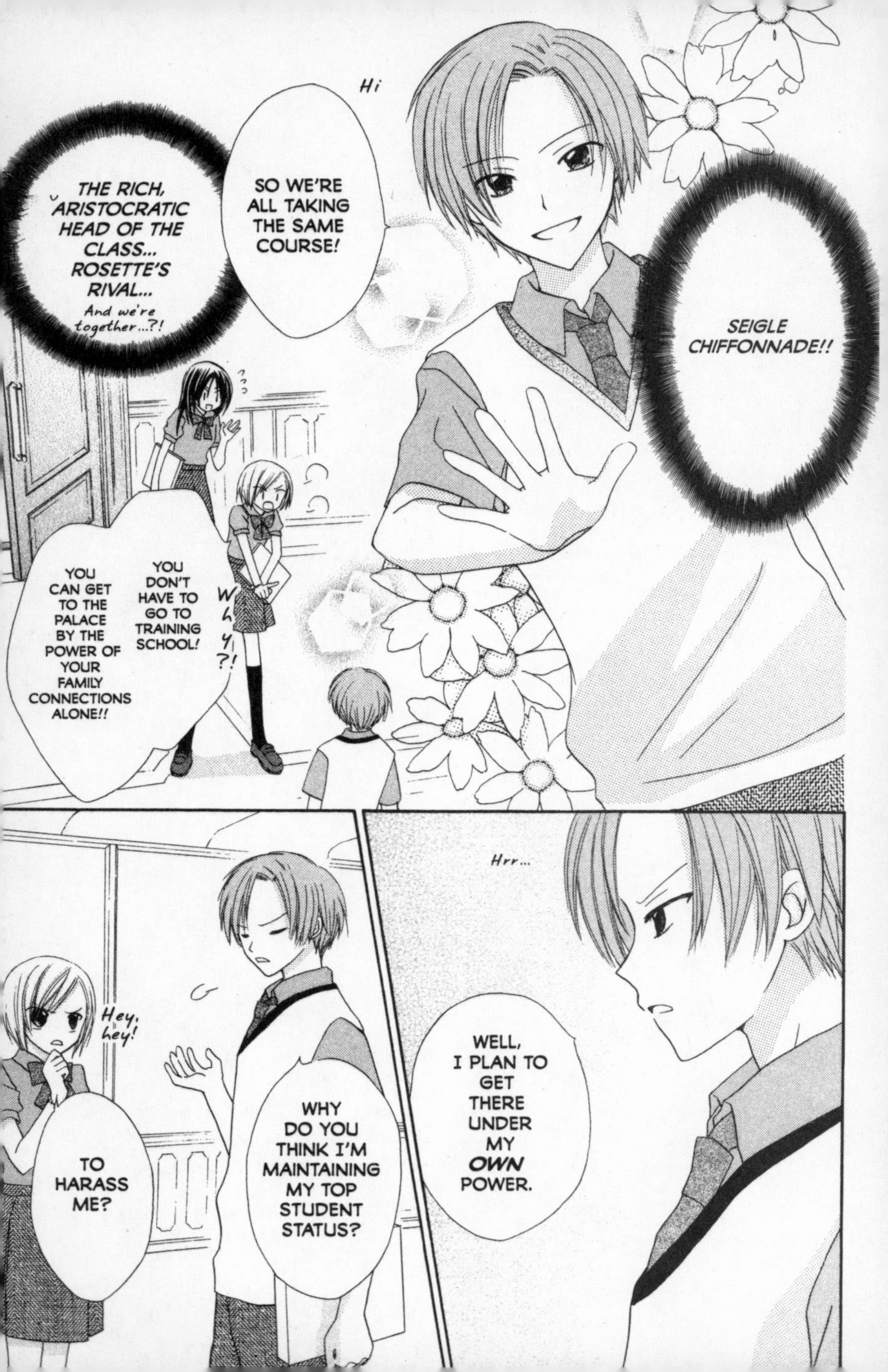
Hi
SO WE'RE ALL TAKING THE SAME COURSE!
THE RICH, ARISTOCRATIC HEAD OF THE CLASS... ROSETTE'S RIVAL...
And we're together...?!
SEIGLE CHIFFONNADE!!
YOU DON'T HAVE TO GO TO TRAINING SCHOOL!
Why?!
YOU CAN GET TO THE PALACE BY THE POWER OF YOUR FAMILY CONNECTIONS ALONE!!
Hrr...
WELL, I PLAN TO GET THERE UNDER MY *OWN* POWER.
WHY DO YOU THINK I'M MAINTAINING MY TOP STUDENT STATUS?
Hey, hey!
TO HARASS ME?

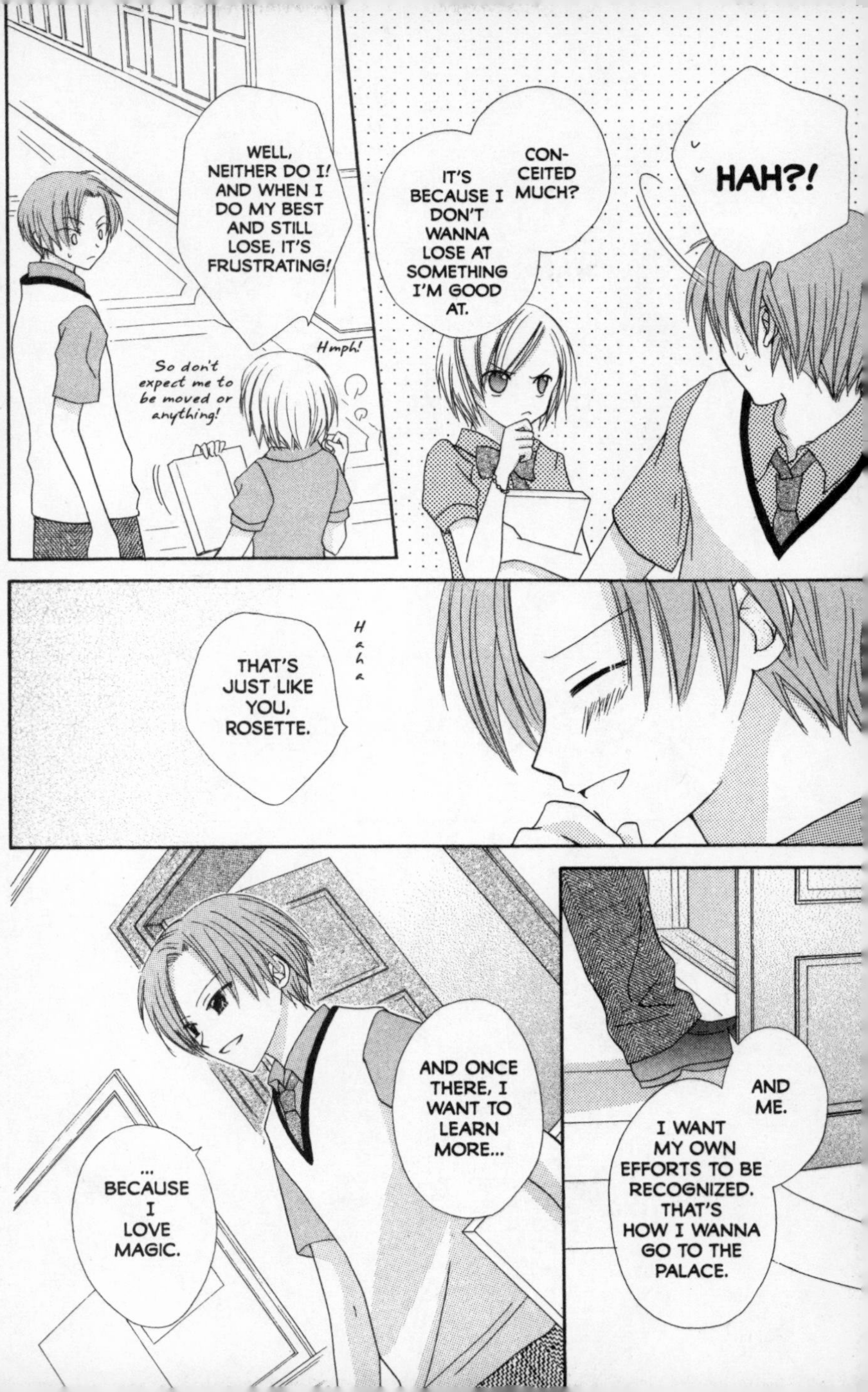
HAH?!
CON-CEITED MUCH?
IT'S BECAUSE I DON'T WANNA LOSE AT SOMETHING I'M GOOD AT.
WELL, NEITHER DO I! AND WHEN I DO MY BEST AND STILL LOSE, IT'S FRUSTRATING!
Hmph!
So don't expect me to be moved or anything!
Haha
THAT'S JUST LIKE YOU, ROSETTE.
AND ME.
I WANT MY OWN EFFORTS TO BE RECOGNIZED. THAT'S HOW I WANNA GO TO THE PALACE.
AND ONCE THERE, I WANT TO LEARN MORE...
...BECAUSE I LOVE MAGIC.

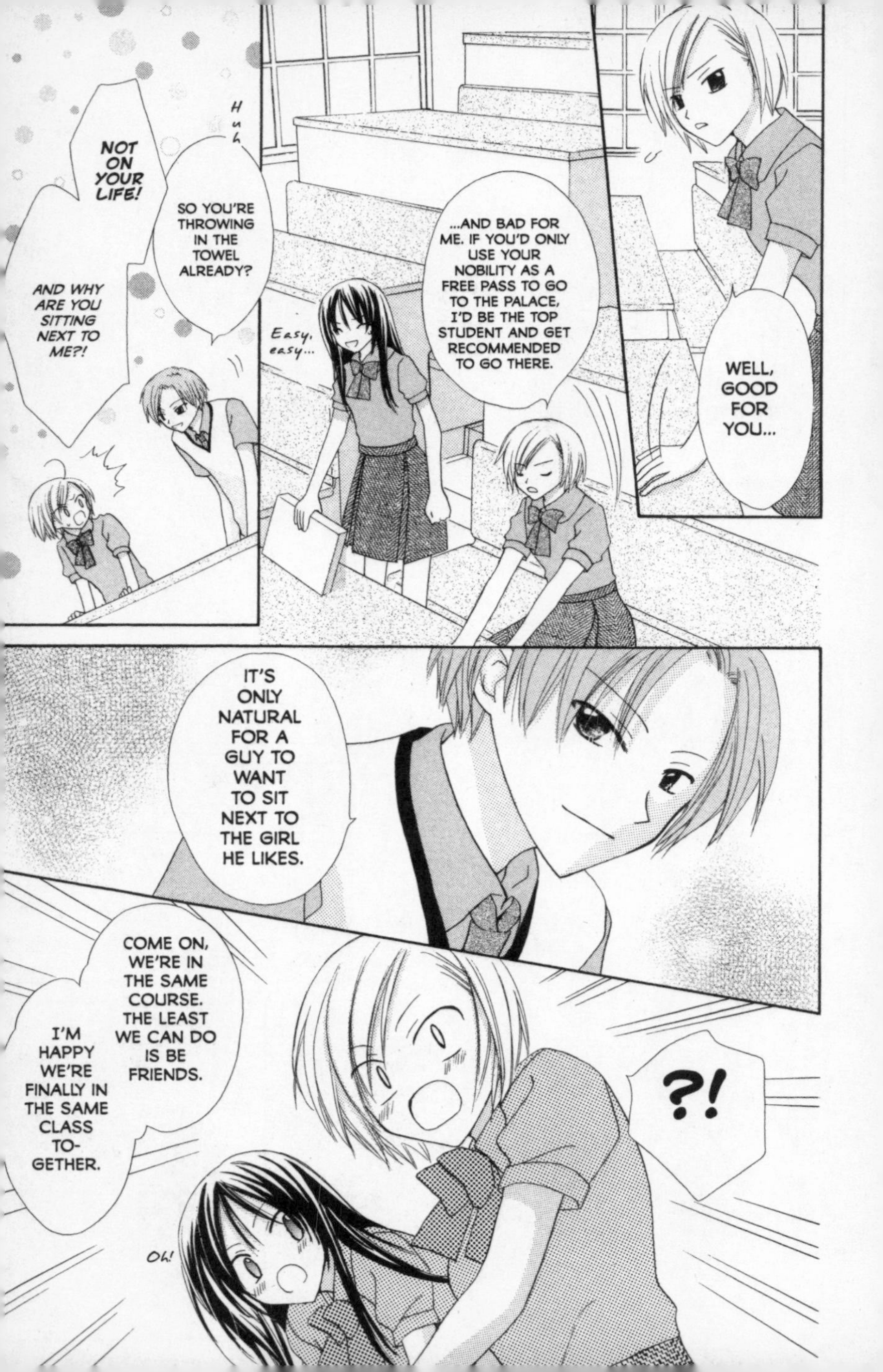
WELL, GOOD FOR YOU...
...AND BAD FOR ME. IF YOU'D ONLY USE YOUR NOBILITY AS A FREE PASS TO GO TO THE PALACE, I'D BE THE TOP STUDENT AND GET RECOMMENDED TO GO THERE.
Easy, easy...
Huh
SO YOU'RE THROWING IN THE TOWEL ALREADY?
NOT ON YOUR LIFE!
AND WHY ARE YOU SITTING NEXT TO ME?!
IT'S ONLY NATURAL FOR A GUY TO WANT TO SIT NEXT TO THE GIRL HE LIKES.
?!
COME ON, WE'RE IN THE SAME COURSE. THE LEAST WE CAN DO IS BE FRIENDS.
I'M HAPPY WE'RE FINALLY IN THE SAME CLASS TO-GETHER.
Oh!

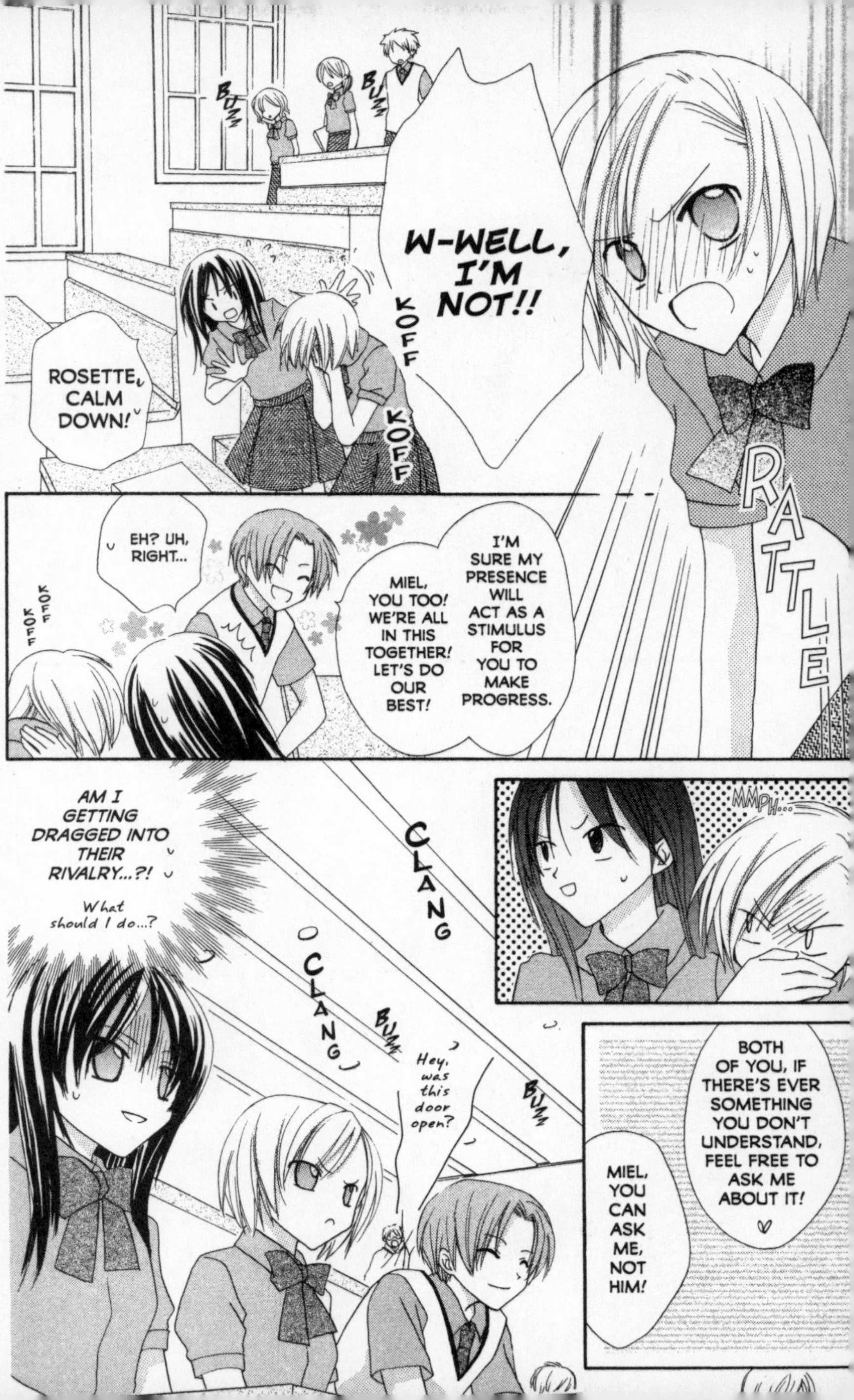
W-WELL, I'M NOT!!
RATTLE
BUZZ
BUZZ
KOFF
KOFF
ROSETTE, CALM DOWN!
I'M SURE MY PRESENCE WILL ACT AS A STIMULUS FOR YOU TO MAKE PROGRESS.
MIEL, YOU TOO! WE'RE ALL IN THIS TOGETHER! LET'S DO OUR BEST!
EH? UH, RIGHT...
KOFF KOFF
MMPH...
BOTH OF YOU, IF THERE'S EVER SOMETHING YOU DON'T UNDERSTAND, FEEL FREE TO ASK ME ABOUT IT!
MIEL, YOU CAN ASK ME, NOT HIM!
AM I GETTING DRAGGED INTO THEIR RIVALRY...?!
What should I do...?
CLANG
CLANG
CLANG
BUM
BUM
Hey, was this door open?

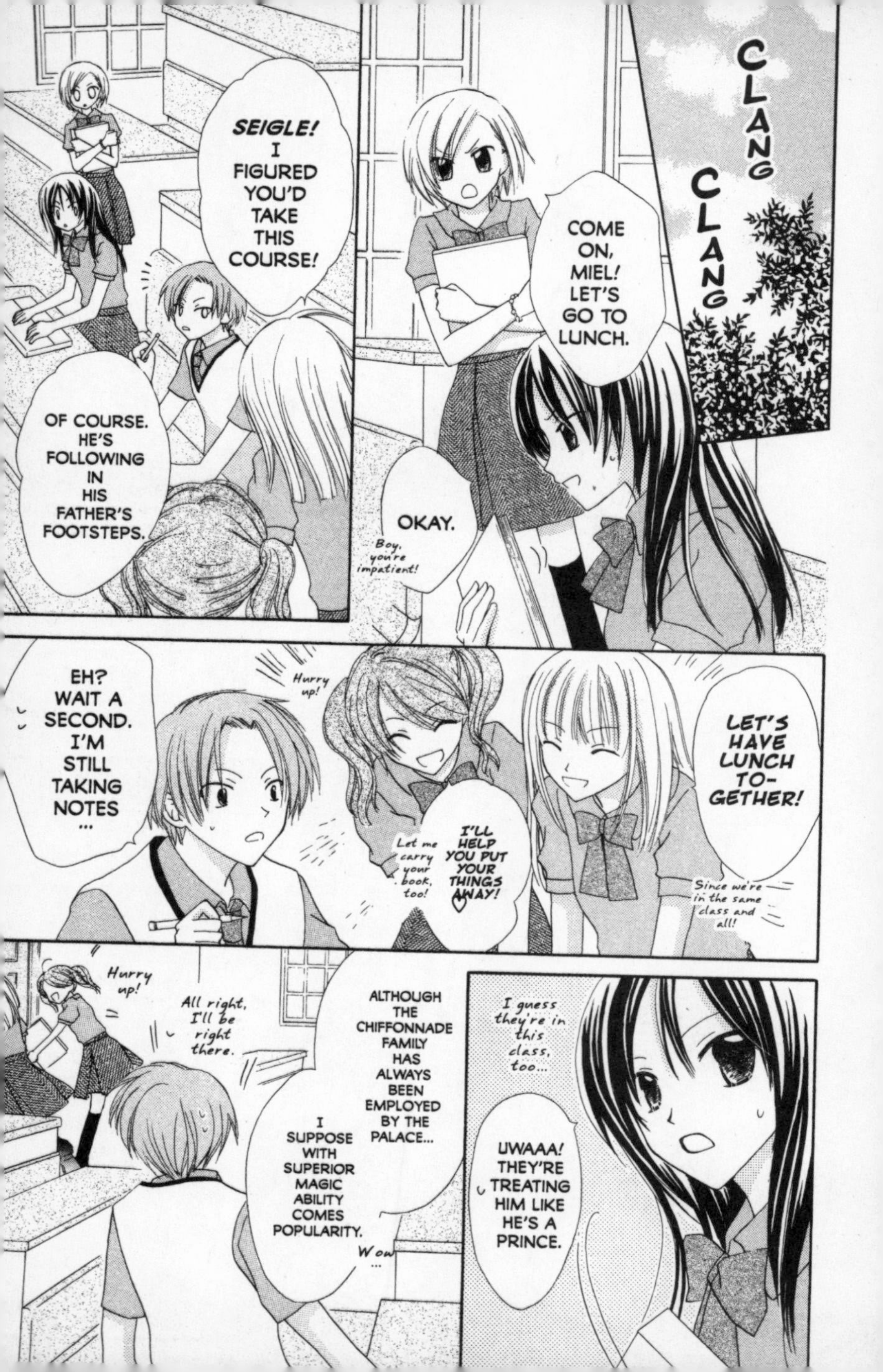
CLANG
CLANG
COME ON, MIEL! LET'S GO TO LUNCH.
OKAY.
Boy, you're impatient!
SEIGLE! I FIGURED YOU'D TAKE THIS COURSE!
OF COURSE. HE'S FOLLOWING IN HIS FATHER'S FOOTSTEPS.
LET'S HAVE LUNCH TO-GETHER!
Since we're in the same class and all!
I'LL HELP YOU PUT YOUR THINGS AWAY!
Let me carry your book, too!
Hurry up!
EH? WAIT A SECOND. I'M STILL TAKING NOTES ...
I guess they're in this class, too...
UWAAA! THEY'RE TREATING HIM LIKE HE'S A PRINCE.
ALTHOUGH THE CHIFFONNADE FAMILY HAS ALWAYS BEEN EMPLOYED BY THE PALACE...
I SUPPOSE WITH SUPERIOR MAGIC ABILITY COMES POPULARITY.
Wow ...
All right, I'll be right there.
Hurry up!

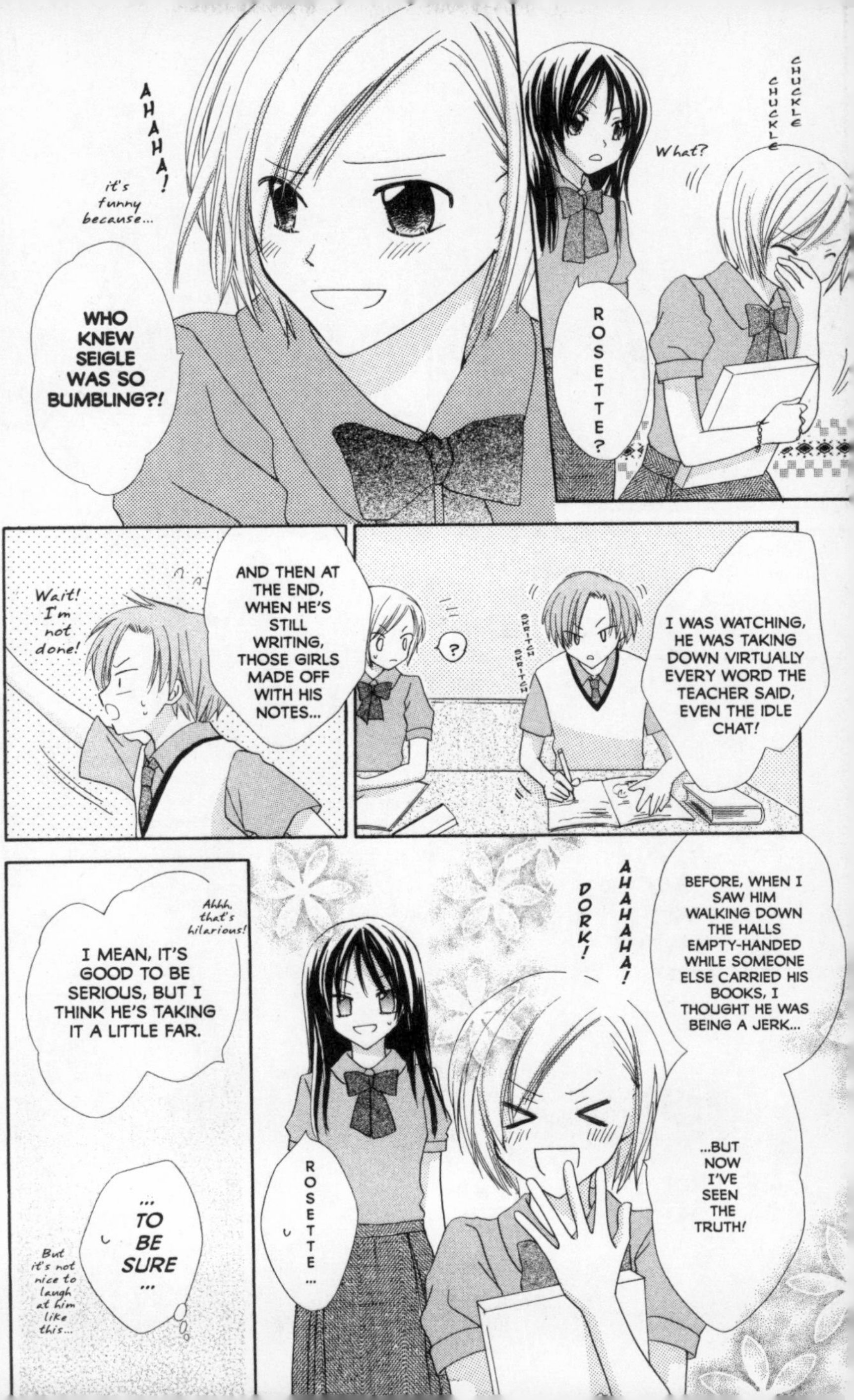
CHUCKLE CHUCKLE
What?
ROSETTE?
AHAHA!
it's funny because...
WHO KNEW SEIGLE WAS SO BUMBLING?!
I WAS WATCHING, HE WAS TAKING DOWN VIRTUALLY EVERY WORD THE TEACHER SAID, EVEN THE IDLE CHAT!
SKRITCH SKRITCH
?
AND THEN AT THE END, WHEN HE'S STILL WRITING, THOSE GIRLS MADE OFF WITH HIS NOTES...
Wait! I'm not done!
BEFORE, WHEN I SAW HIM WALKING DOWN THE HALLS EMPTY-HANDED WHILE SOMEONE ELSE CARRIED HIS BOOKS, I THOUGHT HE WAS BEING A JERK...
AHAHAHA!
DORK!
...BUT NOW I'VE SEEN THE TRUTH!
ROSETTE...
Ahhh, that's hilarious!
I MEAN, IT'S GOOD TO BE SERIOUS, BUT I THINK HE'S TAKING IT A LITTLE FAR.
...TO BE SURE...
But it's not nice to laugh at him like this...

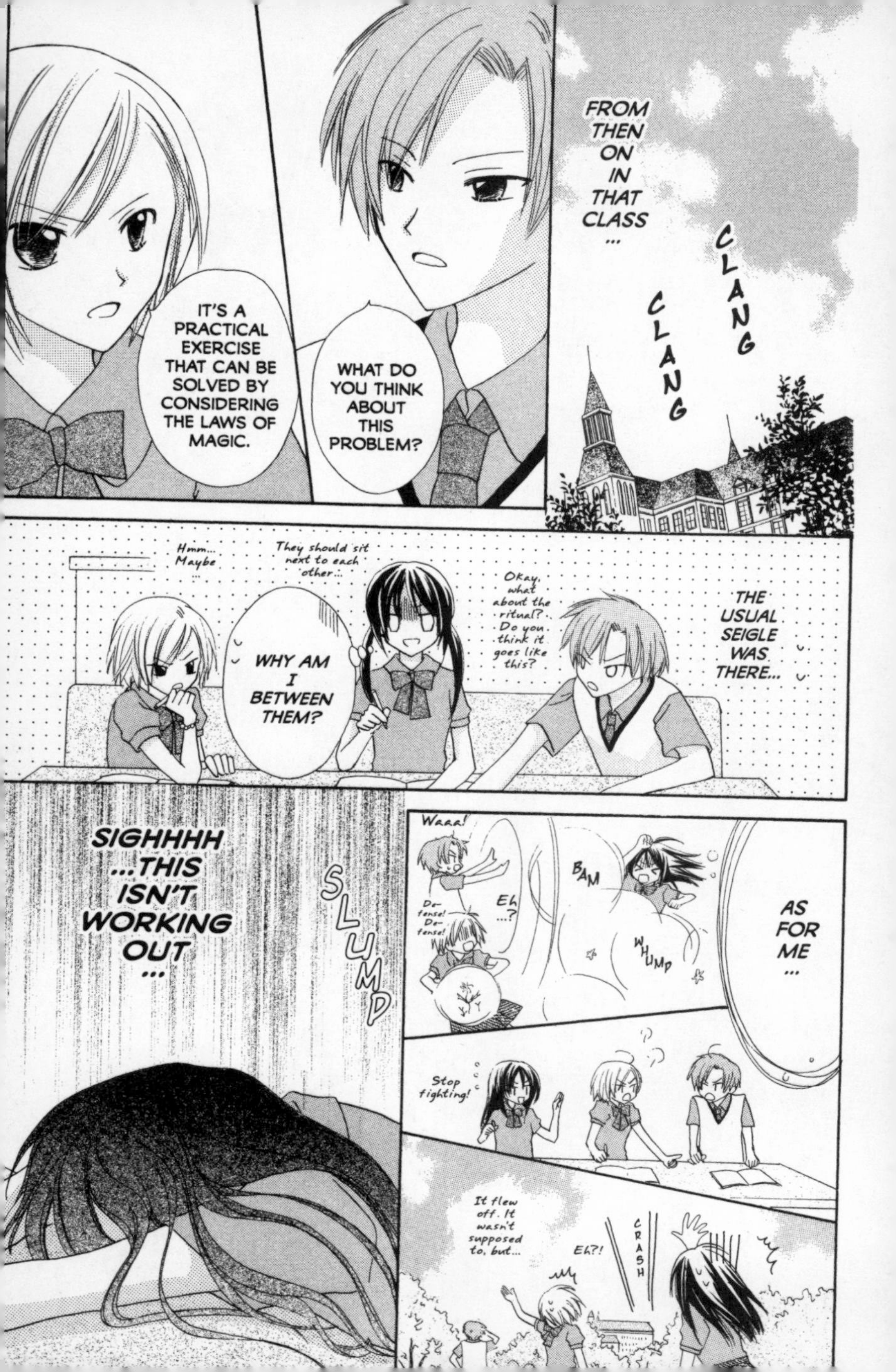

FROM THEN ON IN THAT CLASS ...
CLANG
CLANG
WHAT DO YOU THINK ABOUT THIS PROBLEM?
IT'S A PRACTICAL EXERCISE THAT CAN BE SOLVED BY CONSIDERING THE LAWS OF MAGIC.
THE USUAL SEIGLE WAS THERE...
Okay, what about the ritual? Do you think it goes like this?
They should sit next to each other...
WHY AM I BETWEEN THEM?
Hmm... Maybe ...
AS FOR ME ...
BAM
Waaa!
Eh ...?
WHUMP
Defense! Defense!
Stop fighting!
CRASH
Eh?!
It flew off. It wasn't supposed to, but...
SIGHHHH ...THIS ISN'T WORKING OUT ...
SLUMP

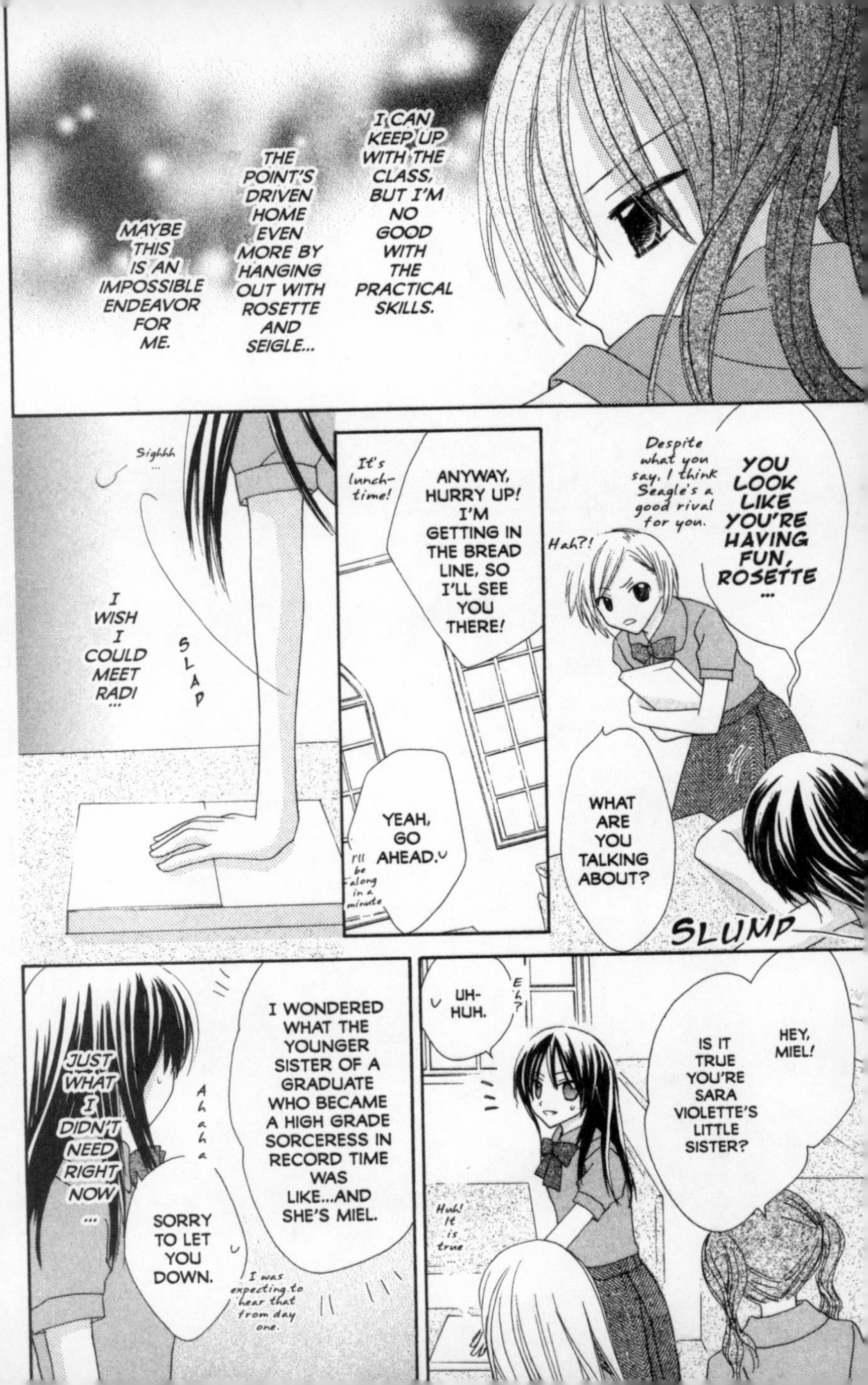
I CAN KEEP UP WITH THE CLASS, BUT I'M NO GOOD WITH THE PRACTICAL SKILLS.
THE POINT'S DRIVEN HOME EVEN MORE BY HANGING OUT WITH ROSETTE AND SEIGLE...
MAYBE THIS IS AN IMPOSSIBLE ENDEAVOR FOR ME.
YOU LOOK LIKE YOU'RE HAVING FUN, ROSETTE...
Despite what you say, I think Seagle's a good rival for you.
Hah?!
WHAT ARE YOU TALKING ABOUT?
SLUMP
ANYWAY, HURRY UP! I'M GETTING IN THE BREAD LINE, SO I'LL SEE YOU THERE!
It's lunch-time!
YEAH, GO AHEAD.
I'll be along in a minute...
Sighhh...
I WISH I COULD MEET RADI...
SLAP
HEY, MIEL!
IS IT TRUE YOU'RE SARA VIOLETTE'S LITTLE SISTER?
Eh?
UH-HUH.
Huh! It is true...
I WONDERED WHAT THE YOUNGER SISTER OF A GRADUATE WHO BECAME A HIGH GRADE SORCERESS IN RECORD TIME WAS LIKE...AND SHE'S MIEL.
Ahaha
SORRY TO LET YOU DOWN.
I was expecting to hear that from day one.
JUST WHAT I DIDN'T NEED RIGHT NOW...

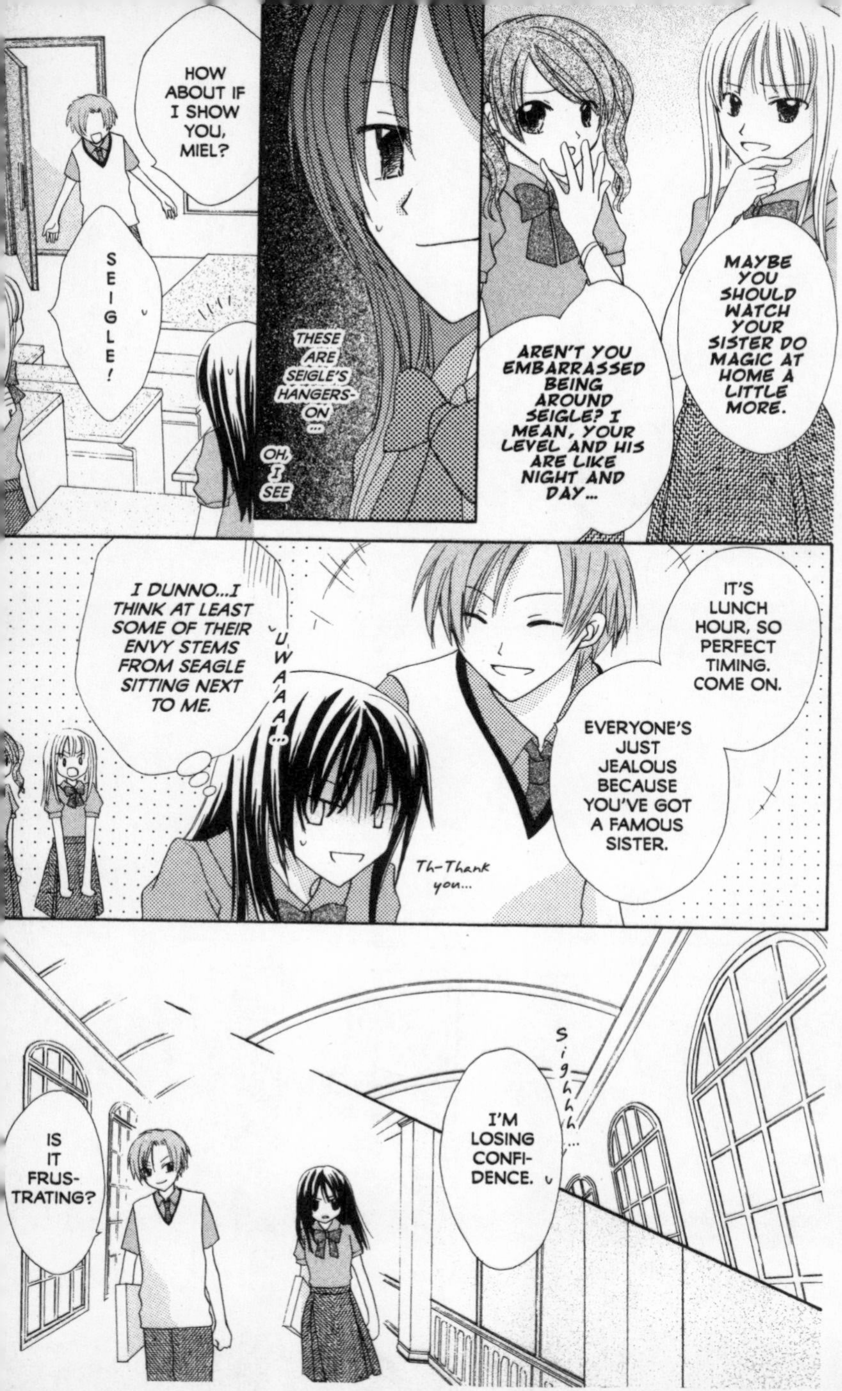
MAYBE YOU SHOULD WATCH YOUR SISTER DO MAGIC AT HOME A LITTLE MORE.
AREN'T YOU EMBARRASSED BEING AROUND SEIGLE? I MEAN, YOUR LEVEL AND HIS ARE LIKE NIGHT AND DAY...
THESE ARE SEIGLE'S HANGERS-ON...
OH, I SEE
HOW ABOUT IF I SHOW YOU, MIEL?
SEIGLE!
IT'S LUNCH HOUR, SO PERFECT TIMING. COME ON.
EVERYONE'S JUST JEALOUS BECAUSE YOU'VE GOT A FAMOUS SISTER.
Th-Thank you...
UWAAA...
I DUNNO...I THINK AT LEAST SOME OF THEIR ENVY STEMS FROM SEAGLE SITTING NEXT TO ME.
Sighhh...
I'M LOSING CONFI-DENCE.
IS IT FRUS-TRATING?

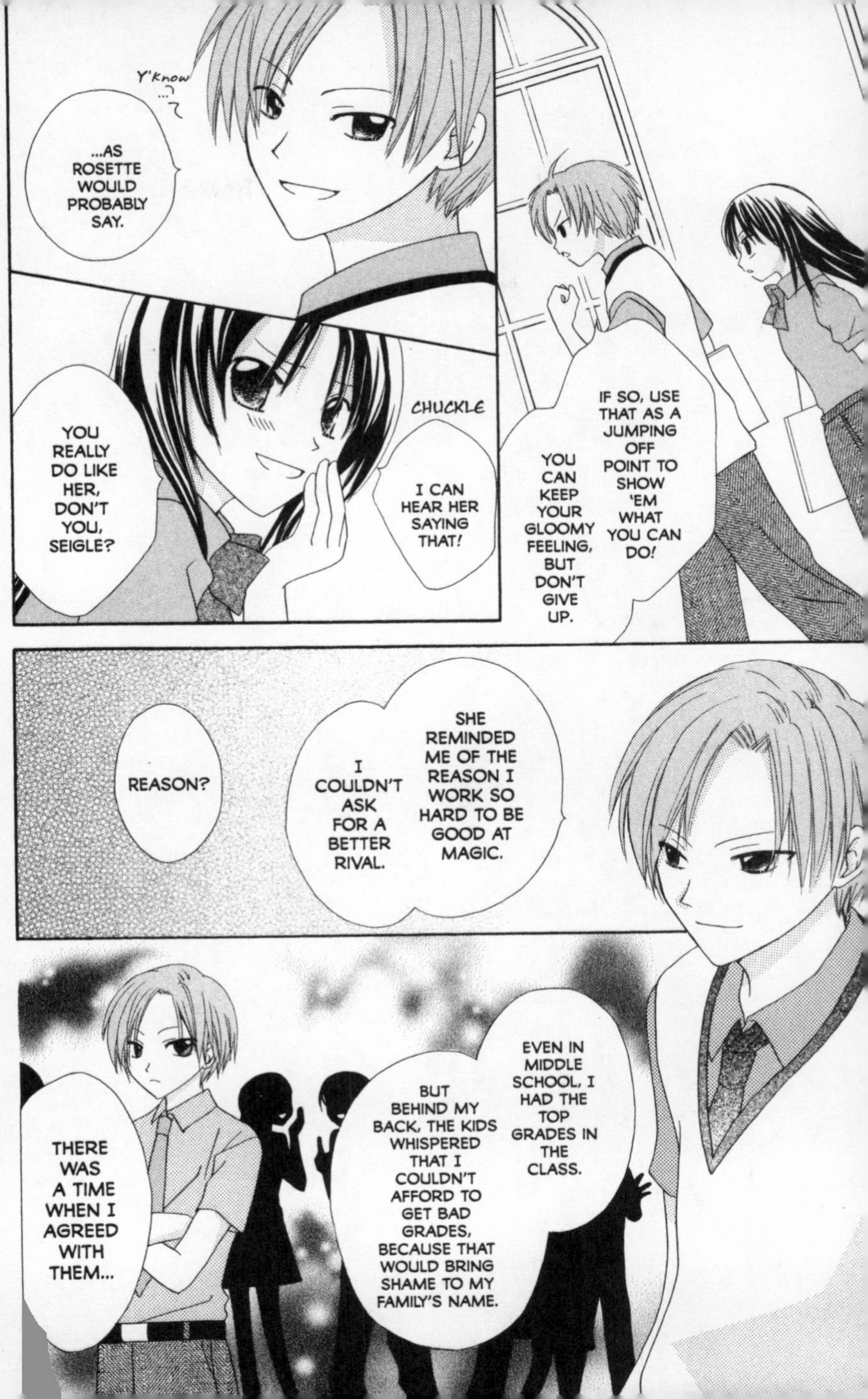
YOU CAN KEEP YOUR GLOOMY FEELING, BUT DON'T GIVE UP.
IF SO, USE THAT AS A JUMPING OFF POINT TO SHOW 'EM WHAT YOU CAN DO!
Y'Know...
...AS ROSETTE WOULD PROBABLY SAY.
CHUCKLE
I CAN HEAR HER SAYING THAT!
YOU REALLY DO LIKE HER, DON'T YOU, SEIGLE?
I COULDN'T ASK FOR A BETTER RIVAL.
SHE REMINDED ME OF THE REASON I WORK SO HARD TO BE GOOD AT MAGIC.
REASON?
EVEN IN MIDDLE SCHOOL, I HAD THE TOP GRADES IN THE CLASS.
BUT BEHIND MY BACK, THE KIDS WHISPERED THAT I COULDN'T AFFORD TO GET BAD GRADES, BECAUSE THAT WOULD BRING SHAME TO MY FAMILY'S NAME.
THERE WAS A TIME WHEN I AGREED WITH THEM...

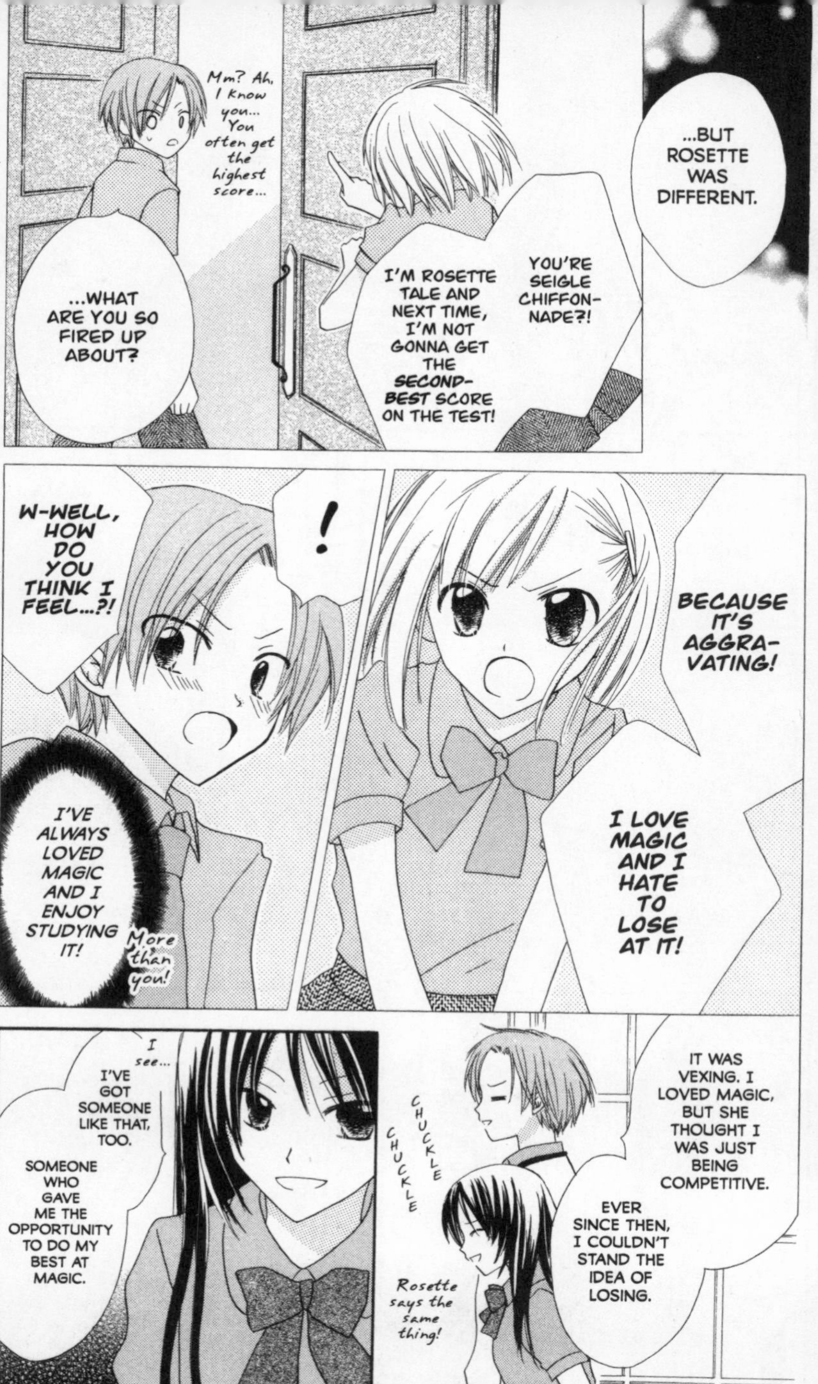
...BUT ROSETTE WAS DIFFERENT.
YOU'RE SEIGLE CHIFFONNADE?!
I'M ROSETTE TALE AND NEXT TIME, I'M NOT GONNA GET THE SECOND-BEST SCORE ON THE TEST!
Mm? Ah, I know you... You often get the highest score...
...WHAT ARE YOU SO FIRED UP ABOUT?
BECAUSE IT'S AGGRAVATING!
I LOVE MAGIC AND I HATE TO LOSE AT IT!
!
W-WELL, HOW DO YOU THINK I FEEL...?!
I'VE ALWAYS LOVED MAGIC AND I ENJOY STUDYING IT!
More than you!
IT WAS VEXING. I LOVED MAGIC, BUT SHE THOUGHT I WAS JUST BEING COMPETITIVE.
EVER SINCE THEN, I COULDN'T STAND THE IDEA OF LOSING.
CHUCKLE CHUCKLE
Rosette says the same thing!
I see...
I'VE GOT SOMEONE LIKE THAT, TOO.
SOMEONE WHO GAVE ME THE OPPORTUNITY TO DO MY BEST AT MAGIC.

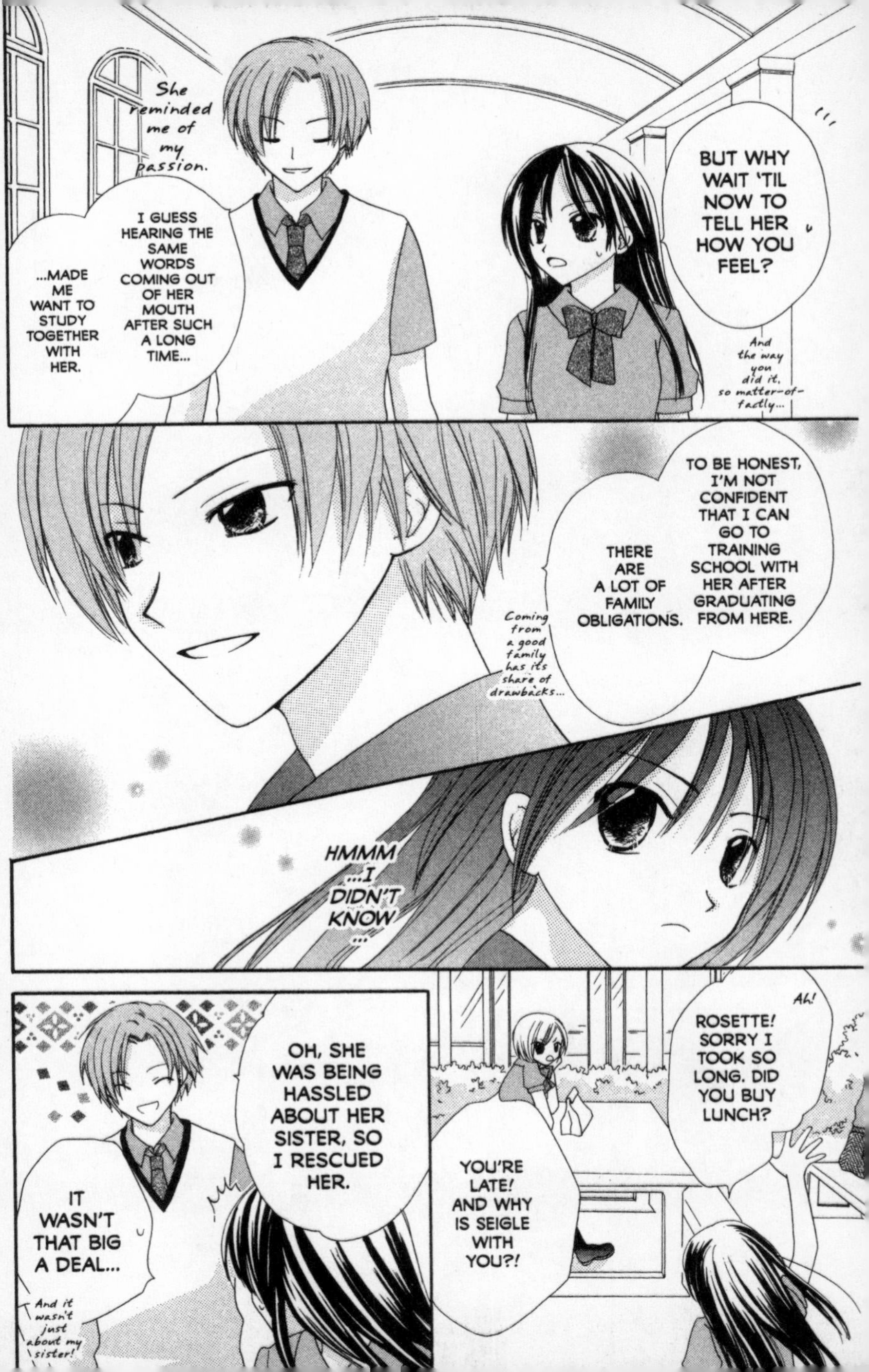
BUT WHY WAIT 'TIL NOW TO TELL HER HOW YOU FEEL?
And the way you did it, so matter-of-factly...
She reminded me of my passion.
I GUESS HEARING THE SAME WORDS COMING OUT OF HER MOUTH AFTER SUCH A LONG TIME...
...MADE ME WANT TO STUDY TOGETHER WITH HER.
TO BE HONEST, I'M NOT CONFIDENT THAT I CAN GO TO TRAINING SCHOOL WITH HER AFTER GRADUATING FROM HERE.
THERE ARE A LOT OF FAMILY OBLIGATIONS.
Coming from a good family has its share of drawbacks...
HMMM ...I DIDN'T KNOW ...
Ah!
ROSETTE! SORRY I TOOK SO LONG. DID YOU BUY LUNCH?
YOU'RE LATE! AND WHY IS SEIGLE WITH YOU?!
OH, SHE WAS BEING HASSLED ABOUT HER SISTER, SO I RESCUED HER.
IT WASN'T THAT BIG A DEAL...
And it wasn't just about my sister!

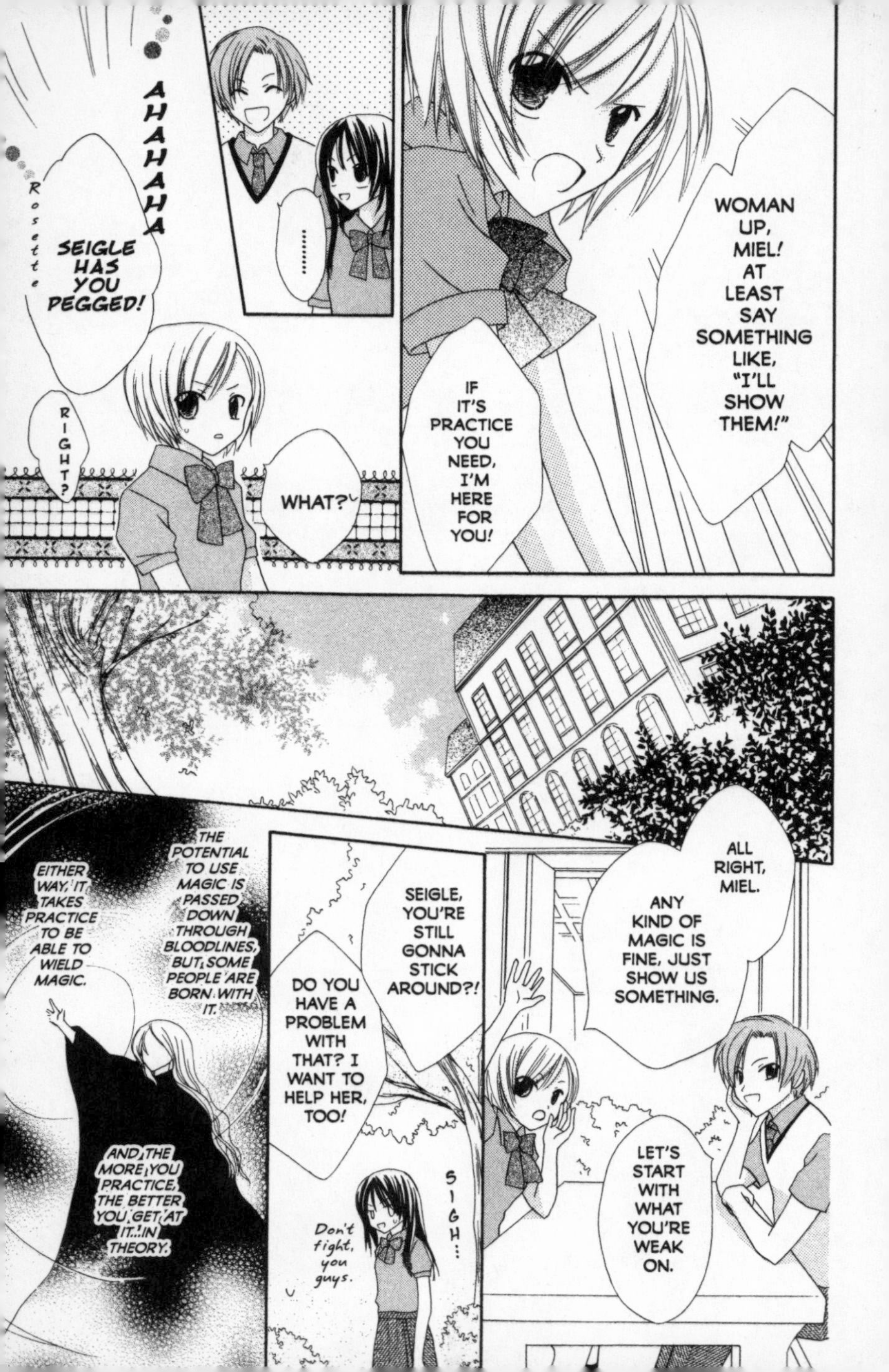
WOMAN UP, MIEL! AT LEAST SAY SOMETHING LIKE, "I'LL SHOW THEM!"
IF IT'S PRACTICE YOU NEED, I'M HERE FOR YOU!
......
AHAHAHA
SEIGLE HAS YOU PEGGED!
Rosette
WHAT?
RIGHT?
ALL RIGHT, MIEL.
ANY KIND OF MAGIC IS FINE, JUST SHOW US SOMETHING.
SEIGLE, YOU'RE STILL GONNA STICK AROUND?!
LET'S START WITH WHAT YOU'RE WEAK ON.
DO YOU HAVE A PROBLEM WITH THAT? I WANT TO HELP HER, TOO!
SIGH...
Don't fight, you guys.
THE POTENTIAL TO USE MAGIC IS PASSED DOWN THROUGH BLOODLINES, BUT SOME PEOPLE ARE BORN WITH IT.
EITHER WAY, IT TAKES PRACTICE TO BE ABLE TO WIELD MAGIC.
AND THE MORE YOU PRACTICE, THE BETTER YOU GET AT IT...IN THEORY.

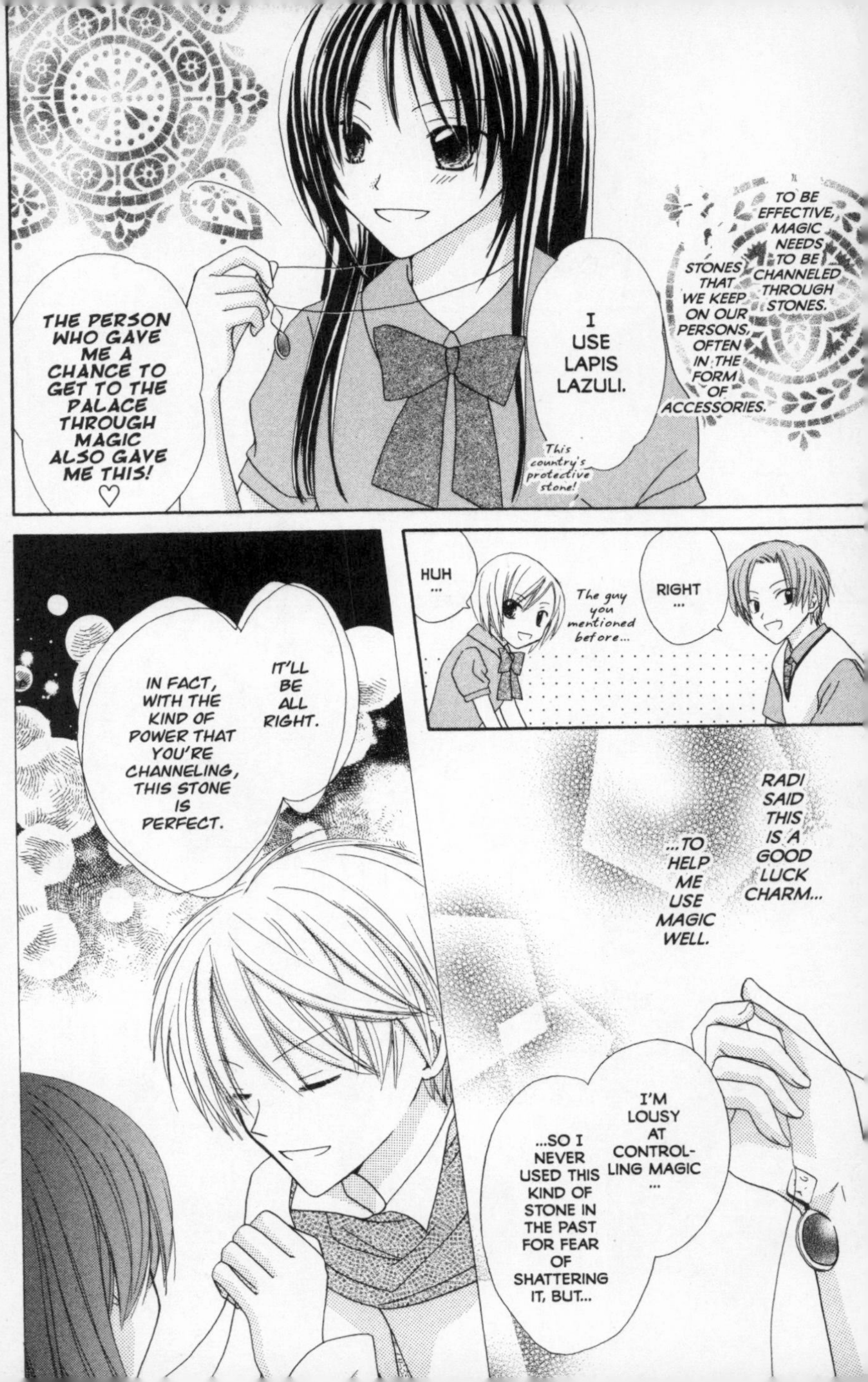
TO BE EFFECTIVE, MAGIC NEEDS TO BE CHANNELED THROUGH STONES.
STONES THAT WE KEEP ON OUR PERSONS, OFTEN IN THE FORM OF ACCESSORIES.
I USE LAPIS LAZULI.
This country's protective stone!
THE PERSON WHO GAVE ME A CHANCE TO GET TO THE PALACE THROUGH MAGIC ALSO GAVE ME THIS! ♡
RIGHT ...
The guy you mentioned before...
HUH ...
RADI SAID THIS IS A GOOD LUCK CHARM...
...TO HELP ME USE MAGIC WELL.
I'M LOUSY AT CONTROL-LING MAGIC ...
...SO I NEVER USED THIS KIND OF STONE IN THE PAST FOR FEAR OF SHATTERING IT, BUT...
IT'LL BE ALL RIGHT.
IN FACT, WITH THE KIND OF POWER THAT YOU'RE CHANNELING, THIS STONE IS PERFECT.

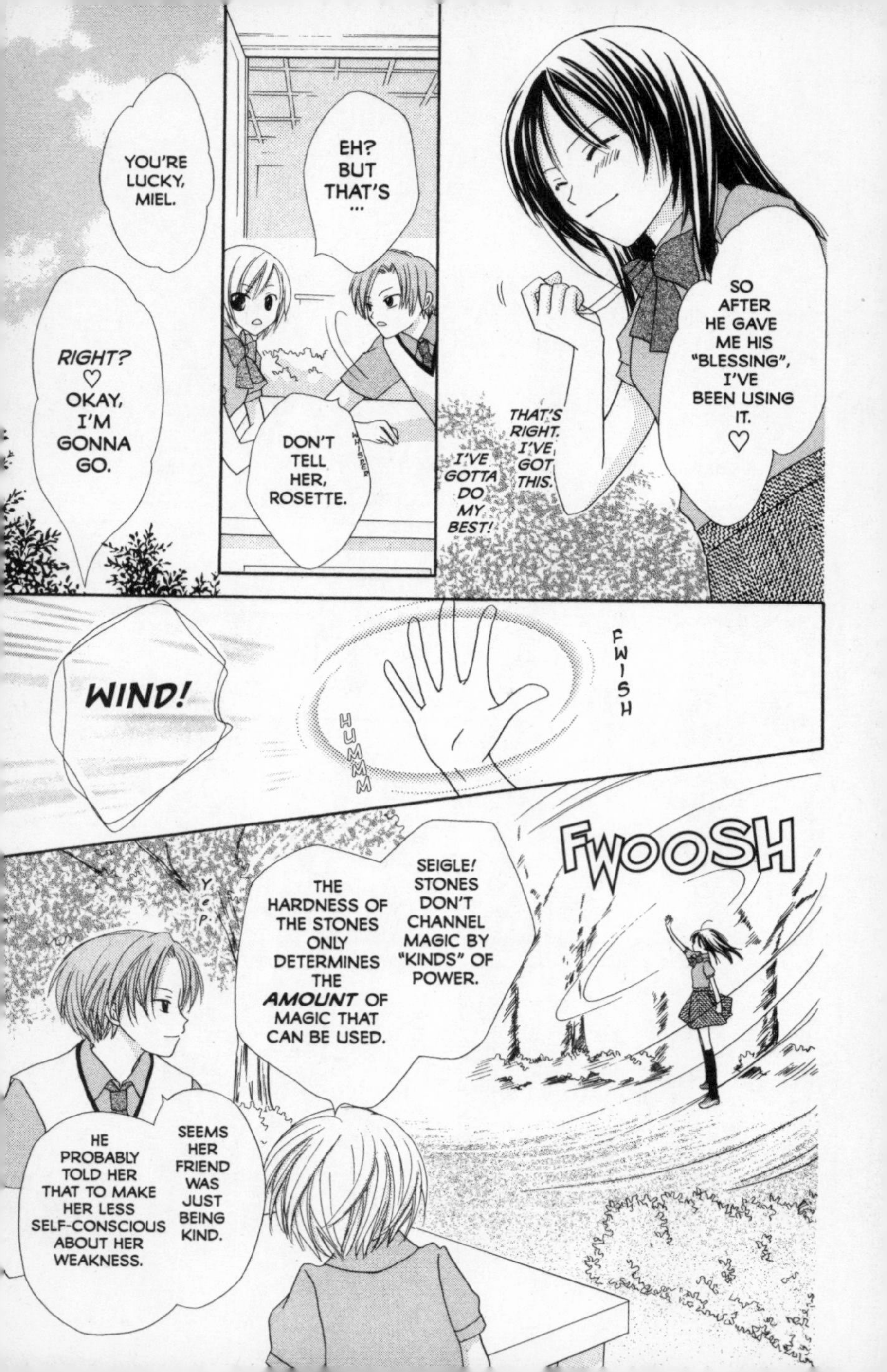
SO AFTER HE GAVE ME HIS "BLESSING", I'VE BEEN USING IT. ♡
THAT'S RIGHT. I'VE GOT THIS.
I'VE GOTTA DO MY BEST!
EH? BUT THAT'S ...
WHISPER
DON'T TELL HER, ROSETTE.
YOU'RE LUCKY, MIEL.
RIGHT? ♡ OKAY, I'M GONNA GO.
FWISH
HUMMM
WIND!
FWOOSH
SEIGLE! STONES DON'T CHANNEL MAGIC BY "KINDS" OF POWER.
THE HARDNESS OF THE STONES ONLY DETERMINES THE AMOUNT OF MAGIC THAT CAN BE USED.
YEP.
SEEMS HER FRIEND WAS JUST BEING KIND.
HE PROBABLY TOLD HER THAT TO MAKE HER LESS SELF-CONSCIOUS ABOUT HER WEAKNESS.

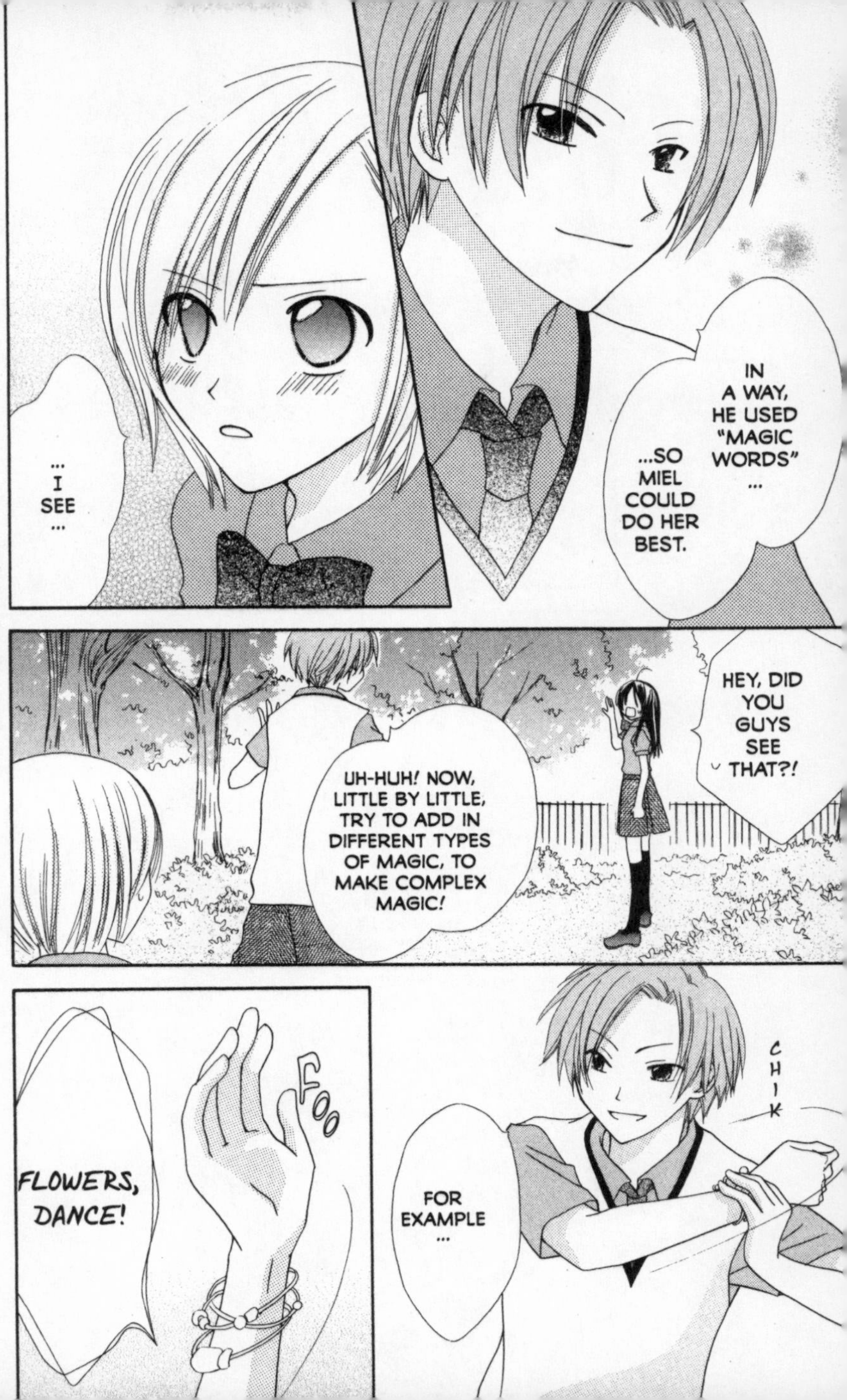

IN A WAY, HE USED "MAGIC WORDS"...
...SO MIEL COULD DO HER BEST.
...I SEE...
HEY, DID YOU GUYS SEE THAT?!
UH-HUH! NOW, LITTLE BY LITTLE, TRY TO ADD IN DIFFERENT TYPES OF MAGIC, TO MAKE COMPLEX MAGIC!
CHIK
FOR EXAMPLE...
FOO
FLOWERS, DANCE!

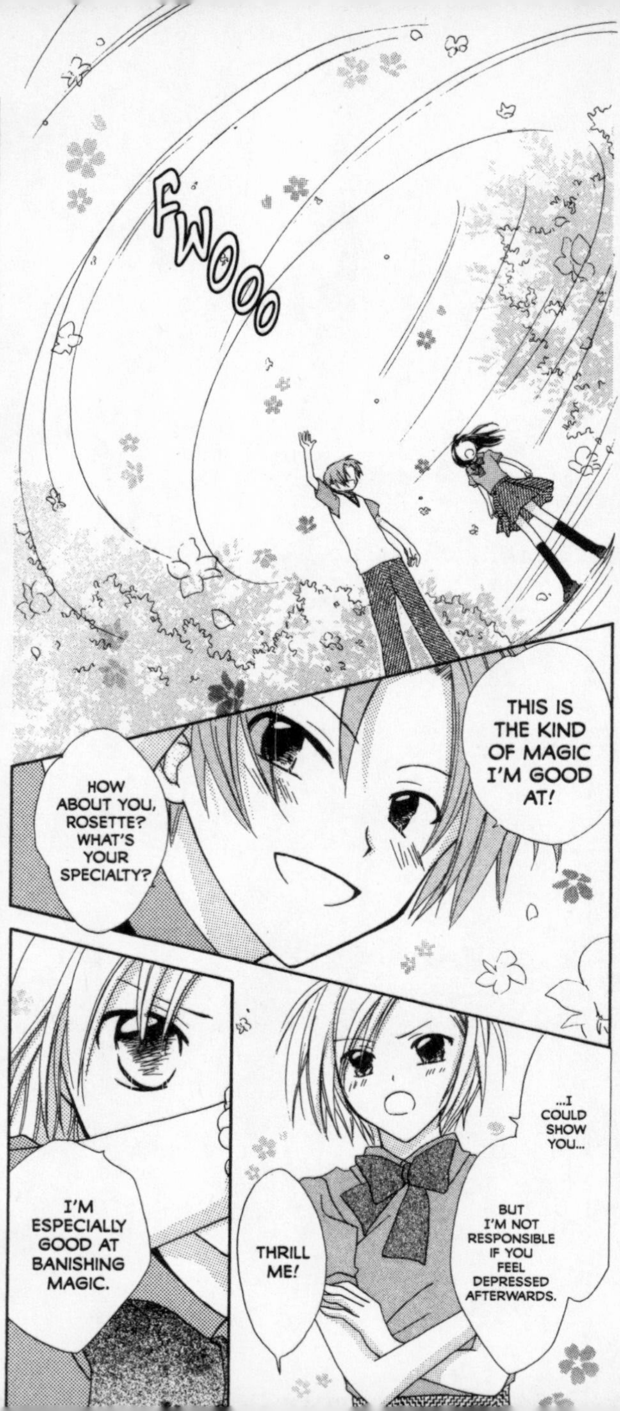
FWOOO
THIS IS THE KIND OF MAGIC I'M GOOD AT!
HOW ABOUT YOU, ROSETTE? WHAT'S YOUR SPECIALTY?
...I COULD SHOW YOU...
BUT I'M NOT RESPONSIBLE IF YOU FEEL DEPRESSED AFTERWARDS.
THRILL ME!
I'M ESPECIALLY GOOD AT BANISHING MAGIC.

HELLO.

LONG TIME NO SEE.

I'M NATSUNA KAWASE.

THIS IS VOLUME 2. THANK YOU FOR GETTING THIS, MY FIFTH PUBLISHED VOLUME.

THIS IS THE FINAL VOLUME OF "THE LAPIS LAZULI CROWN" (ONLY TWO VOLUMES!). THIS ONE ONLY CONTAINS LAPIS LAZULI STORIES. QUITE A BIT OF TIME ELAPSES BETWEEN EACH EPISODE THIS TIME AROUND, SO YOUR IMAGINATION WILL HAVE TO FILL IN A FEW BLANKS HERE AND THERE.

THIS TIME, THERE ARE 9 1/4 PAGE COLUMNS, THE MOST I'VE HAD SO FAR...I THINK I'LL USE THE SPACE AS I DID LAST VOLUME, TO INTRODUCE CHARACTERS AND TALK ABOUT EACH EPISODE.

I HOPE YOU ENJOY THIS VOLUME TO THE END!

1

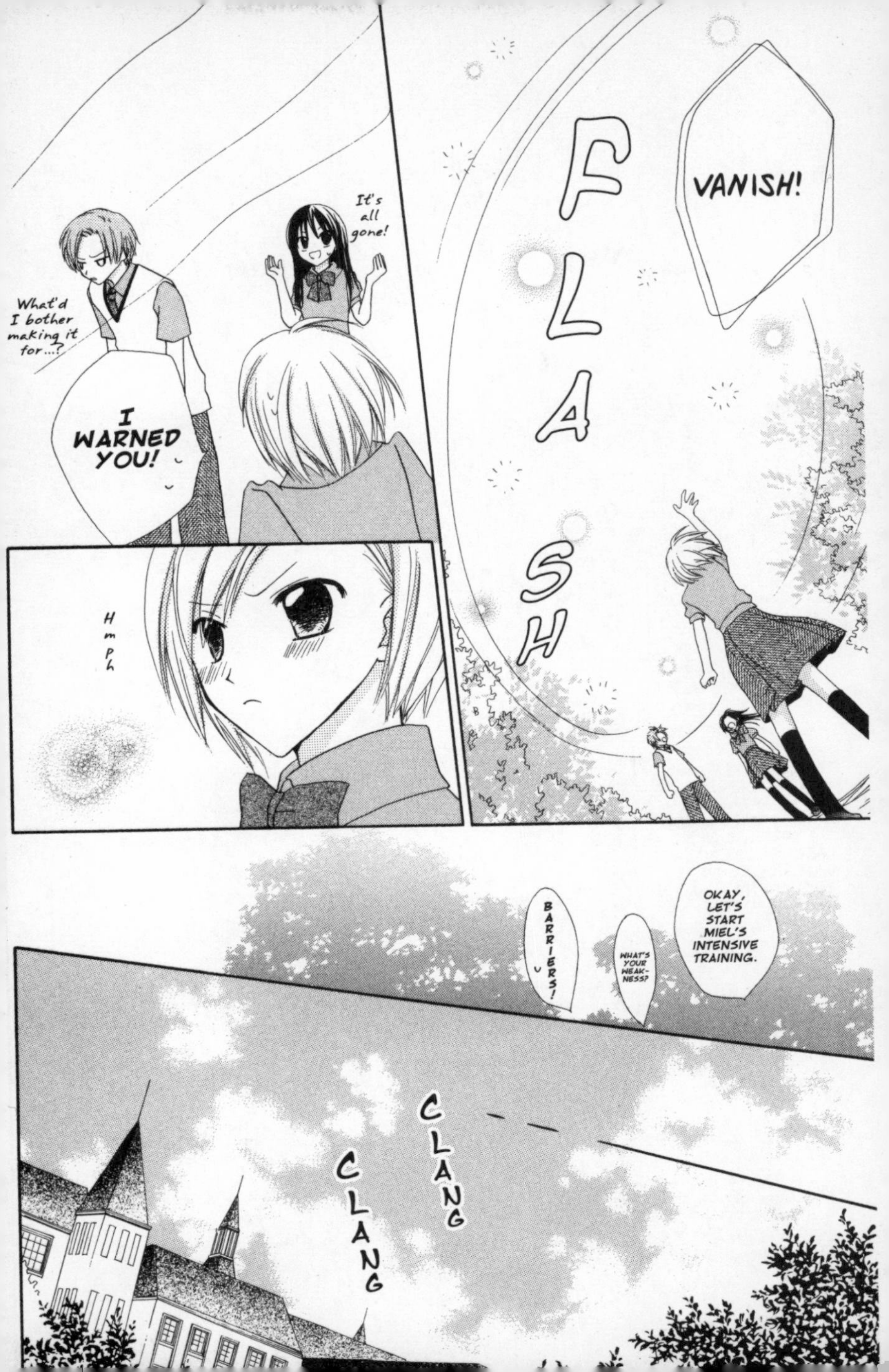
VANISH!
FLASH
It's all gone!
What'd I bother making it for...?
I WARNED YOU!
Hmph
OKAY, LET'S START MIEL'S INTENSIVE TRAINING.
WHAT'S YOUR WEAK-NESS?
BARRIERS!
CLANG
CLANG

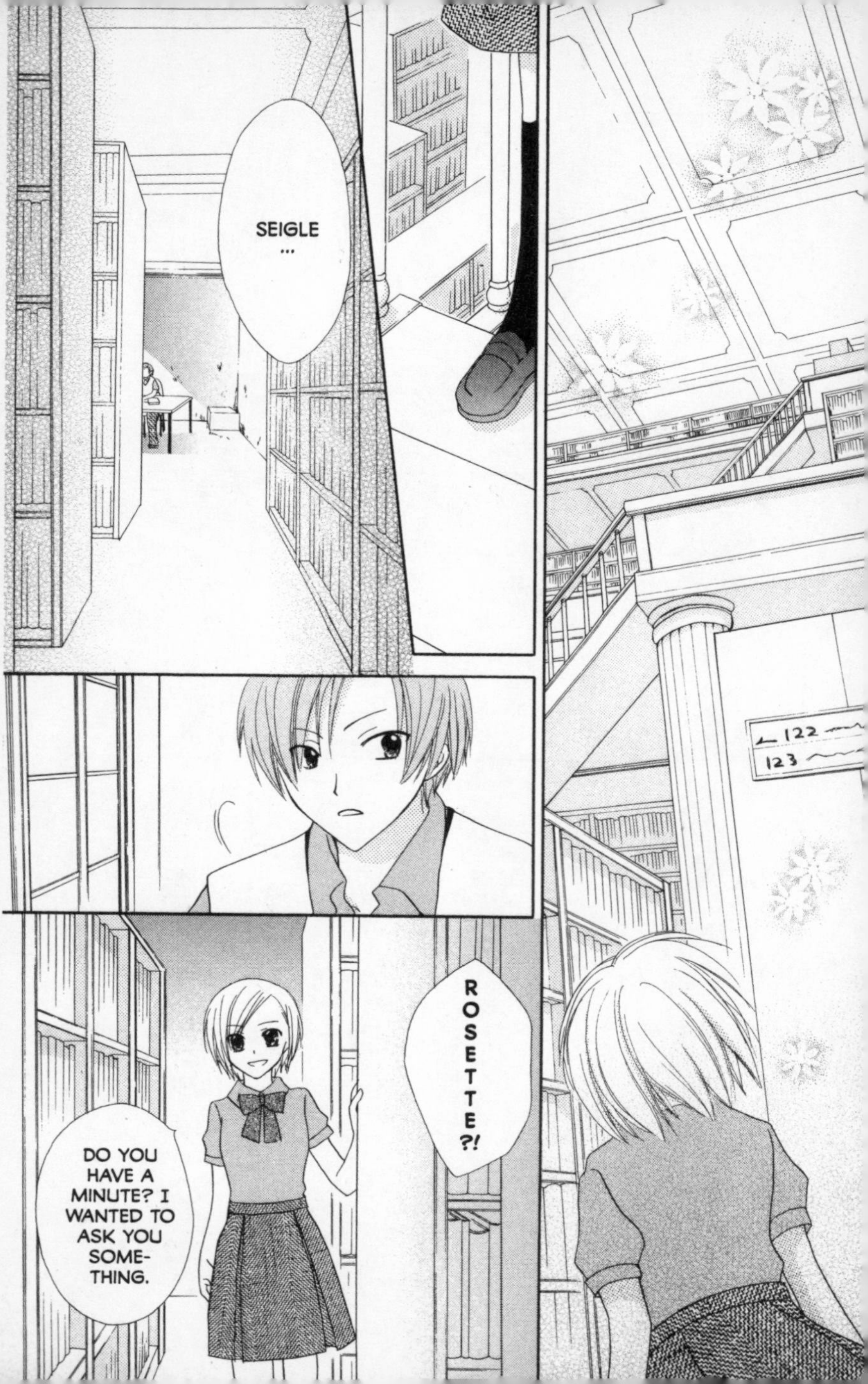
122
123
SEIGLE
...
ROSETTE?!
DO YOU HAVE A MINUTE? I WANTED TO ASK YOU SOME-THING.

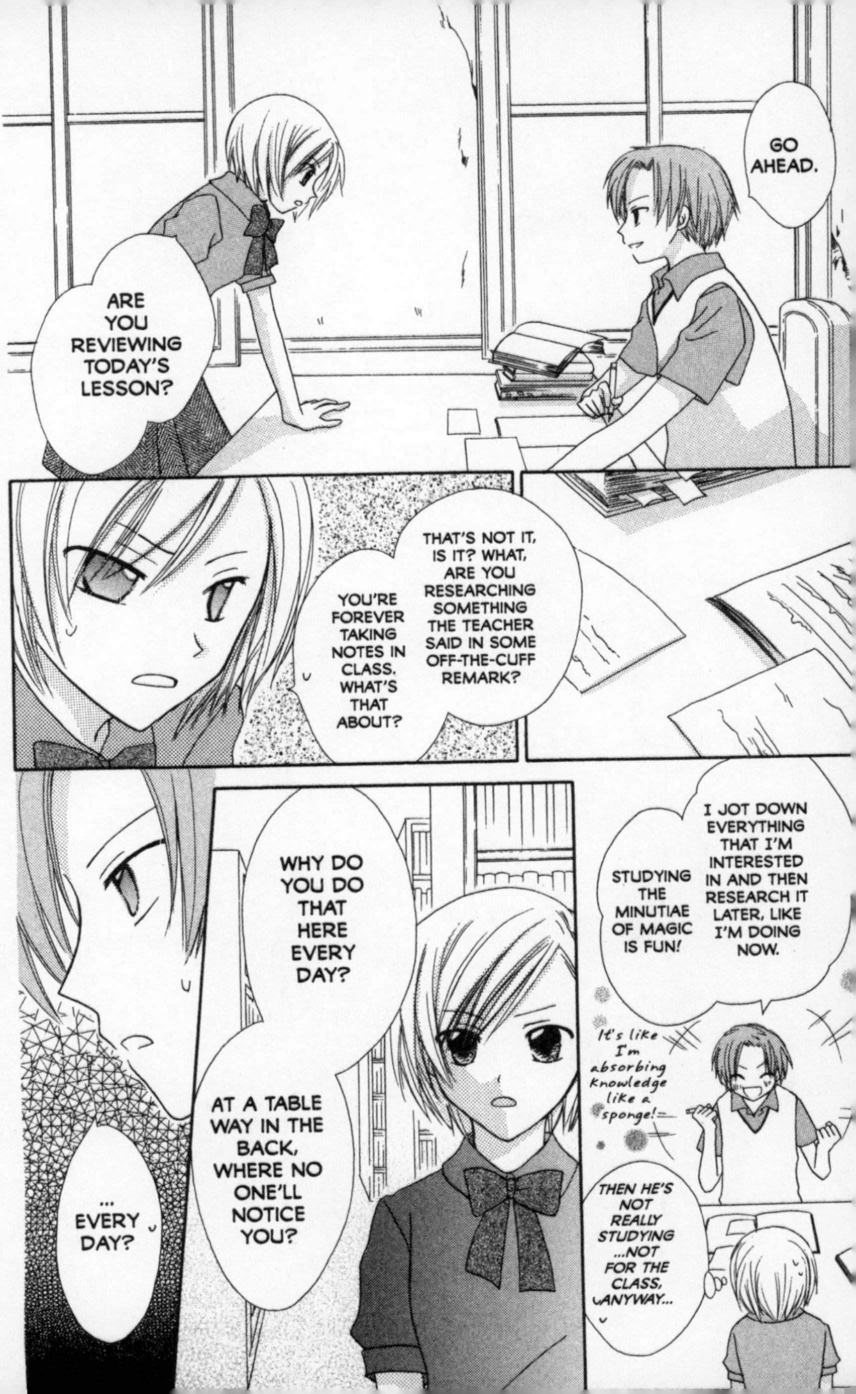
GO AHEAD.
ARE YOU REVIEWING TODAY'S LESSON?
THAT'S NOT IT, IS IT? WHAT, ARE YOU RESEARCHING SOMETHING THE TEACHER SAID IN SOME OFF-THE-CUFF REMARK?
YOU'RE FOREVER TAKING NOTES IN CLASS. WHAT'S THAT ABOUT?
I JOT DOWN EVERYTHING THAT I'M INTERESTED IN AND THEN RESEARCH IT LATER, LIKE I'M DOING NOW.
STUDYING THE MINUTIAE OF MAGIC IS FUN!
It's like I'm absorbing knowledge like a sponge!
THEN HE'S NOT REALLY STUDYING ...NOT FOR THE CLASS, ANYWAY...
WHY DO YOU DO THAT HERE EVERY DAY?
AT A TABLE WAY IN THE BACK, WHERE NO ONE'LL NOTICE YOU?
... EVERY DAY?

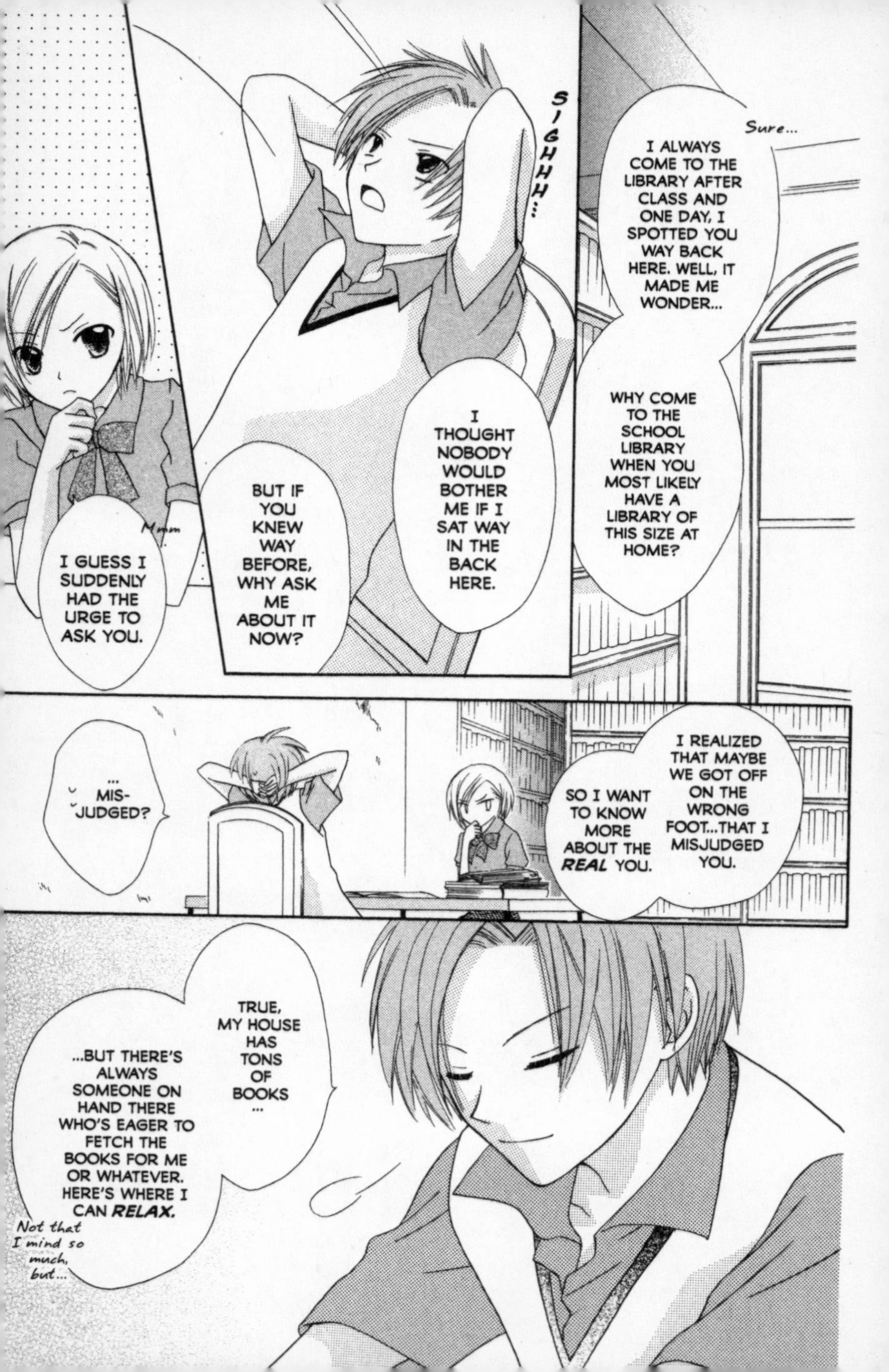
Sure...
I ALWAYS COME TO THE LIBRARY AFTER CLASS AND ONE DAY, I SPOTTED YOU WAY BACK HERE. WELL, IT MADE ME WONDER...
WHY COME TO THE SCHOOL LIBRARY WHEN YOU MOST LIKELY HAVE A LIBRARY OF THIS SIZE AT HOME?
SIGHHH...
I THOUGHT NOBODY WOULD BOTHER ME IF I SAT WAY IN THE BACK HERE.
BUT IF YOU KNEW WAY BEFORE, WHY ASK ME ABOUT IT NOW?
Mmm
I GUESS I SUDDENLY HAD THE URGE TO ASK YOU.
I REALIZED THAT MAYBE WE GOT OFF ON THE WRONG FOOT...THAT I MISJUDGED YOU.
SO I WANT TO KNOW MORE ABOUT THE ***REAL*** YOU.
... MIS-JUDGED?
TRUE, MY HOUSE HAS TONS OF BOOKS ...
...BUT THERE'S ALWAYS SOMEONE ON HAND THERE WHO'S EAGER TO FETCH THE BOOKS FOR ME OR WHATEVER. HERE'S WHERE I CAN ***RELAX.***
Not that I mind so much, but...

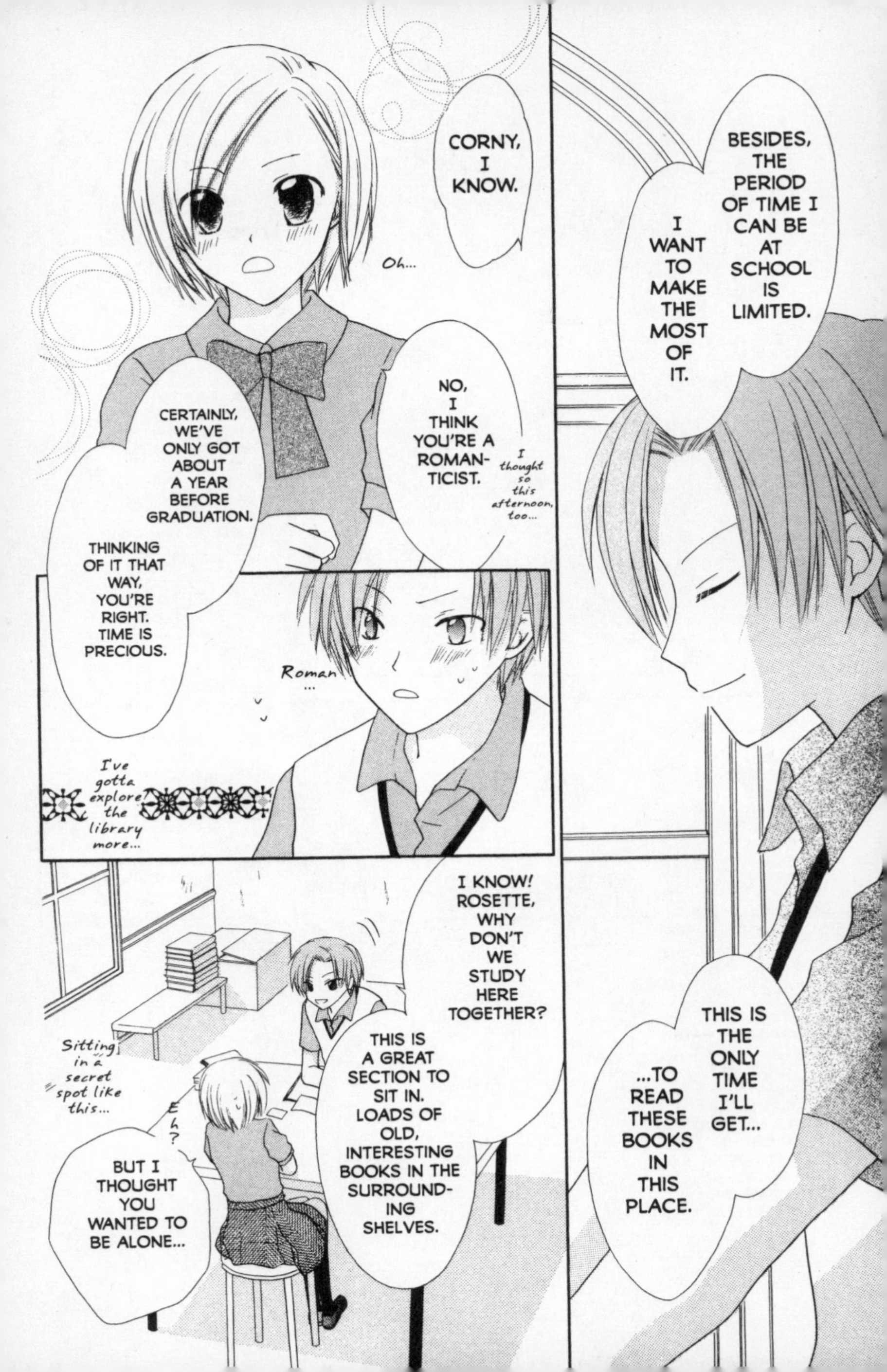
BESIDES, THE PERIOD OF TIME I CAN BE AT SCHOOL IS LIMITED.
I WANT TO MAKE THE MOST OF IT.
THIS IS THE ONLY TIME I'LL GET...
...TO READ THESE BOOKS IN THIS PLACE.
CORNY, I KNOW.
Oh...
NO, I THINK YOU'RE A ROMANTICIST.
I thought so this afternoon, too...
CERTAINLY, WE'VE ONLY GOT ABOUT A YEAR BEFORE GRADUATION.
THINKING OF IT THAT WAY, YOU'RE RIGHT. TIME IS PRECIOUS.
Roman...
I've gotta explore the library more...
I KNOW! ROSETTE, WHY DON'T WE STUDY HERE TOGETHER?
THIS IS A GREAT SECTION TO SIT IN. LOADS OF OLD, INTERESTING BOOKS IN THE SURROUNDING SHELVES.
Eh?
BUT I THOUGHT YOU WANTED TO BE ALONE...
Sitting in a secret spot like this...

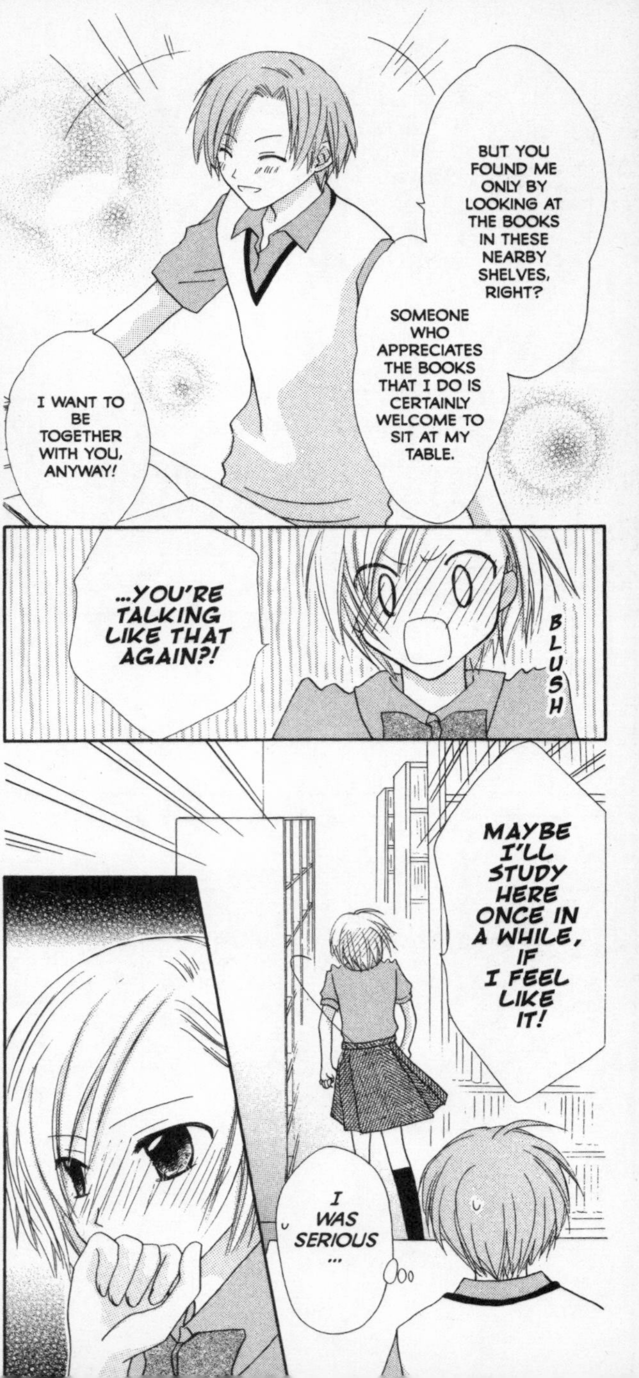
BUT YOU FOUND ME ONLY BY LOOKING AT THE BOOKS IN THESE NEARBY SHELVES, RIGHT?
SOMEONE WHO APPRECIATES THE BOOKS THAT I DO IS CERTAINLY WELCOME TO SIT AT MY TABLE.
I WANT TO BE TOGETHER WITH YOU, ANYWAY!
BLUSH
...YOU'RE TALKING LIKE THAT AGAIN?!
MAYBE I'LL STUDY HERE ONCE IN A WHILE, IF I FEEL LIKE IT!
I WAS SERIOUS ...

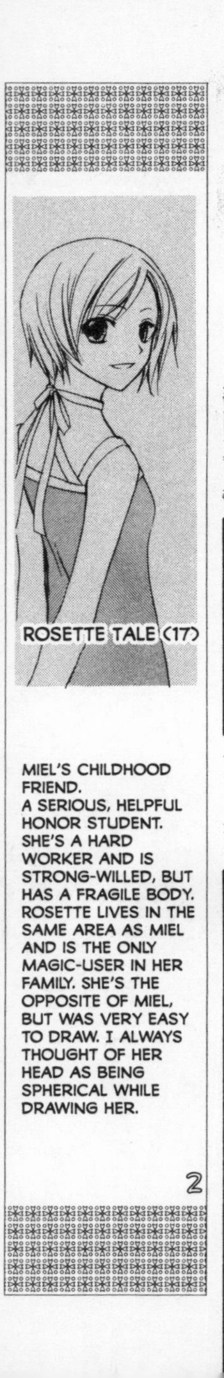

ROSETTE TALE (17)

MIEL'S CHILDHOOD FRIEND.
A SERIOUS, HELPFUL HONOR STUDENT. SHE'S A HARD WORKER AND IS STRONG-WILLED, BUT HAS A FRAGILE BODY. ROSETTE LIVES IN THE SAME AREA AS MIEL AND IS THE ONLY MAGIC-USER IN HER FAMILY. SHE'S THE OPPOSITE OF MIEL, BUT WAS VERY EASY TO DRAW. I ALWAYS THOUGHT OF HER HEAD AS BEING SPHERICAL WHILE DRAWING HER.

2

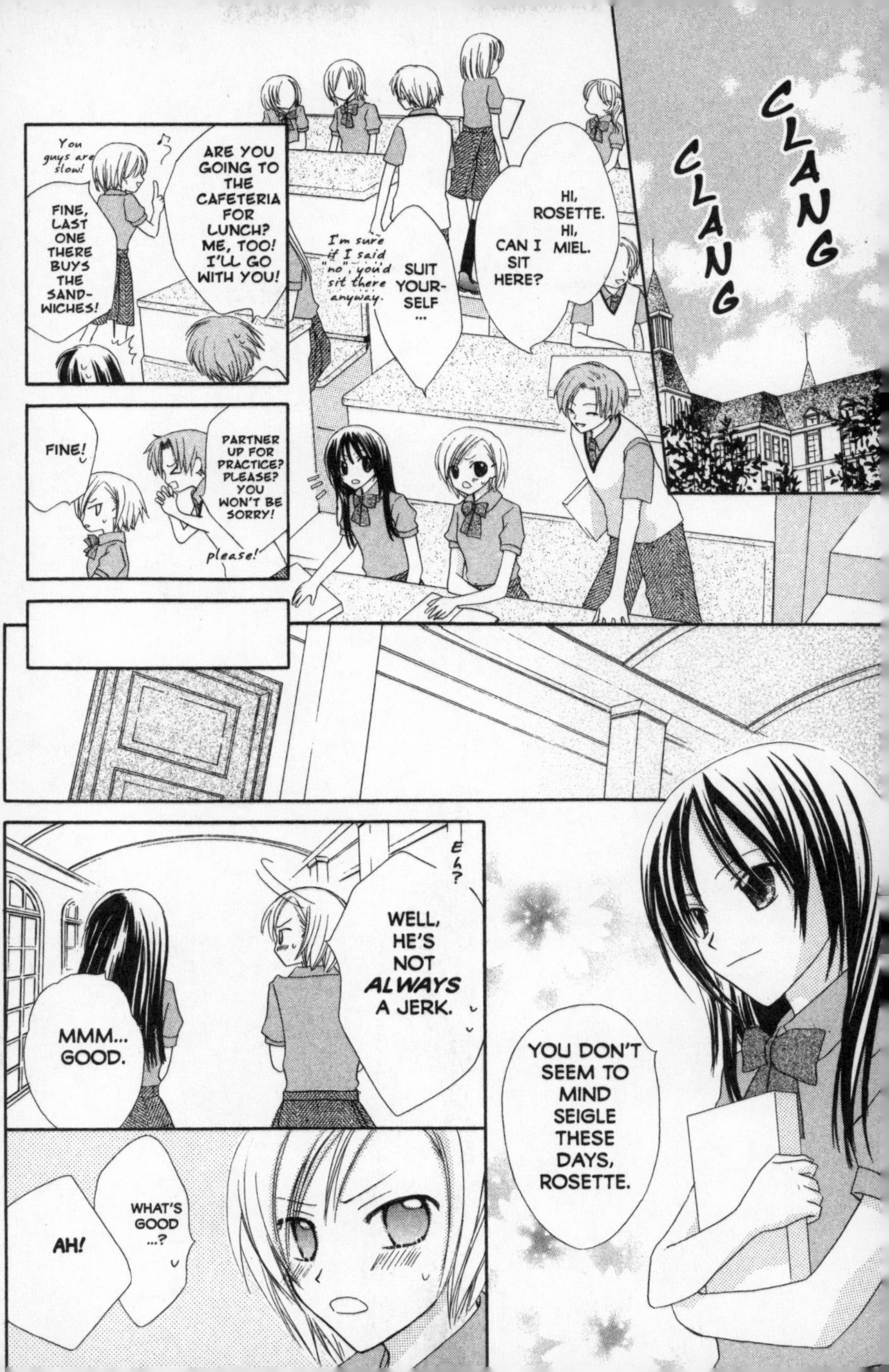
CLANG
CLANG
HI, ROSETTE. HI, MIEL.
CAN I SIT HERE?
SUIT YOURSELF ...
I'm sure if I said "no", you'd sit there anyway.
ARE YOU GOING TO THE CAFETERIA FOR LUNCH? ME, TOO! I'LL GO WITH YOU!
You guys are slow!
FINE, LAST ONE THERE BUYS THE SANDWICHES!
PARTNER UP FOR PRACTICE? PLEASE? YOU WON'T BE SORRY!
please!
FINE!
YOU DON'T SEEM TO MIND SEIGLE THESE DAYS, ROSETTE.
Eh?
WELL, HE'S NOT *ALWAYS* A JERK.
MMM... GOOD.
WHAT'S GOOD ...?
AH!

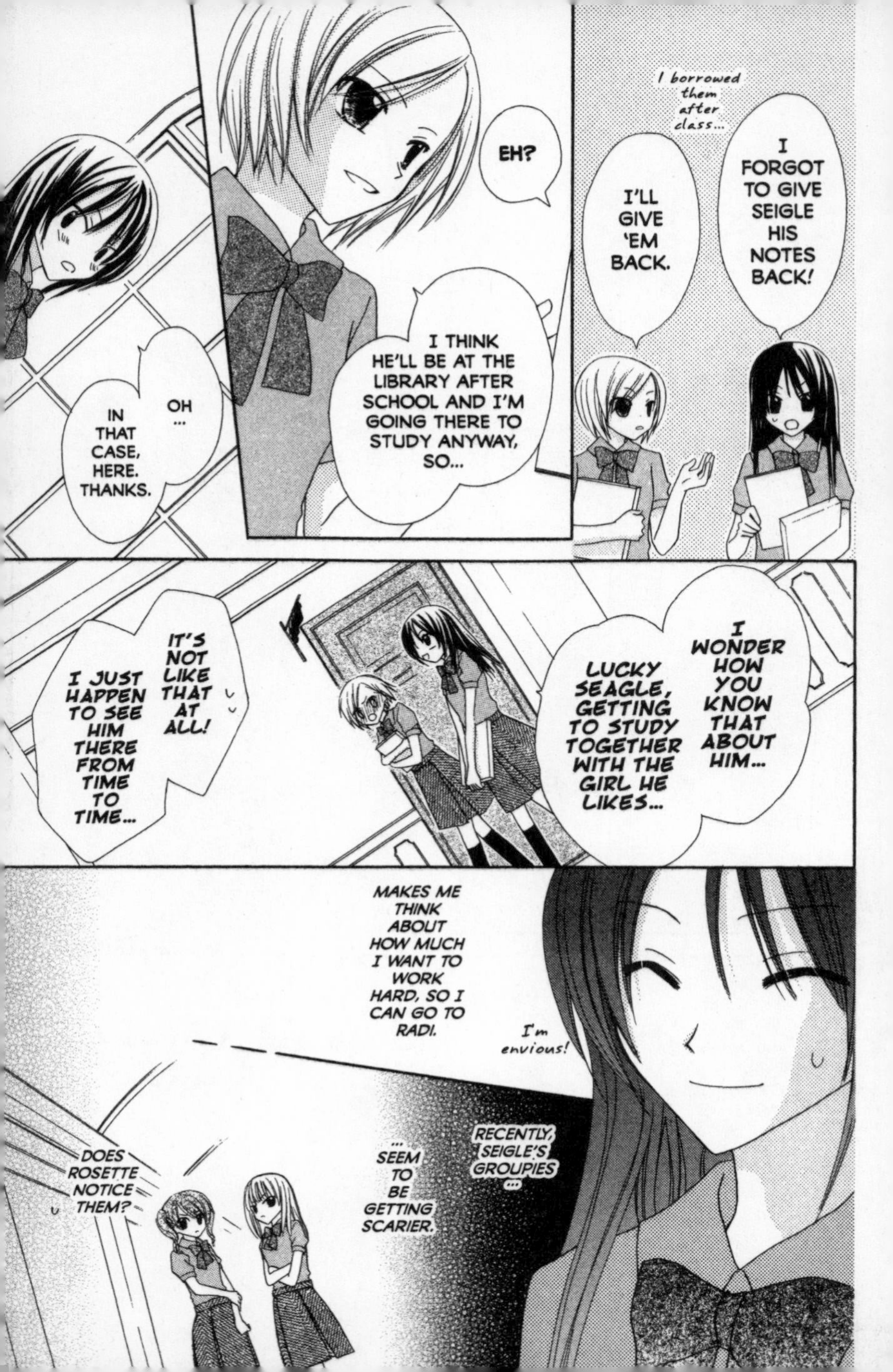
I borrowed them after class...
I FORGOT TO GIVE SEIGLE HIS NOTES BACK!
I'LL GIVE 'EM BACK.
EH?
I THINK HE'LL BE AT THE LIBRARY AFTER SCHOOL AND I'M GOING THERE TO STUDY ANYWAY, SO...
OH...
IN THAT CASE, HERE. THANKS.
I WONDER HOW YOU KNOW THAT ABOUT HIM...
LUCKY SEAGLE, GETTING TO STUDY TOGETHER WITH THE GIRL HE LIKES...
IT'S NOT LIKE THAT AT ALL!
I JUST HAPPEN TO SEE HIM THERE FROM TIME TO TIME...
I'm envious!
MAKES ME THINK ABOUT HOW MUCH I WANT TO WORK HARD, SO I CAN GO TO RADI.
RECENTLY, SEIGLE'S GROUPIES...
...SEEM TO BE GETTING SCARIER.
DOES ROSETTE NOTICE THEM?

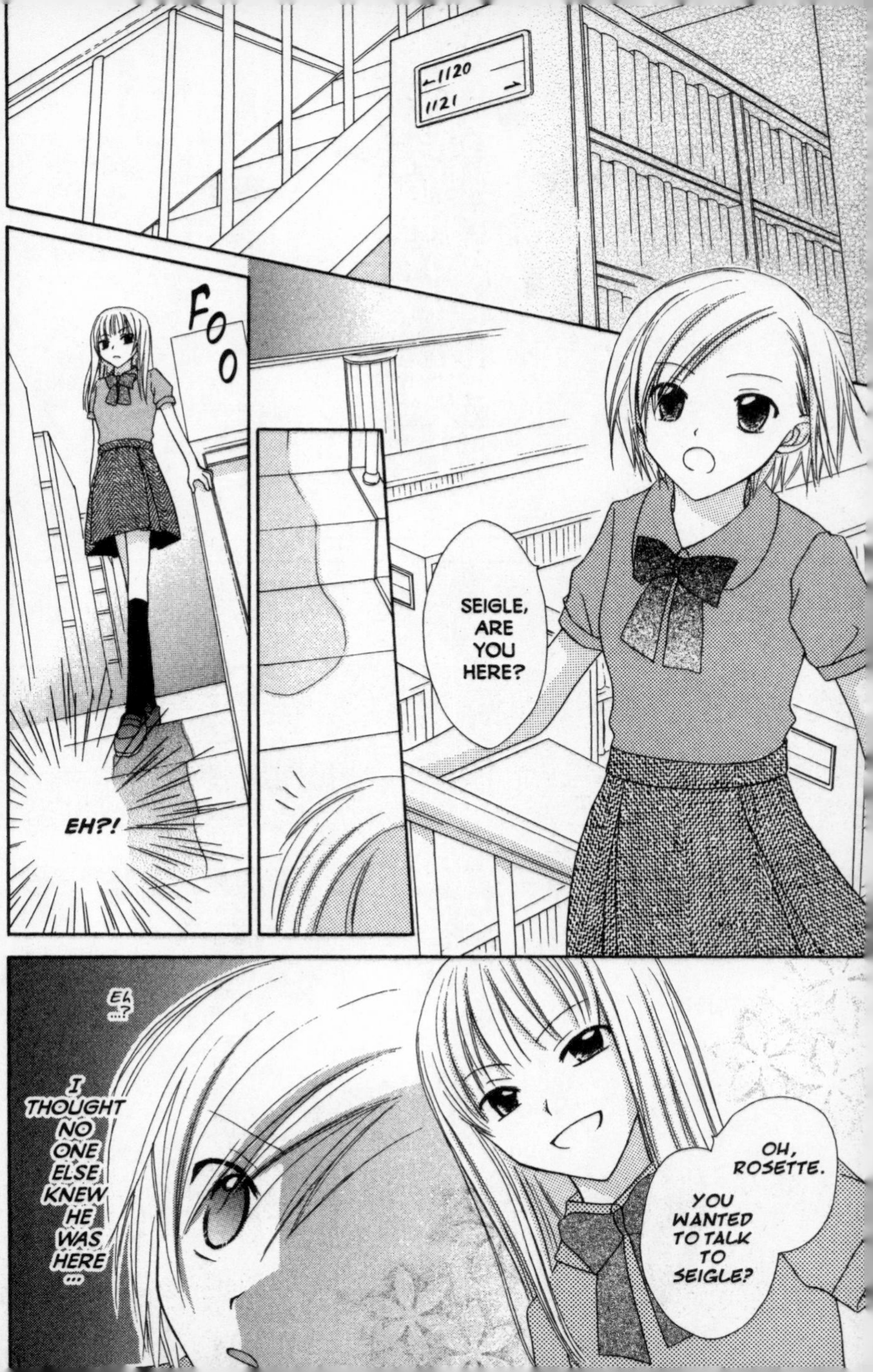

←1120
1121 →
SEIGLE, ARE YOU HERE?
FOO
EH?!
OH, ROSETTE.
YOU WANTED TO TALK TO SEIGLE?
EH ...?
I THOUGHT NO ONE ELSE KNEW HE WAS HERE ...

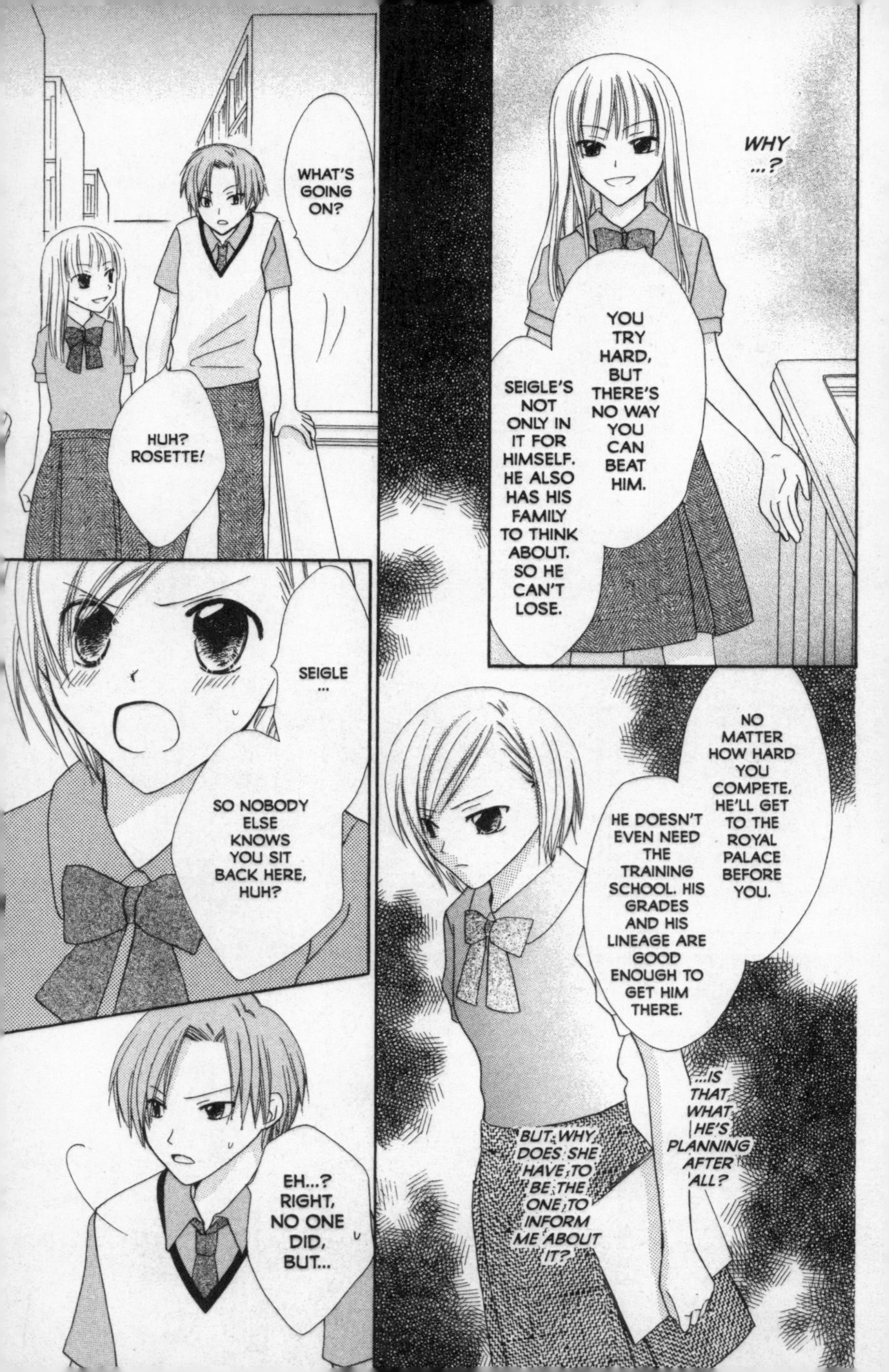
WHY ...?
YOU TRY HARD, BUT THERE'S NO WAY YOU CAN BEAT HIM.
SEIGLE'S NOT ONLY IN IT FOR HIMSELF. HE ALSO HAS HIS FAMILY TO THINK ABOUT. SO HE CAN'T LOSE.
NO MATTER HOW HARD YOU COMPETE, HE'LL GET TO THE ROYAL PALACE BEFORE YOU.
HE DOESN'T EVEN NEED THE TRAINING SCHOOL. HIS GRADES AND HIS LINEAGE ARE GOOD ENOUGH TO GET HIM THERE.
...IS THAT WHAT HE'S PLANNING AFTER ALL?
BUT WHY DOES SHE HAVE TO BE THE ONE TO INFORM ME ABOUT IT?
WHAT'S GOING ON?
HUH? ROSETTE!
SEIGLE ...
SO NOBODY ELSE KNOWS YOU SIT BACK HERE, HUH?
EH...? RIGHT, NO ONE DID, BUT...

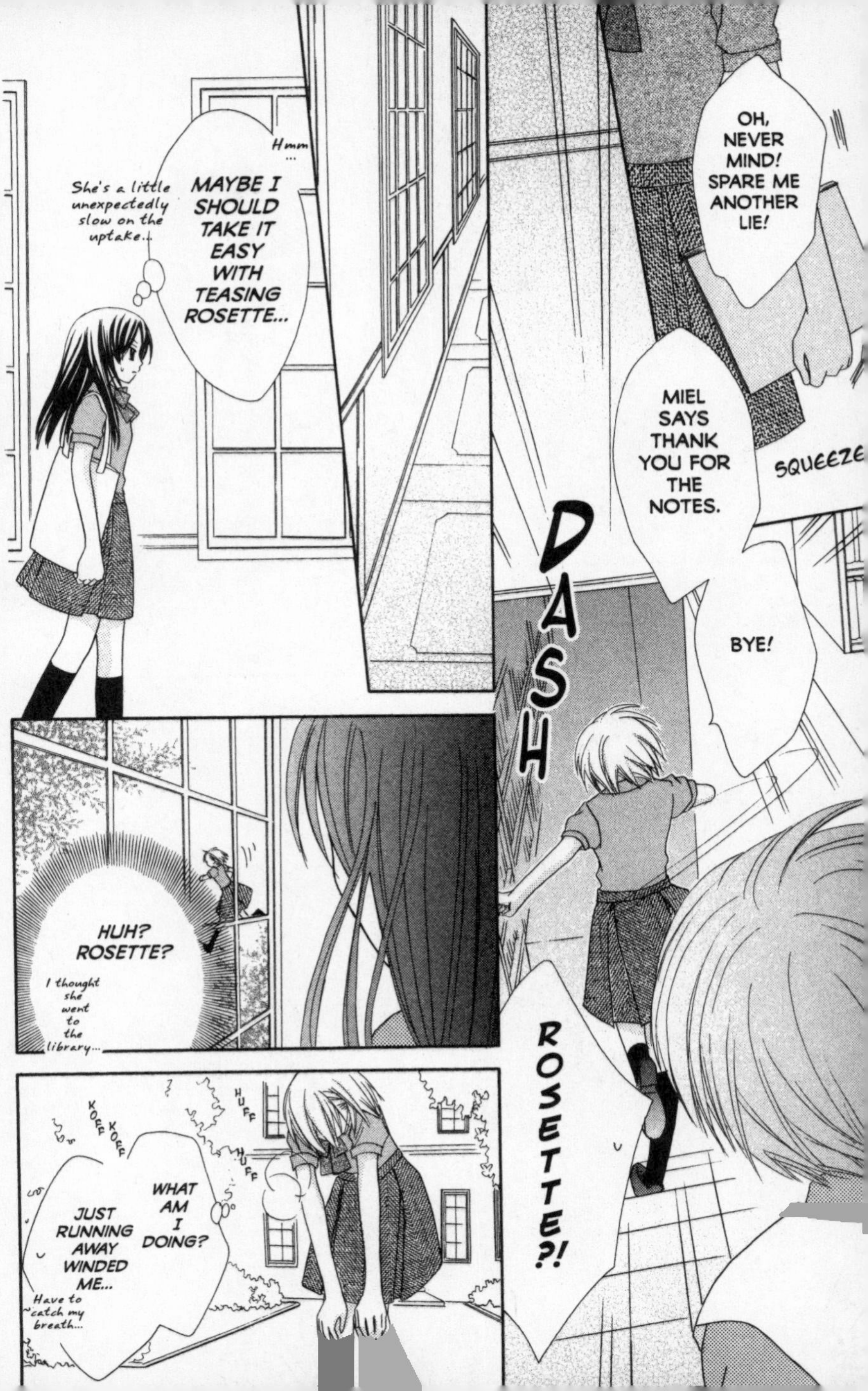
OH, NEVER MIND! SPARE ME ANOTHER LIE!
MIEL SAYS THANK YOU FOR THE NOTES.
SQUEEZE
BYE!
DASH
ROSETTE?!
Hmm...
MAYBE I SHOULD TAKE IT EASY WITH TEASING ROSETTE...
She's a little unexpectedly slow on the uptake...
HUH? ROSETTE?
I thought she went to the library...
HUFF HUFF
WHAT AM I DOING?
KOFF KOFF
JUST RUNNING AWAY WINDED ME...
Have to catch my breath...

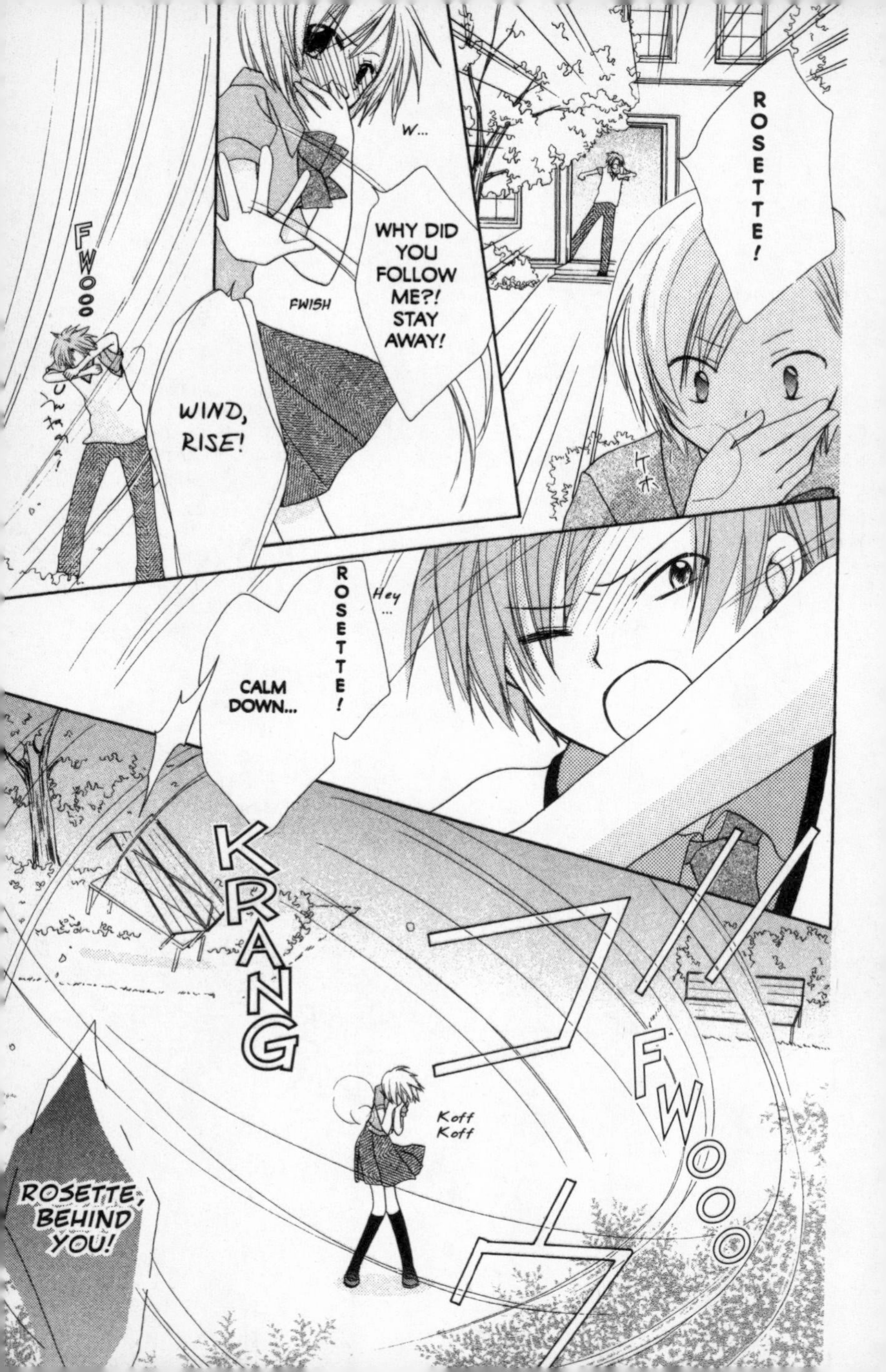
ROSETTE!
W...
WHY DID YOU FOLLOW ME?! STAY AWAY!
FWISH
WIND, RISE!
FWOOO
ROSETTE!
Hey...
CALM DOWN...
KRANG
FWOOO
Koff Koff
ROSETTE, BEHIND YOU!

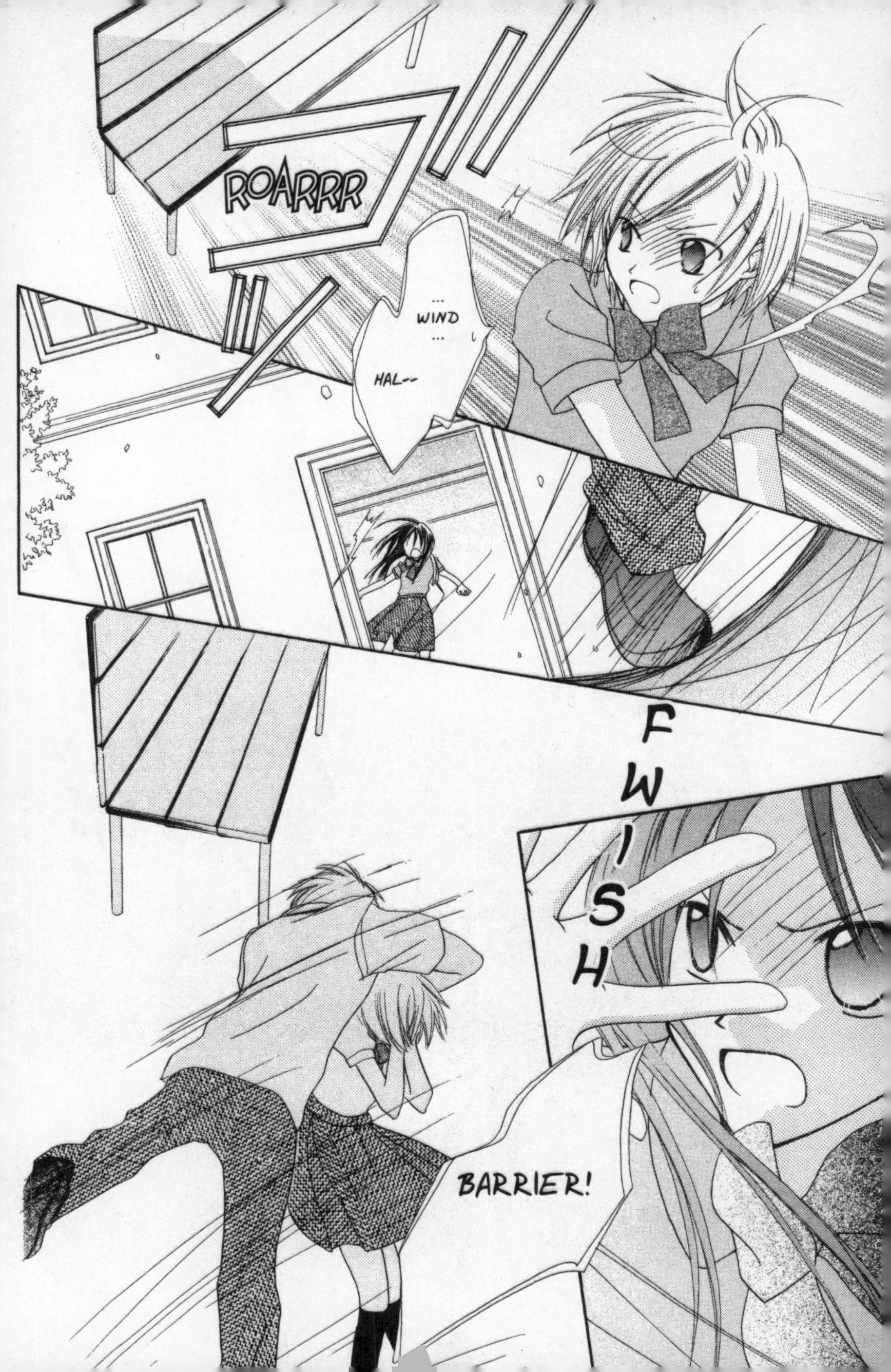
ROARRR
... WIND ... HAL--
FWISH
BARRIER!

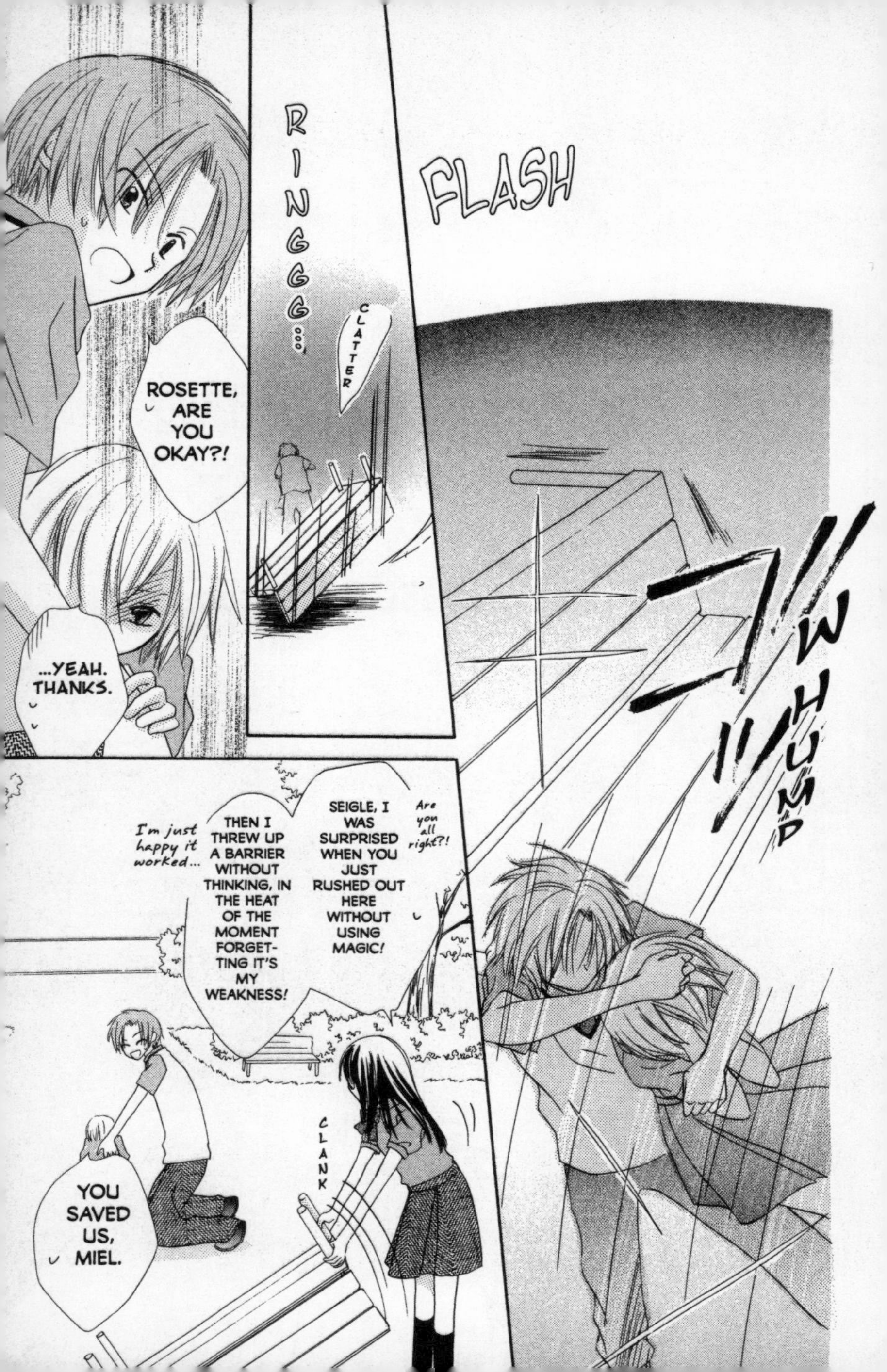
FLASH
WHUMP
RINGGG...
CLATTER
ROSETTE, ARE YOU OKAY?!
...YEAH. THANKS.
Are you all right?!
SEIGLE, I WAS SURPRISED WHEN YOU JUST RUSHED OUT HERE WITHOUT USING MAGIC!
THEN I THREW UP A BARRIER WITHOUT THINKING, IN THE HEAT OF THE MOMENT FORGETTING IT'S MY WEAKNESS!
I'm just happy it worked...
CLANK
YOU SAVED US, MIEL.

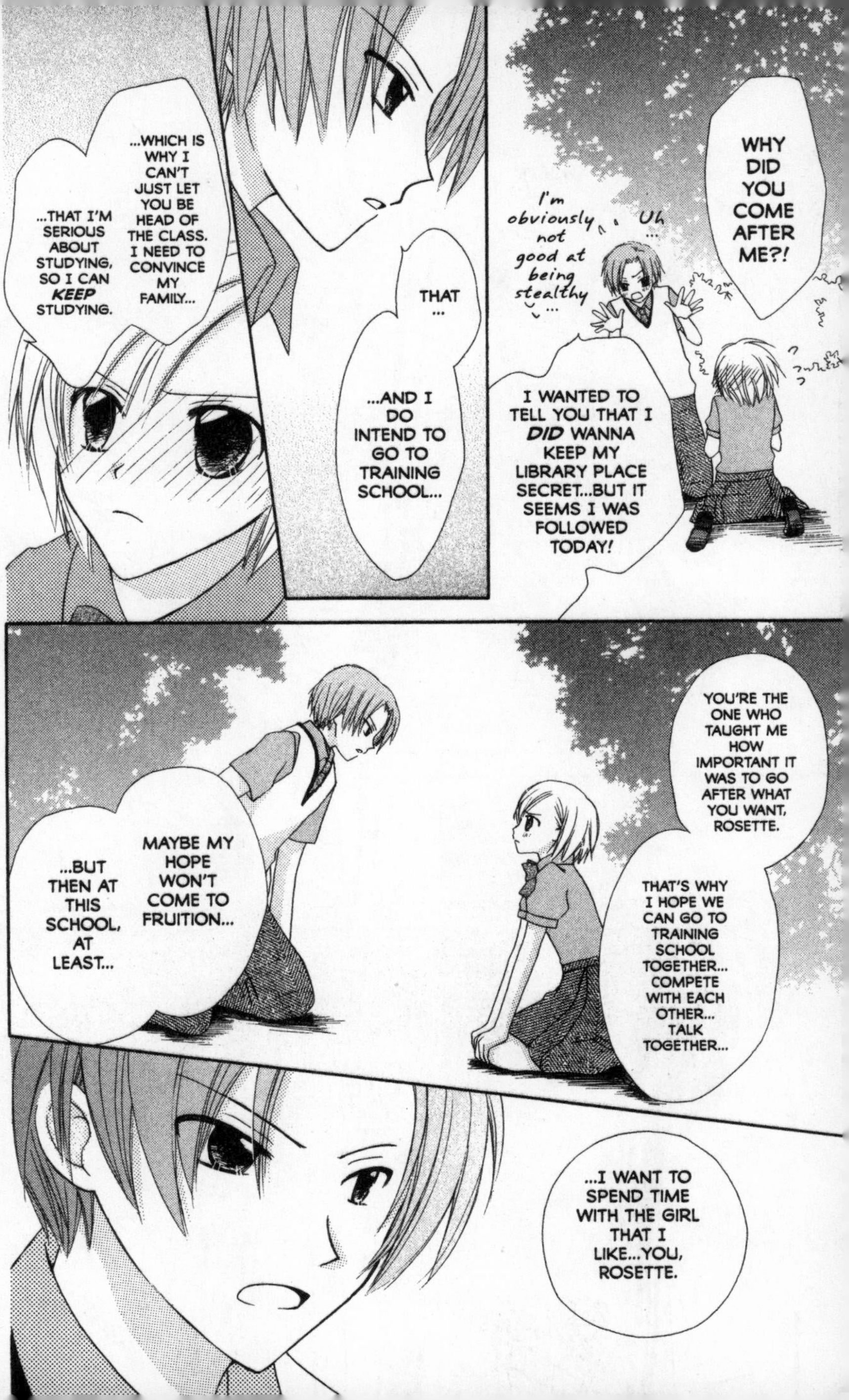
WHY DID YOU COME AFTER ME?!
Uh ...
I'm obviously not good at being stealthy ...
I WANTED TO TELL YOU THAT I *DID* WANNA KEEP MY LIBRARY PLACE SECRET...BUT IT SEEMS I WAS FOLLOWED TODAY!
THAT ...
...AND I DO INTEND TO GO TO TRAINING SCHOOL...
...WHICH IS WHY I CAN'T JUST LET YOU BE HEAD OF THE CLASS. I NEED TO CONVINCE MY FAMILY...
...THAT I'M SERIOUS ABOUT STUDYING, SO I CAN *KEEP* STUDYING.
YOU'RE THE ONE WHO TAUGHT ME HOW IMPORTANT IT WAS TO GO AFTER WHAT YOU WANT, ROSETTE.
THAT'S WHY I HOPE WE CAN GO TO TRAINING SCHOOL TOGETHER... COMPETE WITH EACH OTHER... TALK TOGETHER...
MAYBE MY HOPE WON'T COME TO FRUITION...
...BUT THEN AT THIS SCHOOL, AT LEAST...
...I WANT TO SPEND TIME WITH THE GIRL THAT I LIKE...YOU, ROSETTE.

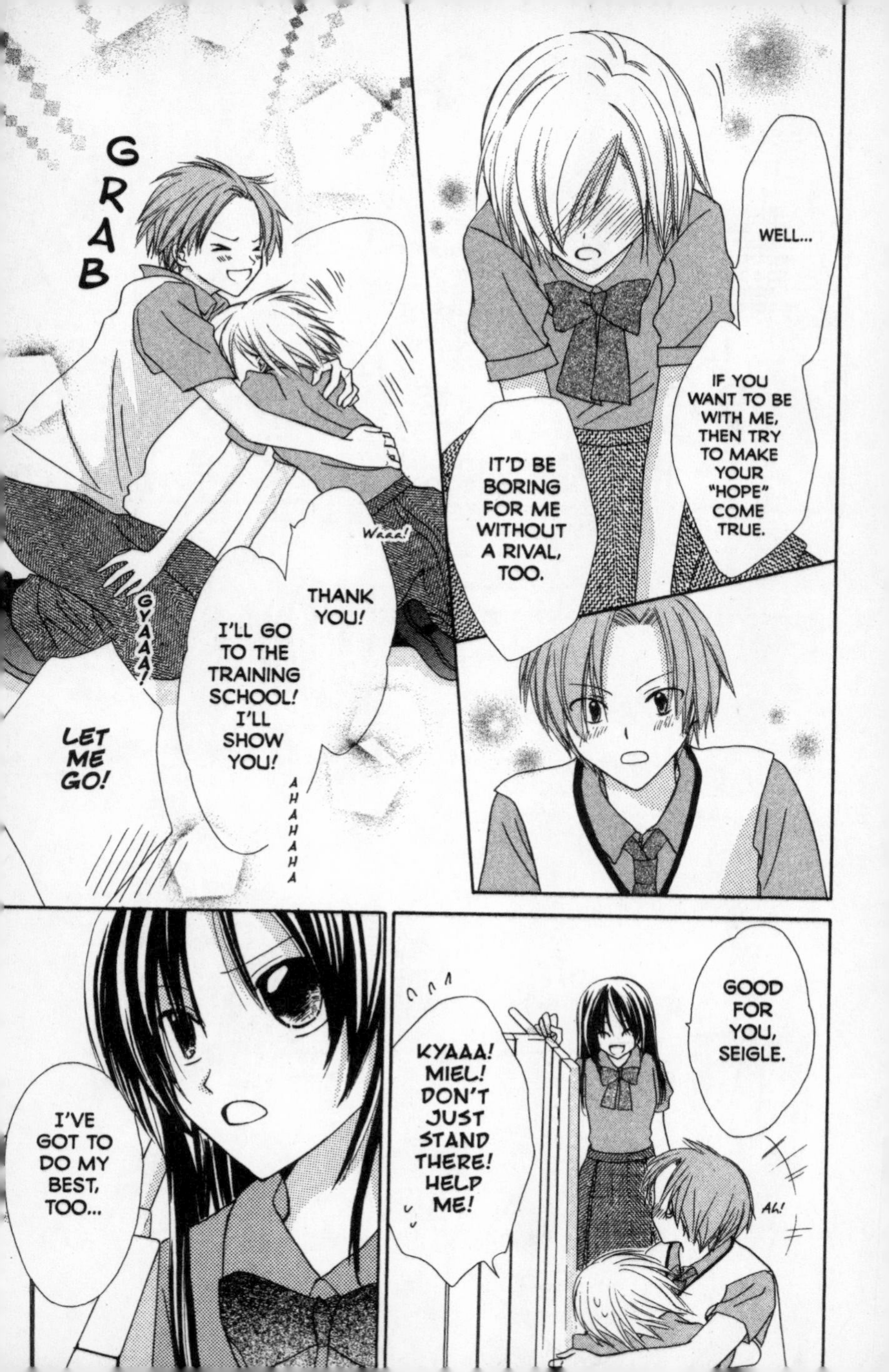
WELL...
IF YOU WANT TO BE WITH ME, THEN TRY TO MAKE YOUR "HOPE" COME TRUE.
IT'D BE BORING FOR ME WITHOUT A RIVAL, TOO.
GRAB
Waaa!
THANK YOU! I'LL GO TO THE TRAINING SCHOOL! I'LL SHOW YOU!
AHAHAHAHA
GYAAA!
LET ME GO!
GOOD FOR YOU, SEIGLE.
KYAAA! MIEL! DON'T JUST STAND THERE! HELP ME!
Ah!
I'VE GOT TO DO MY BEST, TOO...

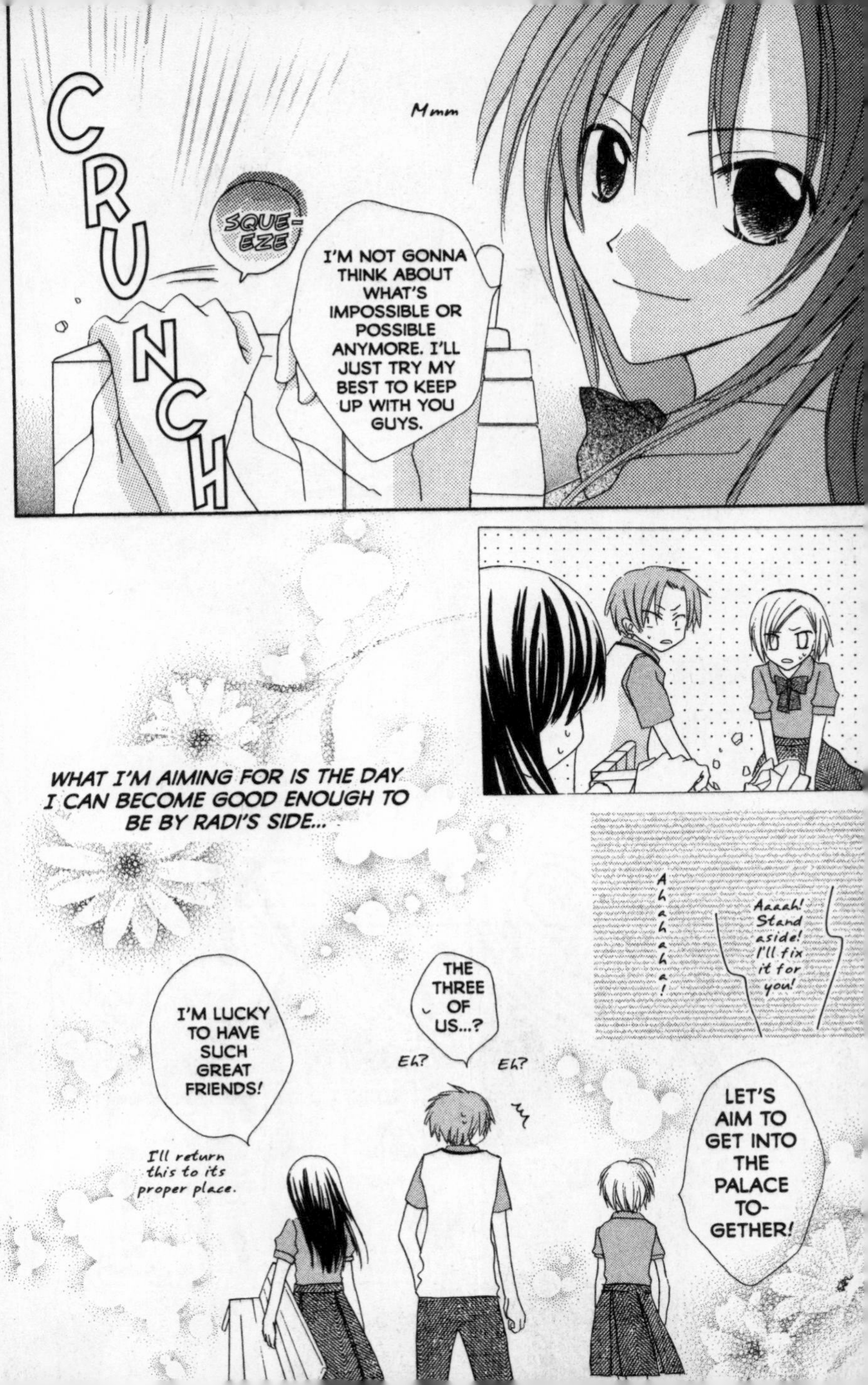
Mmm
I'M NOT GONNA THINK ABOUT WHAT'S IMPOSSIBLE OR POSSIBLE ANYMORE. I'LL JUST TRY MY BEST TO KEEP UP WITH YOU GUYS.
SQUE-EZE
CRUNCH
Aaaah! Stand aside! I'll fix it for you!
Ahahaha!
WHAT I'M AIMING FOR IS THE DAY I CAN BECOME GOOD ENOUGH TO BE BY RADI'S SIDE...
LET'S AIM TO GET INTO THE PALACE TO-GETHER!
Eh?
THE THREE OF US...?
Eh?
I'M LUCKY TO HAVE SUCH GREAT FRIENDS!
I'll return this to its proper place.

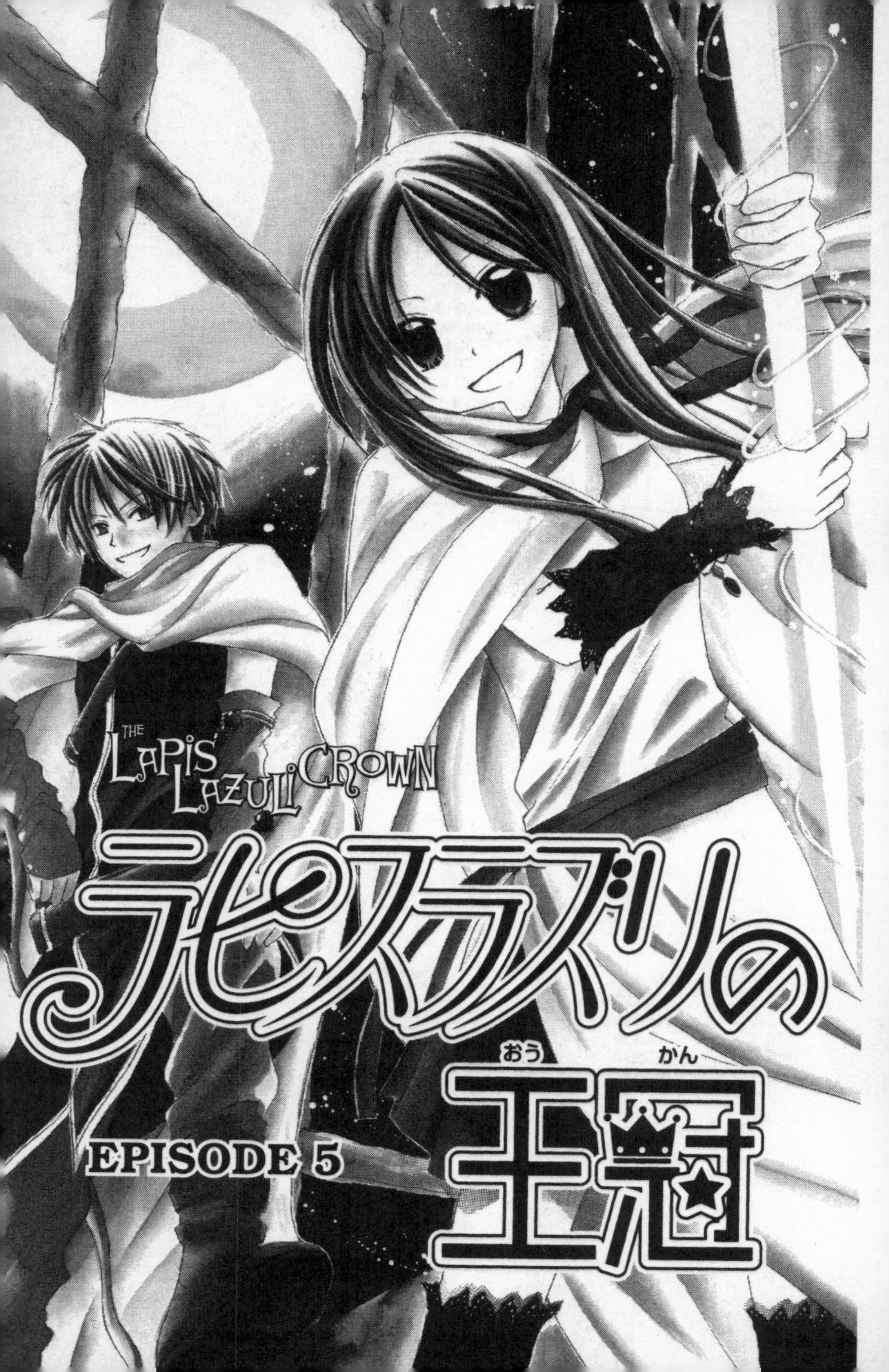
THE LAPIS LAZULI CROWN
ラピスラズリの
王冠（おうかん）
EPISODE 5

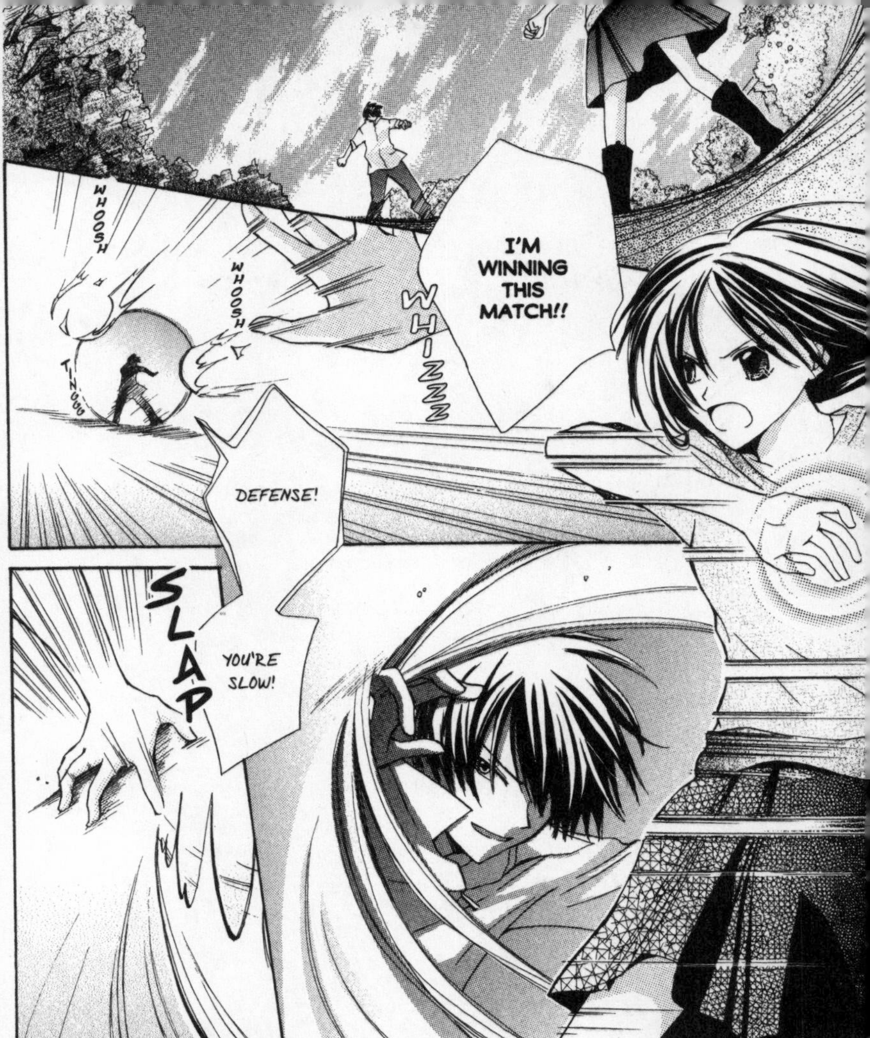
I'M WINNING THIS MATCH!!
WHIZZZ
WHOOSH
WHOOSH
TINGGG
DEFENSE!
YOU'RE SLOW!
SLAP

GUIDE TO THE KINGDOM OF SAVARIN 3

SARACEL

THE SECOND MAJOR CITY IN THE SOUTHERN PART OF THE COUNTRY. NEAR BOTH THE SEA AND MOUNTAINS, THIS TOWN HAS MANY HEALTH RESORTS AND VILLAS. IT'S A QUIET, POPULAR TOWN, AND NOT SO FAR FROM ZALA.

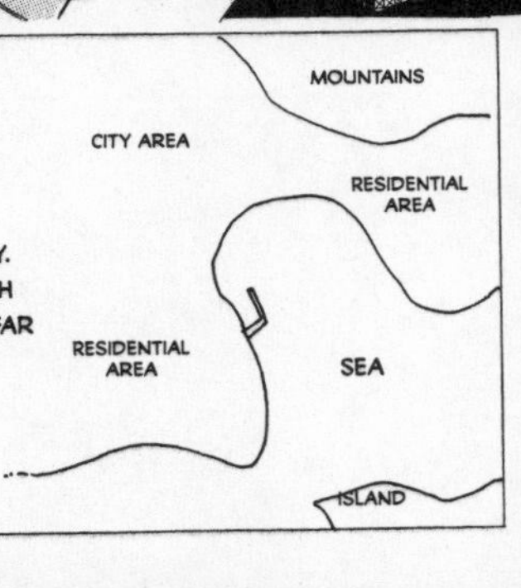
MOUNTAINS
CITY AREA
RESIDENTIAL AREA
RESIDENTIAL AREA
SEA
ISLAND

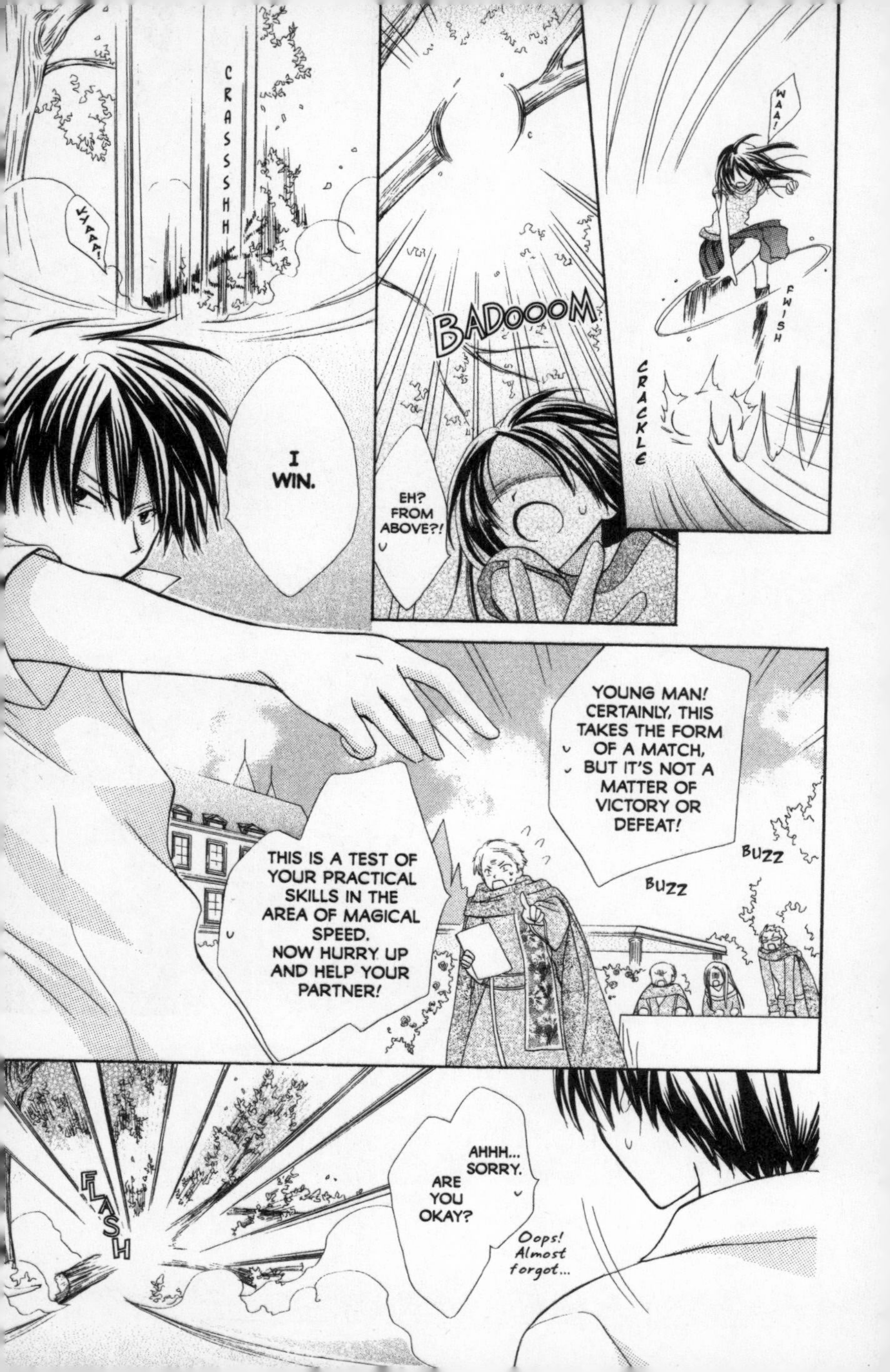
WAA!
FWISH
CRACKLE
BADOOOM
EH? FROM ABOVE?!
CRASSSHH
KYAAA!
I WIN.
YOUNG MAN! CERTAINLY, THIS TAKES THE FORM OF A MATCH, BUT IT'S NOT A MATTER OF VICTORY OR DEFEAT!
BUZZ
BUZZ
THIS IS A TEST OF YOUR PRACTICAL SKILLS IN THE AREA OF MAGICAL SPEED. NOW HURRY UP AND HELP YOUR PARTNER!
AHHH... SORRY. ARE YOU OKAY?
Oops! Almost forgot...
FLASH

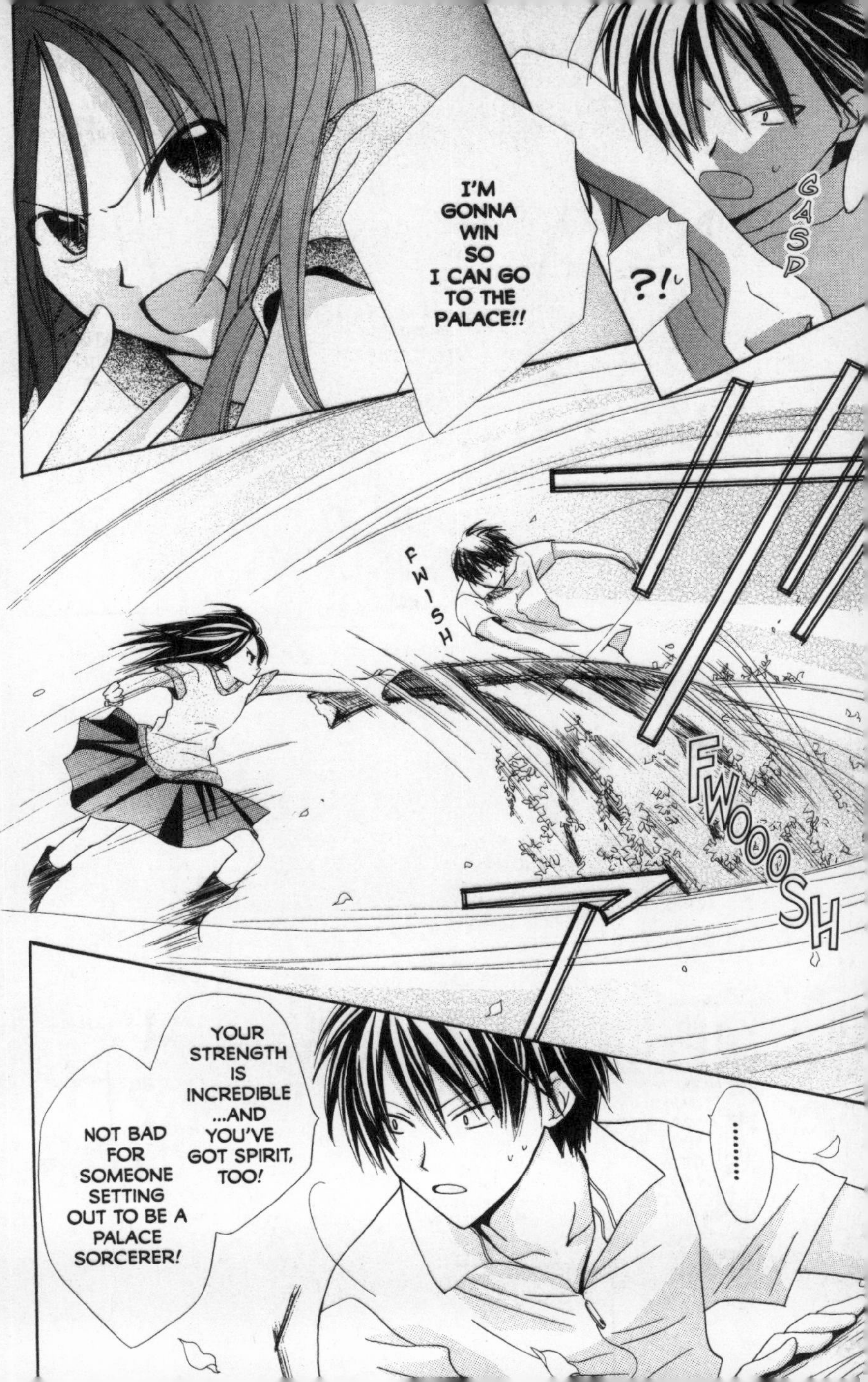
GASP
?!
I'M GONNA WIN SO I CAN GO TO THE PALACE!!
FWISH
FWOOOSH
......
YOUR STRENGTH IS INCREDIBLE ...AND YOU'VE GOT SPIRIT, TOO!
NOT BAD FOR SOMEONE SETTING OUT TO BE A PALACE SORCERER!

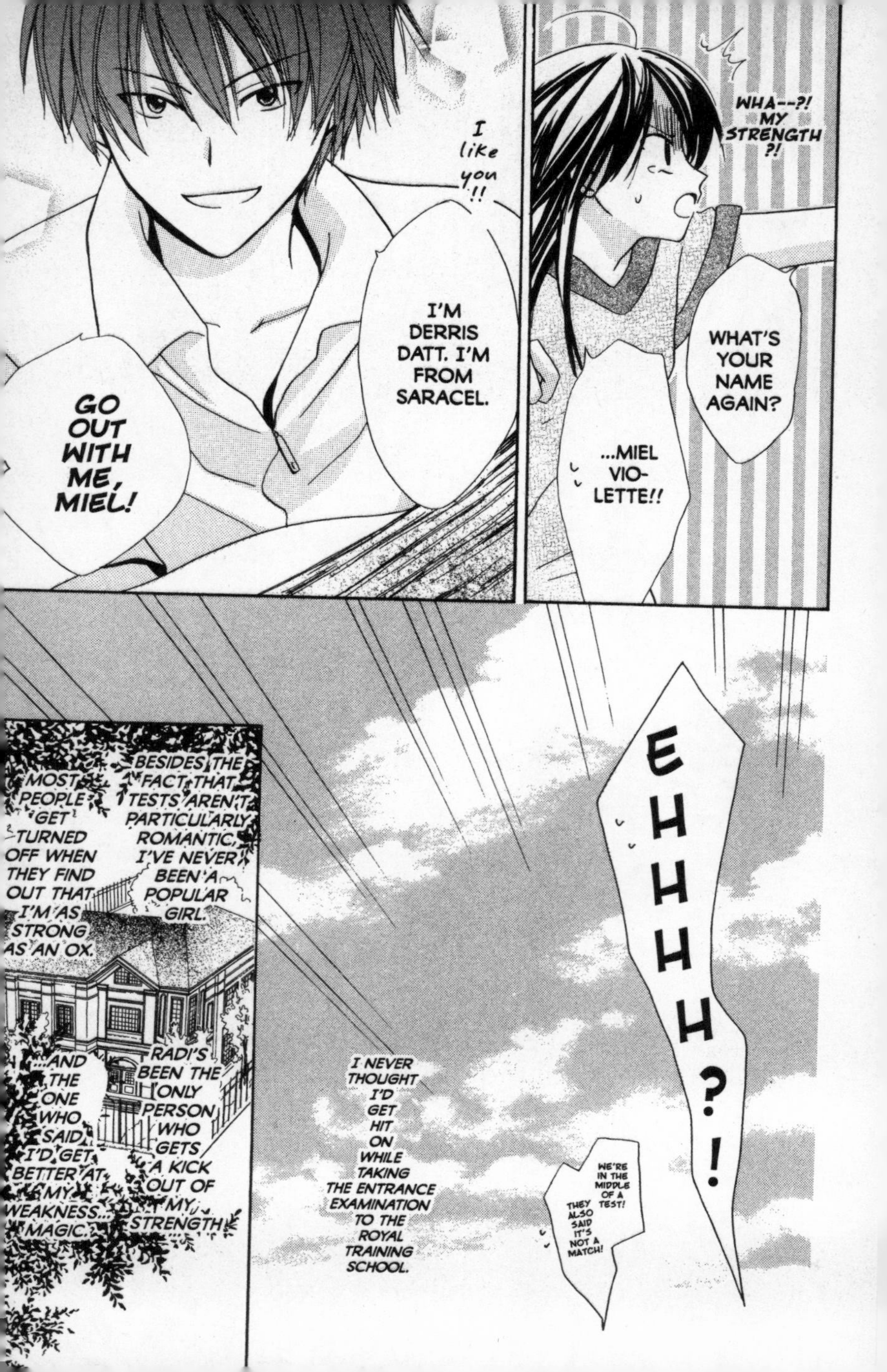
WHA--?! MY STRENGTH ?!
WHAT'S YOUR NAME AGAIN?
...MIEL VIO-LETTE!!
I like you !!
I'M DERRIS DATT. I'M FROM SARACEL.
GO OUT WITH ME, MIEL!
EHHHH?!
WE'RE IN THE MIDDLE OF A TEST! THEY ALSO SAID IT'S NOT A MATCH!
I NEVER THOUGHT I'D GET HIT ON WHILE TAKING THE ENTRANCE EXAMINATION TO THE ROYAL TRAINING SCHOOL.
BESIDES THE FACT THAT TESTS AREN'T PARTICULARLY ROMANTIC, I'VE NEVER BEEN A POPULAR GIRL.
MOST PEOPLE GET TURNED OFF WHEN THEY FIND OUT THAT I'M AS STRONG AS AN OX.
RADI'S BEEN THE ONLY PERSON WHO GETS A KICK OUT OF MY STRENGTH...
...AND THE ONE WHO SAID I'D GET BETTER AT MY WEAKNESS... MAGIC.

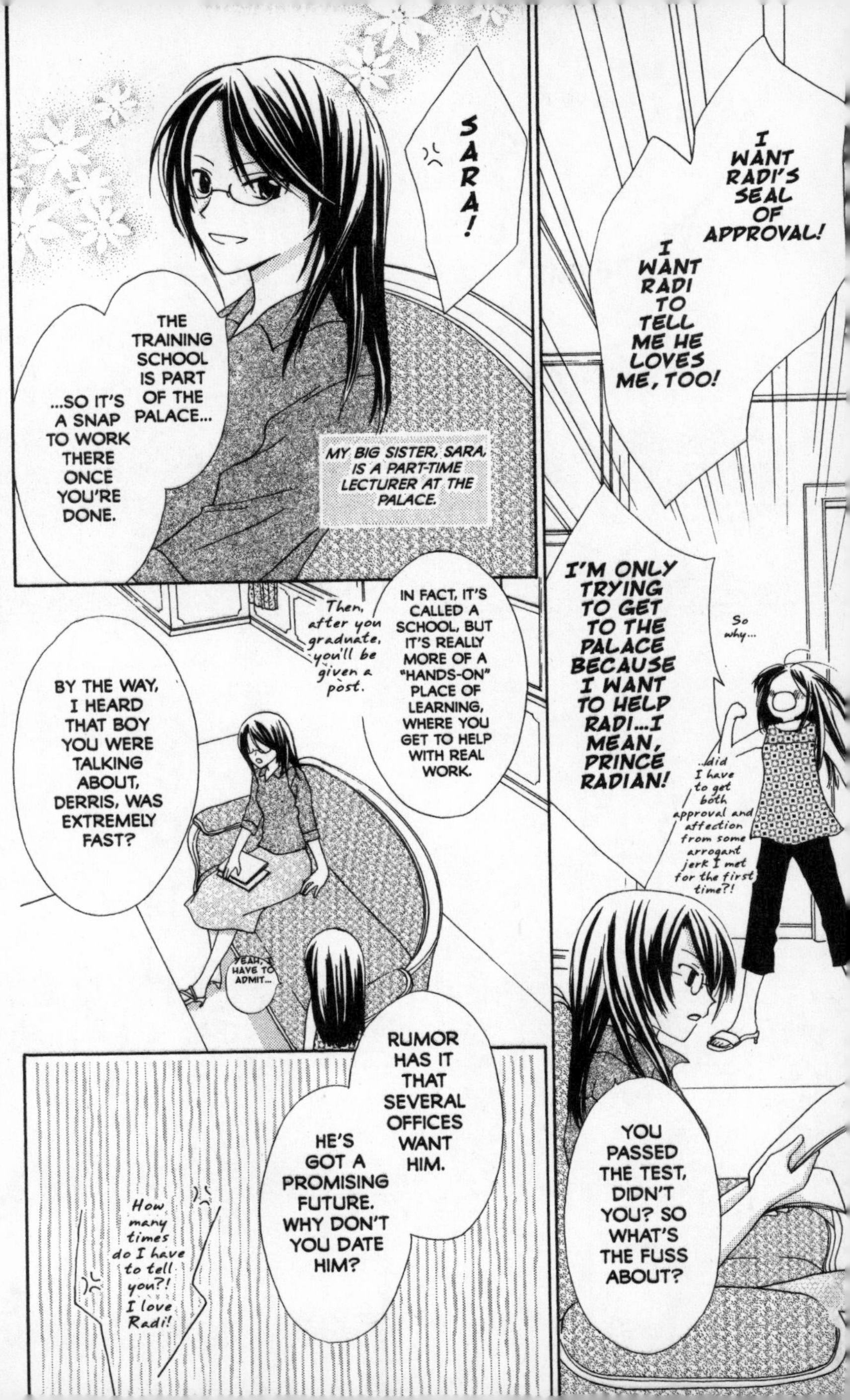

I WANT RADI'S SEAL OF APPROVAL!
I WANT RADI TO TELL ME HE LOVES ME, TOO!
I'M ONLY TRYING TO GET TO THE PALACE BECAUSE I WANT TO HELP RADI...I MEAN, PRINCE RADIAN!
So why...
...did I have to get both approval and affection from some arrogant jerk I met for the first time?!
YOU PASSED THE TEST, DIDN'T YOU? SO WHAT'S THE FUSS ABOUT?
SARA!
THE TRAINING SCHOOL IS PART OF THE PALACE...
...SO IT'S A SNAP TO WORK THERE ONCE YOU'RE DONE.
MY BIG SISTER, SARA, IS A PART-TIME LECTURER AT THE PALACE.
IN FACT, IT'S CALLED A SCHOOL, BUT IT'S REALLY MORE OF A "HANDS-ON" PLACE OF LEARNING, WHERE YOU GET TO HELP WITH REAL WORK.
Then, after you graduate, you'll be given a post.
BY THE WAY, I HEARD THAT BOY YOU WERE TALKING ABOUT, DERRIS, WAS EXTREMELY FAST?
YEAH, I HAVE TO ADMIT...
RUMOR HAS IT THAT SEVERAL OFFICES WANT HIM.
HE'S GOT A PROMISING FUTURE. WHY DON'T YOU DATE HIM?
How many times do I have to tell you?! I love Radi!

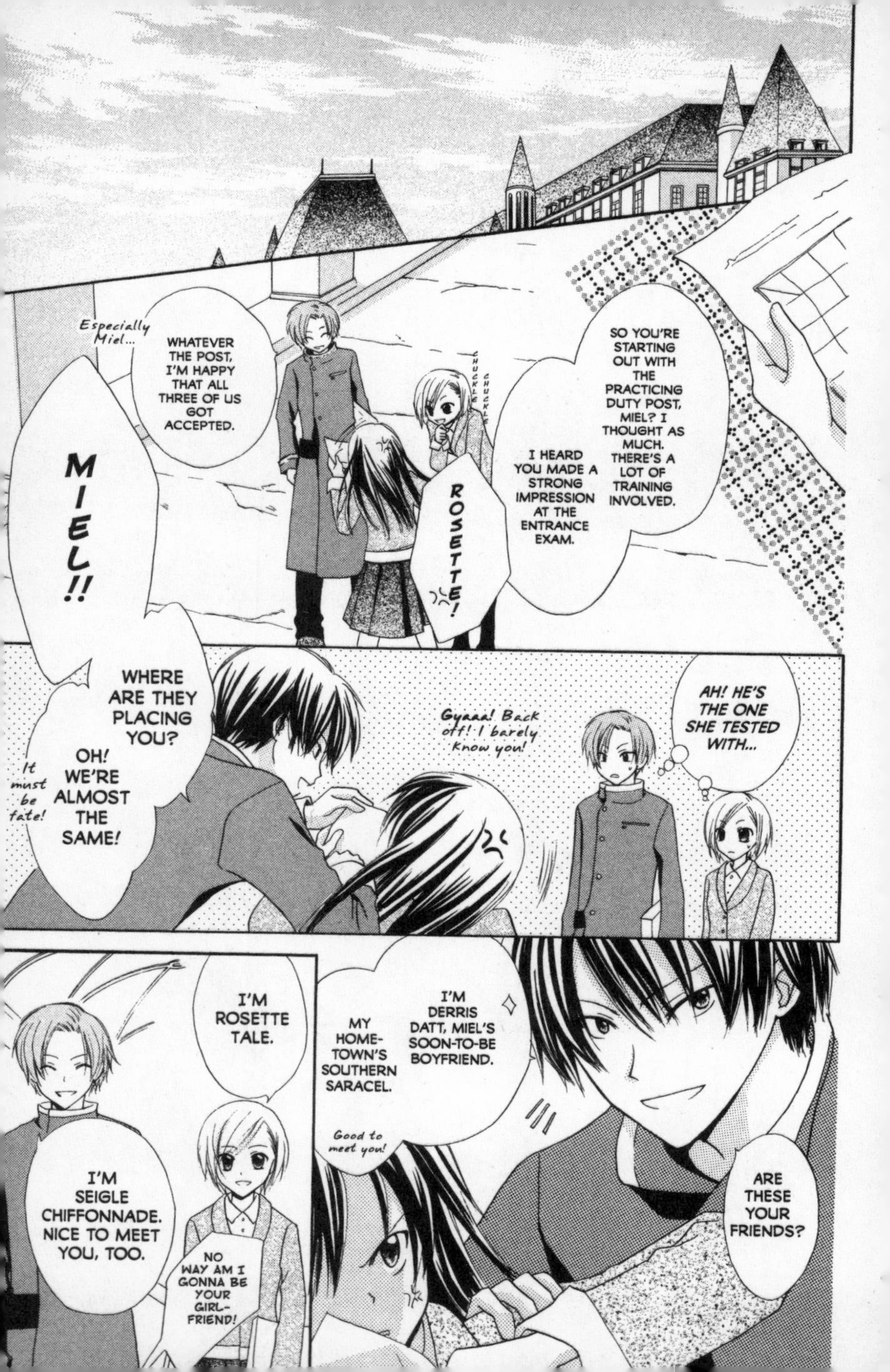

SO YOU'RE STARTING OUT WITH THE PRACTICING DUTY POST, MIEL? I THOUGHT AS MUCH. THERE'S A LOT OF TRAINING INVOLVED.
I HEARD YOU MADE A STRONG IMPRESSION AT THE ENTRANCE EXAM.
CHUCKLE CHUCKLE
ROSETTE!
WHATEVER THE POST, I'M HAPPY THAT ALL THREE OF US GOT ACCEPTED.
Especially Miel...
MIEL!!
AH! HE'S THE ONE SHE TESTED WITH...
Gyaaa! Back off! I barely know you!
WHERE ARE THEY PLACING YOU?
OH! WE'RE ALMOST THE SAME!
It must be fate!
ARE THESE YOUR FRIENDS?
I'M DERRIS DATT, MIEL'S SOON-TO-BE BOYFRIEND.
MY HOME-TOWN'S SOUTHERN SARACEL.
Good to meet you!
NO WAY AM I GONNA BE YOUR GIRL-FRIEND!
I'M ROSETTE TALE.
I'M SEIGLE CHIFFONNADE. NICE TO MEET YOU, TOO.

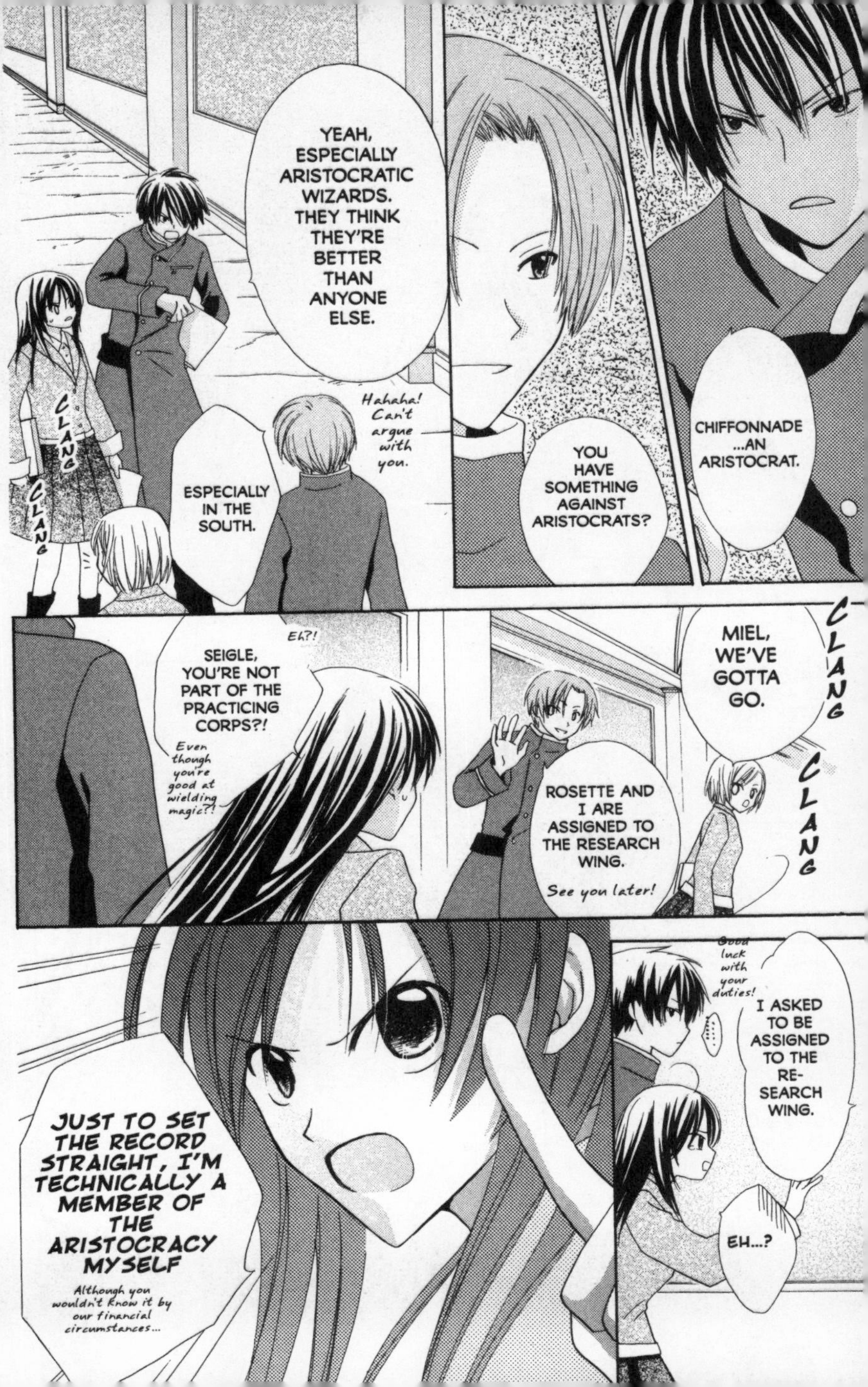
CHIFFONNADE ...AN ARISTOCRAT.
YOU HAVE SOMETHING AGAINST ARISTOCRATS?
YEAH, ESPECIALLY ARISTOCRATIC WIZARDS. THEY THINK THEY'RE BETTER THAN ANYONE ELSE.
Hahaha! Can't argue with you.
ESPECIALLY IN THE SOUTH.
CLANG
CLANG
CLANG
CLANG
MIEL, WE'VE GOTTA GO.
ROSETTE AND I ARE ASSIGNED TO THE RESEARCH WING.
See you later!
Eh?!
SEIGLE, YOU'RE NOT PART OF THE PRACTICING CORPS?!
Even though you're good at wielding magic?!
Good luck with your duties!
I ASKED TO BE ASSIGNED TO THE RE-SEARCH WING.
EH...?
JUST TO SET THE RECORD STRAIGHT, I'M TECHNICALLY A MEMBER OF THE ARISTOCRACY MYSELF
Although you wouldn't know it by our financial circumstances...

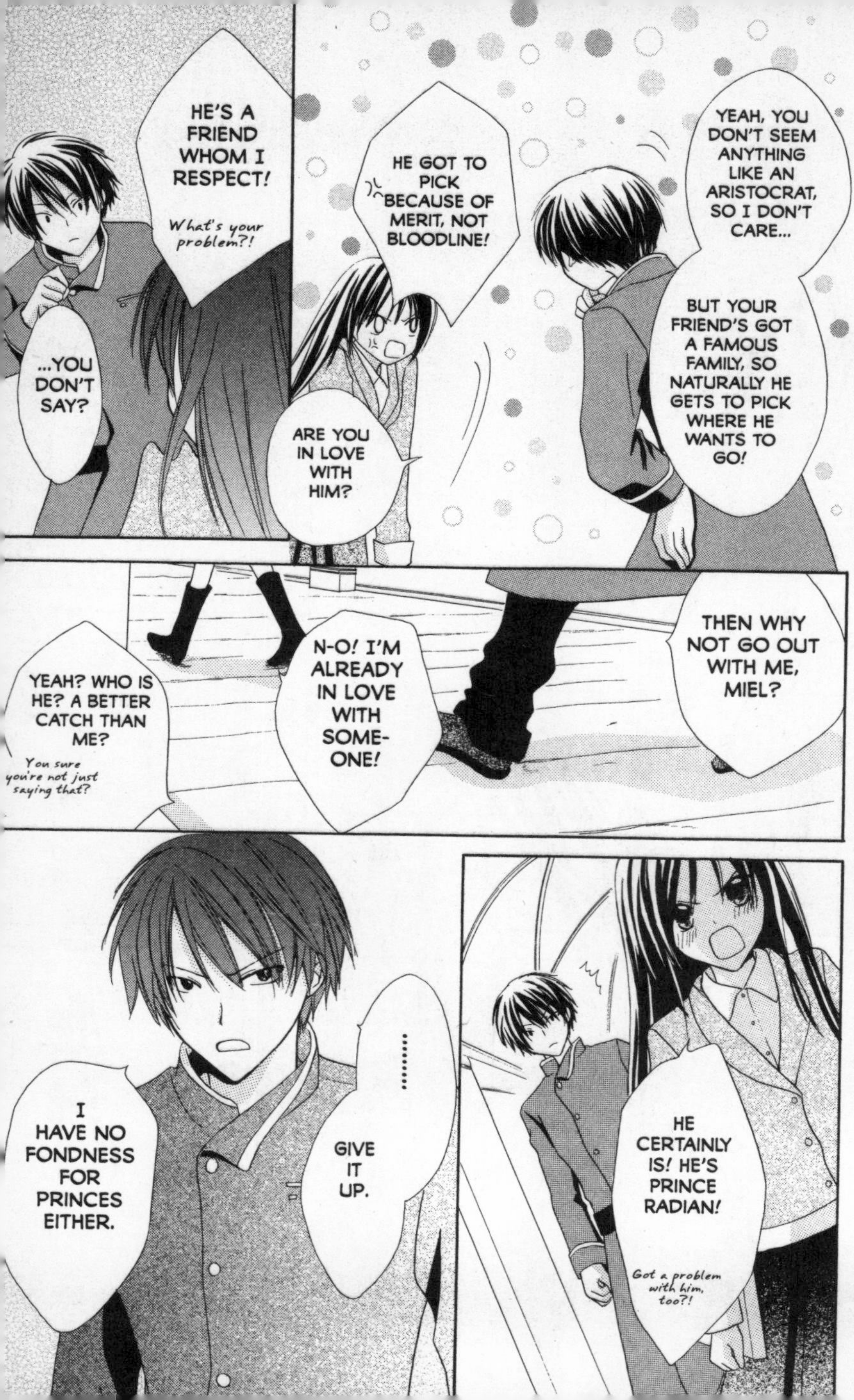
YEAH, YOU DON'T SEEM ANYTHING LIKE AN ARISTOCRAT, SO I DON'T CARE...
BUT YOUR FRIEND'S GOT A FAMOUS FAMILY, SO NATURALLY HE GETS TO PICK WHERE HE WANTS TO GO!
HE GOT TO PICK BECAUSE OF MERIT, NOT BLOODLINE!
ARE YOU IN LOVE WITH HIM?
HE'S A FRIEND WHOM I RESPECT!
What's your problem?!
...YOU DON'T SAY?
THEN WHY NOT GO OUT WITH ME, MIEL?
N-O! I'M ALREADY IN LOVE WITH SOME-ONE!
YEAH? WHO IS HE? A BETTER CATCH THAN ME?
You sure you're not just saying that?
HE CERTAINLY IS! HE'S PRINCE RADIAN!
Got a problem with him, too?!
....
GIVE IT UP.
I HAVE NO FONDNESS FOR PRINCES EITHER.

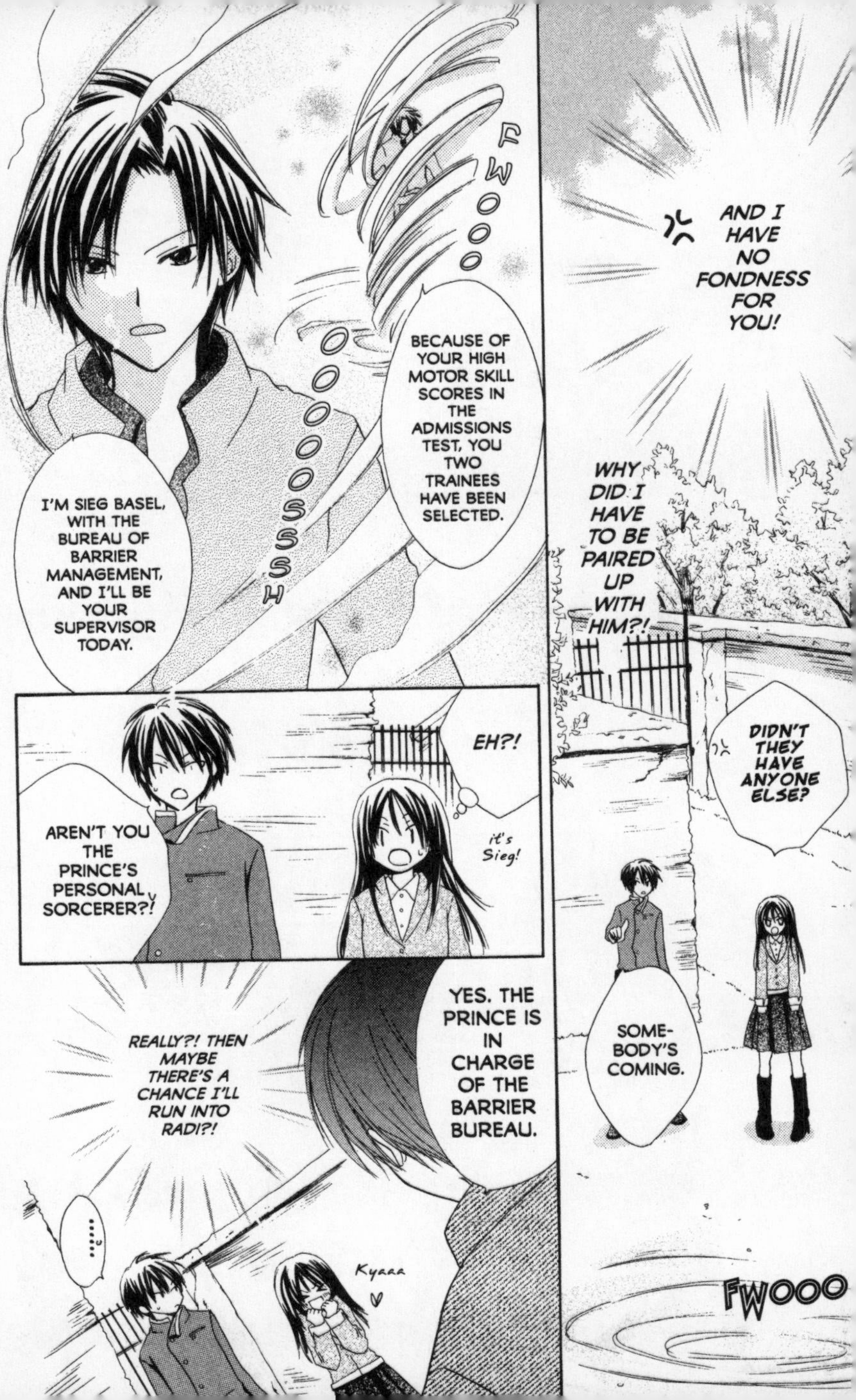
AND I HAVE NO FONDNESS FOR YOU!
WHY DID I HAVE TO BE PAIRED UP WITH HIM?!
DIDN'T THEY HAVE ANYONE ELSE?
SOME-BODY'S COMING.
FWOOO
FWOOOOOOOOOSSSH
BECAUSE OF YOUR HIGH MOTOR SKILL SCORES IN THE ADMISSIONS TEST, YOU TWO TRAINEES HAVE BEEN SELECTED.
I'M SIEG BASEL, WITH THE BUREAU OF BARRIER MANAGEMENT, AND I'LL BE YOUR SUPERVISOR TODAY.
EH?!
it's Sieg!
AREN'T YOU THE PRINCE'S PERSONAL SORCERER?!
YES. THE PRINCE IS IN CHARGE OF THE BARRIER BUREAU.
REALLY?! THEN MAYBE THERE'S A CHANCE I'LL RUN INTO RADI?!
Kyaaa
......

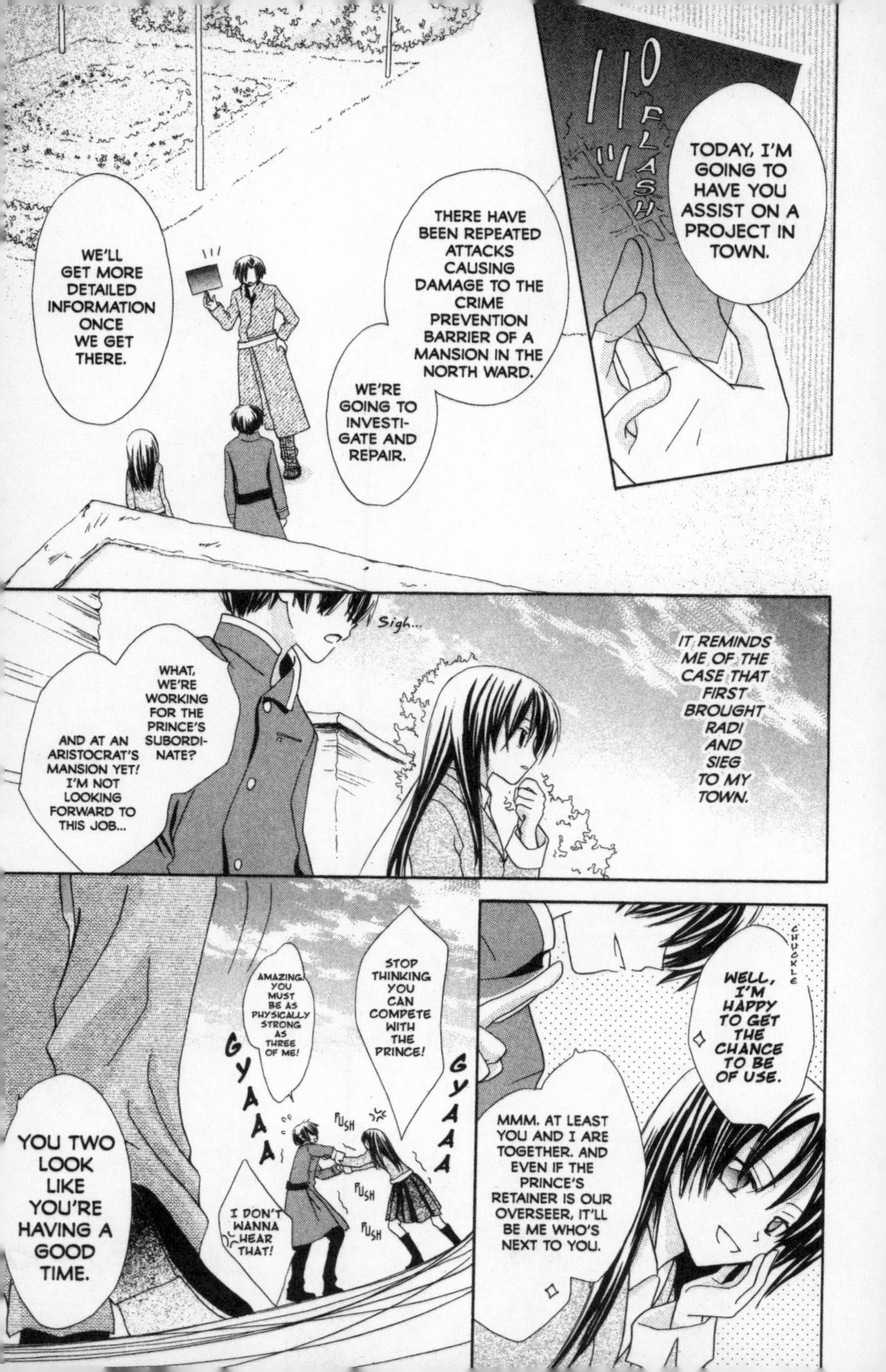
FLASH
TODAY, I'M GOING TO HAVE YOU ASSIST ON A PROJECT IN TOWN.
THERE HAVE BEEN REPEATED ATTACKS CAUSING DAMAGE TO THE CRIME PREVENTION BARRIER OF A MANSION IN THE NORTH WARD.
WE'RE GOING TO INVESTI-GATE AND REPAIR.
WE'LL GET MORE DETAILED INFORMATION ONCE WE GET THERE.
IT REMINDS ME OF THE CASE THAT FIRST BROUGHT RADI AND SIEG TO MY TOWN.
Sigh...
WHAT, WE'RE WORKING FOR THE PRINCE'S SUBORDI-NATE?
AND AT AN ARISTOCRAT'S MANSION YET! I'M NOT LOOKING FORWARD TO THIS JOB...
CHUCKLE
WELL, I'M HAPPY TO GET THE CHANCE TO BE OF USE.
MMM. AT LEAST YOU AND I ARE TOGETHER. AND EVEN IF THE PRINCE'S RETAINER IS OUR OVERSEER, IT'LL BE ME WHO'S NEXT TO YOU.
STOP THINKING YOU CAN COMPETE WITH THE PRINCE!
GYAAA
AMAZING! YOU MUST BE AS PHYSICALLY STRONG AS THREE OF ME!
GYAAA
PUSH
PUSH
PUSH
I DON'T WANNA HEAR THAT!
YOU TWO LOOK LIKE YOU'RE HAVING A GOOD TIME.

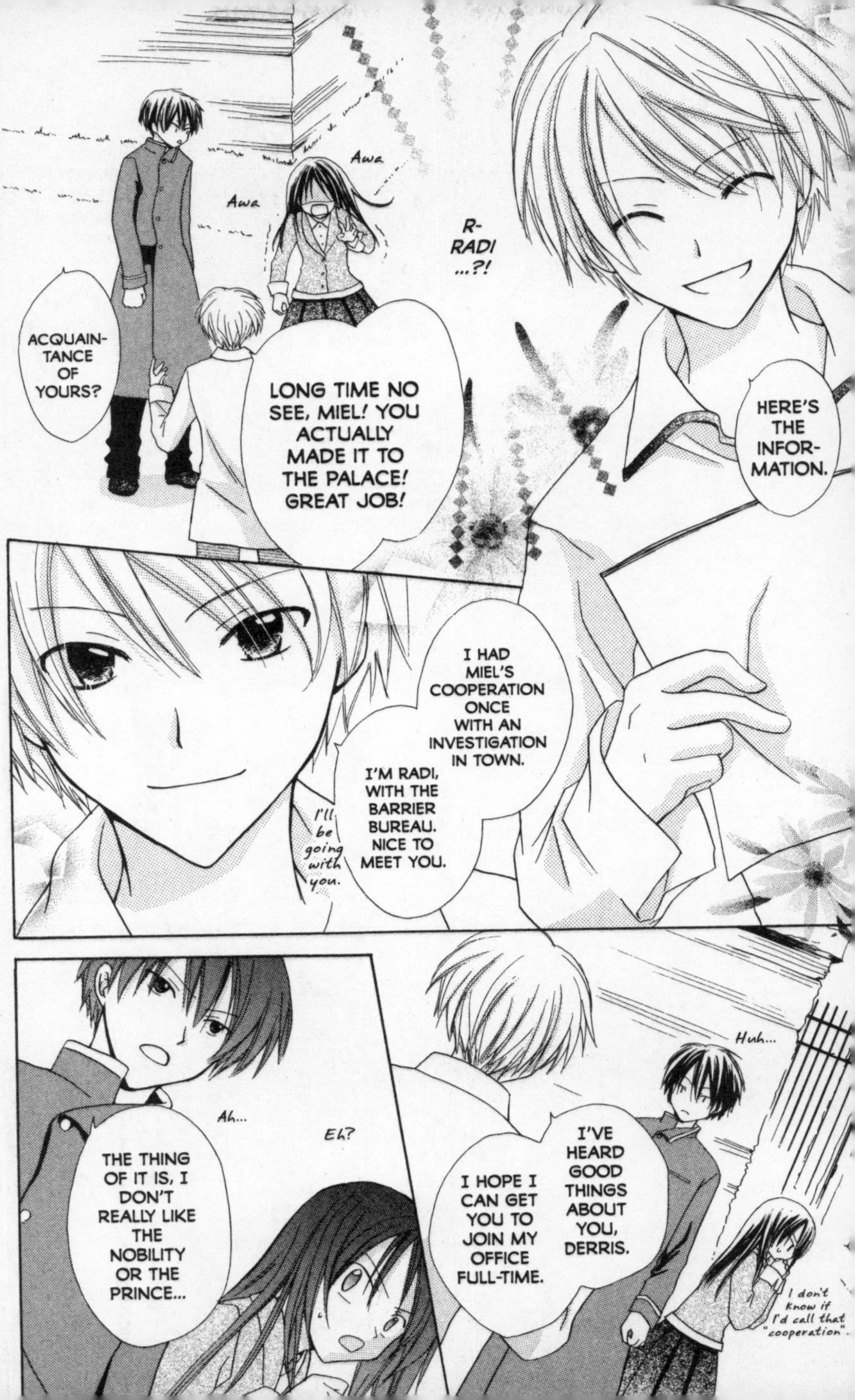
R-RADI ...?!
HERE'S THE INFORMATION.
I HAD MIEL'S COOPERATION ONCE WITH AN INVESTIGATION IN TOWN.
Awa
Awa
ACQUAINTANCE OF YOURS?
LONG TIME NO SEE, MIEL! YOU ACTUALLY MADE IT TO THE PALACE! GREAT JOB!
I'M RADI, WITH THE BARRIER BUREAU. NICE TO MEET YOU.
I'll be going with you.
Huh...
I'VE HEARD GOOD THINGS ABOUT YOU, DERRIS.
I HOPE I CAN GET YOU TO JOIN MY OFFICE FULL-TIME.
I don't know if I'd call that "cooperation".
Eh?
Ah...
THE THING OF IT IS, I DON'T REALLY LIKE THE NOBILITY OR THE PRINCE...

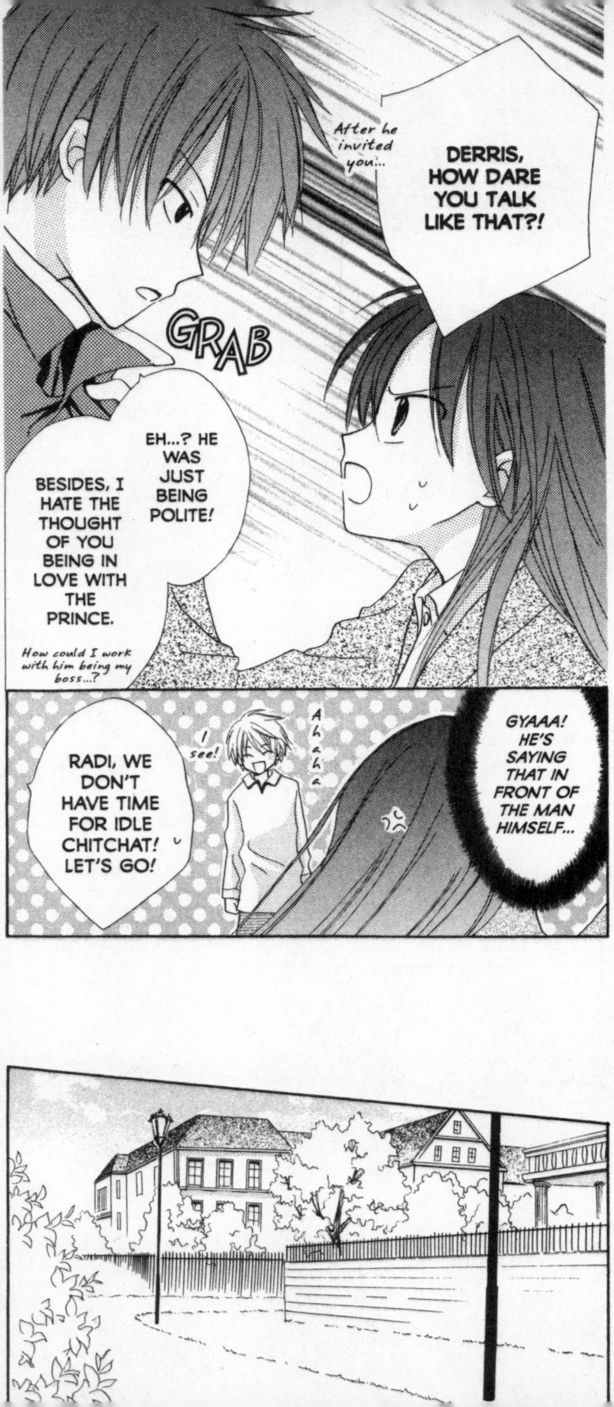
DERRIS, HOW DARE YOU TALK LIKE THAT?!
After he invited you...
GRAB
EH...? HE WAS JUST BEING POLITE!
BESIDES, I HATE THE THOUGHT OF YOU BEING IN LOVE WITH THE PRINCE.
How could I work with him being my boss...?
GYAAA! HE'S SAYING THAT IN FRONT OF THE MAN HIMSELF...
Ahaha
I see!
RADI, WE DON'T HAVE TIME FOR IDLE CHITCHAT! LET'S GO!

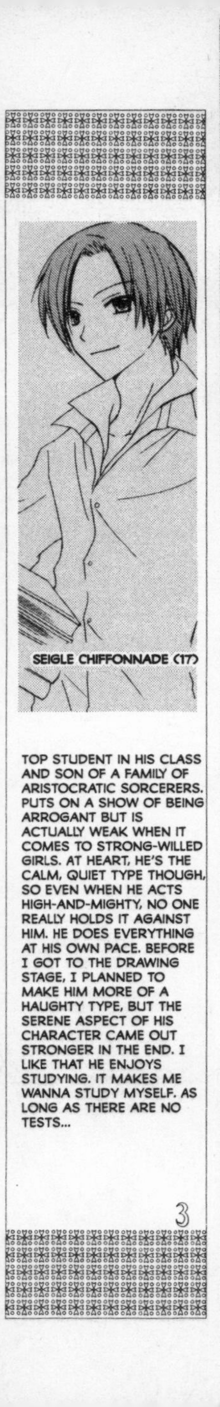
SEIGLE CHIFFONNADE (17)

TOP STUDENT IN HIS CLASS AND SON OF A FAMILY OF ARISTOCRATIC SORCERERS. PUTS ON A SHOW OF BEING ARROGANT BUT IS ACTUALLY WEAK WHEN IT COMES TO STRONG-WILLED GIRLS. AT HEART, HE'S THE CALM, QUIET TYPE THOUGH, SO EVEN WHEN HE ACTS HIGH-AND-MIGHTY, NO ONE REALLY HOLDS IT AGAINST HIM. HE DOES EVERYTHING AT HIS OWN PACE. BEFORE I GOT TO THE DRAWING STAGE, I PLANNED TO MAKE HIM MORE OF A HAUGHTY TYPE, BUT THE SERENE ASPECT OF HIS CHARACTER CAME OUT STRONGER IN THE END. I LIKE THAT HE ENJOYS STUDYING. IT MAKES ME WANNA STUDY MYSELF. AS LONG AS THERE ARE NO TESTS...

3

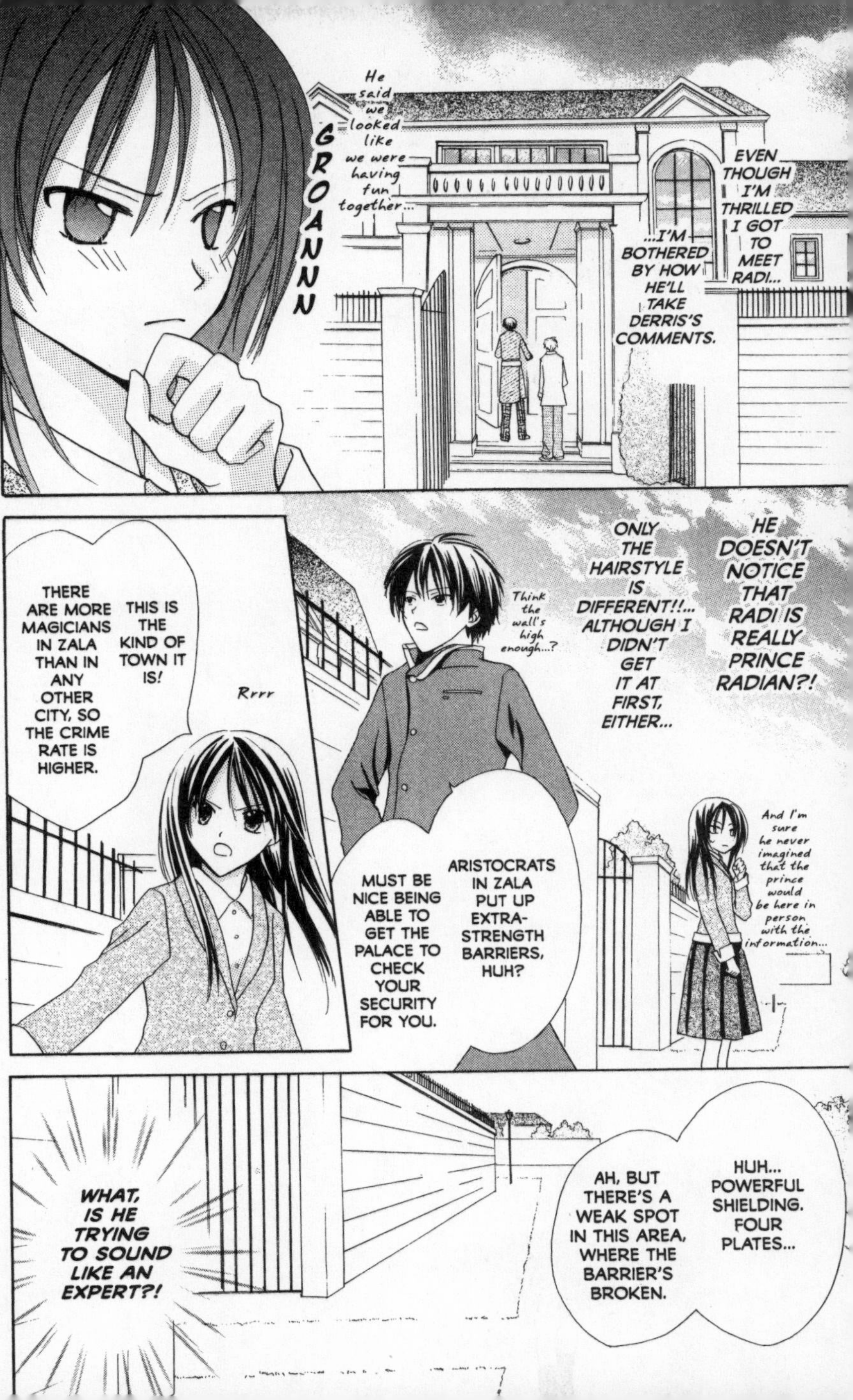
EVEN THOUGH I'M THRILLED I GOT TO MEET RADI...
...I'M BOTHERED BY HOW HE'LL TAKE DERRIS'S COMMENTS.
He said we looked like we were having fun together...
GROANNN
HE DOESN'T NOTICE THAT RADI IS REALLY PRINCE RADIAN?!
ONLY THE HAIRSTYLE IS DIFFERENT!!... ALTHOUGH I DIDN'T GET IT AT FIRST, EITHER...
And I'm sure he never imagined that the prince would be here in person with the information...
Think the wall's high enough...?
ARISTOCRATS IN ZALA PUT UP EXTRA-STRENGTH BARRIERS, HUH?
MUST BE NICE BEING ABLE TO GET THE PALACE TO CHECK YOUR SECURITY FOR YOU.
Rrrr
THIS IS THE KIND OF TOWN IT IS!
THERE ARE MORE MAGICIANS IN ZALA THAN IN ANY OTHER CITY, SO THE CRIME RATE IS HIGHER.
HUH... POWERFUL SHIELDING. FOUR PLATES...
AH, BUT THERE'S A WEAK SPOT IN THIS AREA, WHERE THE BARRIER'S BROKEN.
WHAT, IS HE TRYING TO SOUND LIKE AN EXPERT?!

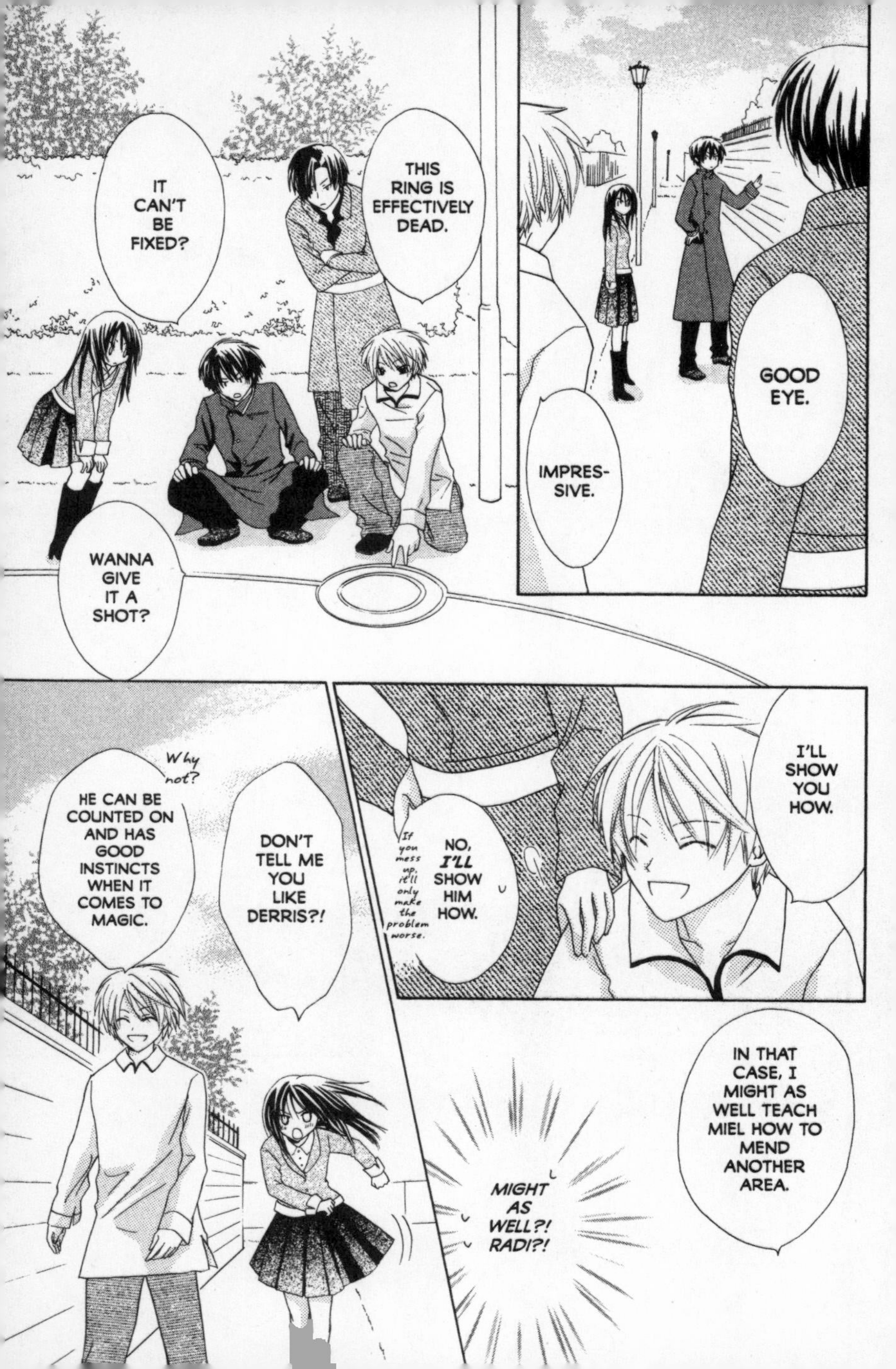
GOOD EYE.
IMPRESSIVE.
THIS RING IS EFFECTIVELY DEAD.
IT CAN'T BE FIXED?
WANNA GIVE IT A SHOT?
I'LL SHOW YOU HOW.
NO, *I'LL* SHOW HIM HOW.
If you mess up, it'll only make the problem worse.
IN THAT CASE, I MIGHT AS WELL TEACH MIEL HOW TO MEND ANOTHER AREA.
MIGHT AS WELL?! RADI?!
DON'T TELL ME YOU LIKE DERRIS?!
Why not?
HE CAN BE COUNTED ON AND HAS GOOD INSTINCTS WHEN IT COMES TO MAGIC.

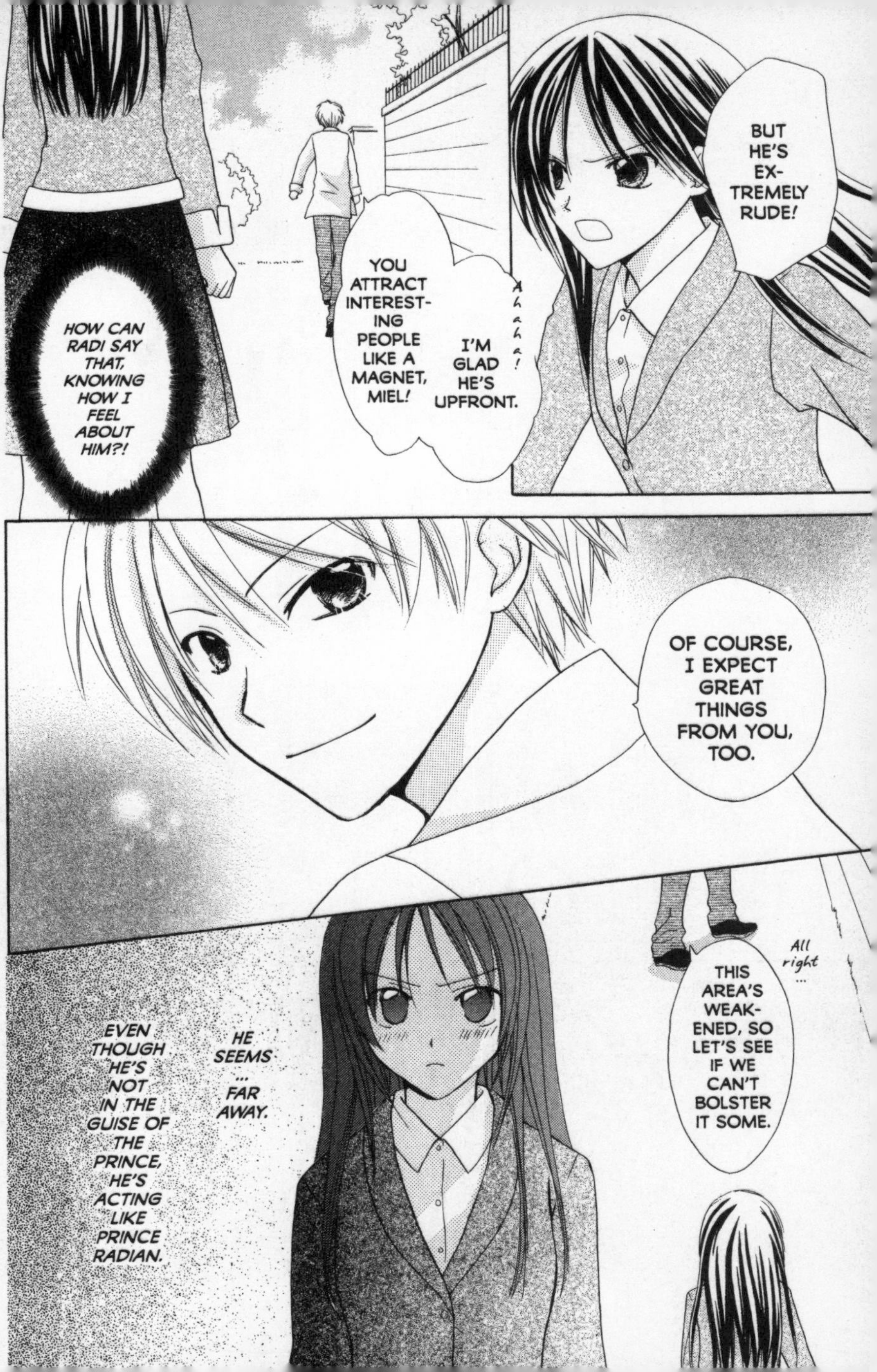
BUT HE'S EX-TREMELY RUDE!
Ahaha!
I'M GLAD HE'S UPFRONT.
YOU ATTRACT INTERESTING PEOPLE LIKE A MAGNET, MIEL!
HOW CAN RADI SAY THAT, KNOWING HOW I FEEL ABOUT HIM?!
OF COURSE, I EXPECT GREAT THINGS FROM YOU, TOO.
All right ...
THIS AREA'S WEAK-ENED, SO LET'S SEE IF WE CAN'T BOLSTER IT SOME.
HE SEEMS ... FAR AWAY.
EVEN THOUGH HE'S NOT IN THE GUISE OF THE PRINCE, HE'S ACTING LIKE PRINCE RADIAN.

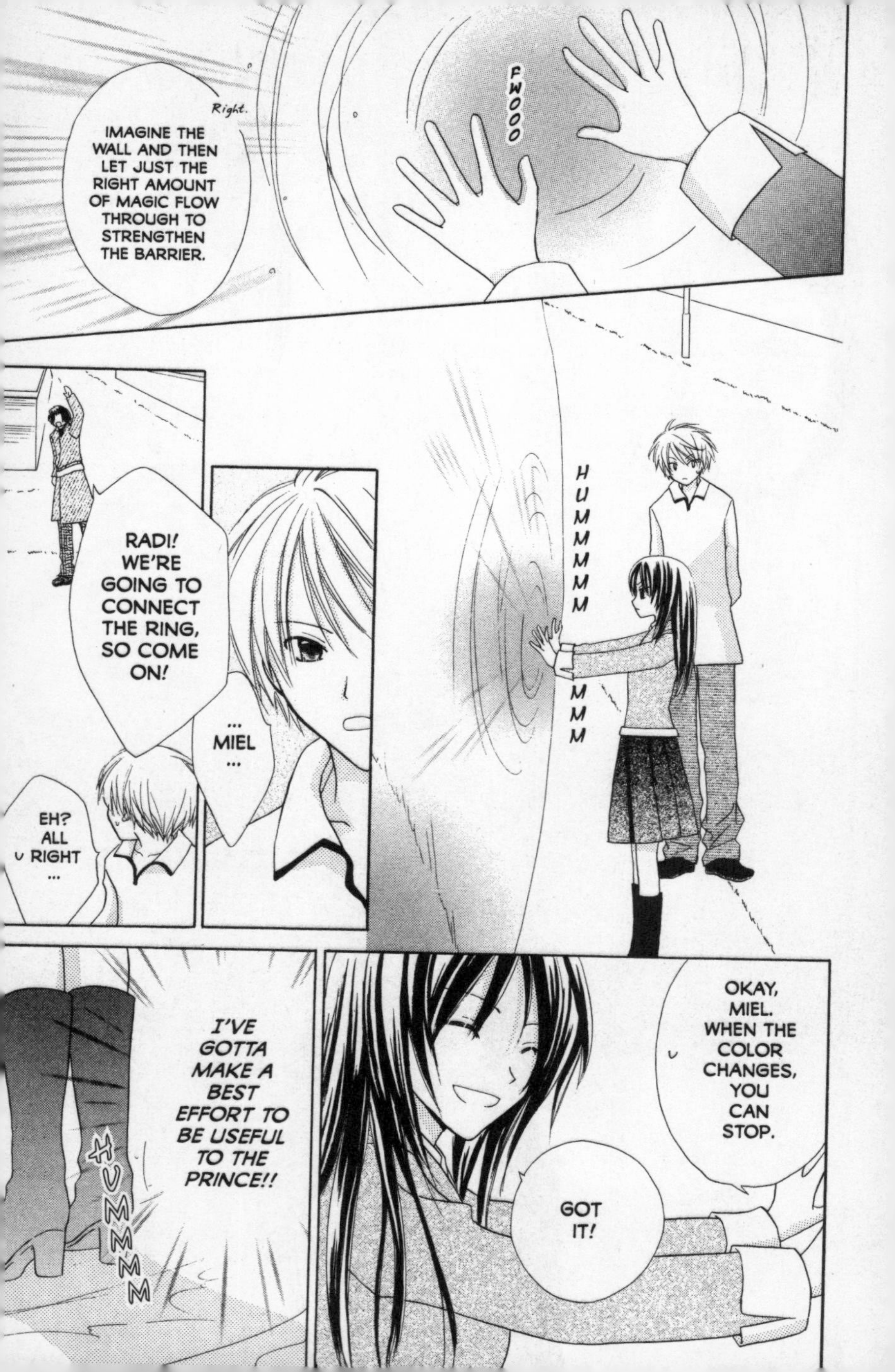
FWOOO
Right.
IMAGINE THE WALL AND THEN LET JUST THE RIGHT AMOUNT OF MAGIC FLOW THROUGH TO STRENGTHEN THE BARRIER.
HUMMMMMM MMM
RADI! WE'RE GOING TO CONNECT THE RING, SO COME ON!
... MIEL ...
EH? ALL RIGHT ...
OKAY, MIEL. WHEN THE COLOR CHANGES, YOU CAN STOP.
GOT IT!
I'VE GOTTA MAKE A BEST EFFORT TO BE USEFUL TO THE PRINCE!!
HUMMMM

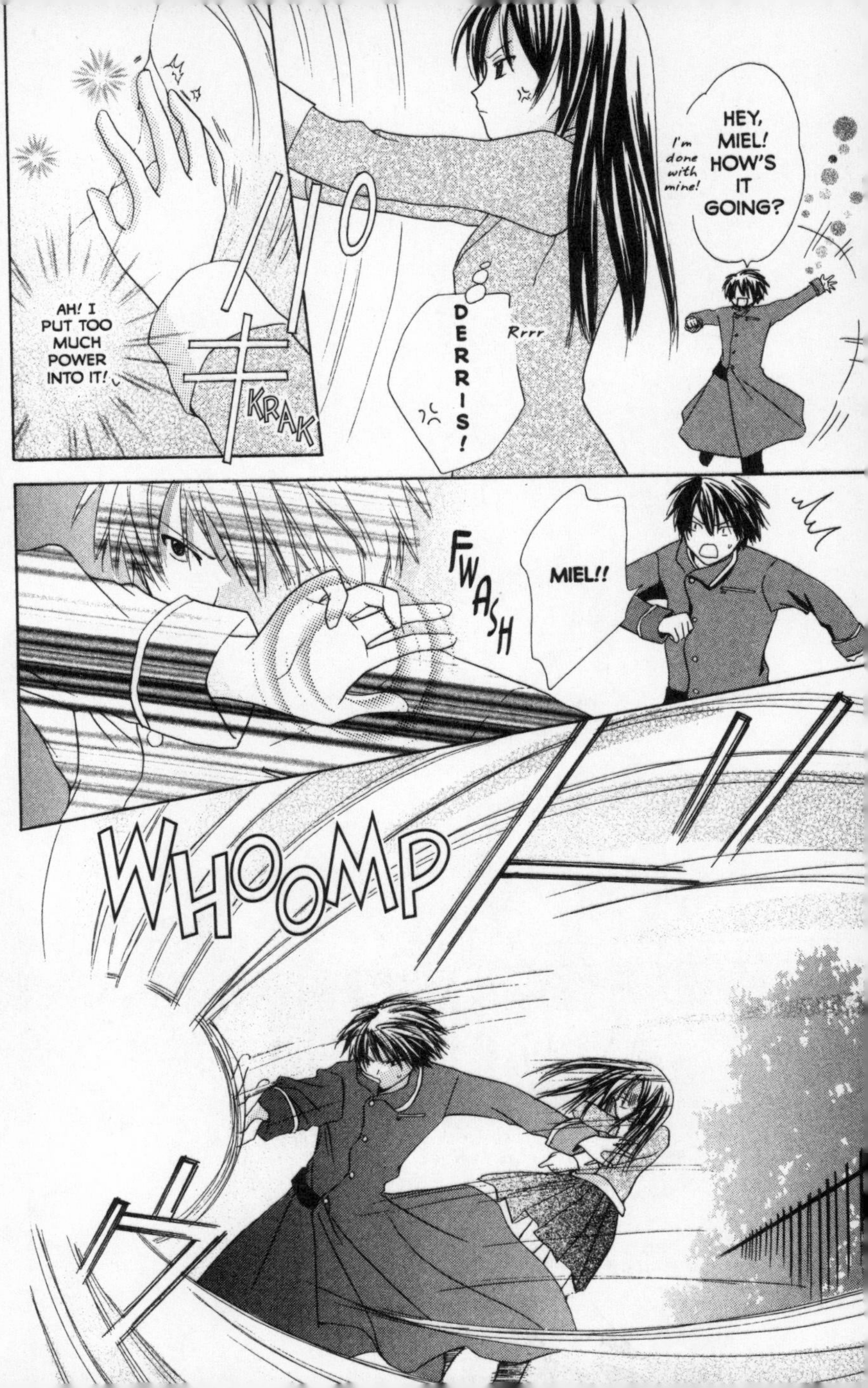

HEY, MIEL! HOW'S IT GOING?
I'm done with mine!
Rrrr
DERRIS!
KRAK
AH! I PUT TOO MUCH POWER INTO IT!
MIEL!!
FWASH
WHOOMP

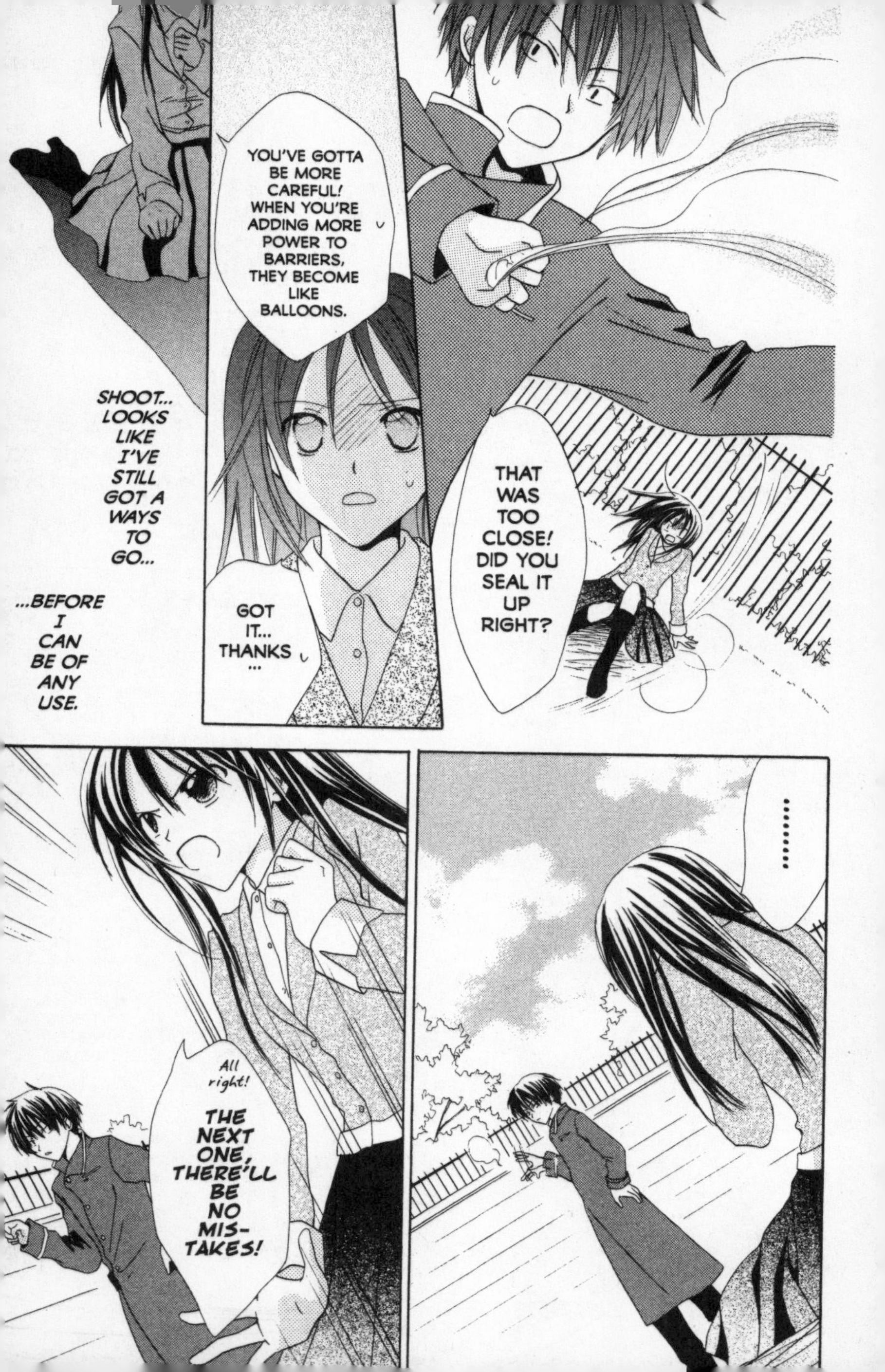
THAT WAS TOO CLOSE! DID YOU SEAL IT UP RIGHT?
YOU'VE GOTTA BE MORE CAREFUL! WHEN YOU'RE ADDING MORE POWER TO BARRIERS, THEY BECOME LIKE BALLOONS.
GOT IT... THANKS ...
SHOOT... LOOKS LIKE I'VE STILL GOT A WAYS TO GO...
...BEFORE I CAN BE OF ANY USE.
......
All right!
THE NEXT ONE, THERE'LL BE NO MIS-TAKES!

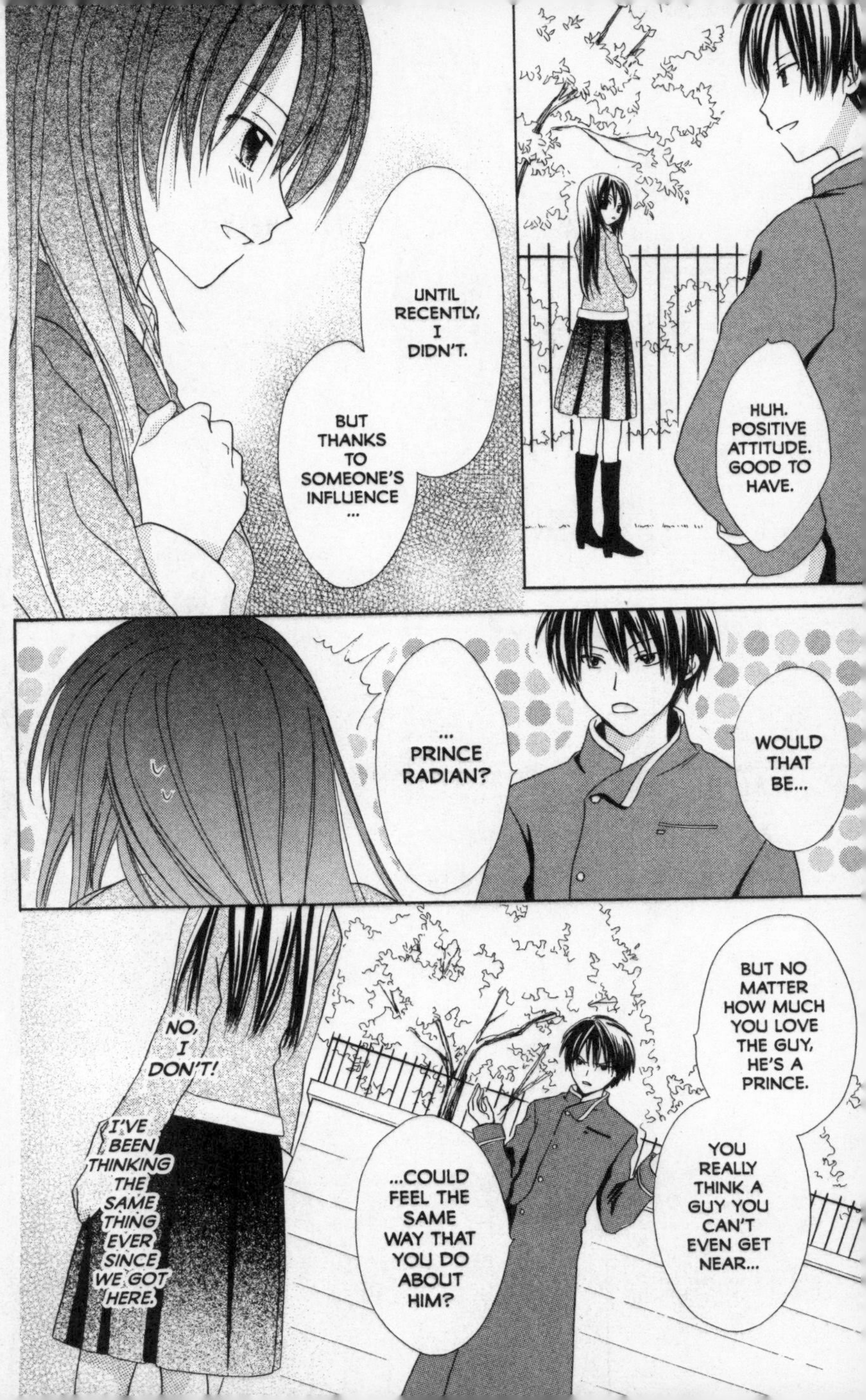
HUH. POSITIVE ATTITUDE. GOOD TO HAVE.
UNTIL RECENTLY, I DIDN'T.
BUT THANKS TO SOMEONE'S INFLUENCE ...
WOULD THAT BE...
... PRINCE RADIAN?
BUT NO MATTER HOW MUCH YOU LOVE THE GUY, HE'S A PRINCE.
YOU REALLY THINK A GUY YOU CAN'T EVEN GET NEAR...
...COULD FEEL THE SAME WAY THAT YOU DO ABOUT HIM?
NO, I DON'T!
I'VE BEEN THINKING THE SAME THING EVER SINCE WE GOT HERE.

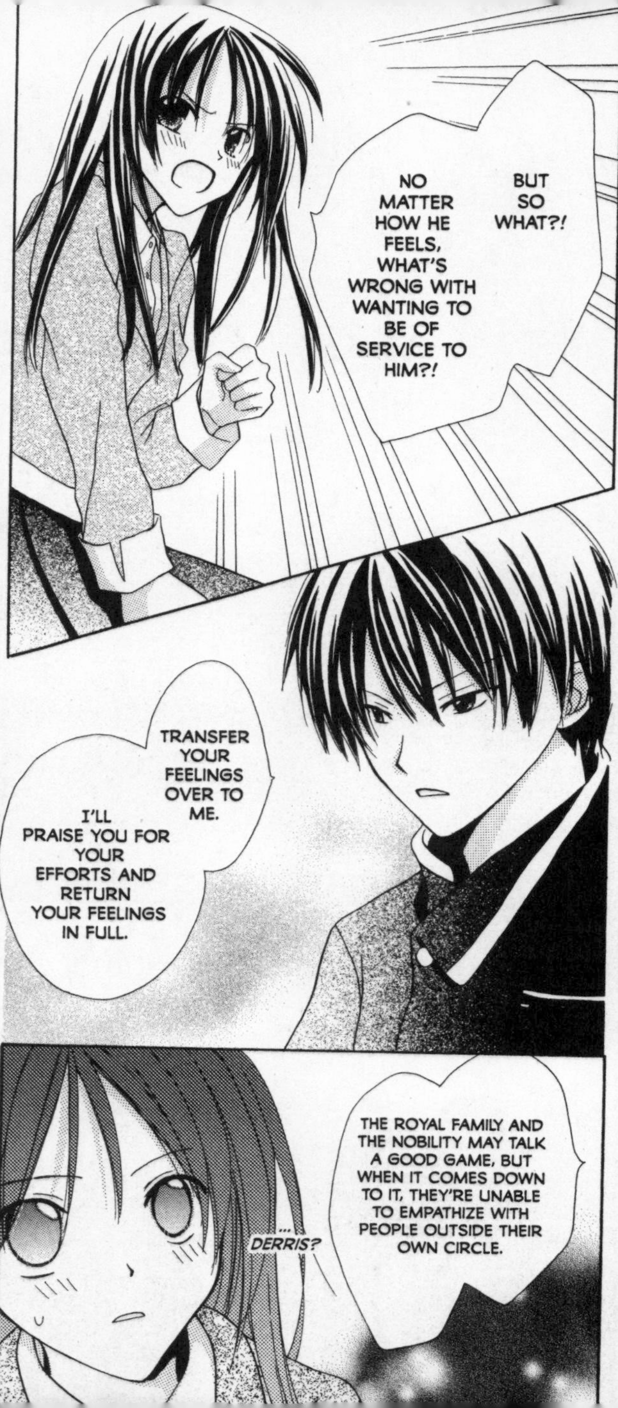
BUT SO WHAT?!
NO MATTER HOW HE FEELS, WHAT'S WRONG WITH WANTING TO BE OF SERVICE TO HIM?!
TRANSFER YOUR FEELINGS OVER TO ME.
I'LL PRAISE YOU FOR YOUR EFFORTS AND RETURN YOUR FEELINGS IN FULL.
THE ROYAL FAMILY AND THE NOBILITY MAY TALK A GOOD GAME, BUT WHEN IT COMES DOWN TO IT, THEY'RE UNABLE TO EMPATHIZE WITH PEOPLE OUTSIDE THEIR OWN CIRCLE.
...DERRIS?

I'LL USE EVERY OTHER COLUMN TO TALK ABOUT THE EPISODES THEMSELVES.

EPISODE FOUR FOCUSES ON ROSETTE AND SEAGLE. IT CONTINUES FROM EPISODE THREE, AT SCHOOL, AND WAS FUN TO DRAW. I LOVE SCHOOL LIBRARIES AND SCHOOL UNIFORMS.

AFTER I FINISHED ALL THE BREAKDOWNS FOR THIS EPISODE, I REALIZED THAT I FORGOT TO LEAVE A 1/4 COLUMN SPACE HERE, SO I HAD TO REDRAW THE PAGE...

I WAS A LITTLE PEEVED (EVEN THOUGH IT WAS MY OWN FAULT FOR NOT DOUBLE-CHECKING).

ANYWAY, I MADE EPISODE FOUR WITH THE INTENTION OF SETTING ROSETTE AND SEAGLE UP AS A COUPLE SO THEY COULD BE USED IN FUTURE EPISODES TOGETHER, BUT ALAS, DUE TO PAGE CONSTRAINTS, I HAD TO CUT OUT THEIR FUTURE "PAGE TIME" TOGETHER...

OH, WELL. I'M GLAD I GOT THE CHANCE TO HAVE THEM SHINE IN EPISODE FOUR, AT LEAST.

4

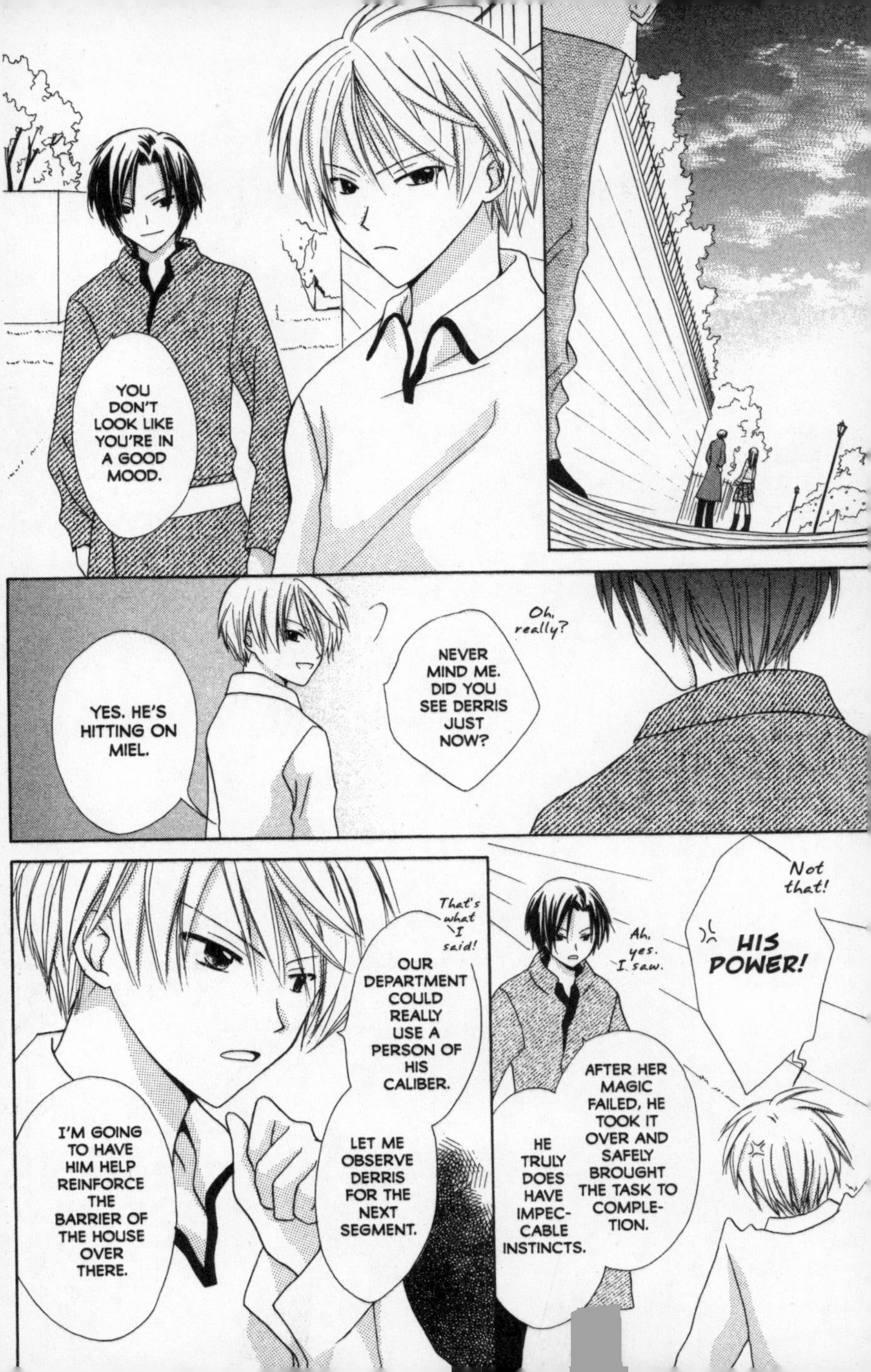
YOU DON'T LOOK LIKE YOU'RE IN A GOOD MOOD.
Oh, really?
NEVER MIND ME. DID YOU SEE DERRIS JUST NOW?
YES. HE'S HITTING ON MIEL.
Not that!
HIS POWER!
Ah, yes. I saw.
AFTER HER MAGIC FAILED, HE TOOK IT OVER AND SAFELY BROUGHT THE TASK TO COMPLE-TION.
HE TRULY DOES HAVE IMPEC-CABLE INSTINCTS.
That's what I said!
OUR DEPARTMENT COULD REALLY USE A PERSON OF HIS CALIBER.
LET ME OBSERVE DERRIS FOR THE NEXT SEGMENT.
I'M GOING TO HAVE HIM HELP REINFORCE THE BARRIER OF THE HOUSE OVER THERE.

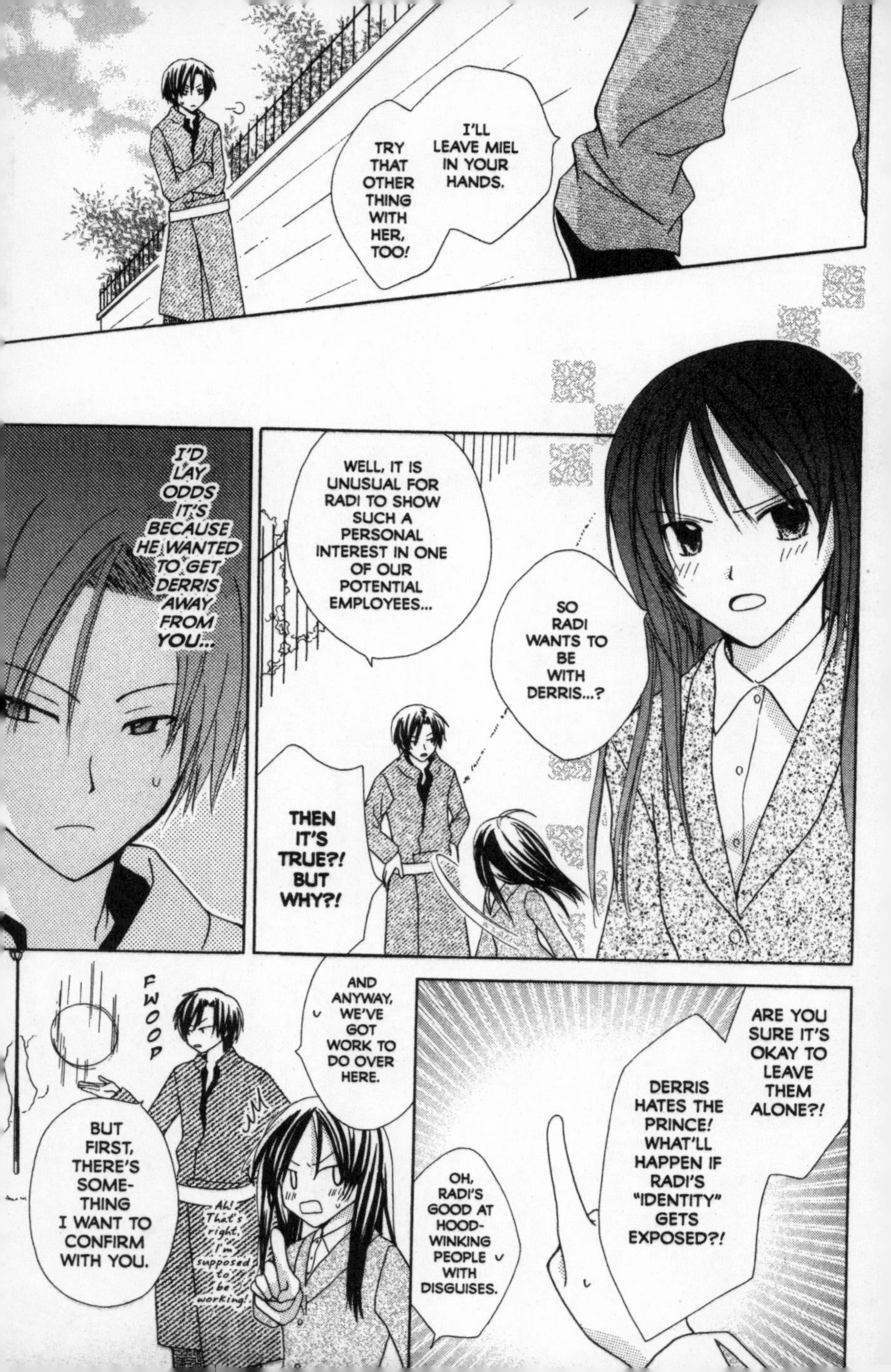
I'LL LEAVE MIEL IN YOUR HANDS. TRY THAT OTHER THING WITH HER, TOO!
SO RADI WANTS TO BE WITH DERRIS...?
WELL, IT IS UNUSUAL FOR RADI TO SHOW SUCH A PERSONAL INTEREST IN ONE OF OUR POTENTIAL EMPLOYEES...
THEN IT'S TRUE?! BUT WHY?!
I'D LAY ODDS IT'S BECAUSE HE WANTED TO GET DERRIS AWAY FROM YOU...
ARE YOU SURE IT'S OKAY TO LEAVE THEM ALONE?!
DERRIS HATES THE PRINCE! WHAT'LL HAPPEN IF RADI'S "IDENTITY" GETS EXPOSED?!
OH, RADI'S GOOD AT HOOD-WINKING PEOPLE WITH DISGUISES.
AND ANYWAY, WE'VE GOT WORK TO DO OVER HERE.
FWOOP
Ah! That's right, I'm supposed to be working!
BUT FIRST, THERE'S SOME-THING I WANT TO CONFIRM WITH YOU.

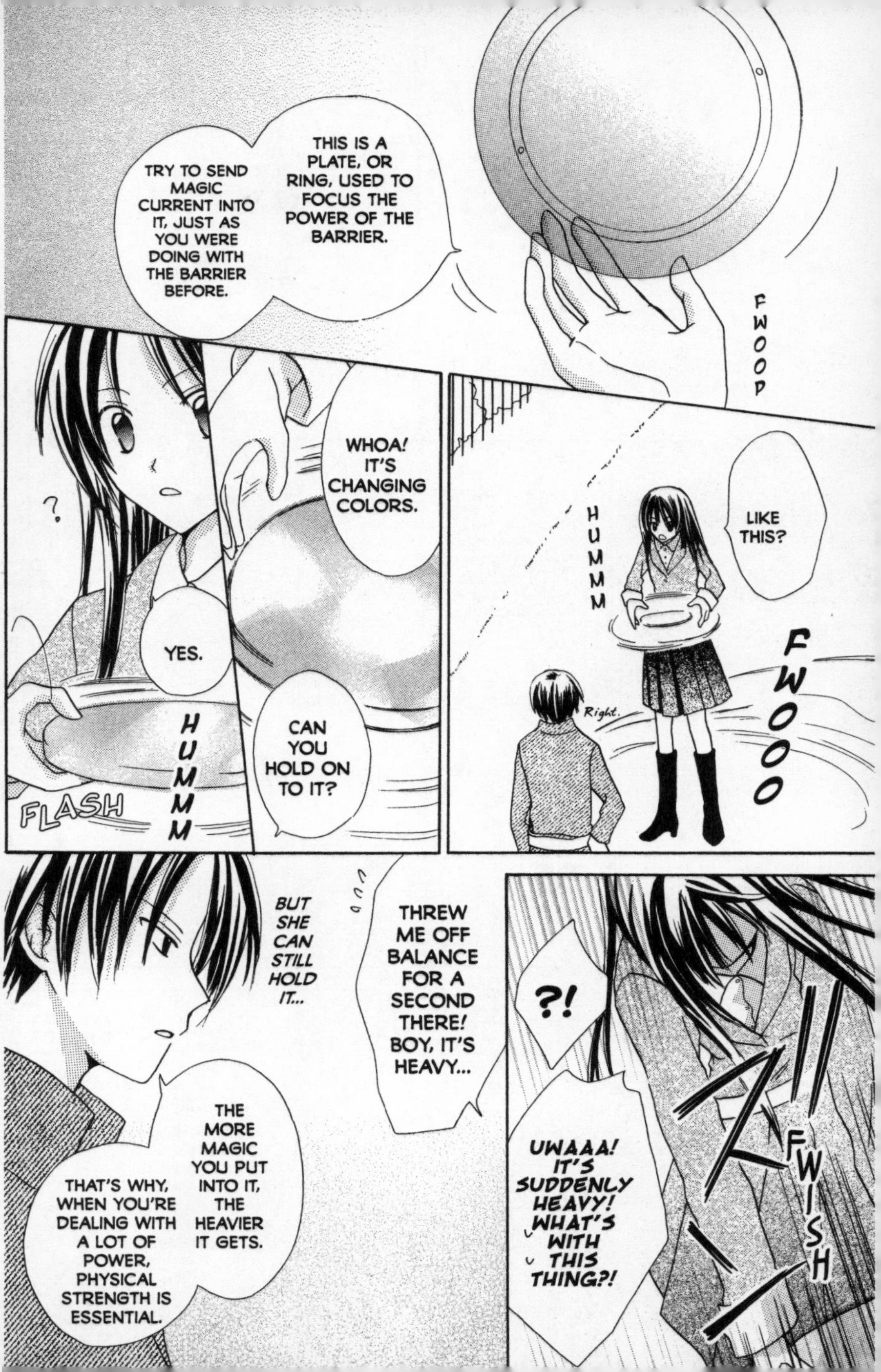
FWOOOP
THIS IS A PLATE, OR RING, USED TO FOCUS THE POWER OF THE BARRIER.
TRY TO SEND MAGIC CURRENT INTO IT, JUST AS YOU WERE DOING WITH THE BARRIER BEFORE.
LIKE THIS?
HUMMM
FWOOOO
Right.
WHOA! IT'S CHANGING COLORS.
CAN YOU HOLD ON TO IT?
HUMMM
?
YES.
FLASH
?!
UWAAA! IT'S SUDDENLY HEAVY! WHAT'S WITH THIS THING?!
FWISH
THREW ME OFF BALANCE FOR A SECOND THERE! BOY, IT'S HEAVY...
BUT SHE CAN STILL HOLD IT...
THE MORE MAGIC YOU PUT INTO IT, THE HEAVIER IT GETS.
THAT'S WHY, WHEN YOU'RE DEALING WITH A LOT OF POWER, PHYSICAL STRENGTH IS ESSENTIAL.

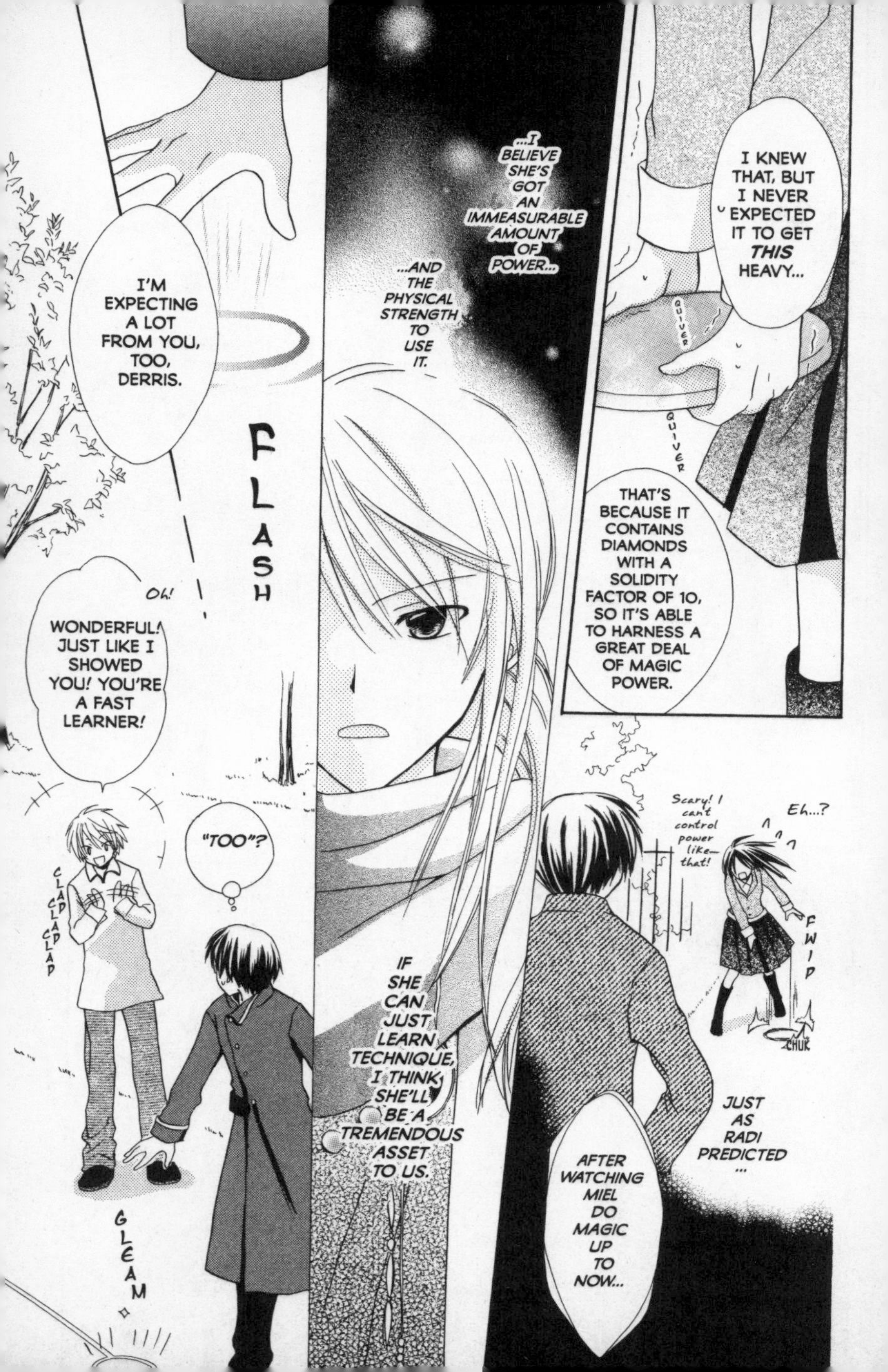
I KNEW THAT, BUT I NEVER EXPECTED IT TO GET THIS HEAVY...
QUIVER
QUIVER
THAT'S BECAUSE IT CONTAINS DIAMONDS WITH A SOLIDITY FACTOR OF 10, SO IT'S ABLE TO HARNESS A GREAT DEAL OF MAGIC POWER.
Eh...?
Scary! I can't control power like that!
FWID
CHUK
JUST AS RADI PREDICTED ...
AFTER WATCHING MIEL DO MAGIC UP TO NOW...
...I BELIEVE SHE'S GOT AN IMMEASURABLE AMOUNT OF POWER...
...AND THE PHYSICAL STRENGTH TO USE IT.
IF SHE CAN JUST LEARN TECHNIQUE, I THINK SHE'LL BE A TREMENDOUS ASSET TO US.
I'M EXPECTING A LOT FROM YOU, TOO, DERRIS.
FLASH
Oh!
WONDERFUL! JUST LIKE I SHOWED YOU! YOU'RE A FAST LEARNER!
CLAP CLAP CLAP
"TOO"?
GLEAM

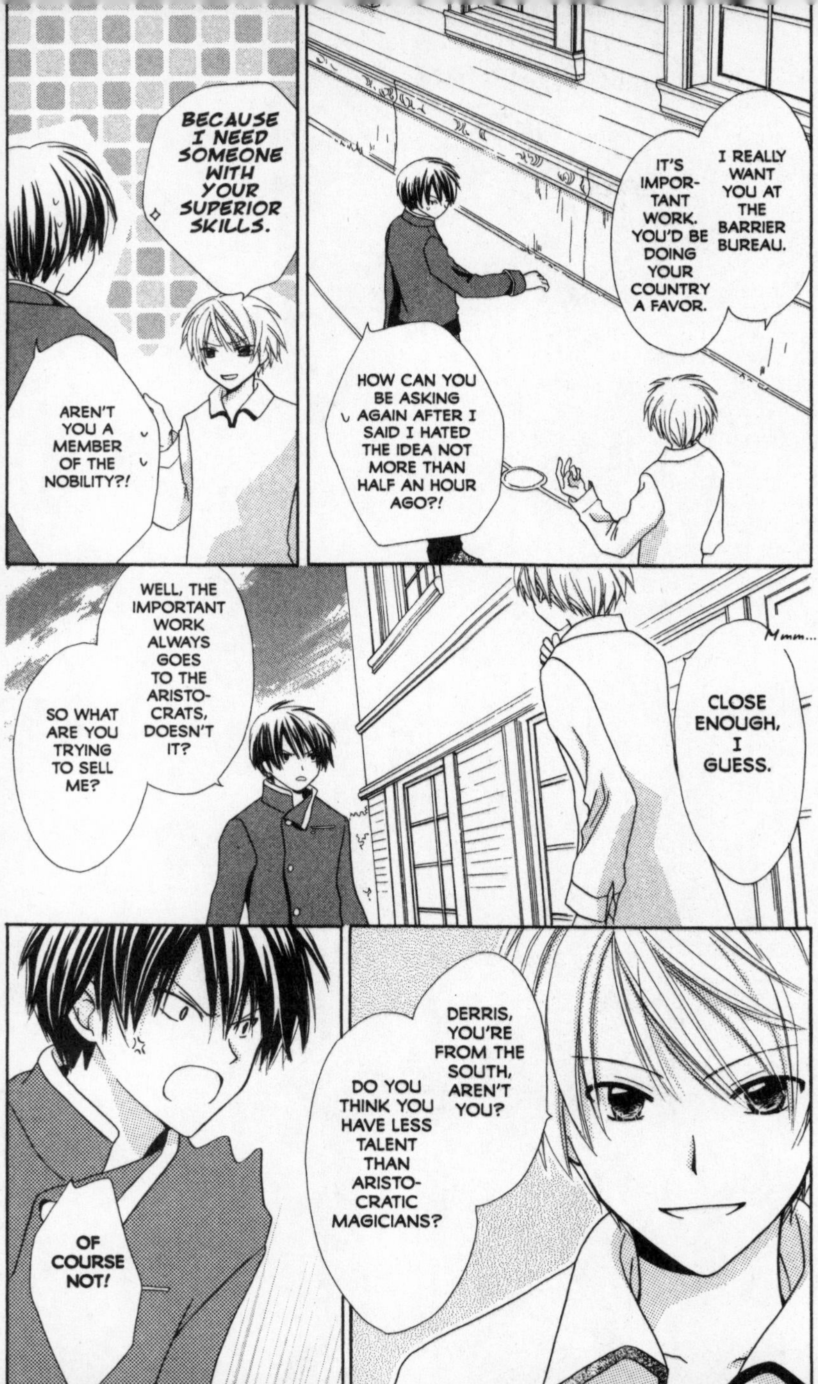
I REALLY WANT YOU AT THE BARRIER BUREAU.
IT'S IMPORTANT WORK. YOU'D BE DOING YOUR COUNTRY A FAVOR.
HOW CAN YOU BE ASKING AGAIN AFTER I SAID I HATED THE IDEA NOT MORE THAN HALF AN HOUR AGO?!
BECAUSE I NEED SOMEONE WITH YOUR SUPERIOR SKILLS.
AREN'T YOU A MEMBER OF THE NOBILITY?!
Mmm...
CLOSE ENOUGH, I GUESS.
WELL, THE IMPORTANT WORK ALWAYS GOES TO THE ARISTOCRATS, DOESN'T IT?
SO WHAT ARE YOU TRYING TO SELL ME?
DERRIS, YOU'RE FROM THE SOUTH, AREN'T YOU?
DO YOU THINK YOU HAVE LESS TALENT THAN ARISTOCRATIC MAGICIANS?
OF COURSE NOT!

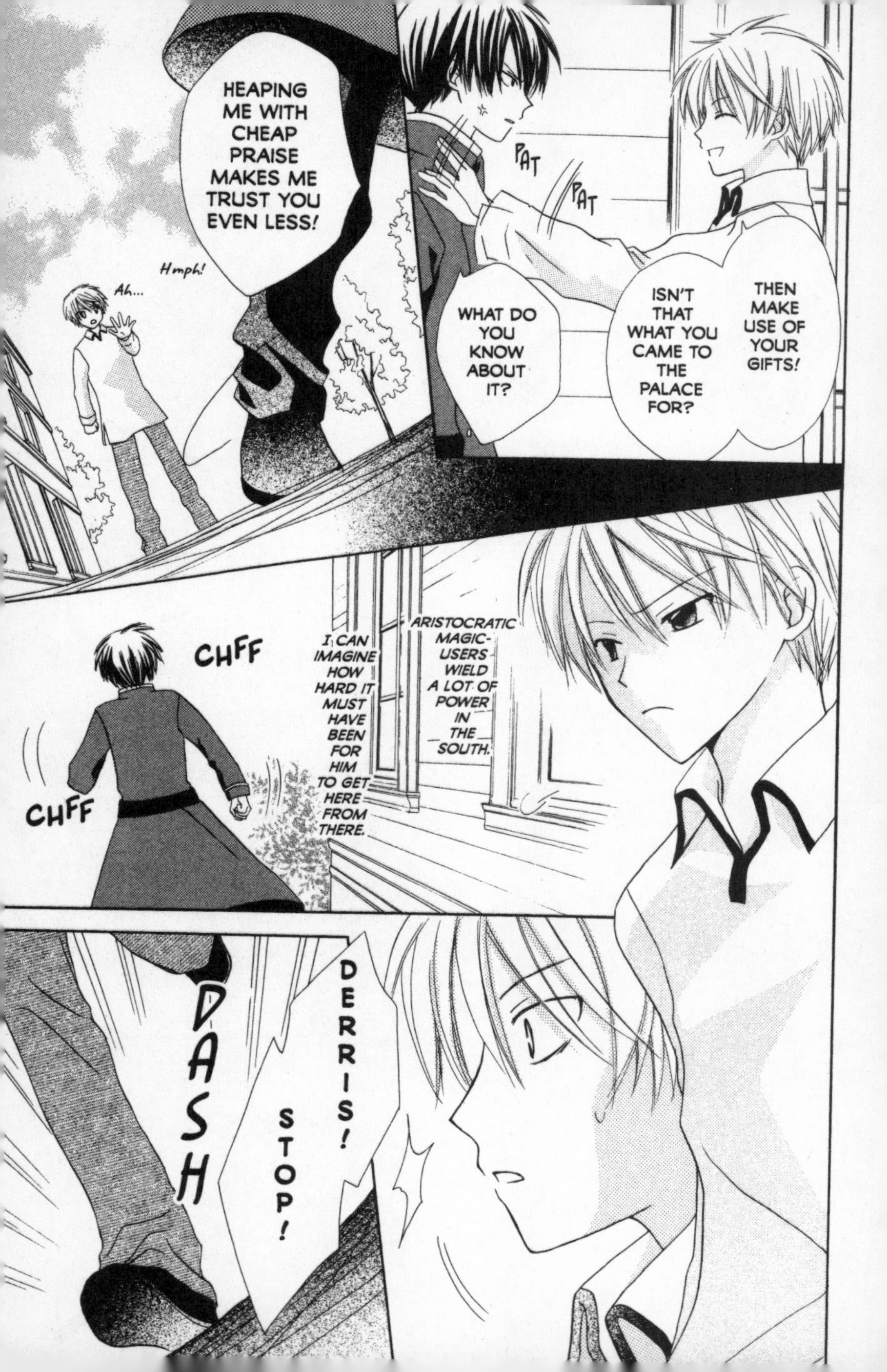
THEN MAKE USE OF YOUR GIFTS!
ISN'T THAT WHAT YOU CAME TO THE PALACE FOR?
PAT
PAT
WHAT DO YOU KNOW ABOUT IT?
HEAPING ME WITH CHEAP PRAISE MAKES ME TRUST YOU EVEN LESS!
Hmph!
Ah...
ARISTOCRATIC MAGIC-USERS WIELD A LOT OF POWER IN THE SOUTH.
I CAN IMAGINE HOW HARD IT MUST HAVE BEEN FOR HIM TO GET HERE FROM THERE.
CHFF
CHFF
DERRIS!
STOP!
DASH

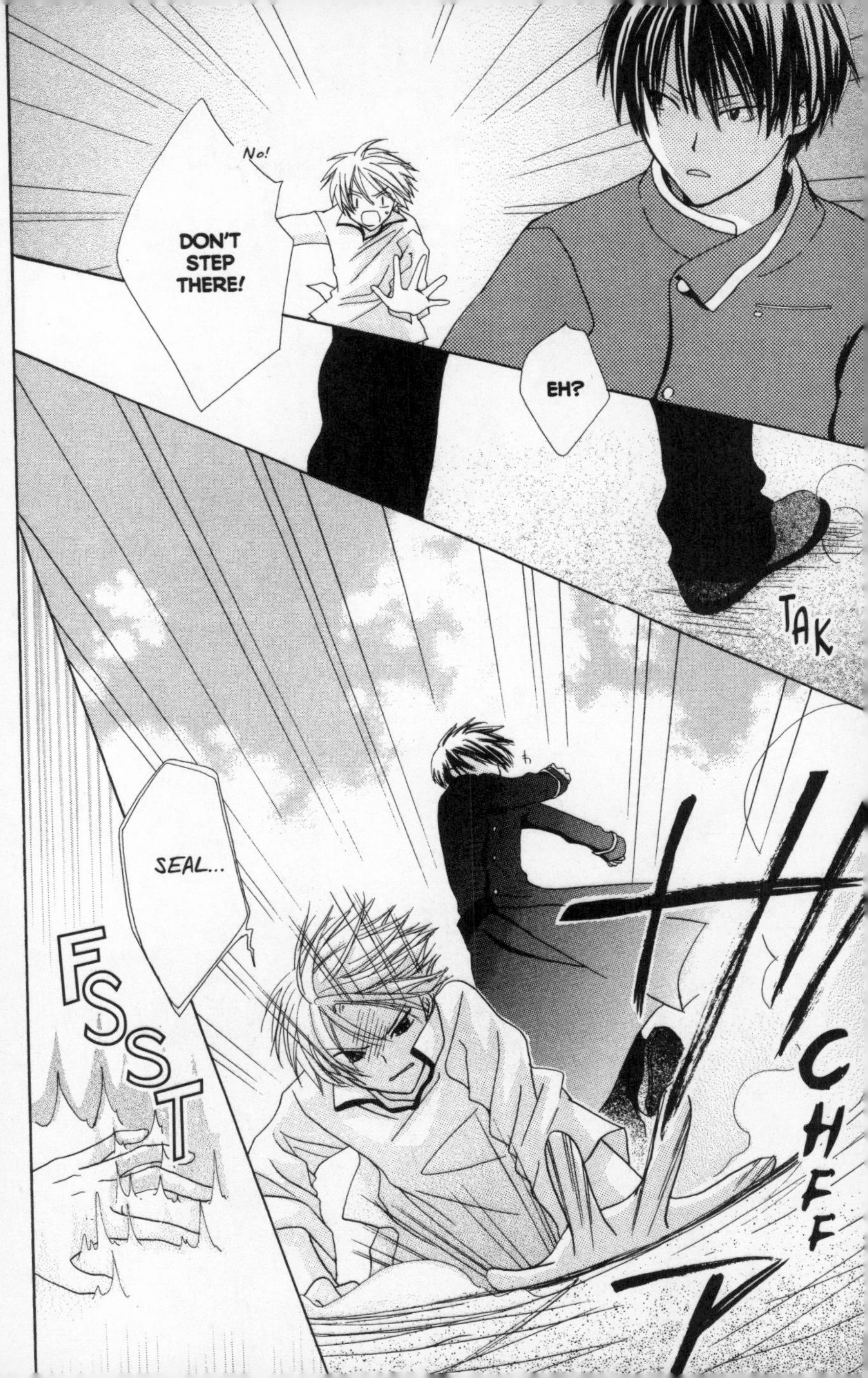
No!
DON'T STEP THERE!
EH?
TAK
CHFF
SEAL...
FSSST

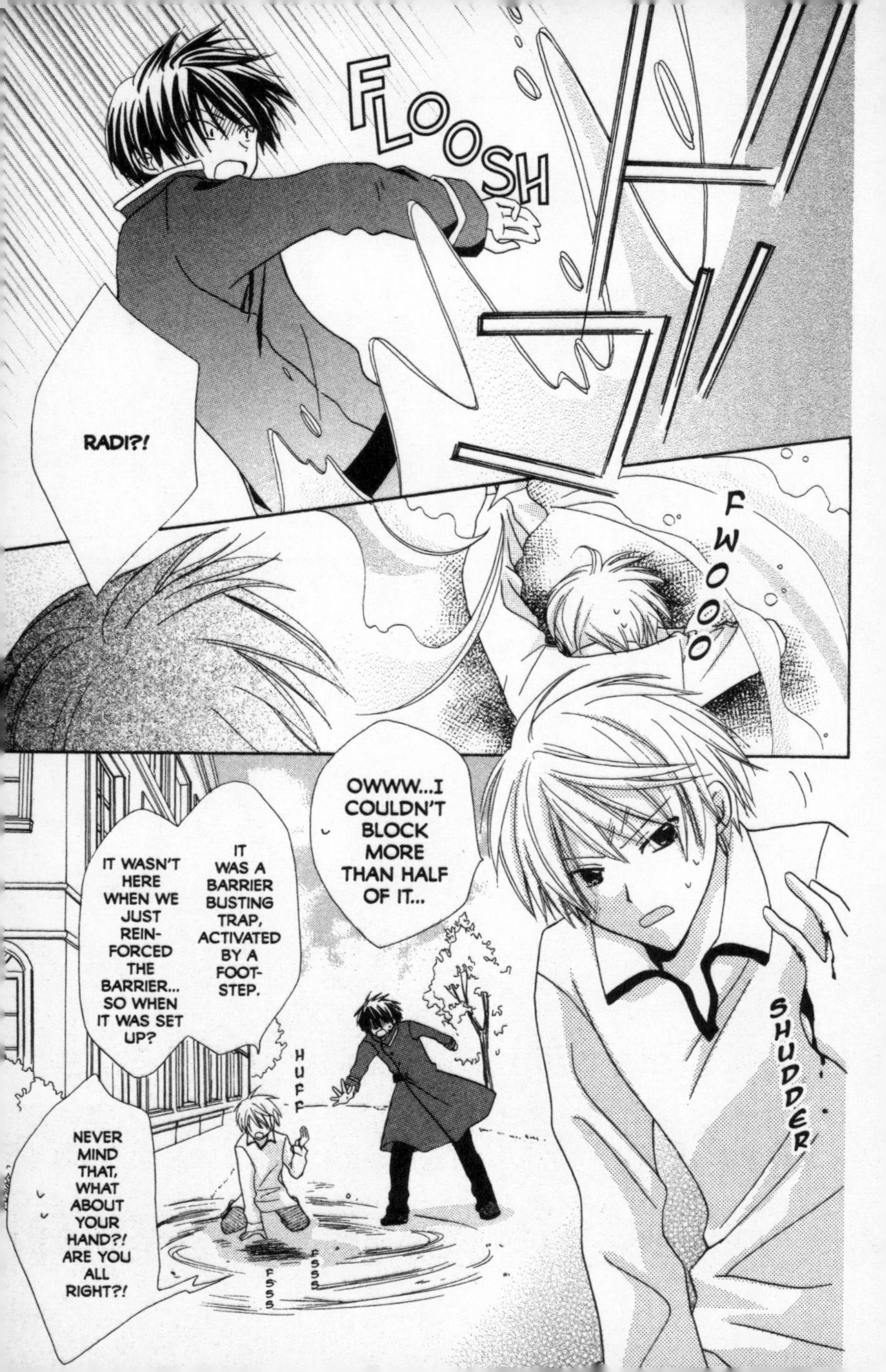
FLOOSH
RADI?!
FWOOOO
OWWW...I COULDN'T BLOCK MORE THAN HALF OF IT...
SHUDDER
IT WAS A BARRIER BUSTING TRAP, ACTIVATED BY A FOOT-STEP.
IT WASN'T HERE WHEN WE JUST REIN-FORCED THE BARRIER... SO WHEN IT WAS SET UP?
HUFF
FSSS
FSSS
NEVER MIND THAT, WHAT ABOUT YOUR HAND?! ARE YOU ALL RIGHT?!

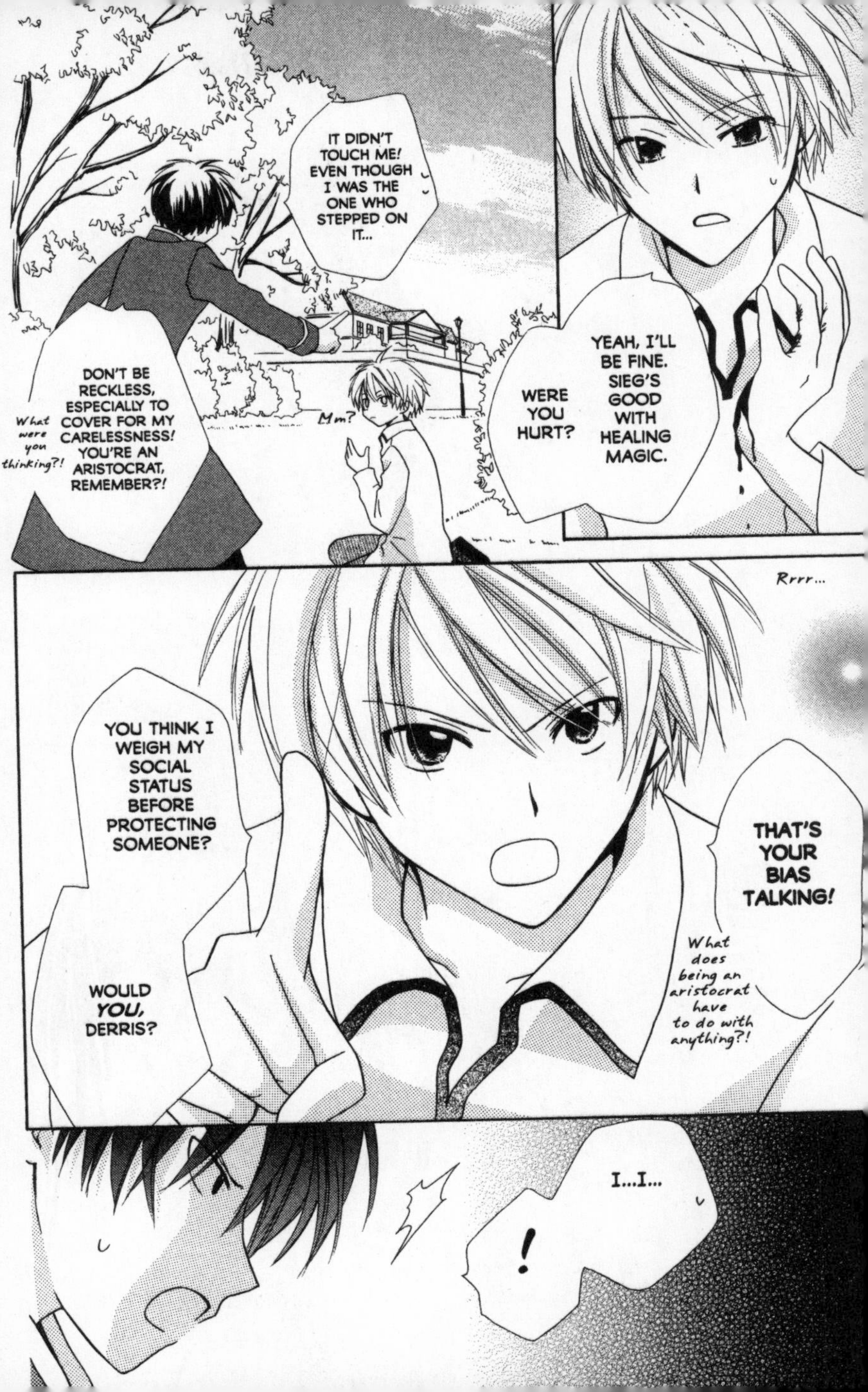
WERE YOU HURT?
YEAH, I'LL BE FINE. SIEG'S GOOD WITH HEALING MAGIC.
IT DIDN'T TOUCH ME! EVEN THOUGH I WAS THE ONE WHO STEPPED ON IT...
Mm?
DON'T BE RECKLESS, ESPECIALLY TO COVER FOR MY CARELESSNESS! YOU'RE AN ARISTOCRAT, REMEMBER?!
What were you thinking?!
Rrrr...
THAT'S YOUR BIAS TALKING!
What does being an aristocrat have to do with anything?!
YOU THINK I WEIGH MY SOCIAL STATUS BEFORE PROTECTING SOMEONE?
WOULD *YOU*, DERRIS?
I...I...
!

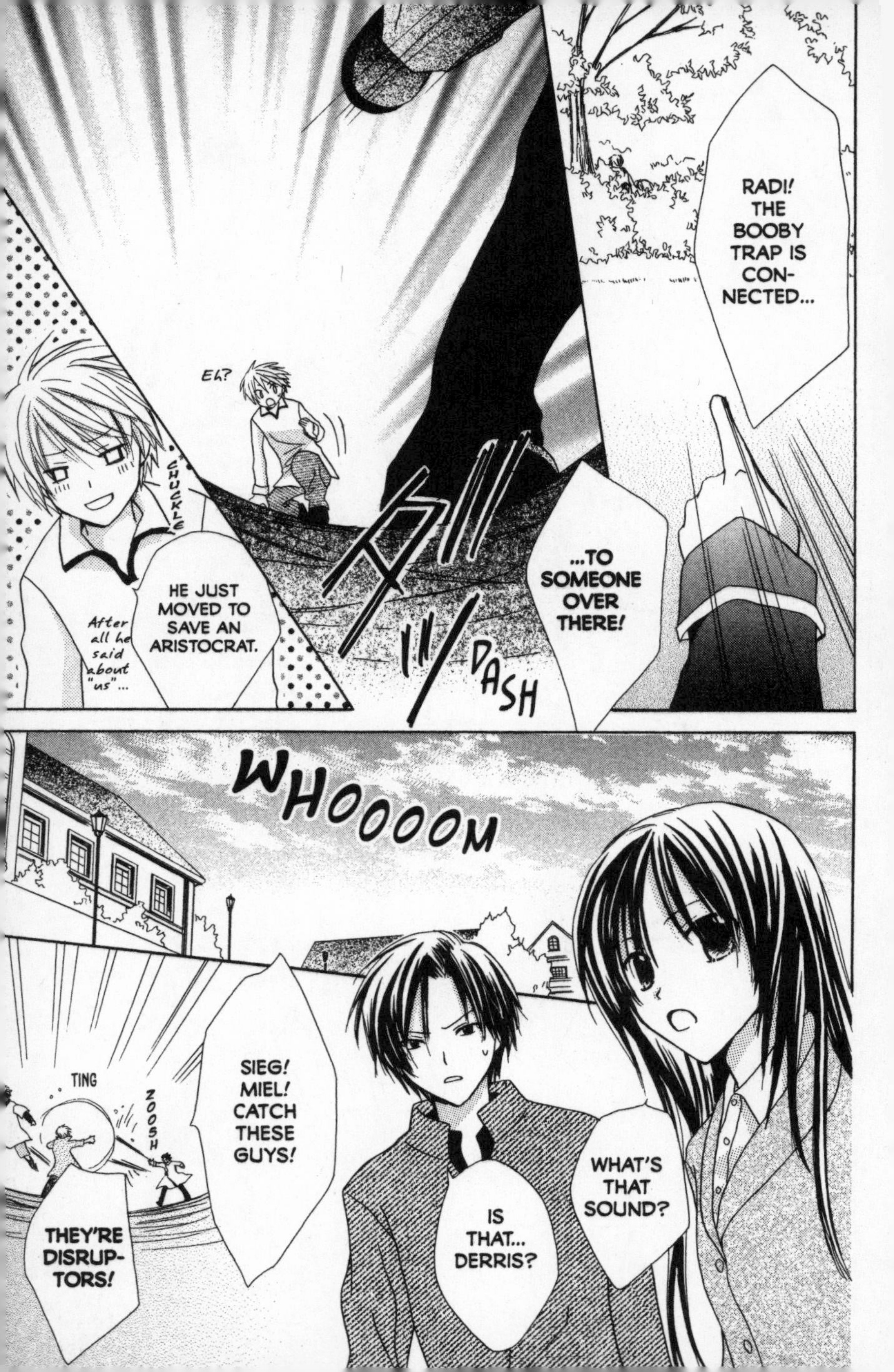
RADI! THE BOOBY TRAP IS CONNECTED...
...TO SOMEONE OVER THERE!
DASH
EH?
CHUCKLE
HE JUST MOVED TO SAVE AN ARISTOCRAT.
After all he said about "us"...
WHOOOOM
WHAT'S THAT SOUND?
IS THAT... DERRIS?
SIEG! MIEL! CATCH THESE GUYS!
THEY'RE DISRUP-TORS!
ZOOSH
TING

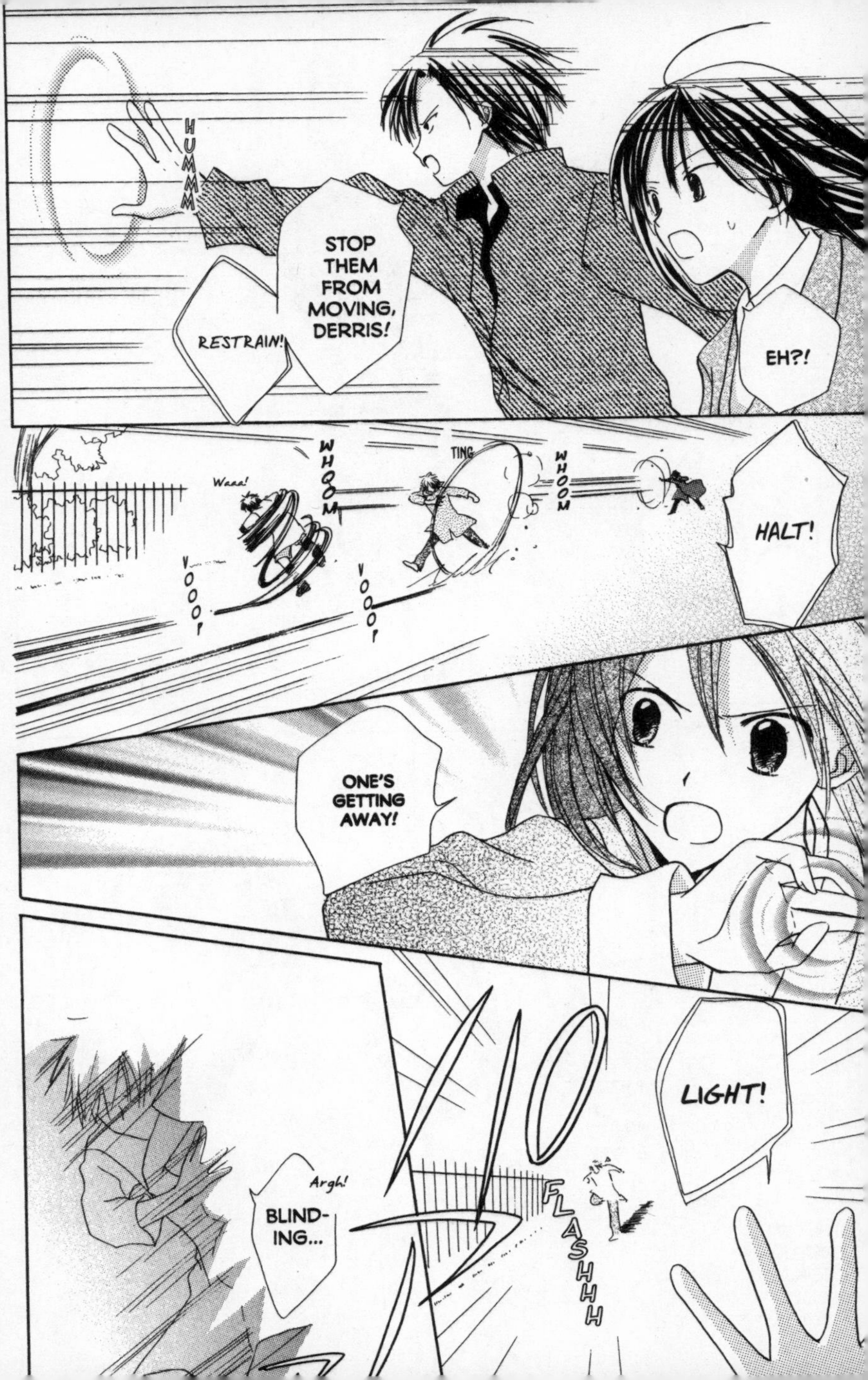
EH?!
STOP THEM FROM MOVING, DERRIS!
HUMMM
RESTRAIN!
HALT!
WHOOM
TING
WHOOM
Waaa!
VOOOP
VOOOP
ONE'S GETTING AWAY!
LIGHT!
FLASHHH
Argh!
BLIND-ING...

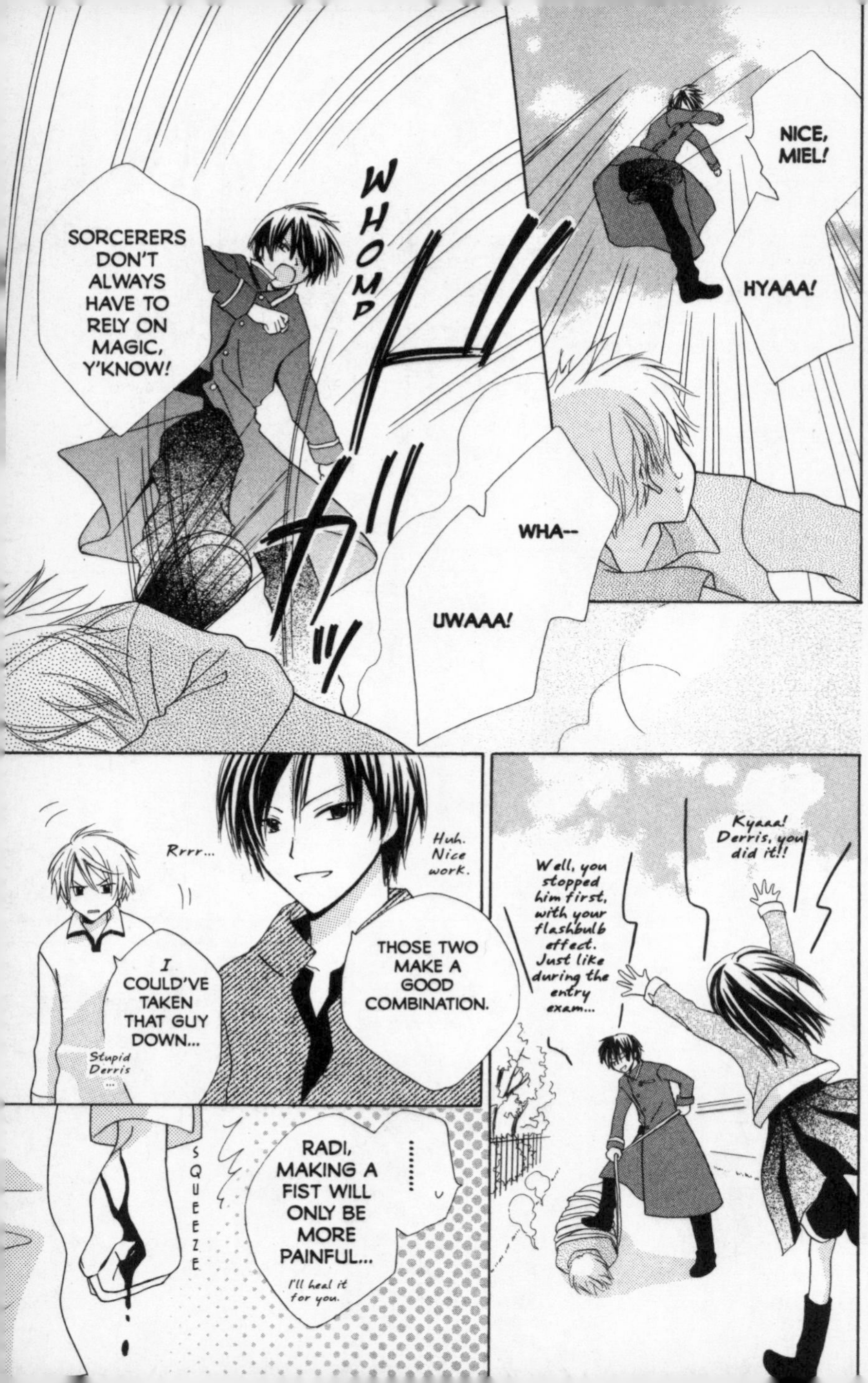
NICE, MIEL!
HYAAA!
WHA--
SORCERERS DON'T ALWAYS HAVE TO RELY ON MAGIC, Y'KNOW!
WHOMP
UWAAA!
Kyaaa! Derris, you did it!!
Well, you stopped him first, with your flashbulb effect. Just like during the entry exam...
Huh. Nice work.
THOSE TWO MAKE A GOOD COMBINATION.
Rrrr...
I COULD'VE TAKEN THAT GUY DOWN...
Stupid Derris...
....
RADI, MAKING A FIST WILL ONLY BE MORE PAINFUL...
I'll heal it for you.
SQUEEZE

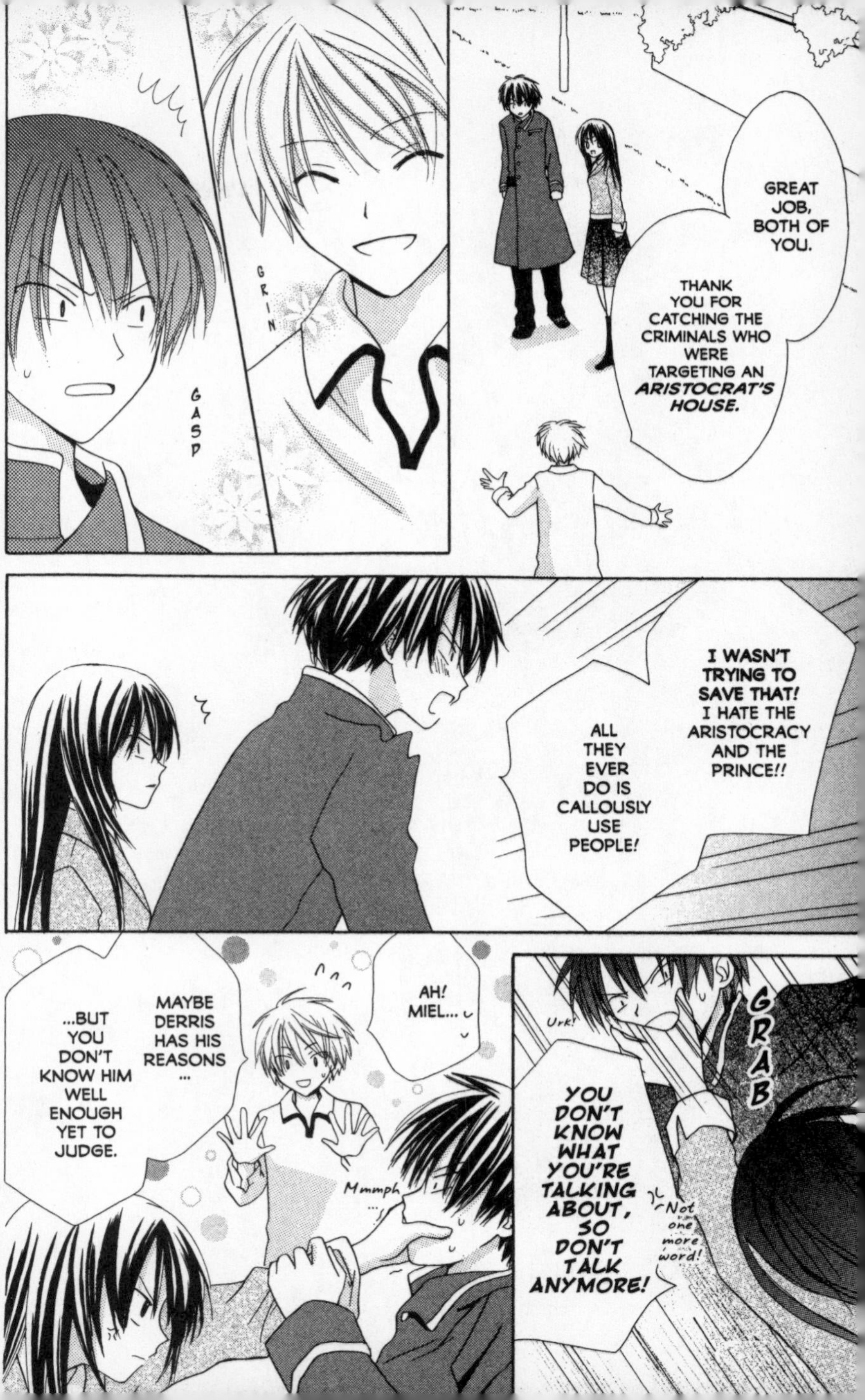
GREAT JOB, BOTH OF YOU.
THANK YOU FOR CATCHING THE CRIMINALS WHO WERE TARGETING AN *ARISTOCRAT'S HOUSE.*
GRIN
GASP
I WASN'T TRYING TO SAVE THAT! I HATE THE ARISTOCRACY AND THE PRINCE!!
ALL THEY EVER DO IS CALLOUSLY USE PEOPLE!
GRAB
Urk!
YOU DON'T KNOW WHAT YOU'RE TALKING ABOUT, SO DON'T TALK ANYMORE!
Not one more word!
AH! MIEL...
MAYBE DERRIS HAS HIS REASONS...
...BUT YOU DON'T KNOW HIM WELL ENOUGH YET TO JUDGE.
Mmmph...

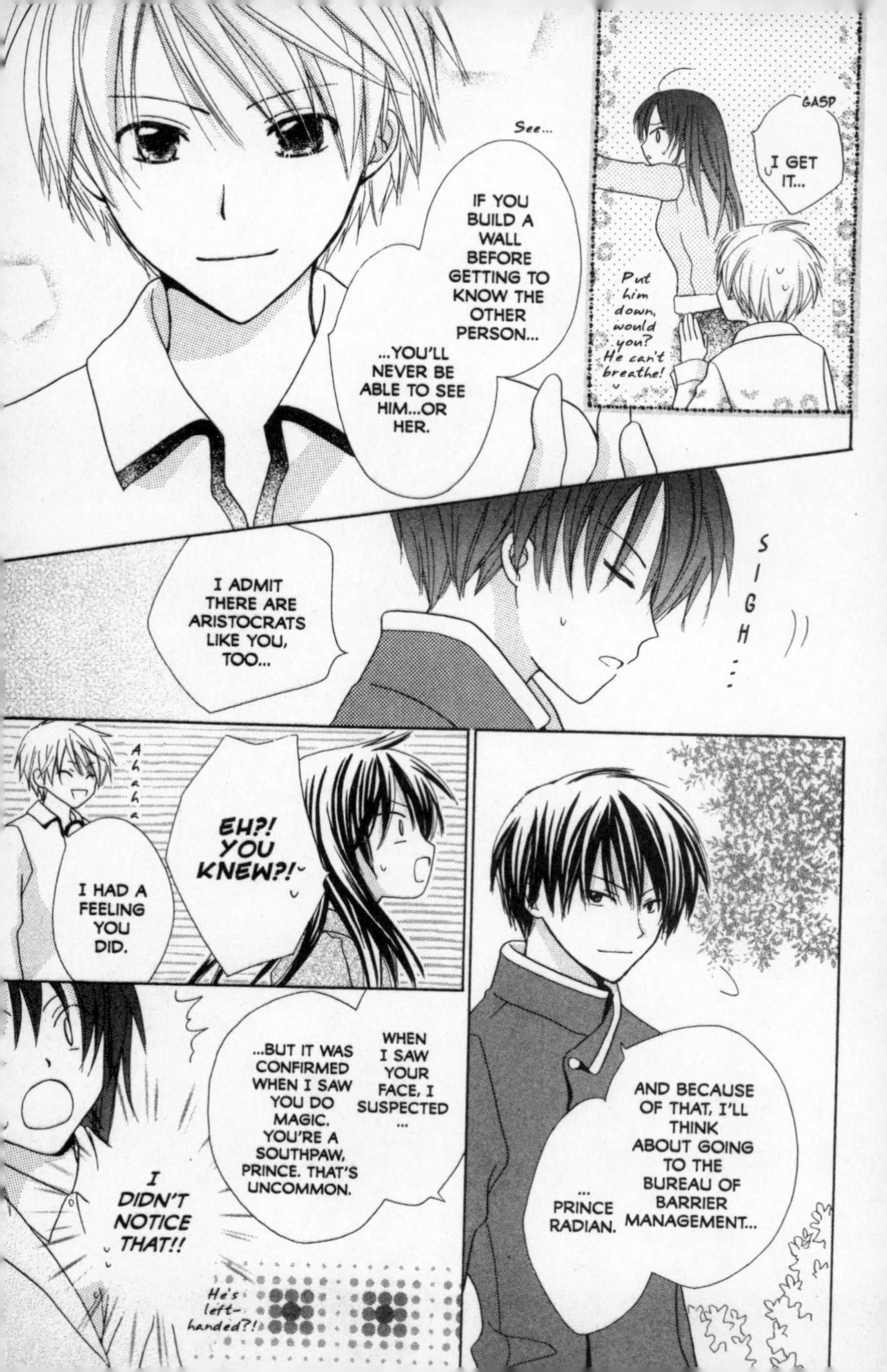
GASP
I GET IT...
Put him down, would you? He can't breathe!
See...
IF YOU BUILD A WALL BEFORE GETTING TO KNOW THE OTHER PERSON...
...YOU'LL NEVER BE ABLE TO SEE HIM...OR HER.
I ADMIT THERE ARE ARISTOCRATS LIKE YOU, TOO...
SIGH...
AND BECAUSE OF THAT, I'LL THINK ABOUT GOING TO THE BUREAU OF BARRIER MANAGEMENT...
...PRINCE RADIAN.
EH?! YOU KNEW?!
Ahaha
I HAD A FEELING YOU DID.
WHEN I SAW YOUR FACE, I SUSPECTED...
...BUT IT WAS CONFIRMED WHEN I SAW YOU DO MAGIC. YOU'RE A SOUTHPAW, PRINCE. THAT'S UNCOMMON.
I DIDN'T NOTICE THAT!!
He's left-handed?!

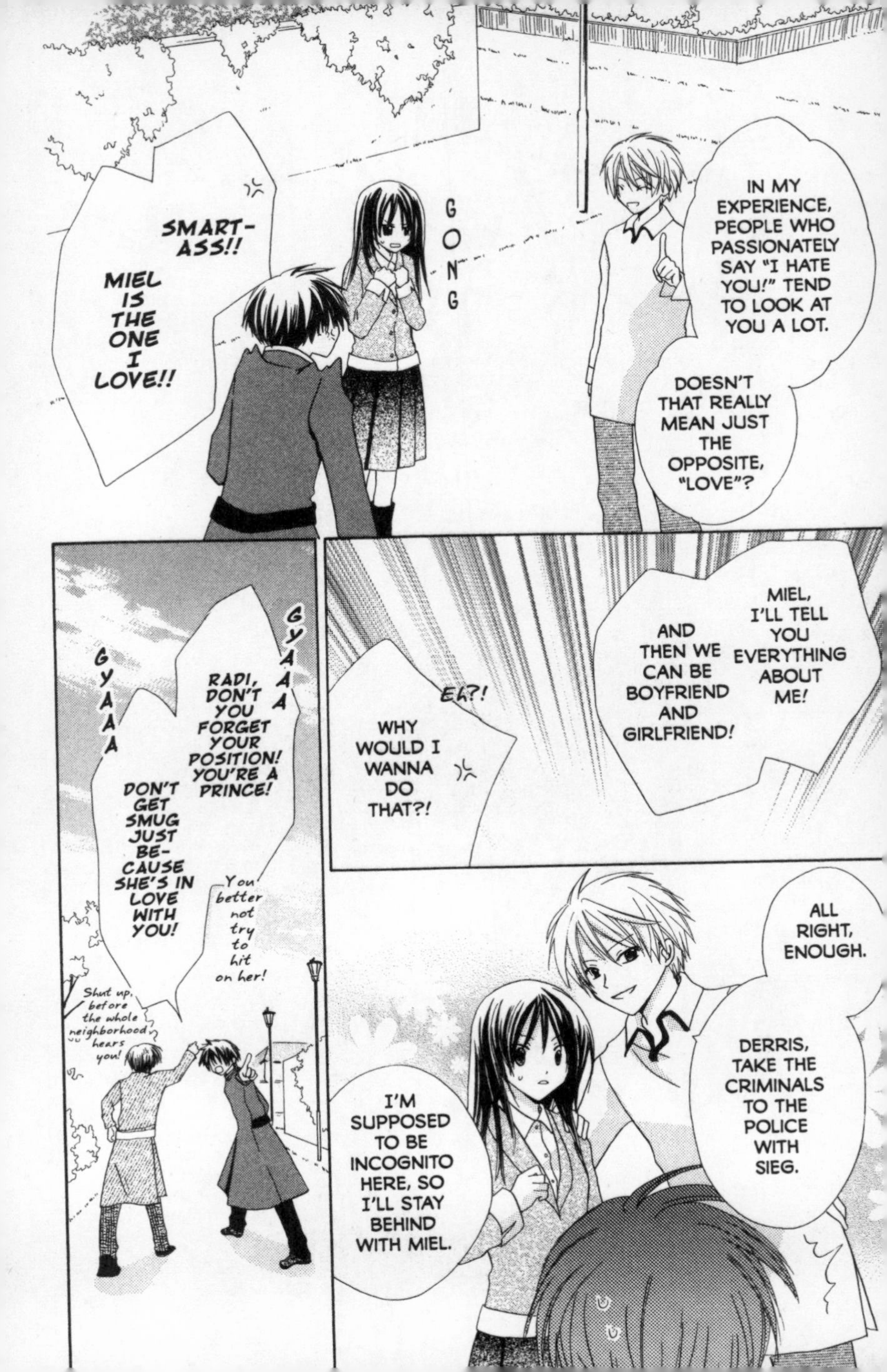
IN MY EXPERIENCE, PEOPLE WHO PASSIONATELY SAY "I HATE YOU!" TEND TO LOOK AT YOU A LOT.
DOESN'T THAT REALLY MEAN JUST THE OPPOSITE, "LOVE"?
GONG
SMART-ASS!!
MIEL IS THE ONE I LOVE!!
MIEL, I'LL TELL YOU EVERYTHING ABOUT ME!
AND THEN WE CAN BE BOYFRIEND AND GIRLFRIEND!
Eh?!
WHY WOULD I WANNA DO THAT?!
ALL RIGHT, ENOUGH.
DERRIS, TAKE THE CRIMINALS TO THE POLICE WITH SIEG.
I'M SUPPOSED TO BE INCOGNITO HERE, SO I'LL STAY BEHIND WITH MIEL.
GYAAA
RADI, DON'T YOU FORGET YOUR POSITION! YOU'RE A PRINCE!
GYAAA
DON'T GET SMUG JUST BE-CAUSE SHE'S IN LOVE WITH YOU!
You better not try to hit on her!
Shut up, before the whole neighborhood hears you!

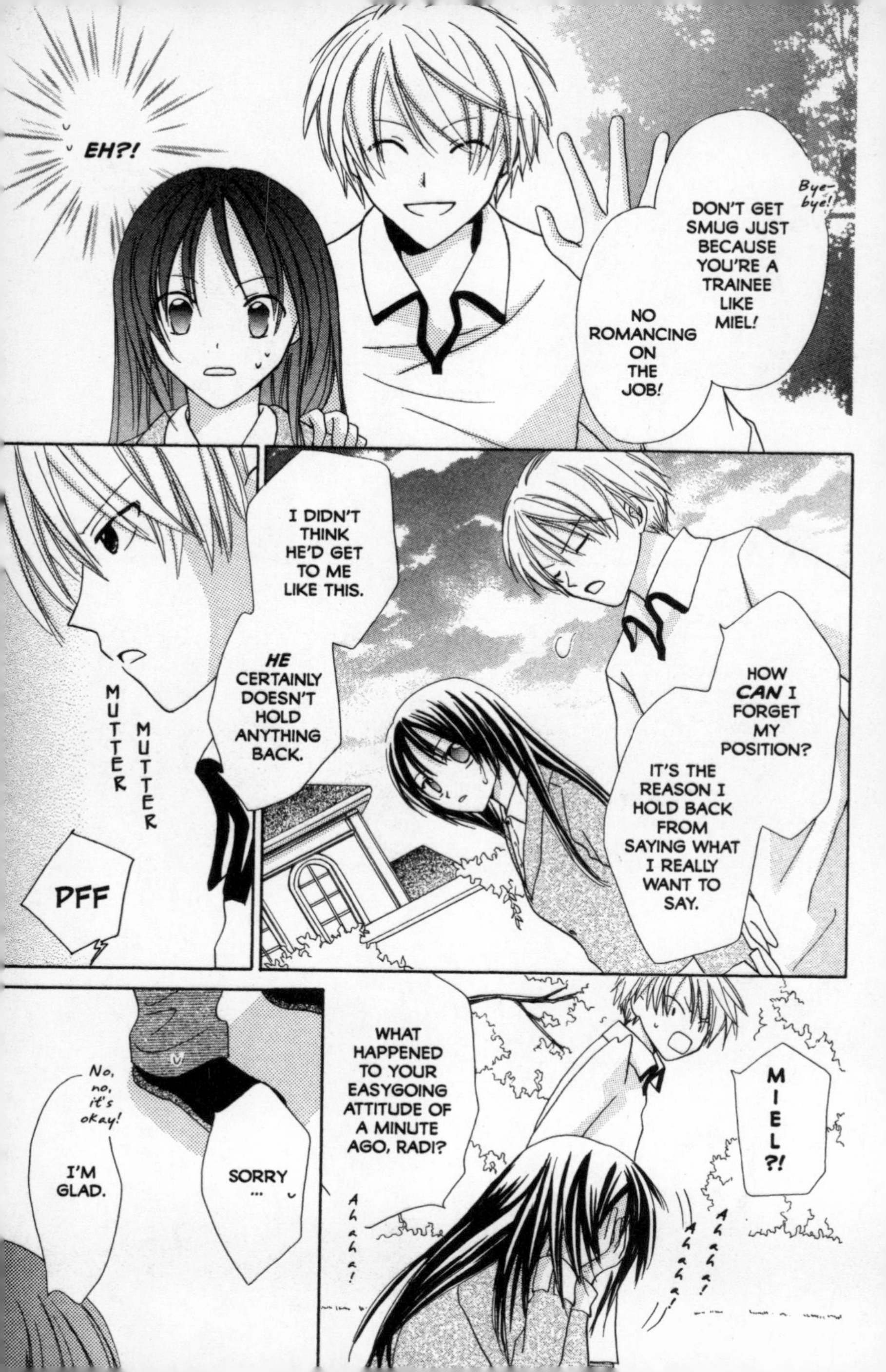
Bye-bye!
DON'T GET SMUG JUST BECAUSE YOU'RE A TRAINEE LIKE MIEL!
NO ROMANCING ON THE JOB!
EH?!
HOW CAN I FORGET MY POSITION?
IT'S THE REASON I HOLD BACK FROM SAYING WHAT I REALLY WANT TO SAY.
I DIDN'T THINK HE'D GET TO ME LIKE THIS.
HE CERTAINLY DOESN'T HOLD ANYTHING BACK.
MUTTER
MUTTER
PFF
MIEL?!
Ahahaha!
Ahahaha!
WHAT HAPPENED TO YOUR EASYGOING ATTITUDE OF A MINUTE AGO, RADI?
Ahahaha!
SORRY...
I'M GLAD.
No, no, it's okay!

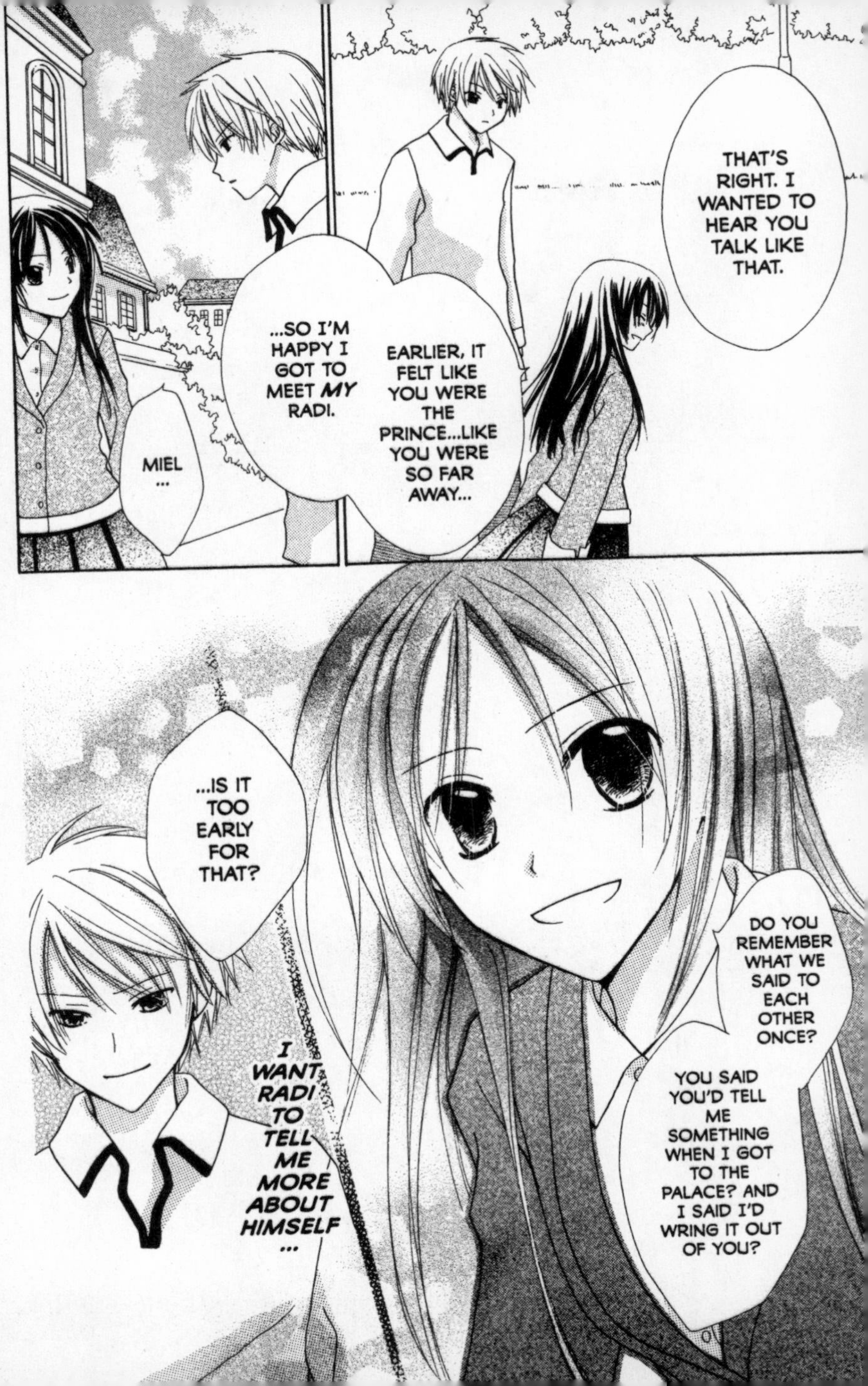
THAT'S RIGHT. I WANTED TO HEAR YOU TALK LIKE THAT.
EARLIER, IT FELT LIKE YOU WERE THE PRINCE...LIKE YOU WERE SO FAR AWAY...
...SO I'M HAPPY I GOT TO MEET *MY* RADI.
MIEL ...
DO YOU REMEMBER WHAT WE SAID TO EACH OTHER ONCE?
YOU SAID YOU'D TELL ME SOMETHING WHEN I GOT TO THE PALACE? AND I SAID I'D WRING IT OUT OF YOU?
...IS IT TOO EARLY FOR THAT?
I WANT RADI TO TELL ME MORE ABOUT HIMSELF ...

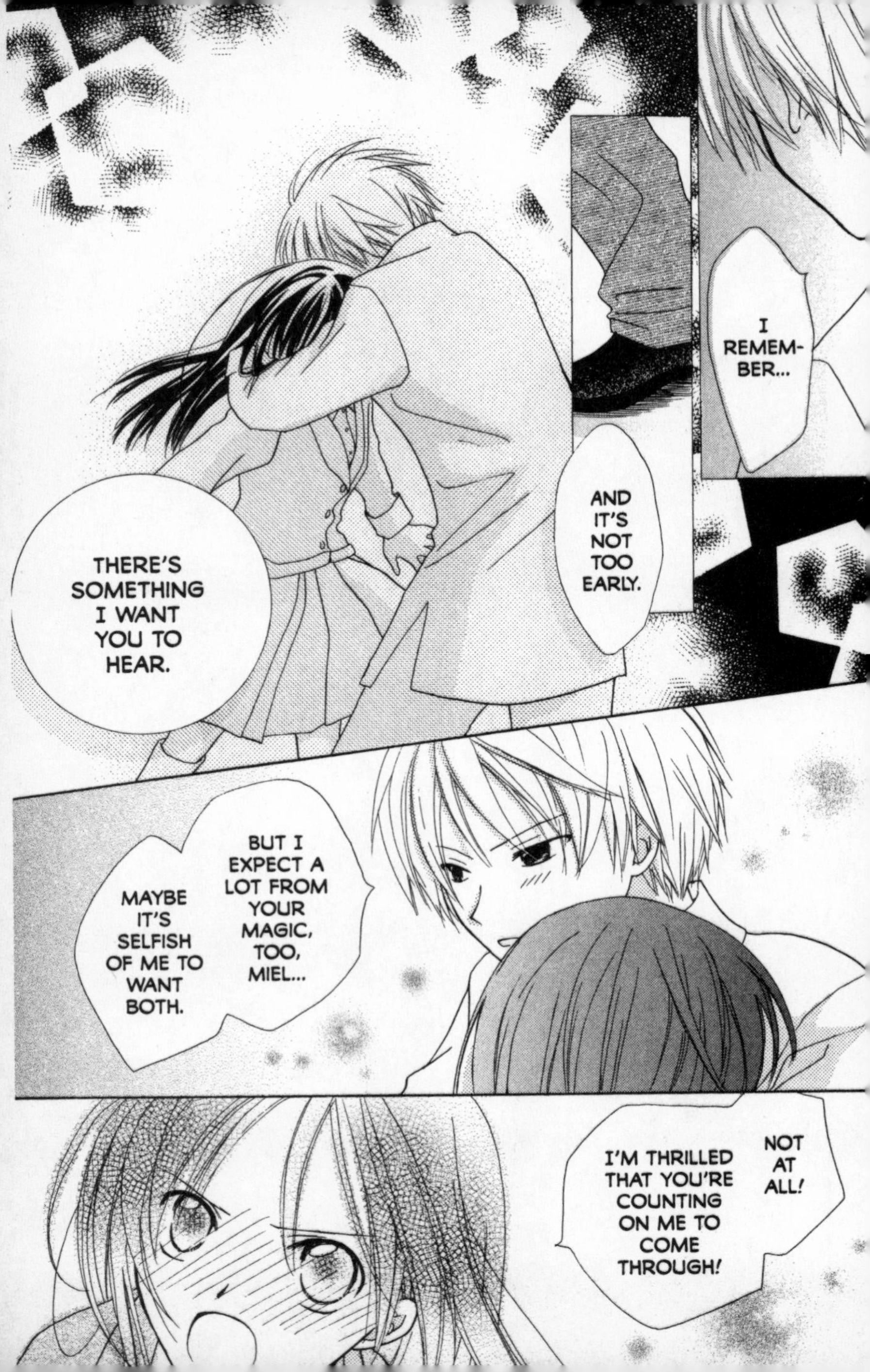
I REMEMBER...
AND IT'S NOT TOO EARLY.
THERE'S SOMETHING I WANT YOU TO HEAR.
BUT I EXPECT A LOT FROM YOUR MAGIC, TOO, MIEL...
MAYBE IT'S SELFISH OF ME TO WANT BOTH.
NOT AT ALL!
I'M THRILLED THAT YOU'RE COUNTING ON ME TO COME THROUGH!

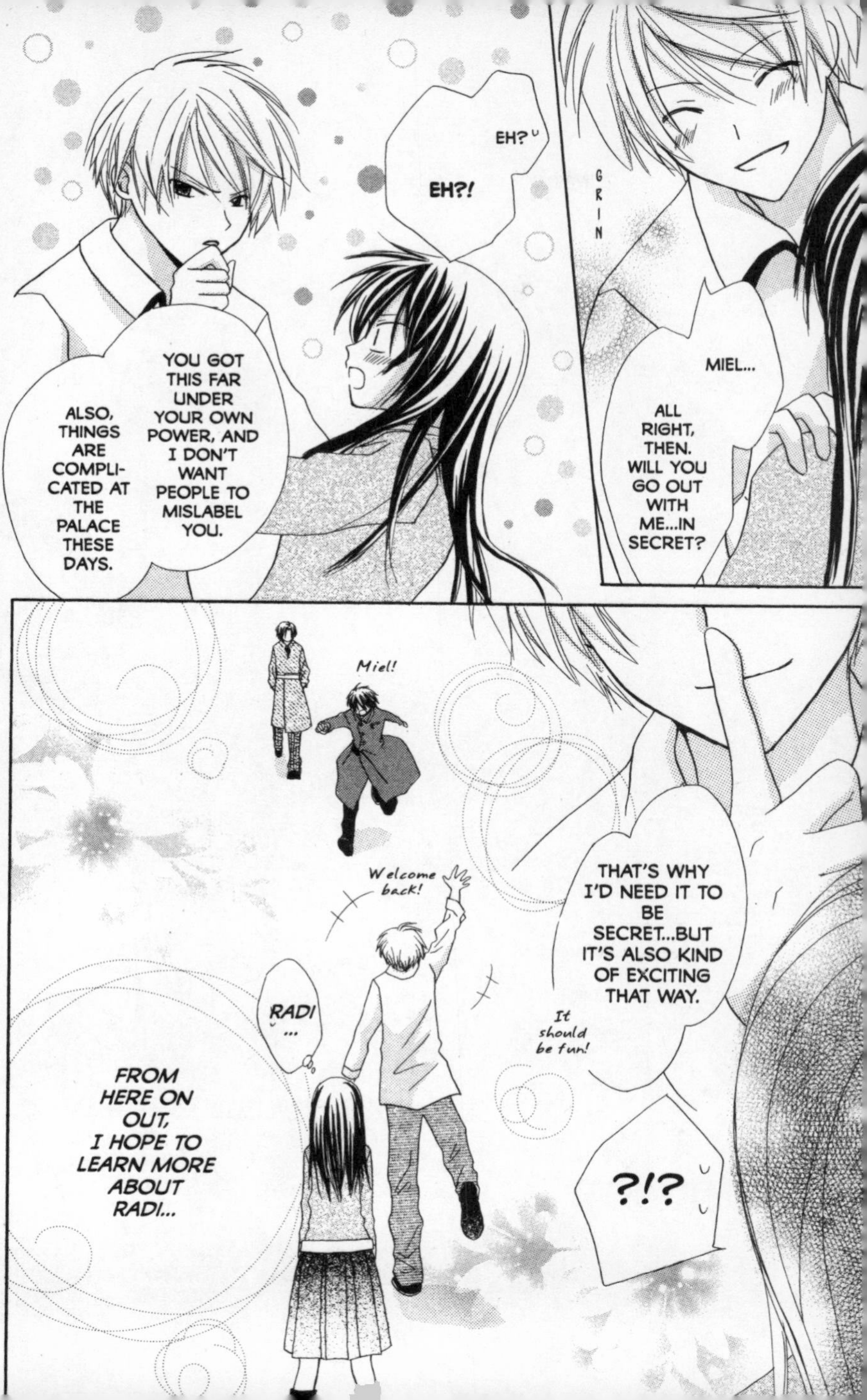
G R I N
MIEL... ALL RIGHT, THEN. WILL YOU GO OUT WITH ME...IN SECRET?
EH?
EH?!
YOU GOT THIS FAR UNDER YOUR OWN POWER, AND I DON'T WANT PEOPLE TO MISLABEL YOU.
ALSO, THINGS ARE COMPLICATED AT THE PALACE THESE DAYS.
THAT'S WHY I'D NEED IT TO BE SECRET...BUT IT'S ALSO KIND OF EXCITING THAT WAY.
It should be fun!
?!?
Miel!
Welcome back!
RADI...
FROM HERE ON OUT, I HOPE TO LEARN MORE ABOUT RADI...

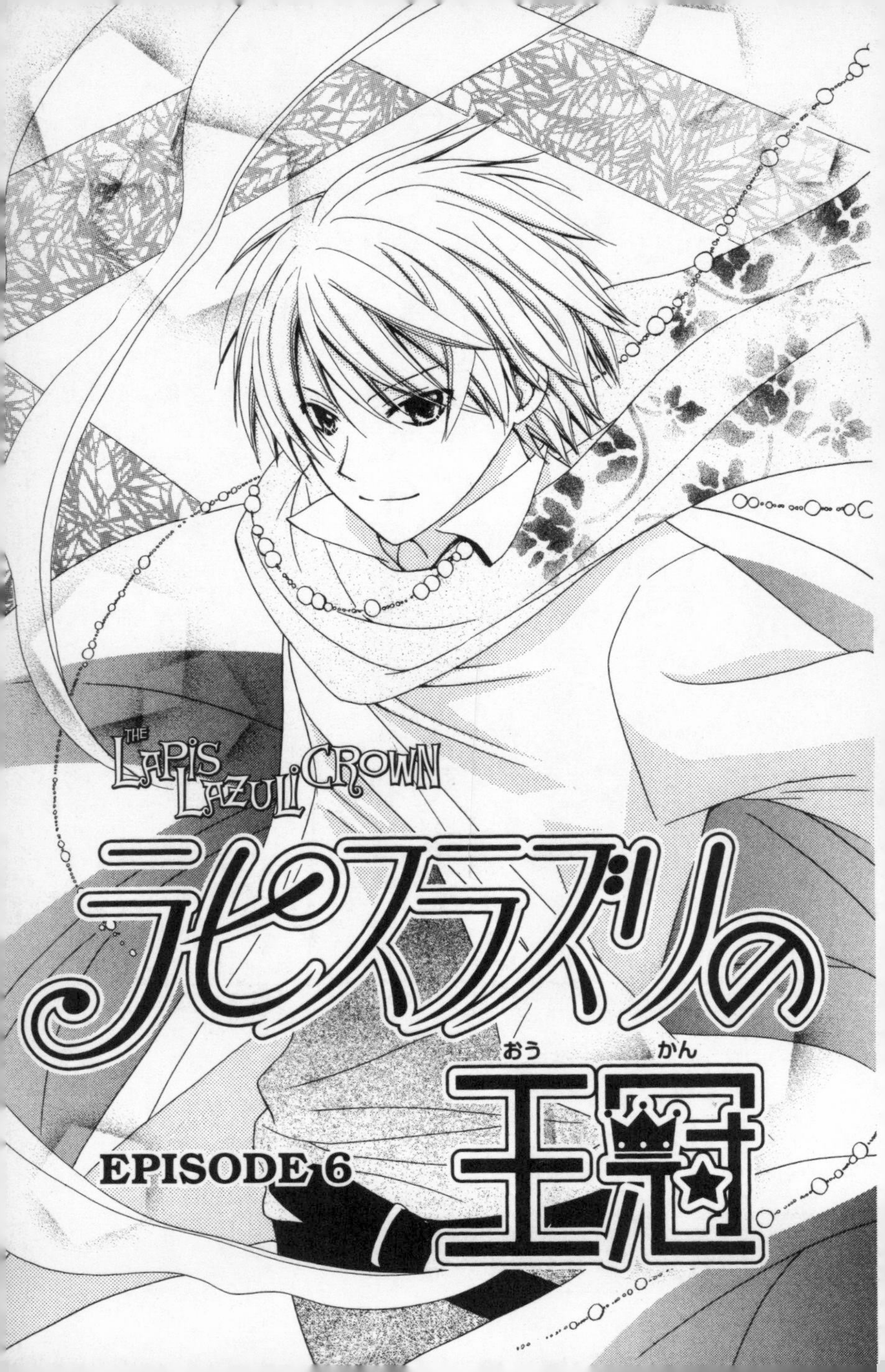
THE LAPIS LAZULI CROWN
ラピスラズリの王冠（おうかん）
EPISODE 6

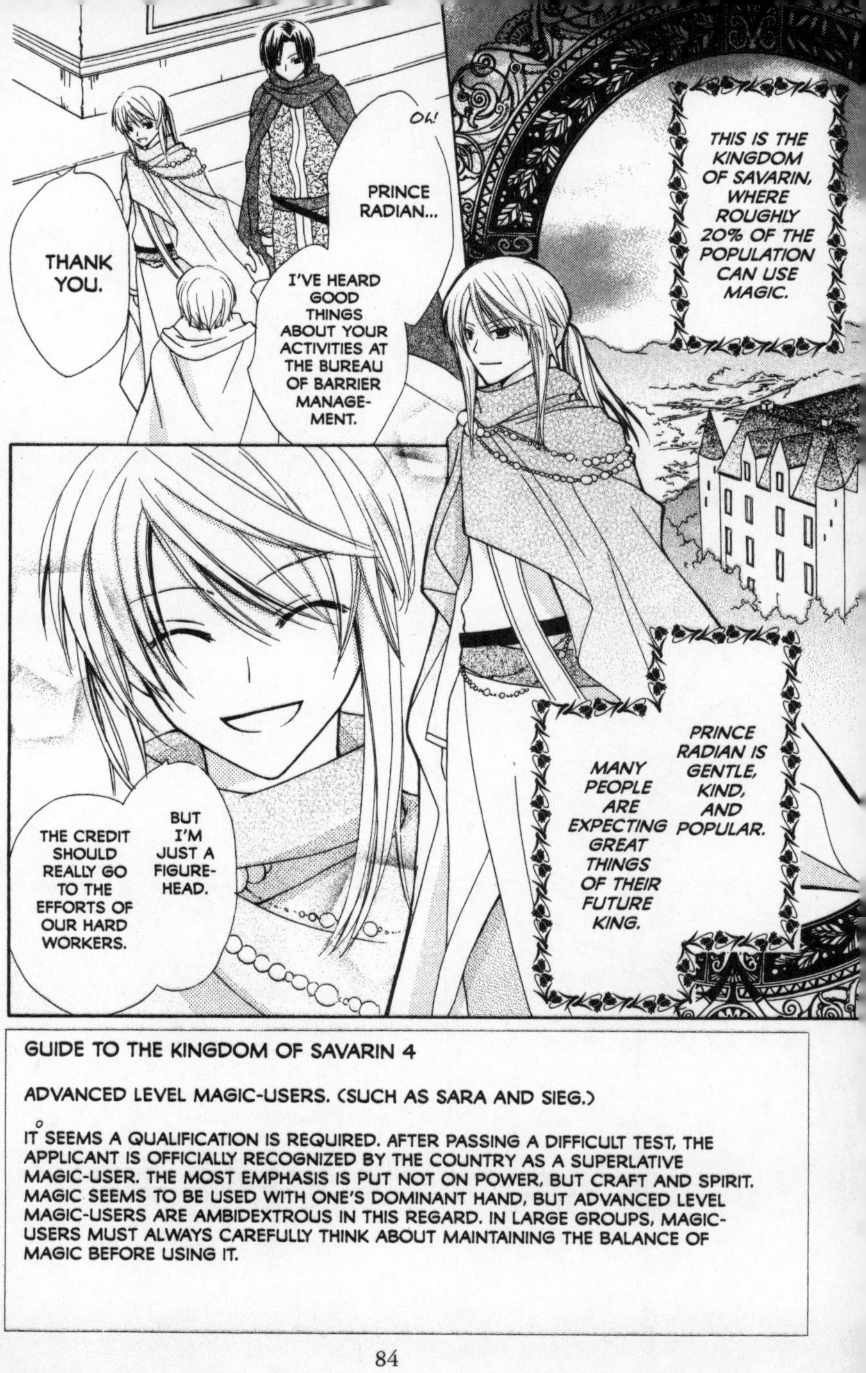
THIS IS THE KINGDOM OF SAVARIN, WHERE ROUGHLY 20% OF THE POPULATION CAN USE MAGIC.
PRINCE RADIAN IS GENTLE, KIND, AND POPULAR.
MANY PEOPLE ARE EXPECTING GREAT THINGS OF THEIR FUTURE KING.
OH!
PRINCE RADIAN...
I'VE HEARD GOOD THINGS ABOUT YOUR ACTIVITIES AT THE BUREAU OF BARRIER MANAGEMENT.
THANK YOU.
BUT I'M JUST A FIGUREHEAD.
THE CREDIT SHOULD REALLY GO TO THE EFFORTS OF OUR HARD WORKERS.

GUIDE TO THE KINGDOM OF SAVARIN 4

ADVANCED LEVEL MAGIC-USERS. (SUCH AS SARA AND SIEG.)

IT SEEMS A QUALIFICATION IS REQUIRED. AFTER PASSING A DIFFICULT TEST, THE APPLICANT IS OFFICIALLY RECOGNIZED BY THE COUNTRY AS A SUPERLATIVE MAGIC-USER. THE MOST EMPHASIS IS PUT NOT ON POWER, BUT CRAFT AND SPIRIT. MAGIC SEEMS TO BE USED WITH ONE'S DOMINANT HAND, BUT ADVANCED LEVEL MAGIC-USERS ARE AMBIDEXTROUS IN THIS REGARD. IN LARGE GROUPS, MAGIC-USERS MUST ALWAYS CAREFULLY THINK ABOUT MAINTAINING THE BALANCE OF MAGIC BEFORE USING IT.

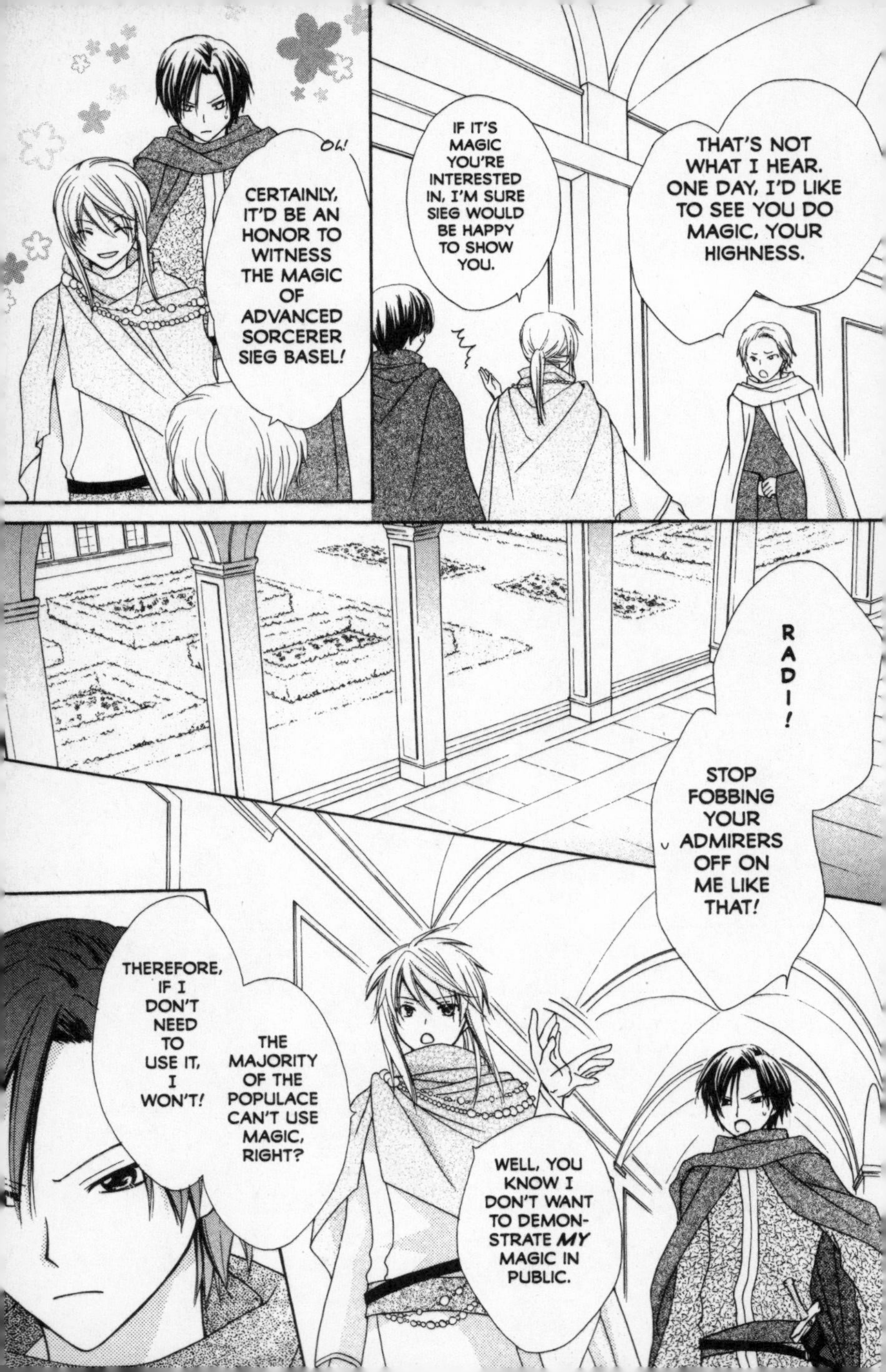
THAT'S NOT WHAT I HEAR. ONE DAY, I'D LIKE TO SEE YOU DO MAGIC, YOUR HIGHNESS.
IF IT'S MAGIC YOU'RE INTERESTED IN, I'M SURE SIEG WOULD BE HAPPY TO SHOW YOU.
OH!
CERTAINLY, IT'D BE AN HONOR TO WITNESS THE MAGIC OF ADVANCED SORCERER SIEG BASEL!
RADI!
STOP FOBBING YOUR ADMIRERS OFF ON ME LIKE THAT!
WELL, YOU KNOW I DON'T WANT TO DEMON-STRATE MY MAGIC IN PUBLIC.
THE MAJORITY OF THE POPULACE CAN'T USE MAGIC, RIGHT?
THEREFORE, IF I DON'T NEED TO USE IT, I WON'T!

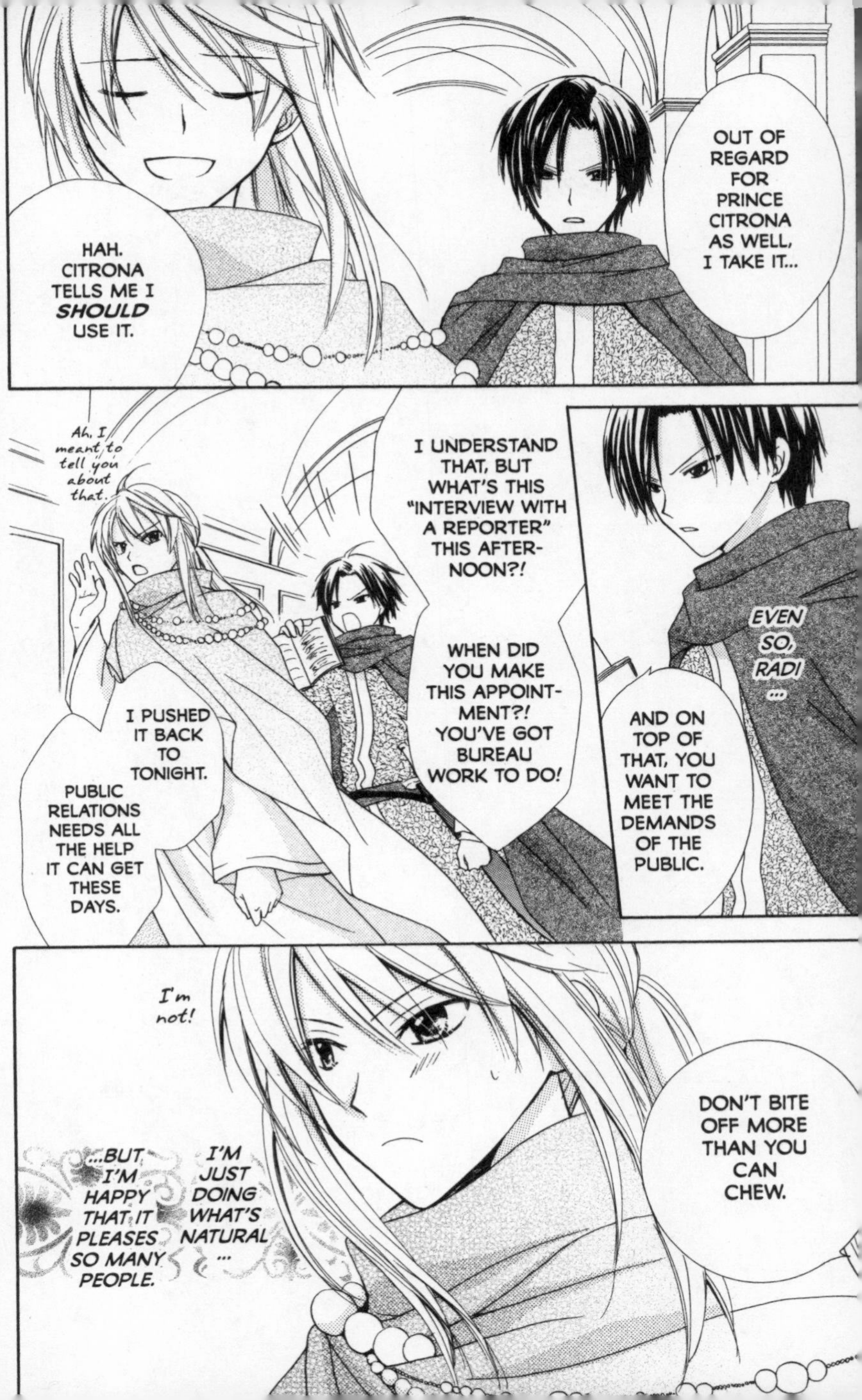
OUT OF REGARD FOR PRINCE CITRONA AS WELL, I TAKE IT...
HAH. CITRONA TELLS ME I ***SHOULD*** USE IT.
EVEN SO, RADI ...
AND ON TOP OF THAT, YOU WANT TO MEET THE DEMANDS OF THE PUBLIC.
I UNDERSTAND THAT, BUT WHAT'S THIS "INTERVIEW WITH A REPORTER" THIS AFTER-NOON?!
WHEN DID YOU MAKE THIS APPOINT-MENT?! YOU'VE GOT BUREAU WORK TO DO!
Ah, I meant to tell you about that.
I PUSHED IT BACK TO TONIGHT.
PUBLIC RELATIONS NEEDS ALL THE HELP IT CAN GET THESE DAYS.
DON'T BITE OFF MORE THAN YOU CAN CHEW.
I'm not!
I'M JUST DOING WHAT'S NATURAL ...
...BUT I'M HAPPY THAT IT PLEASES SO MANY PEOPLE.

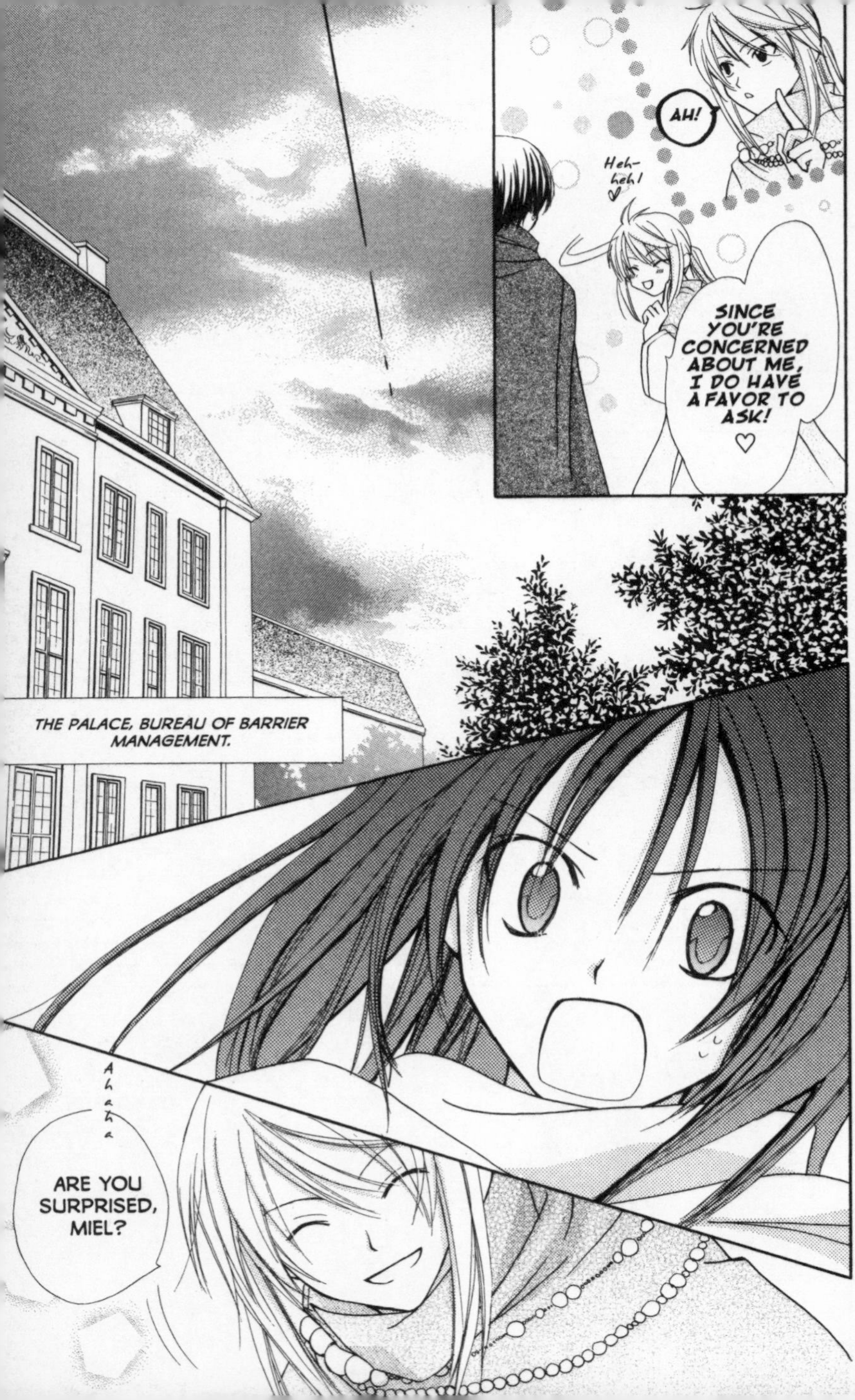
AH!
Heh-heh! ♡
SINCE YOU'RE CONCERNED ABOUT ME, I DO HAVE A FAVOR TO ASK! ♡
THE PALACE, BUREAU OF BARRIER MANAGEMENT.
Ahaha
ARE YOU SURPRISED, MIEL?

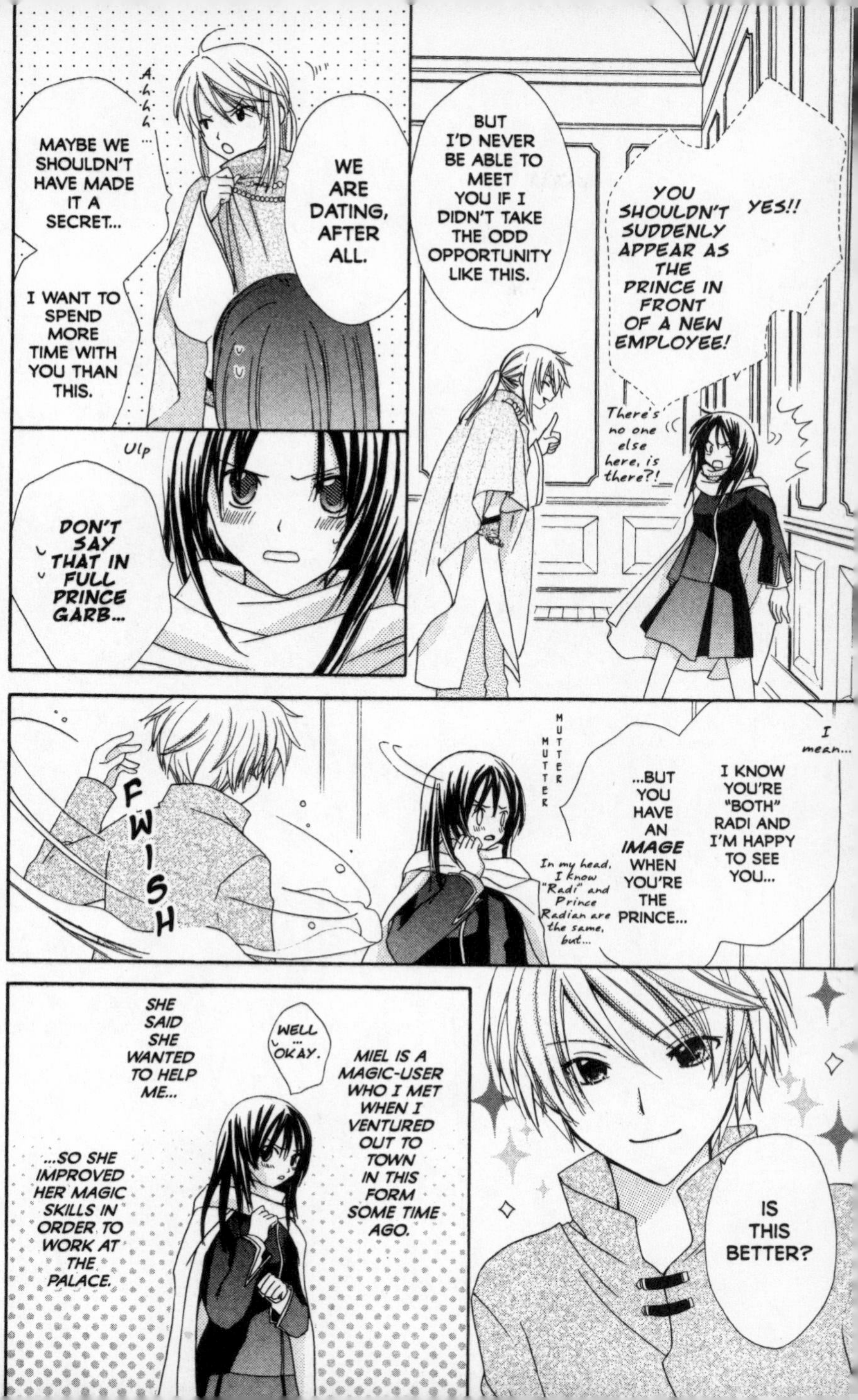
YES!!
YOU SHOULDN'T SUDDENLY APPEAR AS THE PRINCE IN FRONT OF A NEW EMPLOYEE!
BUT I'D NEVER BE ABLE TO MEET YOU IF I DIDN'T TAKE THE ODD OPPORTUNITY LIKE THIS.
There's no one else here, is there?!
WE ARE DATING, AFTER ALL.
Ahhh...
MAYBE WE SHOULDN'T HAVE MADE IT A SECRET...
I WANT TO SPEND MORE TIME WITH YOU THAN THIS.
Ulp
DON'T SAY THAT IN FULL PRINCE GARB...
I mean...
I KNOW YOU'RE "BOTH" RADI AND I'M HAPPY TO SEE YOU...
...BUT YOU HAVE AN IMAGE WHEN YOU'RE THE PRINCE...
MUTTER MUTTER
In my head, I know "Radi" and Prince Radian are the same, but...
FWISH
IS THIS BETTER?
MIEL IS A MAGIC-USER WHO I MET WHEN I VENTURED OUT TO TOWN IN THIS FORM SOME TIME AGO.
WELL... OKAY.
SHE SAID SHE WANTED TO HELP ME...
...SO SHE IMPROVED HER MAGIC SKILLS IN ORDER TO WORK AT THE PALACE.

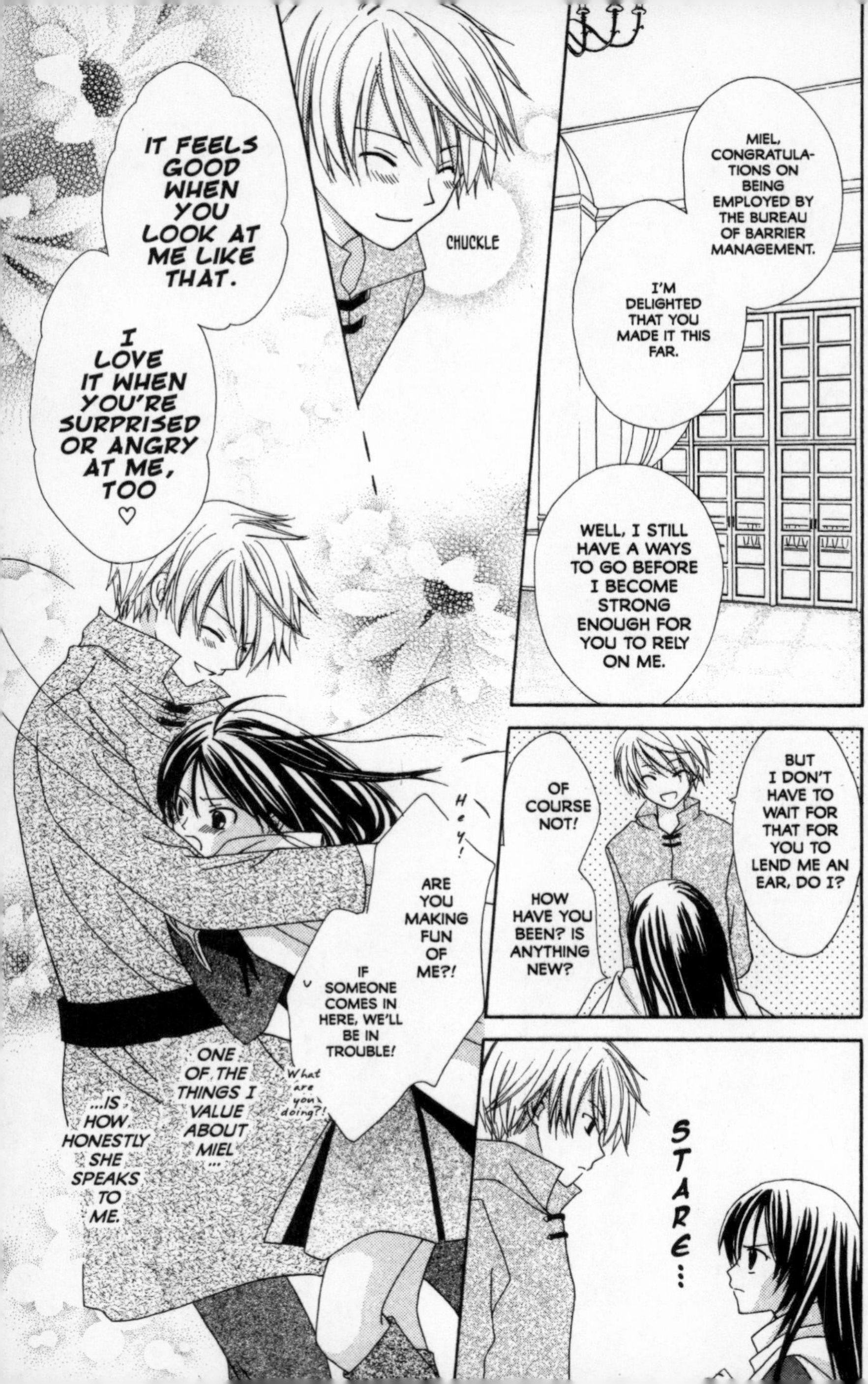
MIEL, CONGRATULATIONS ON BEING EMPLOYED BY THE BUREAU OF BARRIER MANAGEMENT.
I'M DELIGHTED THAT YOU MADE IT THIS FAR.
WELL, I STILL HAVE A WAYS TO GO BEFORE I BECOME STRONG ENOUGH FOR YOU TO RELY ON ME.
BUT I DON'T HAVE TO WAIT FOR THAT FOR YOU TO LEND ME AN EAR, DO I?
OF COURSE NOT!
HOW HAVE YOU BEEN? IS ANYTHING NEW?
STARE...
IT FEELS GOOD WHEN YOU LOOK AT ME LIKE THAT.
CHUCKLE
I LOVE IT WHEN YOU'RE SURPRISED OR ANGRY AT ME, TOO ♡
Hey!
ARE YOU MAKING FUN OF ME?!
IF SOMEONE COMES IN HERE, WE'LL BE IN TROUBLE!
What are you doing?!
ONE OF THE THINGS I VALUE ABOUT MIEL...
...IS HOW HONESTLY SHE SPEAKS TO ME.

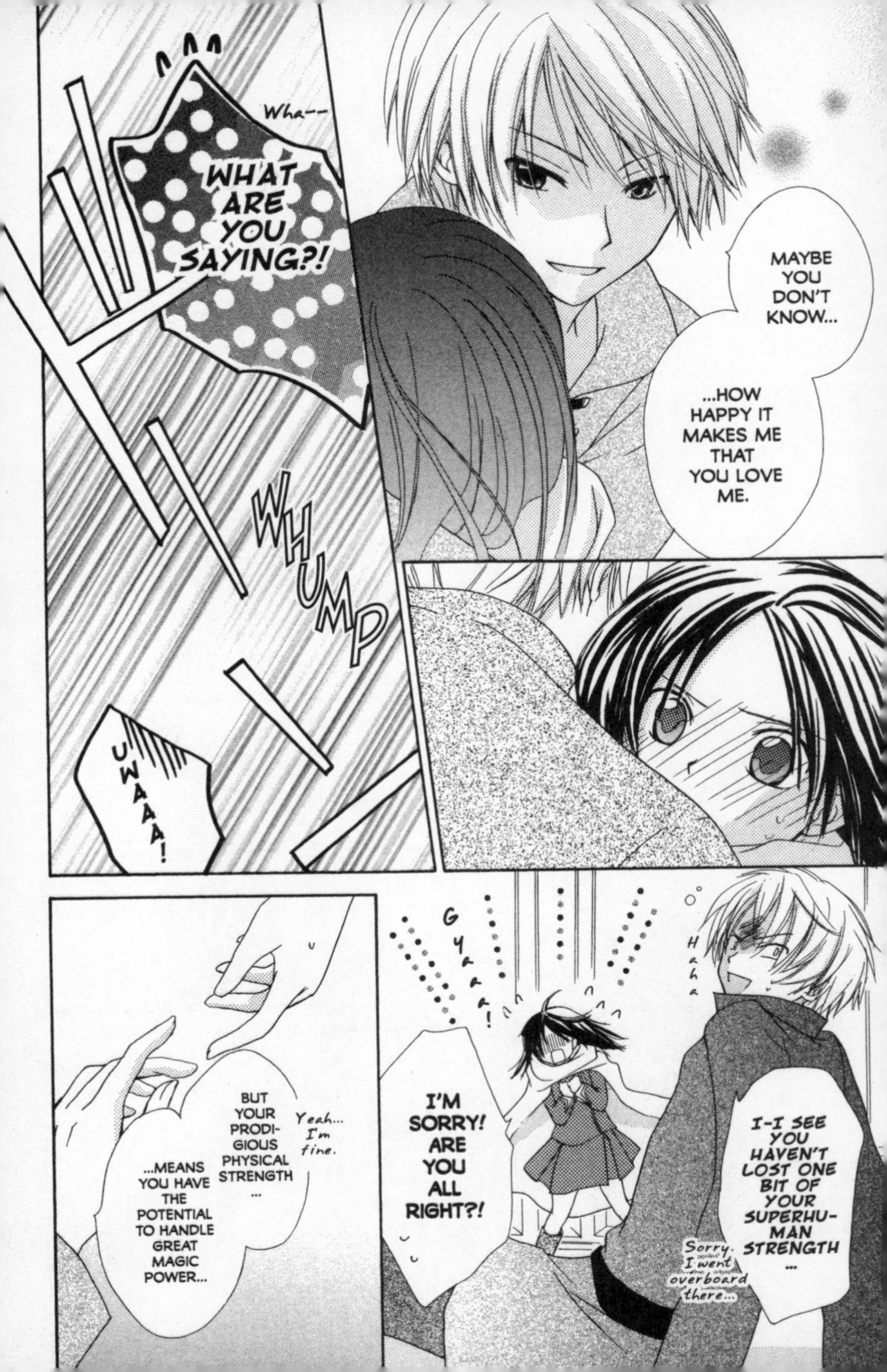
MAYBE YOU DON'T KNOW...
...HOW HAPPY IT MAKES ME THAT YOU LOVE ME.
Wha--
WHAT ARE YOU SAYING?!
WHUMP
UWAAA!
Gyaaaa!
Haha
I-I SEE YOU HAVEN'T LOST ONE BIT OF YOUR SUPERHUMAN STRENGTH...
I'M SORRY! ARE YOU ALL RIGHT?!
Sorry. I went overboard there...
Yeah... I'm fine.
BUT YOUR PRODIGIOUS PHYSICAL STRENGTH...
...MEANS YOU HAVE THE POTENTIAL TO HANDLE GREAT MAGIC POWER...

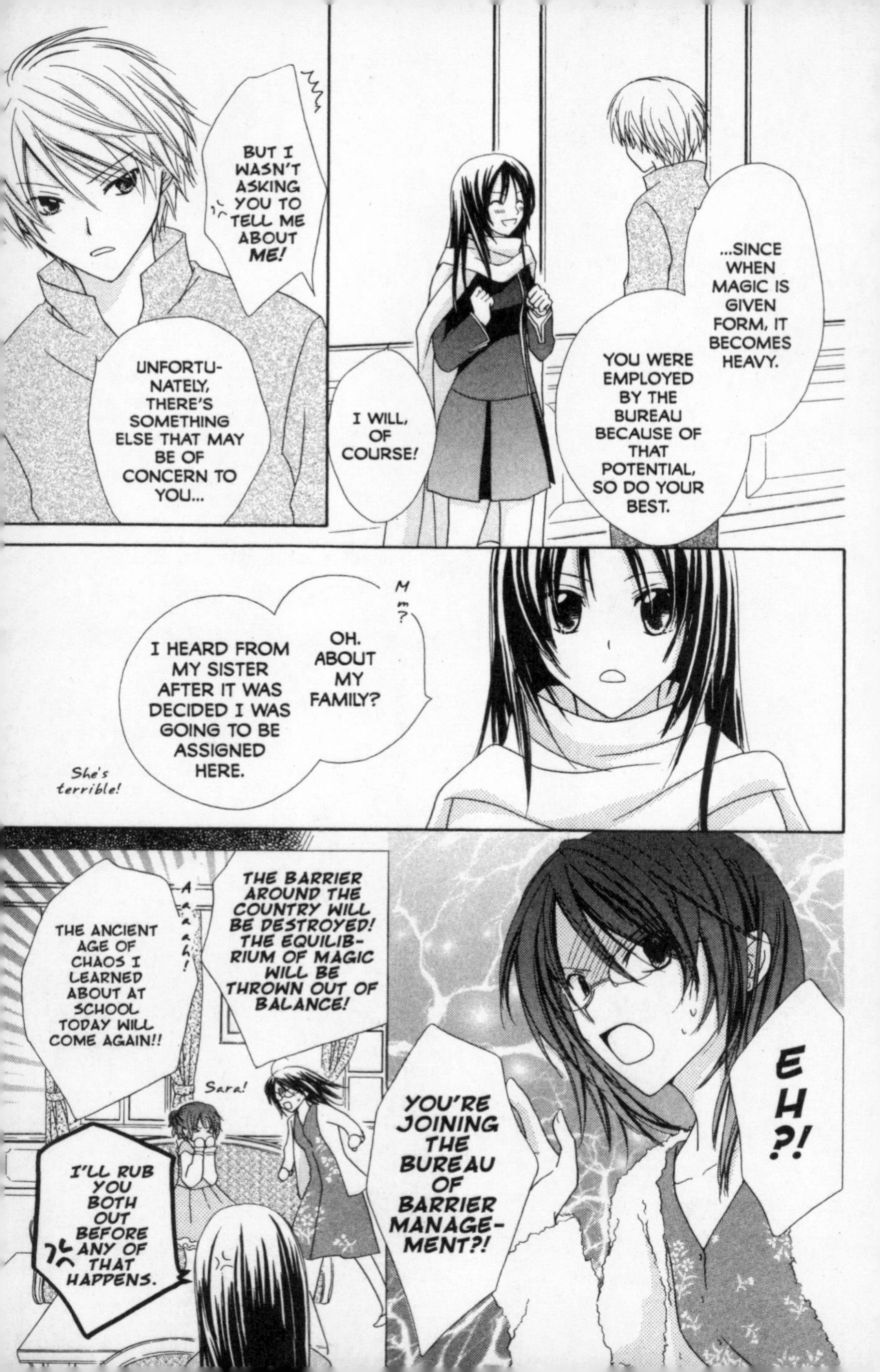
...SINCE WHEN MAGIC IS GIVEN FORM, IT BECOMES HEAVY.
YOU WERE EMPLOYED BY THE BUREAU BECAUSE OF THAT POTENTIAL, SO DO YOUR BEST.
I WILL, OF COURSE!
BUT I WASN'T ASKING YOU TO TELL ME ABOUT *ME!*
UNFORTU-NATELY, THERE'S SOMETHING ELSE THAT MAY BE OF CONCERN TO YOU...
Mm?
OH. ABOUT MY FAMILY?
I HEARD FROM MY SISTER AFTER IT WAS DECIDED I WAS GOING TO BE ASSIGNED HERE.
She's terrible!
EH?!
YOU'RE JOINING THE BUREAU OF BARRIER MANAGE-MENT?!
THE BARRIER AROUND THE COUNTRY WILL BE DESTROYED! THE EQUILIB-RIUM OF MAGIC WILL BE THROWN OUT OF BALANCE!
Aaaah!
THE ANCIENT AGE OF CHAOS I LEARNED ABOUT AT SCHOOL TODAY WILL COME AGAIN!!
Sara!
I'LL RUB YOU BOTH OUT BEFORE ANY OF THAT HAPPENS.

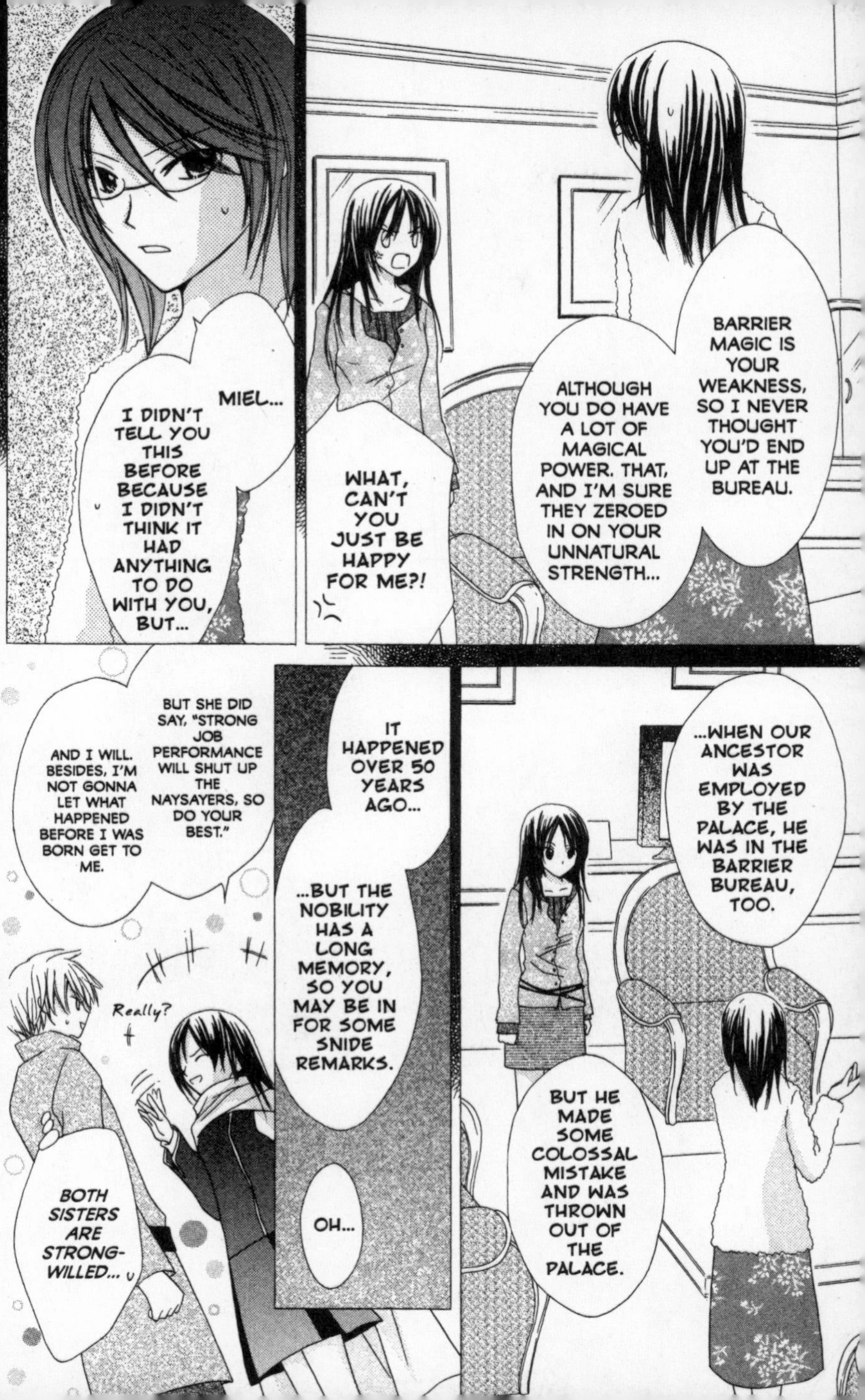
BARRIER MAGIC IS YOUR WEAKNESS, SO I NEVER THOUGHT YOU'D END UP AT THE BUREAU.
ALTHOUGH YOU DO HAVE A LOT OF MAGICAL POWER. THAT, AND I'M SURE THEY ZEROED IN ON YOUR UNNATURAL STRENGTH...
WHAT, CAN'T YOU JUST BE HAPPY FOR ME?!
MIEL...
I DIDN'T TELL YOU THIS BEFORE BECAUSE I DIDN'T THINK IT HAD ANYTHING TO DO WITH YOU, BUT...
...WHEN OUR ANCESTOR WAS EMPLOYED BY THE PALACE, HE WAS IN THE BARRIER BUREAU, TOO.
BUT HE MADE SOME COLOSSAL MISTAKE AND WAS THROWN OUT OF THE PALACE.
IT HAPPENED OVER 50 YEARS AGO...
...BUT THE NOBILITY HAS A LONG MEMORY, SO YOU MAY BE IN FOR SOME SNIDE REMARKS.
OH...
BUT SHE DID SAY, "STRONG JOB PERFORMANCE WILL SHUT UP THE NAYSAYERS, SO DO YOUR BEST."
AND I WILL. BESIDES, I'M NOT GONNA LET WHAT HAPPENED BEFORE I WAS BORN GET TO ME.
Really?
BOTH SISTERS ARE STRONG-WILLED...

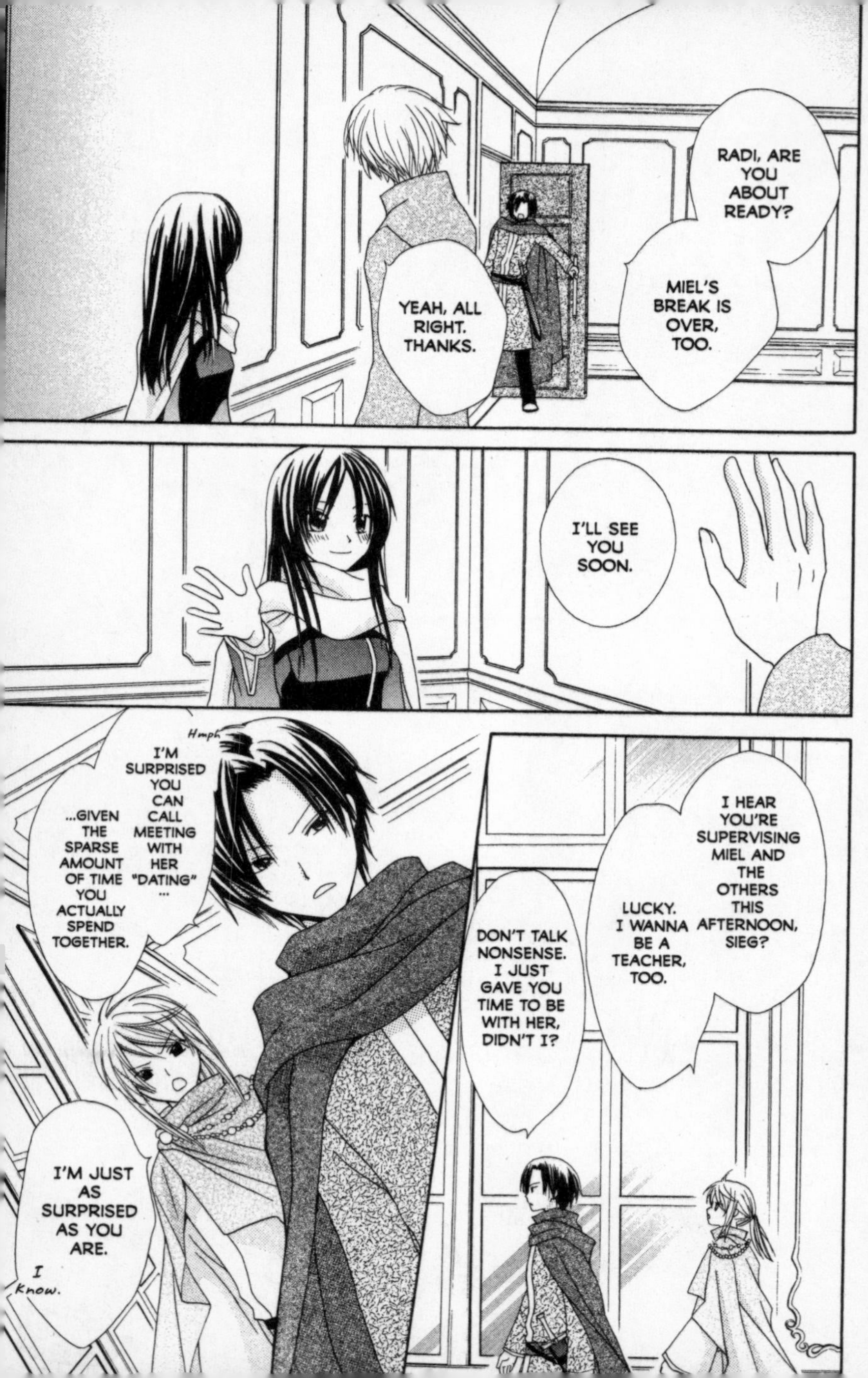
RADI, ARE YOU ABOUT READY?
MIEL'S BREAK IS OVER, TOO.
YEAH, ALL RIGHT. THANKS.
I'LL SEE YOU SOON.
I HEAR YOU'RE SUPERVISING MIEL AND THE OTHERS THIS AFTERNOON, SIEG?
LUCKY. I WANNA BE A TEACHER, TOO.
DON'T TALK NONSENSE. I JUST GAVE YOU TIME TO BE WITH HER, DIDN'T I?
Hmph
I'M SURPRISED YOU CAN CALL MEETING WITH HER "DATING"...
...GIVEN THE SPARSE AMOUNT OF TIME YOU ACTUALLY SPEND TOGETHER.
I'M JUST AS SURPRISED AS YOU ARE.
I know.

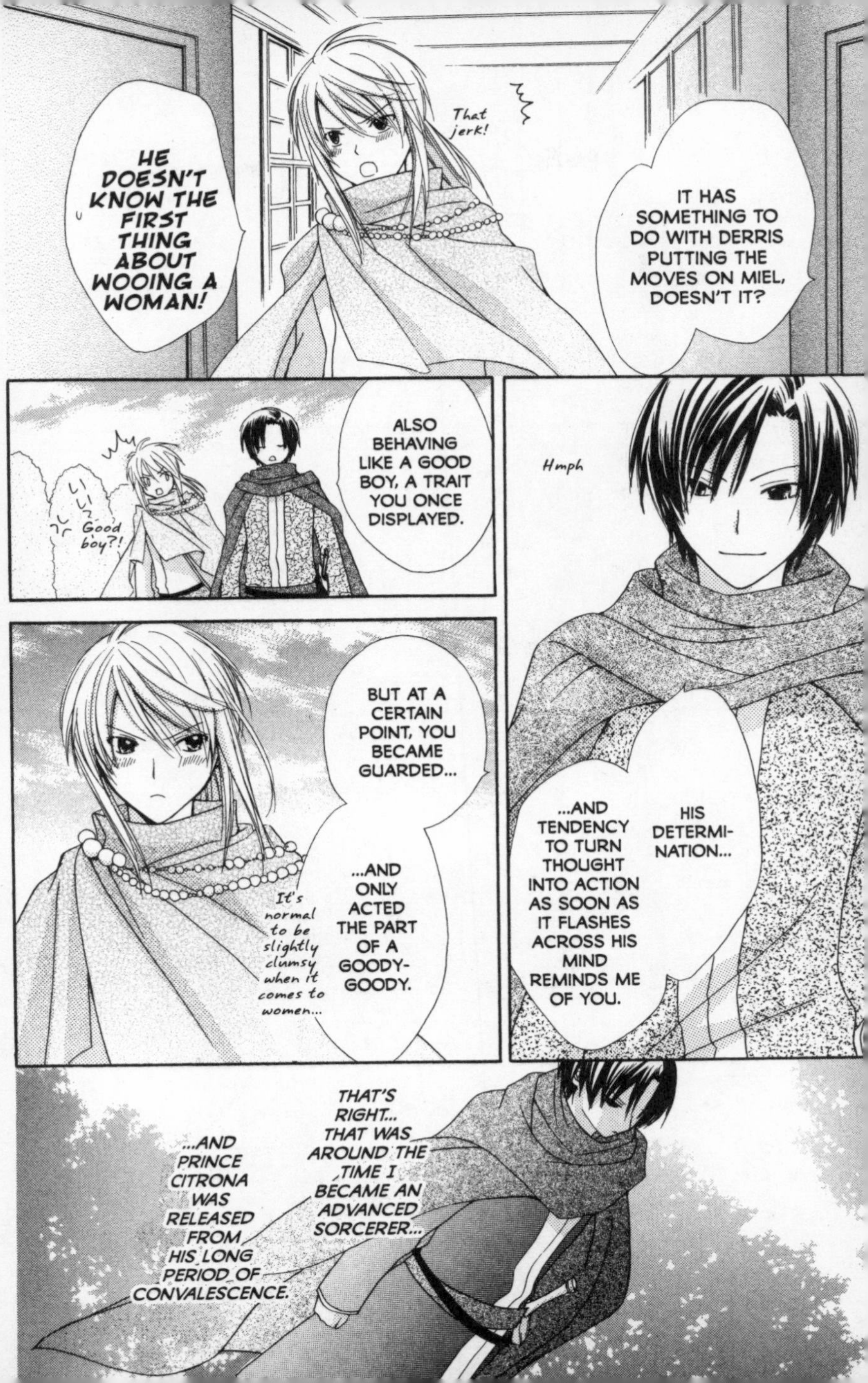
IT HAS SOMETHING TO DO WITH DERRIS PUTTING THE MOVES ON MIEL, DOESN'T IT?
That jerk!
HE DOESN'T KNOW THE FIRST THING ABOUT WOOING A WOMAN!
Hmph
HIS DETERMINATION...
...AND TENDENCY TO TURN THOUGHT INTO ACTION AS SOON AS IT FLASHES ACROSS HIS MIND REMINDS ME OF YOU.
ALSO BEHAVING LIKE A GOOD BOY, A TRAIT YOU ONCE DISPLAYED.
Good boy?!
BUT AT A CERTAIN POINT, YOU BECAME GUARDED...
...AND ONLY ACTED THE PART OF A GOODY-GOODY.
It's normal to be slightly clumsy when it comes to women...
THAT'S RIGHT... THAT WAS AROUND THE TIME I BECAME AN ADVANCED SORCERER...
...AND PRINCE CITRONA WAS RELEASED FROM HIS LONG PERIOD OF CONVALESCENCE.

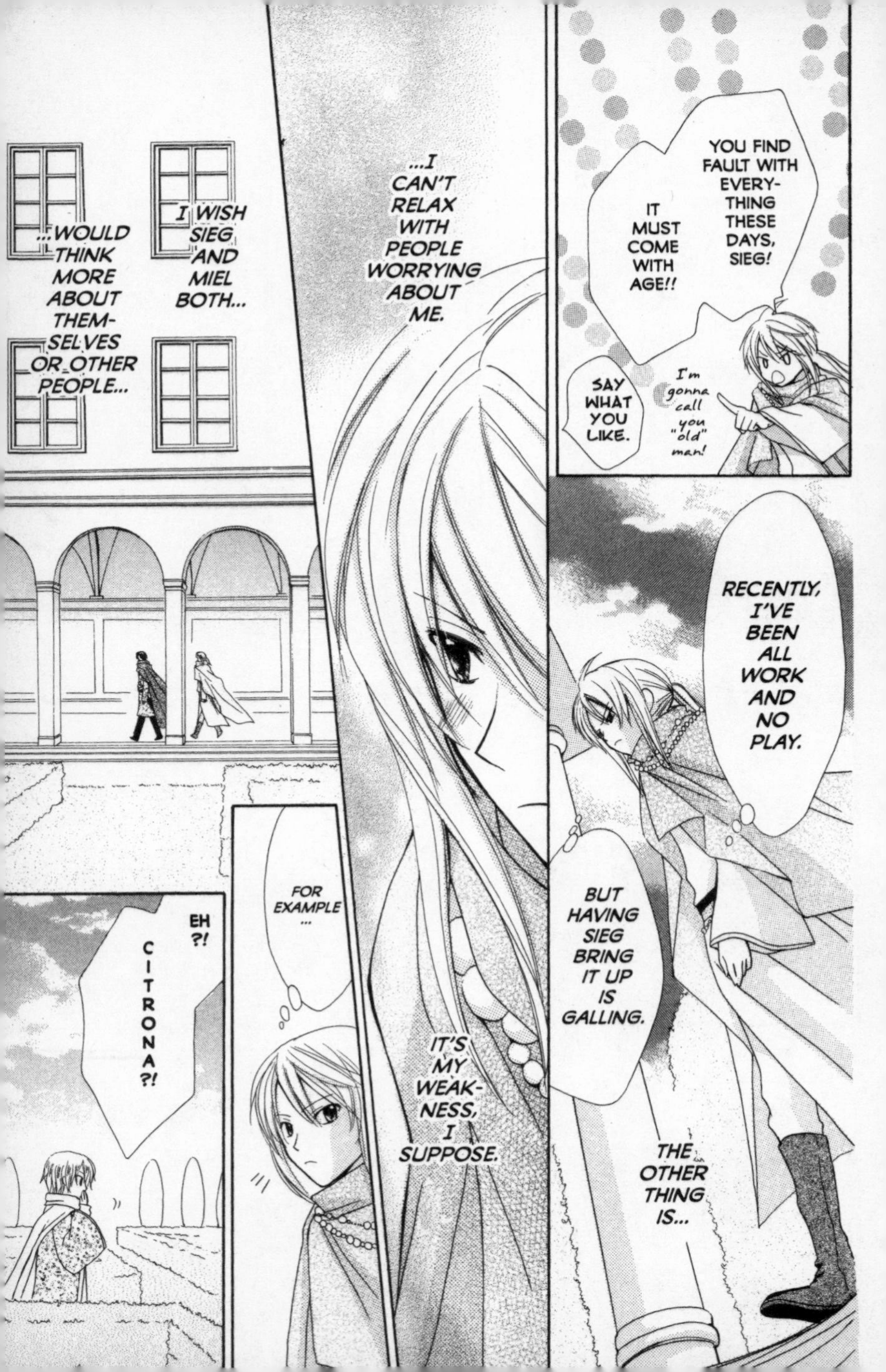
YOU FIND FAULT WITH EVERYTHING THESE DAYS, SIEG!
IT MUST COME WITH AGE!!
I'm gonna call you "old" man!
SAY WHAT YOU LIKE.
RECENTLY, I'VE BEEN ALL WORK AND NO PLAY.
BUT HAVING SIEG BRING IT UP IS GALLING.
THE OTHER THING IS...
...I CAN'T RELAX WITH PEOPLE WORRYING ABOUT ME.
IT'S MY WEAKNESS, I SUPPOSE.
I WISH SIEG AND MIEL BOTH...
...WOULD THINK MORE ABOUT THEMSELVES OR OTHER PEOPLE...
FOR EXAMPLE...
EH?!
CITRONA?!

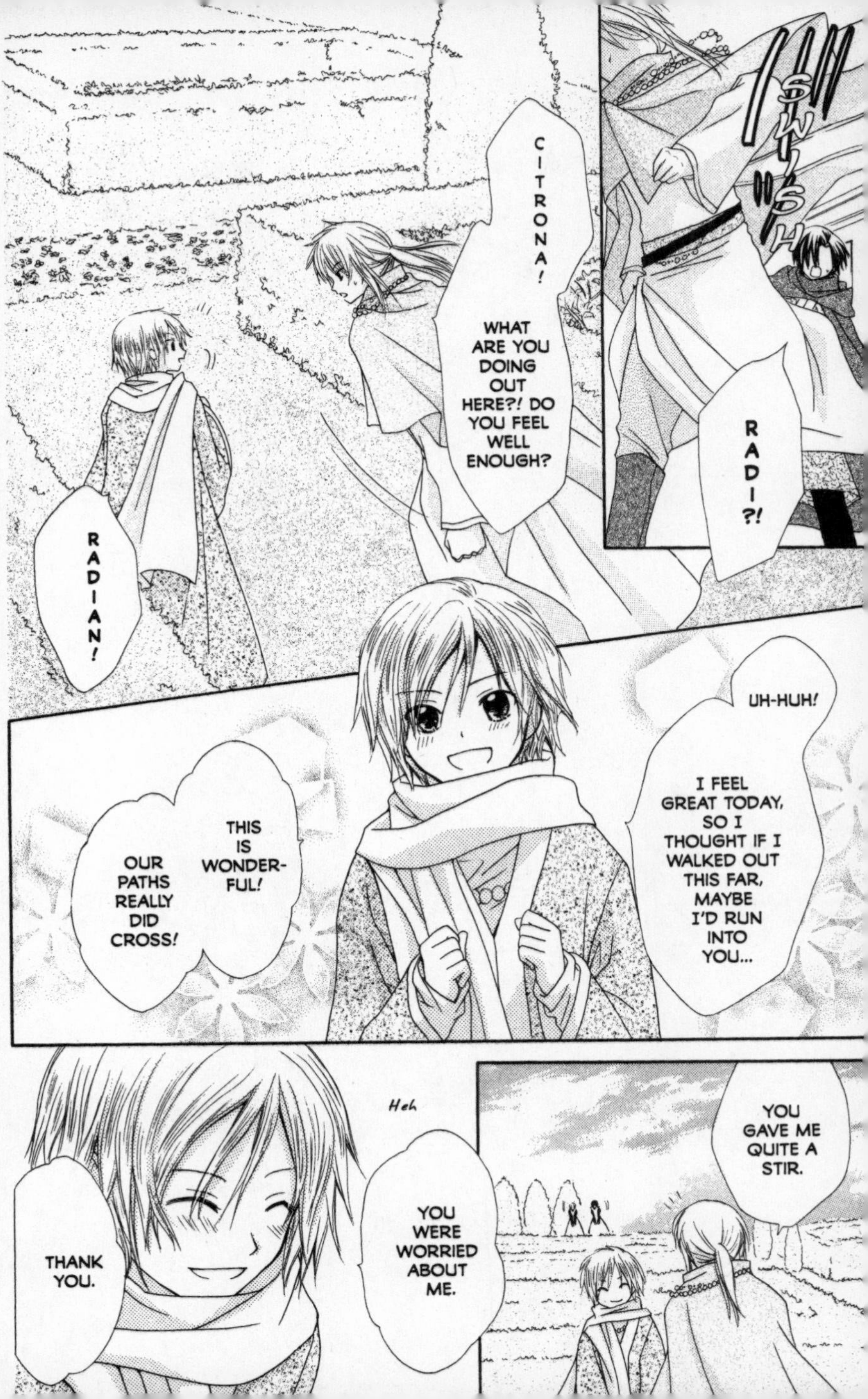
SWISH
RADI?!
CITRONA!
WHAT ARE YOU DOING OUT HERE?! DO YOU FEEL WELL ENOUGH?
RADIAN!
UH-HUH!
I FEEL GREAT TODAY, SO I THOUGHT IF I WALKED OUT THIS FAR, MAYBE I'D RUN INTO YOU...
THIS IS WONDERFUL!
OUR PATHS REALLY DID CROSS!
YOU GAVE ME QUITE A STIR.
Heh
YOU WERE WORRIED ABOUT ME.
THANK YOU.

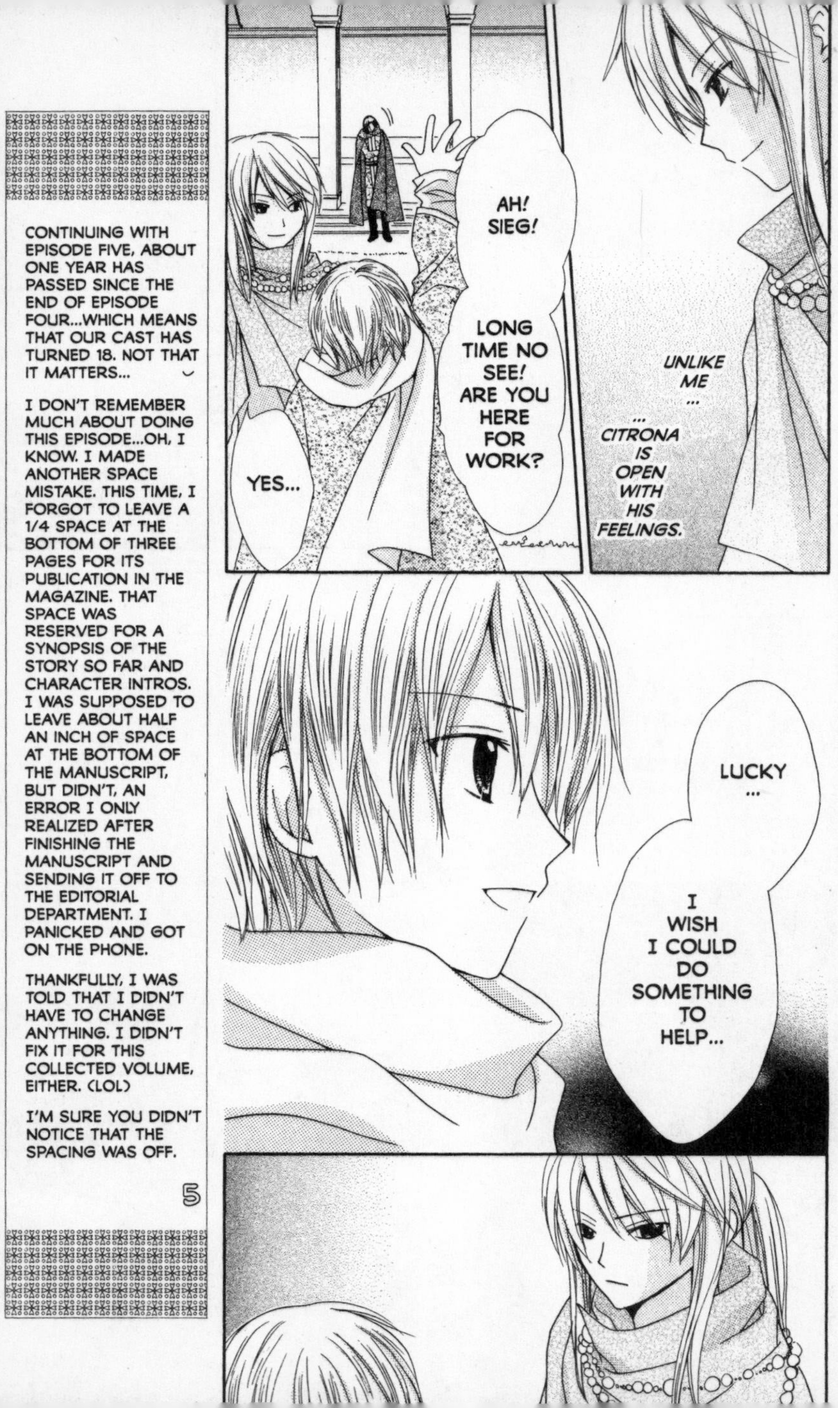
UNLIKE ME ...
... CITRONA IS OPEN WITH HIS FEELINGS.
AH! SIEG!
LONG TIME NO SEE! ARE YOU HERE FOR WORK?
YES...
LUCKY ...
I WISH I COULD DO SOMETHING TO HELP...

CONTINUING WITH EPISODE FIVE, ABOUT ONE YEAR HAS PASSED SINCE THE END OF EPISODE FOUR...WHICH MEANS THAT OUR CAST HAS TURNED 18. NOT THAT IT MATTERS...

I DON'T REMEMBER MUCH ABOUT DOING THIS EPISODE...OH, I KNOW. I MADE ANOTHER SPACE MISTAKE. THIS TIME, I FORGOT TO LEAVE A 1/4 SPACE AT THE BOTTOM OF THREE PAGES FOR ITS PUBLICATION IN THE MAGAZINE. THAT SPACE WAS RESERVED FOR A SYNOPSIS OF THE STORY SO FAR AND CHARACTER INTROS. I WAS SUPPOSED TO LEAVE ABOUT HALF AN INCH OF SPACE AT THE BOTTOM OF THE MANUSCRIPT, BUT DIDN'T, AN ERROR I ONLY REALIZED AFTER FINISHING THE MANUSCRIPT AND SENDING IT OFF TO THE EDITORIAL DEPARTMENT. I PANICKED AND GOT ON THE PHONE.

THANKFULLY, I WAS TOLD THAT I DIDN'T HAVE TO CHANGE ANYTHING. I DIDN'T FIX IT FOR THIS COLLECTED VOLUME, EITHER. (LOL)

I'M SURE YOU DIDN'T NOTICE THAT THE SPACING WAS OFF.

5

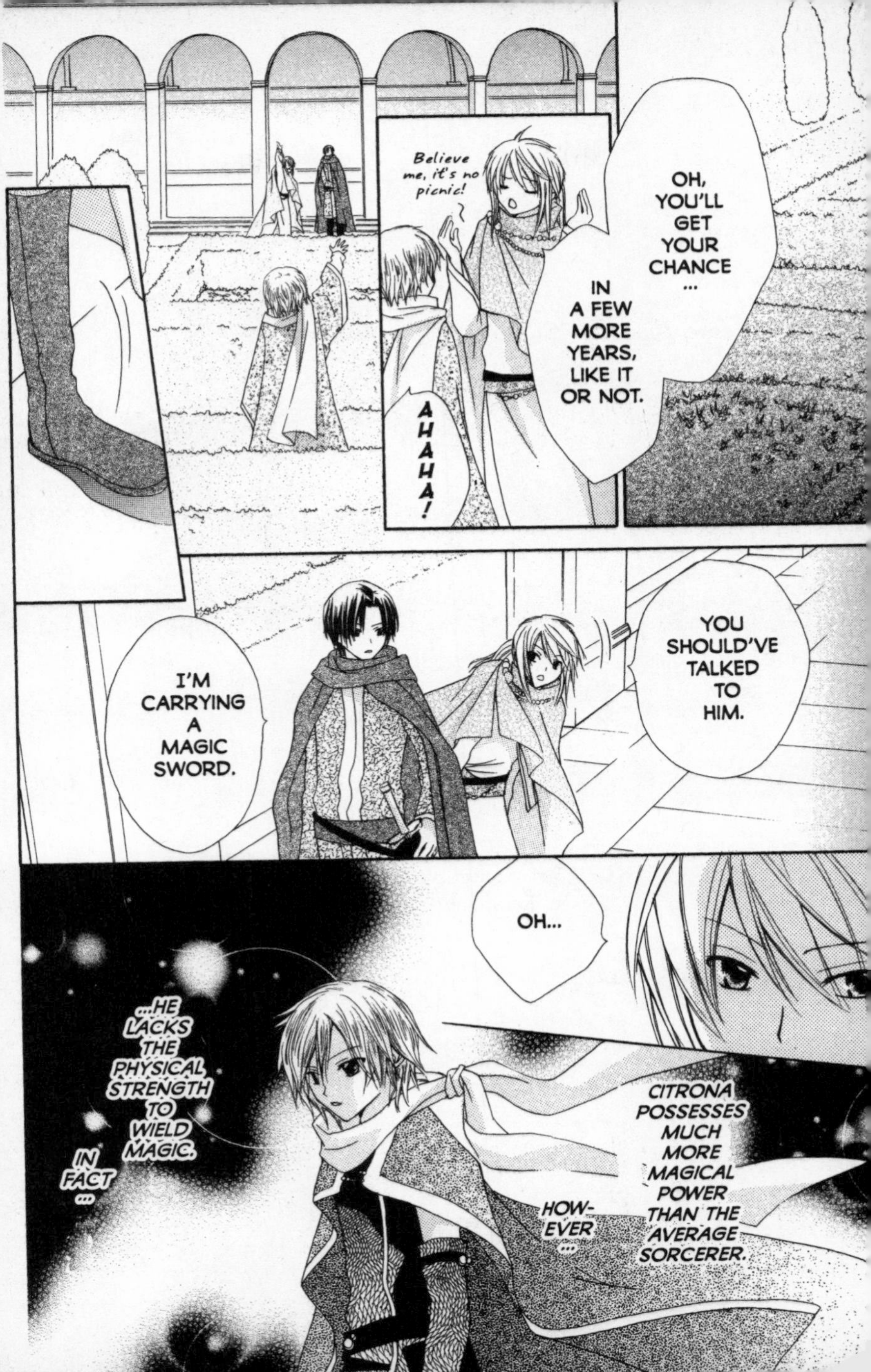
OH, YOU'LL GET YOUR CHANCE ...
IN A FEW MORE YEARS, LIKE IT OR NOT.
Believe me, it's no picnic!
AHAHA!
YOU SHOULD'VE TALKED TO HIM.
I'M CARRYING A MAGIC SWORD.
OH...
CITRONA POSSESSES MUCH MORE MAGICAL POWER THAN THE AVERAGE SORCERER.
HOW-EVER ...
...HE LACKS THE PHYSICAL STRENGTH TO WIELD MAGIC.
IN FACT ...

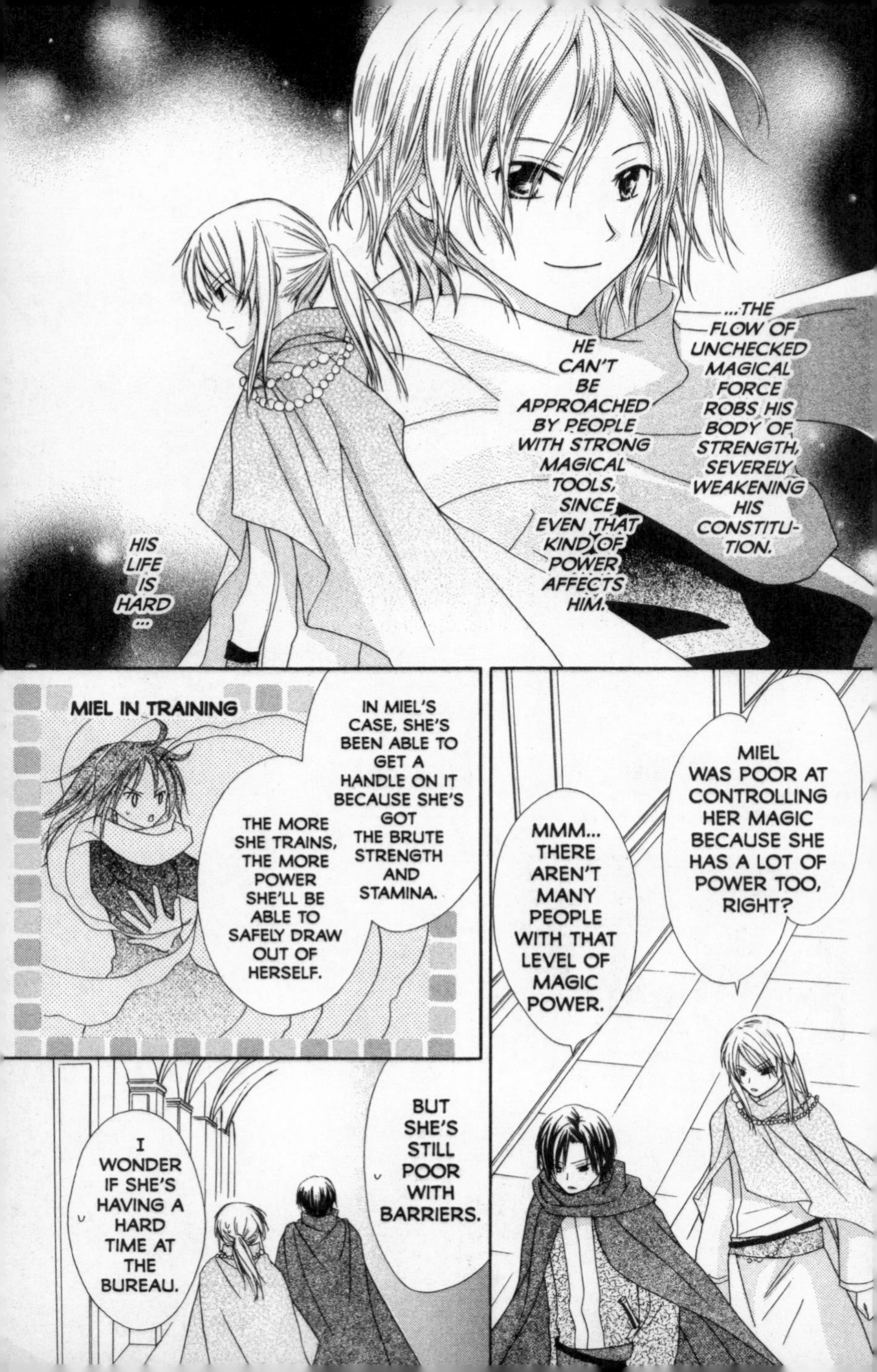
...THE FLOW OF UNCHECKED MAGICAL FORCE ROBS HIS BODY OF STRENGTH, SEVERELY WEAKENING HIS CONSTITUTION.
HE CAN'T BE APPROACHED BY PEOPLE WITH STRONG MAGICAL TOOLS, SINCE EVEN THAT KIND OF POWER AFFECTS HIM.
HIS LIFE IS HARD...
MIEL WAS POOR AT CONTROLLING HER MAGIC BECAUSE SHE HAS A LOT OF POWER TOO, RIGHT?
MMM... THERE AREN'T MANY PEOPLE WITH THAT LEVEL OF MAGIC POWER.
MIEL IN TRAINING
IN MIEL'S CASE, SHE'S BEEN ABLE TO GET A HANDLE ON IT BECAUSE SHE'S GOT THE BRUTE STRENGTH AND STAMINA.
THE MORE SHE TRAINS, THE MORE POWER SHE'LL BE ABLE TO SAFELY DRAW OUT OF HERSELF.
BUT SHE'S STILL POOR WITH BARRIERS.
I WONDER IF SHE'S HAVING A HARD TIME AT THE BUREAU.

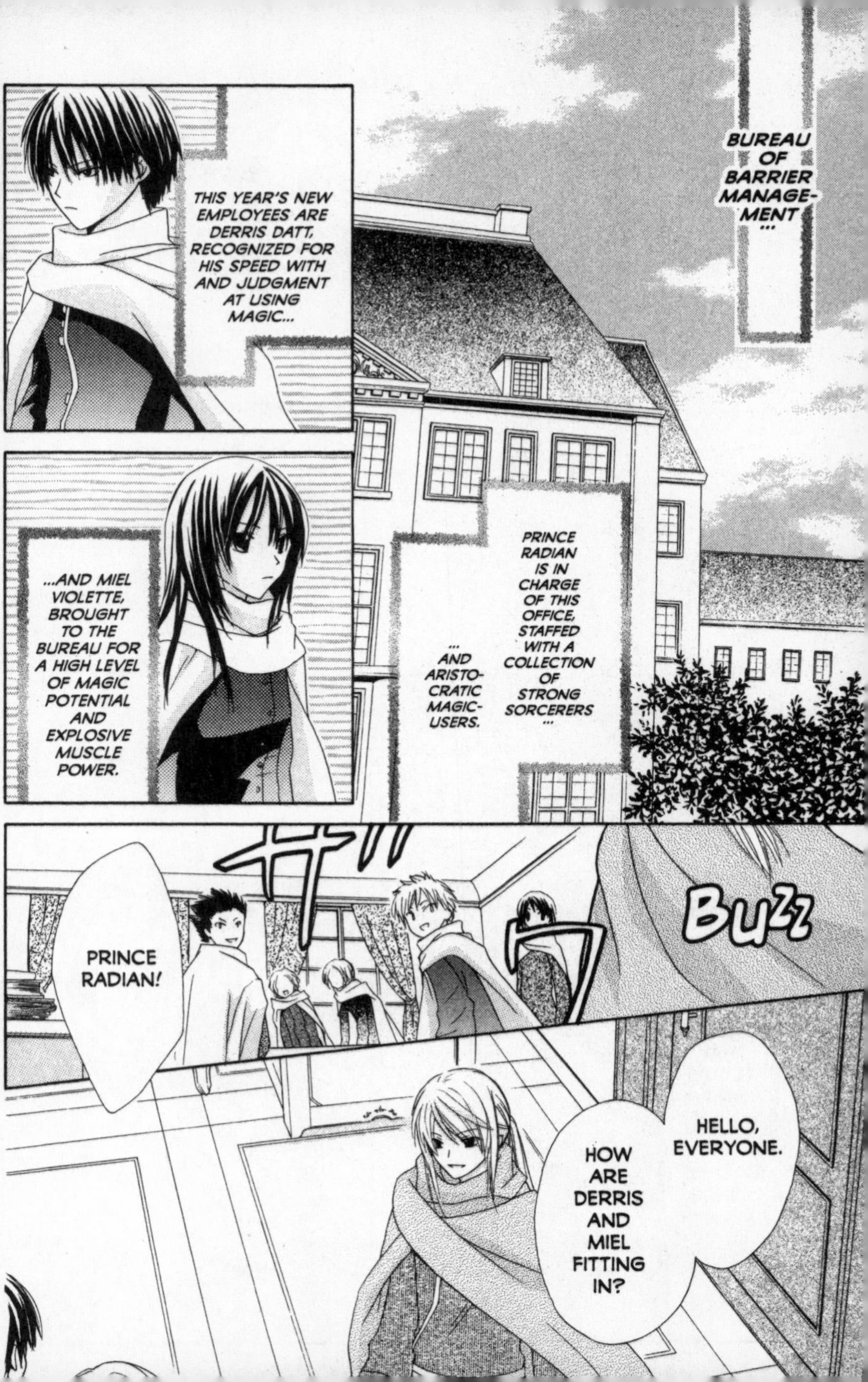
BUREAU OF BARRIER MANAGEMENT...
PRINCE RADIAN IS IN CHARGE OF THIS OFFICE, STAFFED WITH A COLLECTION OF STRONG SORCERERS...
...AND ARISTOCRATIC MAGIC-USERS.
THIS YEAR'S NEW EMPLOYEES ARE DERRIS DATT, RECOGNIZED FOR HIS SPEED WITH AND JUDGMENT AT USING MAGIC...
...AND MIEL VIOLETTE, BROUGHT TO THE BUREAU FOR A HIGH LEVEL OF MAGIC POTENTIAL AND EXPLOSIVE MUSCLE POWER.
Buzz
PRINCE RADIAN!
HELLO, EVERYONE.
HOW ARE DERRIS AND MIEL FITTING IN?

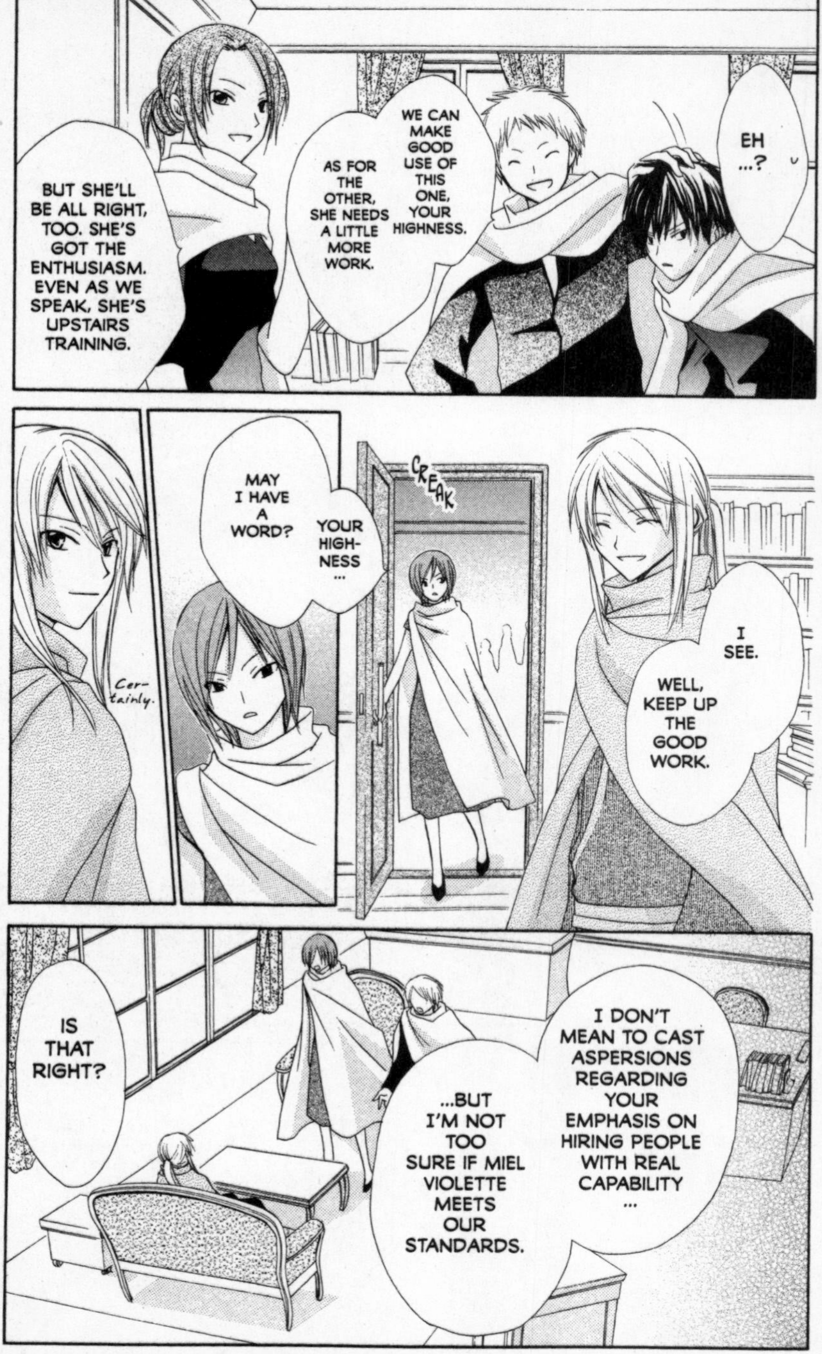
EH ...?
WE CAN MAKE GOOD USE OF THIS ONE, YOUR HIGHNESS.
AS FOR THE OTHER, SHE NEEDS A LITTLE MORE WORK.
BUT SHE'LL BE ALL RIGHT, TOO. SHE'S GOT THE ENTHUSIASM. EVEN AS WE SPEAK, SHE'S UPSTAIRS TRAINING.
I SEE.
WELL, KEEP UP THE GOOD WORK.
CREAK
YOUR HIGHNESS ...
MAY I HAVE A WORD?
Certainly.
I DON'T MEAN TO CAST ASPERSIONS REGARDING YOUR EMPHASIS ON HIRING PEOPLE WITH REAL CAPABILITY ...
...BUT I'M NOT TOO SURE IF MIEL VIOLETTE MEETS OUR STANDARDS.
IS THAT RIGHT?

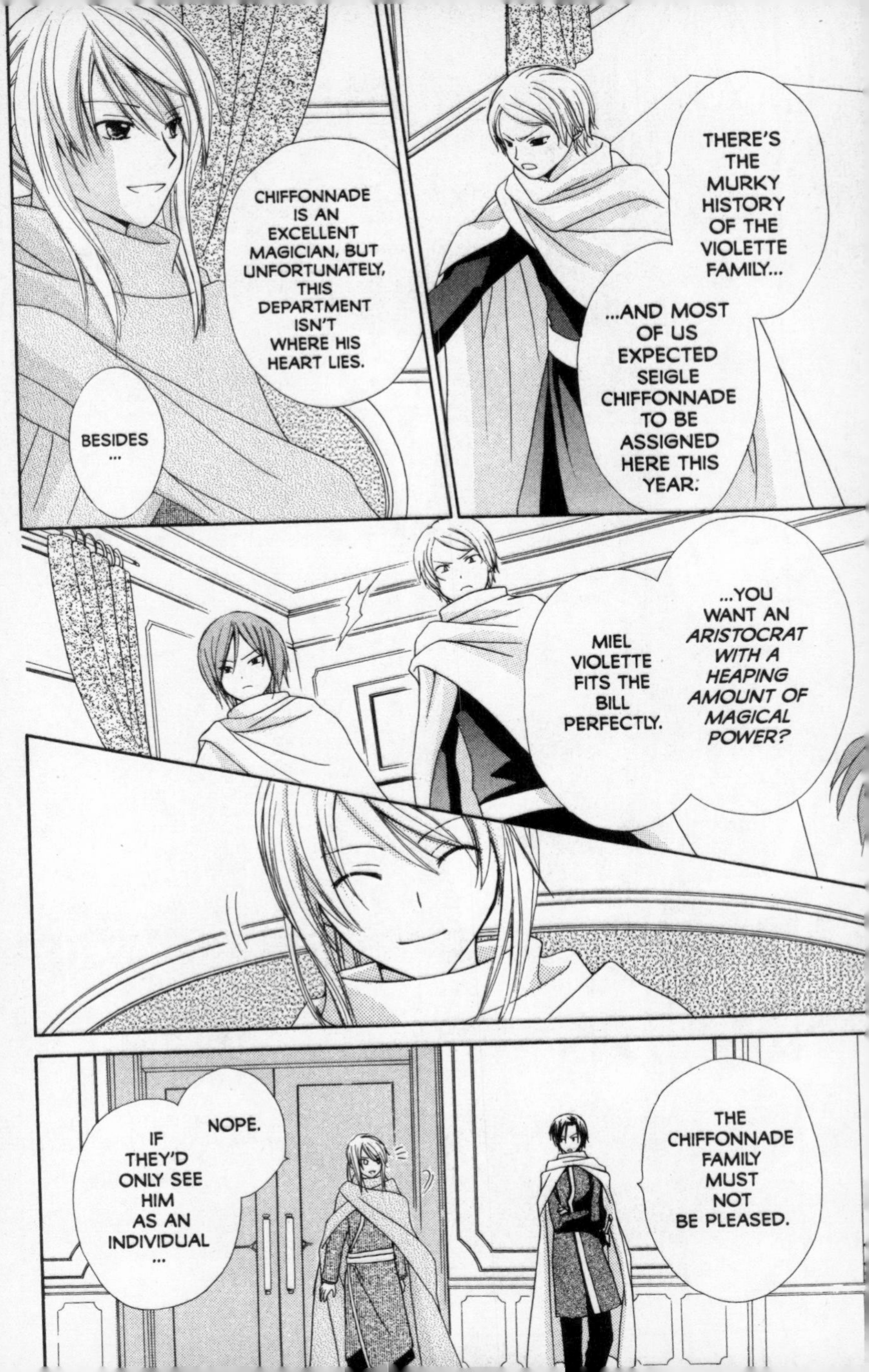
THERE'S THE MURKY HISTORY OF THE VIOLETTE FAMILY...
...AND MOST OF US EXPECTED SEIGLE CHIFFONNADE TO BE ASSIGNED HERE THIS YEAR.
CHIFFONNADE IS AN EXCELLENT MAGICIAN, BUT UNFORTUNATELY, THIS DEPARTMENT ISN'T WHERE HIS HEART LIES.
BESIDES ...
...YOU WANT AN *ARISTOCRAT WITH A HEAPING AMOUNT OF MAGICAL POWER?*
MIEL VIOLETTE FITS THE BILL PERFECTLY.
THE CHIFFONNADE FAMILY MUST NOT BE PLEASED.
NOPE.
IF THEY'D ONLY SEE HIM AS AN INDIVIDUAL ...

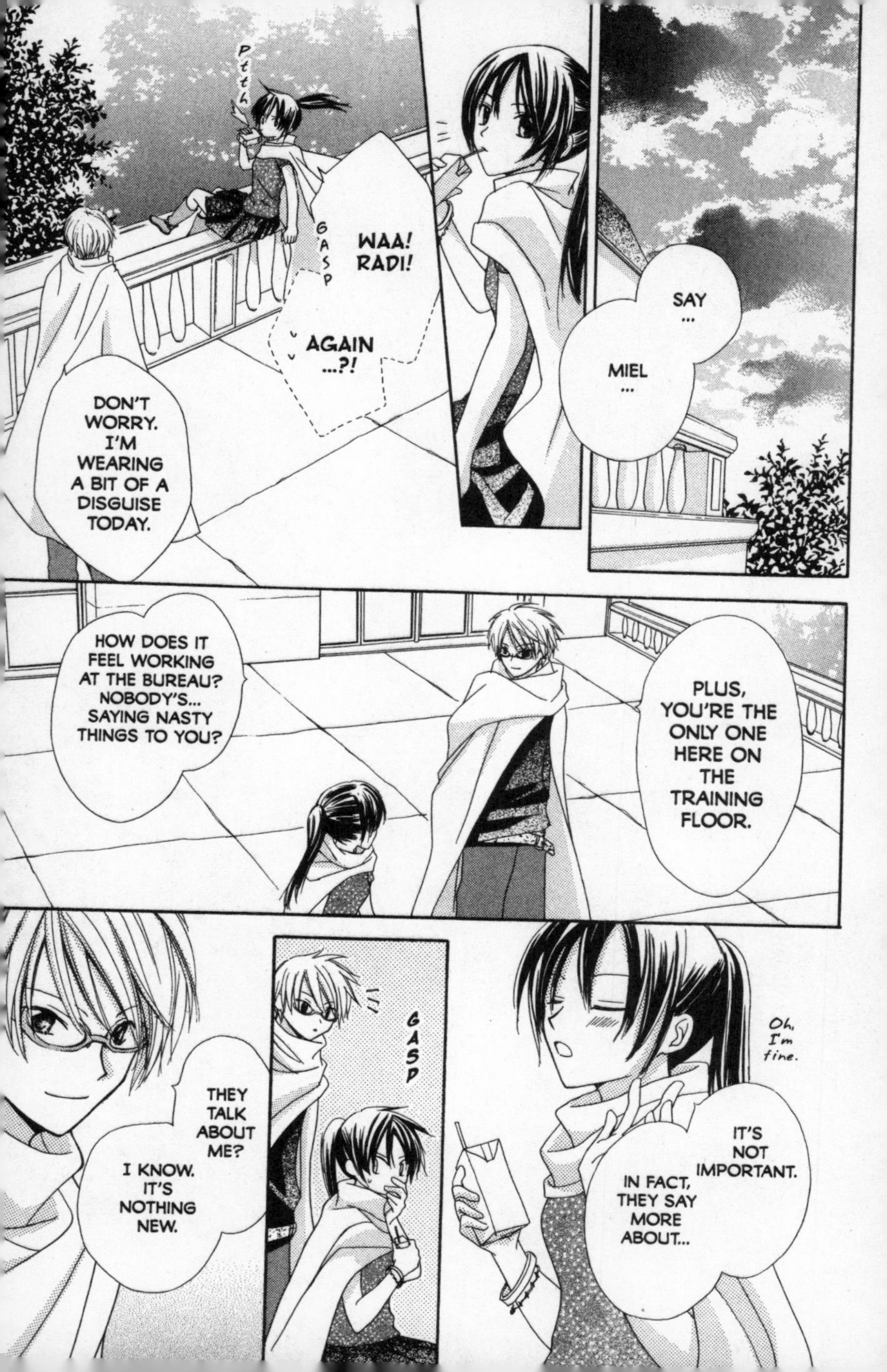
SAY ...
MIEL ...
Ptth
GASP
WAA! RADI!
AGAIN ...?!
DON'T WORRY. I'M WEARING A BIT OF A DISGUISE TODAY.
PLUS, YOU'RE THE ONLY ONE HERE ON THE TRAINING FLOOR.
HOW DOES IT FEEL WORKING AT THE BUREAU? NOBODY'S... SAYING NASTY THINGS TO YOU?
Oh, I'm fine.
IT'S NOT IMPORTANT.
IN FACT, THEY SAY MORE ABOUT...
GASP
THEY TALK ABOUT ME?
I KNOW. IT'S NOTHING NEW.

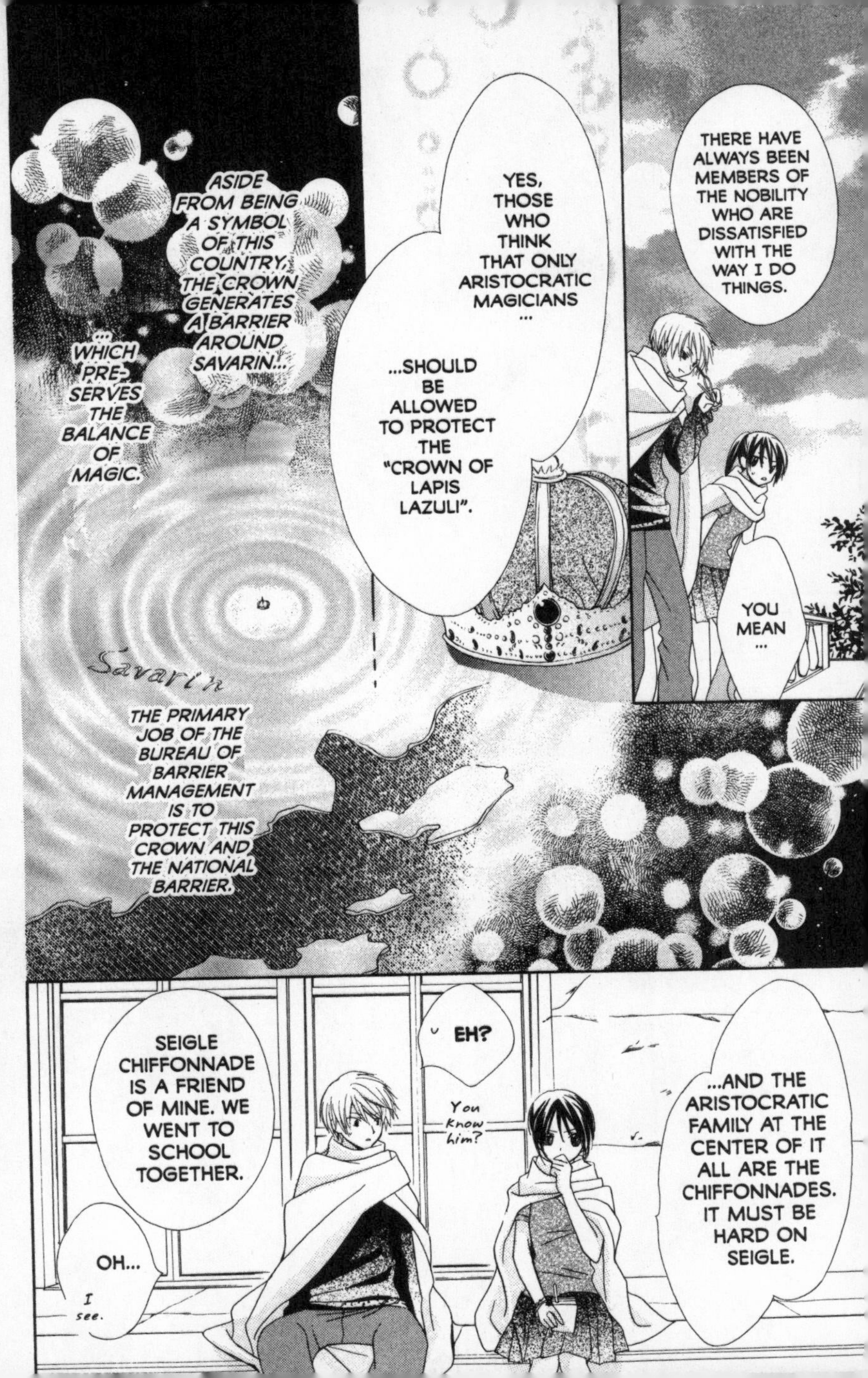
THERE HAVE ALWAYS BEEN MEMBERS OF THE NOBILITY WHO ARE DISSATISFIED WITH THE WAY I DO THINGS.
YOU MEAN ...
YES, THOSE WHO THINK THAT ONLY ARISTOCRATIC MAGICIANS ...
...SHOULD BE ALLOWED TO PROTECT THE "CROWN OF LAPIS LAZULI".
ASIDE FROM BEING A SYMBOL OF THIS COUNTRY, THE CROWN GENERATES A BARRIER AROUND SAVARIN...
... WHICH PRE-SERVES THE BALANCE OF MAGIC.
Savarin
THE PRIMARY JOB OF THE BUREAU OF BARRIER MANAGEMENT IS TO PROTECT THIS CROWN AND THE NATIONAL BARRIER.
...AND THE ARISTOCRATIC FAMILY AT THE CENTER OF IT ALL ARE THE CHIFFONNADES. IT MUST BE HARD ON SEIGLE.
EH?
You know him?
SEIGLE CHIFFONNADE IS A FRIEND OF MINE. WE WENT TO SCHOOL TOGETHER.
OH...
I see.

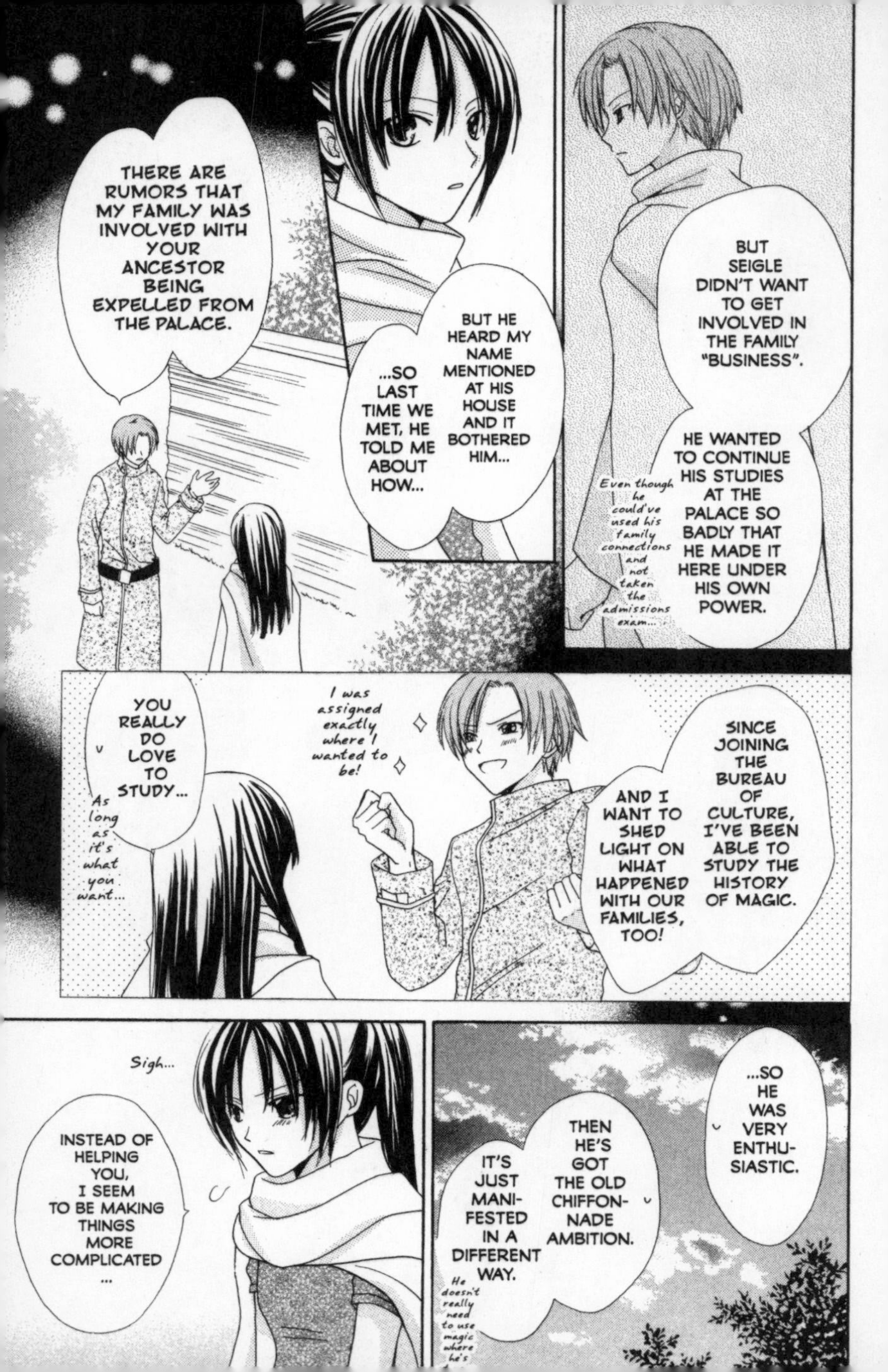
BUT SEIGLE DIDN'T WANT TO GET INVOLVED IN THE FAMILY "BUSINESS".
HE WANTED TO CONTINUE HIS STUDIES AT THE PALACE SO BADLY THAT HE MADE IT HERE UNDER HIS OWN POWER.
Even though he could've used his family connections and not taken the admissions exam...
BUT HE HEARD MY NAME MENTIONED AT HIS HOUSE AND IT BOTHERED HIM...
...SO LAST TIME WE MET, HE TOLD ME ABOUT HOW...
THERE ARE RUMORS THAT MY FAMILY WAS INVOLVED WITH YOUR ANCESTOR BEING EXPELLED FROM THE PALACE.
SINCE JOINING THE BUREAU OF CULTURE, I'VE BEEN ABLE TO STUDY THE HISTORY OF MAGIC.
AND I WANT TO SHED LIGHT ON WHAT HAPPENED WITH OUR FAMILIES, TOO!
I was assigned exactly where I wanted to be!
YOU REALLY DO LOVE TO STUDY...
As long as it's what you want...
...SO HE WAS VERY ENTHUSIASTIC.
THEN HE'S GOT THE OLD CHIFFONNADE AMBITION.
IT'S JUST MANIFESTED IN A DIFFERENT WAY.
He doesn't really need to use magic where he's
Sigh...
INSTEAD OF HELPING YOU, I SEEM TO BE MAKING THINGS MORE COMPLICATED ...

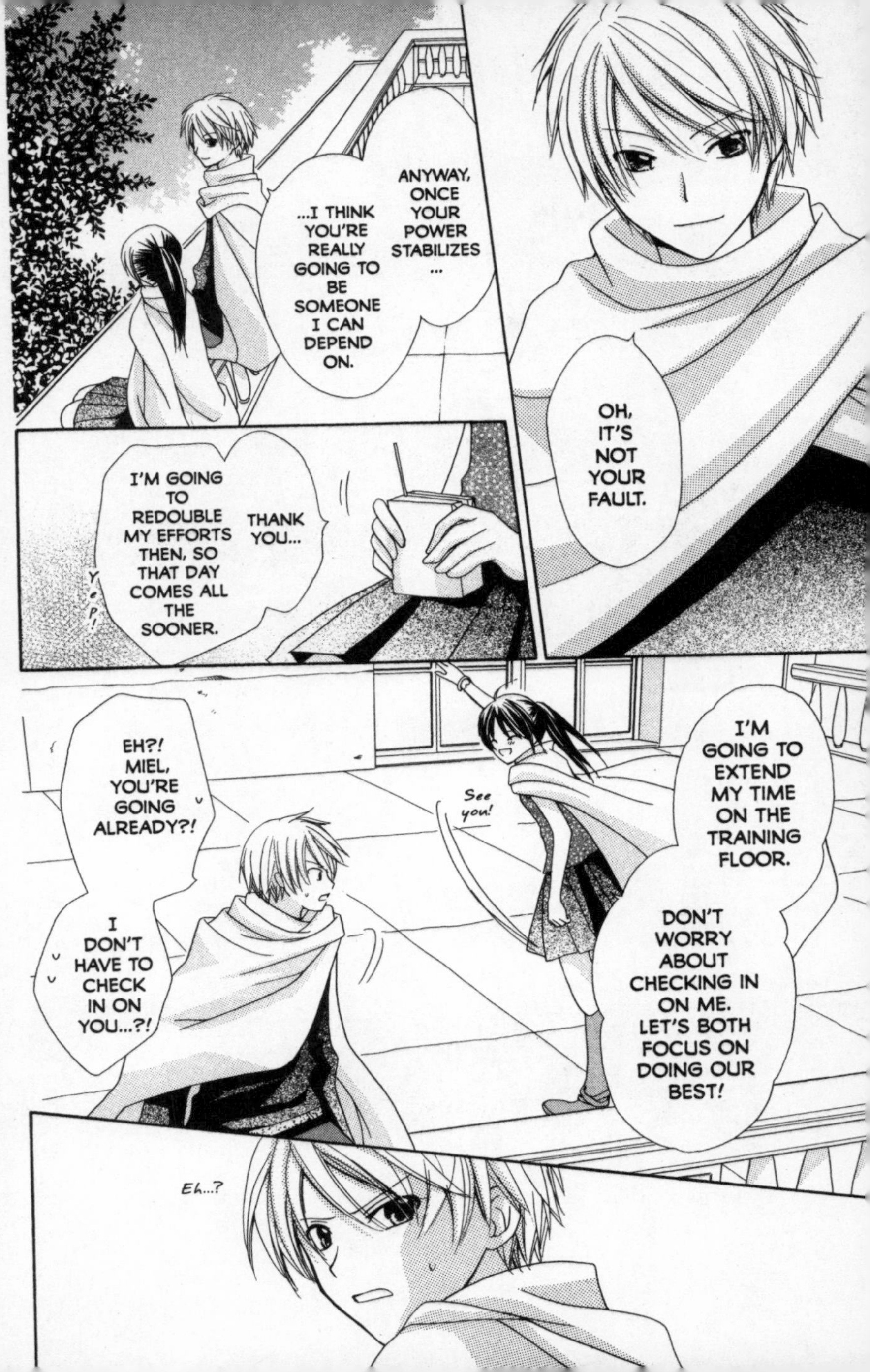
OH, IT'S NOT YOUR FAULT.
ANYWAY, ONCE YOUR POWER STABILIZES...
...I THINK YOU'RE REALLY GOING TO BE SOMEONE I CAN DEPEND ON.
THANK YOU...
I'M GOING TO REDOUBLE MY EFFORTS THEN, SO THAT DAY COMES ALL THE SOONER.
Yep!
I'M GOING TO EXTEND MY TIME ON THE TRAINING FLOOR.
DON'T WORRY ABOUT CHECKING IN ON ME. LET'S BOTH FOCUS ON DOING OUR BEST!
See you!
EH?! MIEL, YOU'RE GOING ALREADY?!
I DON'T HAVE TO CHECK IN ON YOU...?!
Eh...?

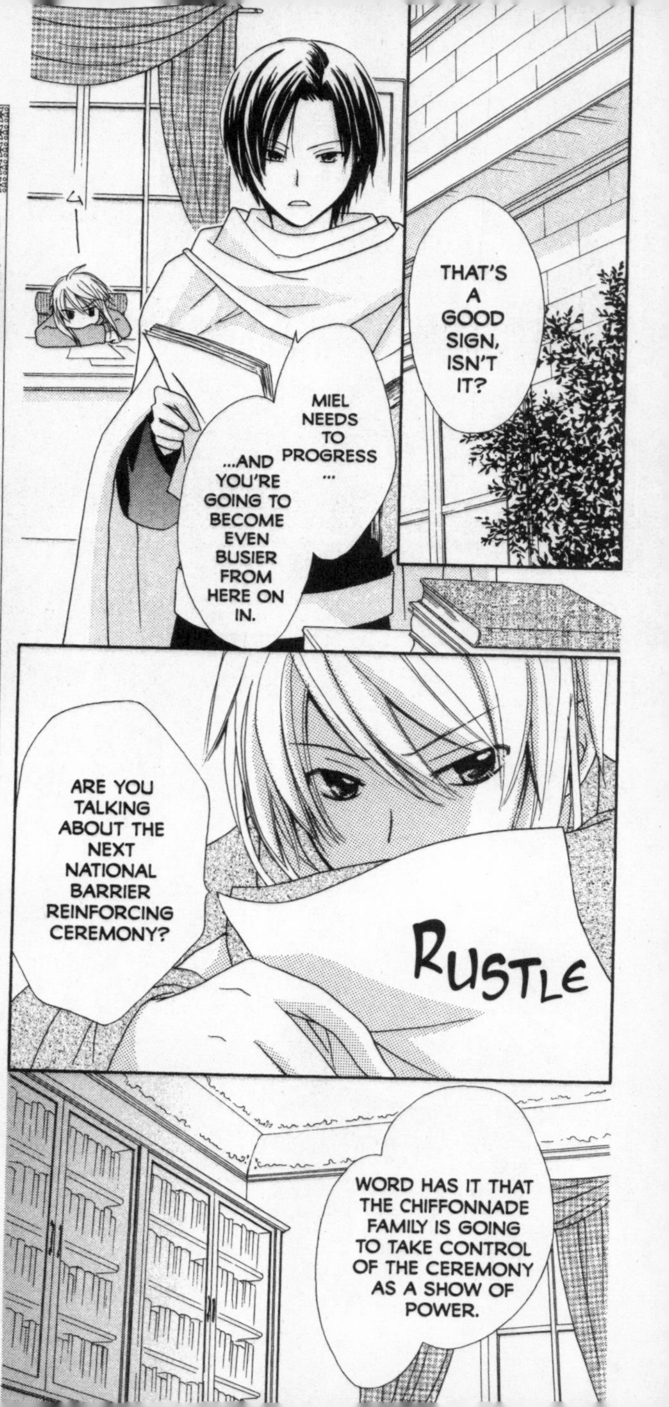
THAT'S A GOOD SIGN, ISN'T IT?
MIEL NEEDS TO PROGRESS ...
...AND YOU'RE GOING TO BECOME EVEN BUSIER FROM HERE ON IN.
RUSTLE
ARE YOU TALKING ABOUT THE NEXT NATIONAL BARRIER REINFORCING CEREMONY?
WORD HAS IT THAT THE CHIFFONNADE FAMILY IS GOING TO TAKE CONTROL OF THE CEREMONY AS A SHOW OF POWER.

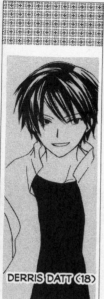

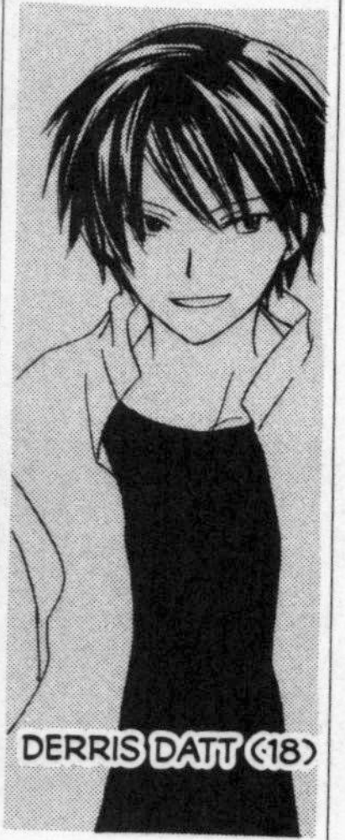
DERRIS DATT (18)

GRADUATED FROM THE ROYAL SCHOOL OF MAGIC IN SARACEL.
A DETERMINED AND POSITIVE THINKER TO THE POINT OF ARROGANCE. HATES THE NOBILITY BECAUSE IN HIS HOME AREA, THEY CONTROL MANY MAGIC-RELATED INDUSTRIES. IN ORDER TO CHANGE THAT ONE DAY FOR THE SAKE OF THOSE WHO COME AFTER HIM, HE'S COME TO THE PALACE.

HE'S AFFECTIONATE AND HAS A WEAKNESS FOR PEOPLE WHO ARE WORLDLY-WISE. HE'S A GOOD GUY AND I LIKE TO THINK I MADE THE MOST OF HIS APPEARANCES, BUT I ONLY WISH HE COULD'VE HAD MORE "SCREEN TIME" (SAME WAY I FEEL ABOUT ALL THE "FRIEND CHARACTERS"...).

6

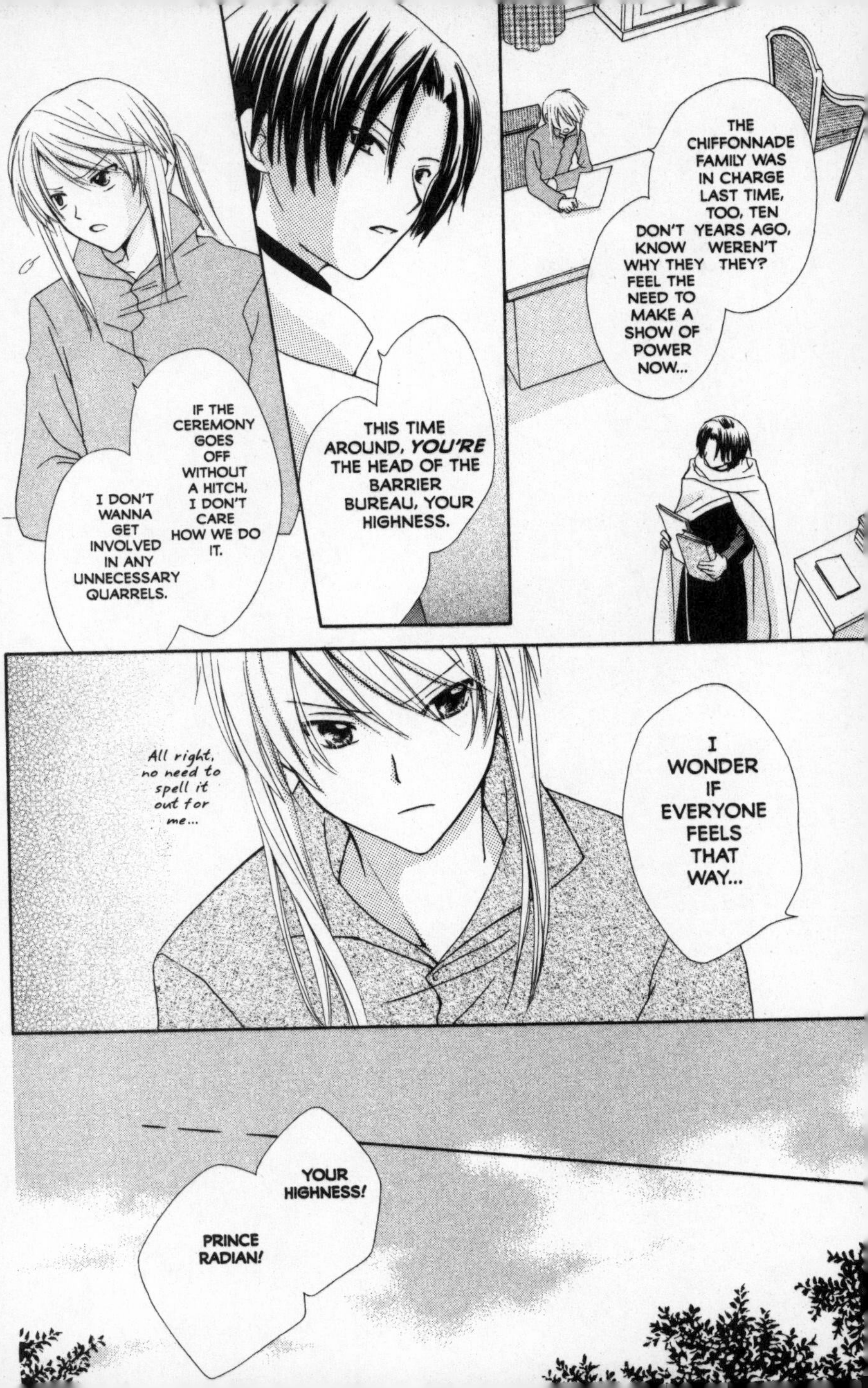
THE CHIFFONNADE FAMILY WAS IN CHARGE LAST TIME, TOO, TEN YEARS AGO, WEREN'T THEY?
DON'T KNOW WHY THEY FEEL THE NEED TO MAKE A SHOW OF POWER NOW...
THIS TIME AROUND, *YOU'RE* THE HEAD OF THE BARRIER BUREAU, YOUR HIGHNESS.
IF THE CEREMONY GOES OFF WITHOUT A HITCH, I DON'T CARE HOW WE DO IT.
I DON'T WANNA GET INVOLVED IN ANY UNNECESSARY QUARRELS.
I WONDER IF EVERYONE FEELS THAT WAY...
All right, no need to spell it out for me...
YOUR HIGHNESS!
PRINCE RADIAN!

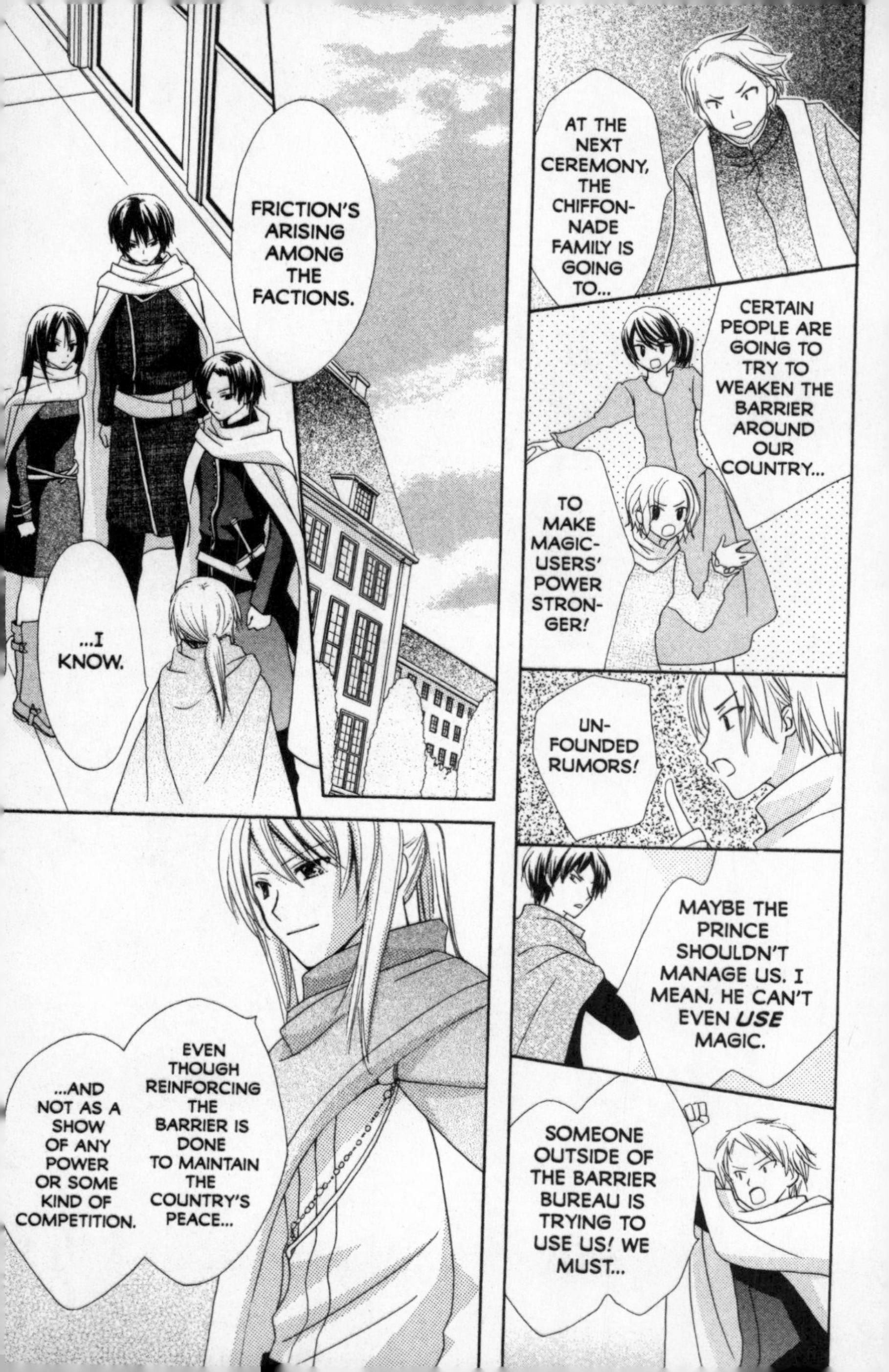
AT THE NEXT CEREMONY, THE CHIFFON-NADE FAMILY IS GOING TO...
CERTAIN PEOPLE ARE GOING TO TRY TO WEAKEN THE BARRIER AROUND OUR COUNTRY...
TO MAKE MAGIC-USERS' POWER STRONGER!
UN-FOUNDED RUMORS!
MAYBE THE PRINCE SHOULDN'T MANAGE US. I MEAN, HE CAN'T EVEN *USE* MAGIC.
SOMEONE OUTSIDE OF THE BARRIER BUREAU IS TRYING TO USE US! WE MUST...
FRICTION'S ARISING AMONG THE FACTIONS.
...I KNOW.
EVEN THOUGH REINFORCING THE BARRIER IS DONE TO MAINTAIN THE COUNTRY'S PEACE...
...AND NOT AS A SHOW OF ANY POWER OR SOME KIND OF COMPETITION.

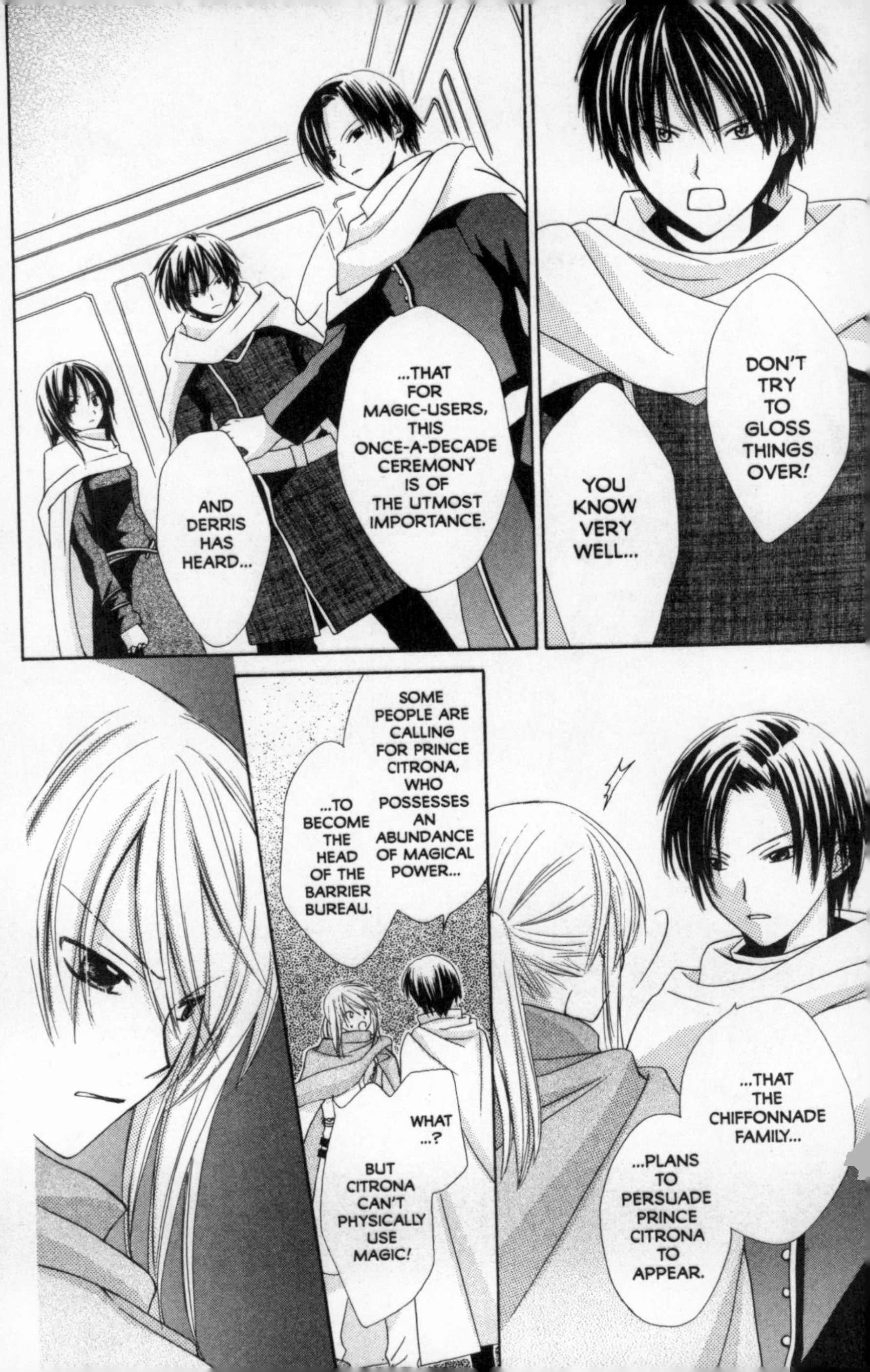
DON'T TRY TO GLOSS THINGS OVER!
YOU KNOW VERY WELL...
...THAT FOR MAGIC-USERS, THIS ONCE-A-DECADE CEREMONY IS OF THE UTMOST IMPORTANCE.
AND DERRIS HAS HEARD...
...THAT THE CHIFFONNADE FAMILY...
...PLANS TO PERSUADE PRINCE CITRONA TO APPEAR.
SOME PEOPLE ARE CALLING FOR PRINCE CITRONA, WHO POSSESSES AN ABUNDANCE OF MAGICAL POWER...
...TO BECOME THE HEAD OF THE BARRIER BUREAU.
WHAT ...?
BUT CITRONA CAN'T PHYSICALLY USE MAGIC!

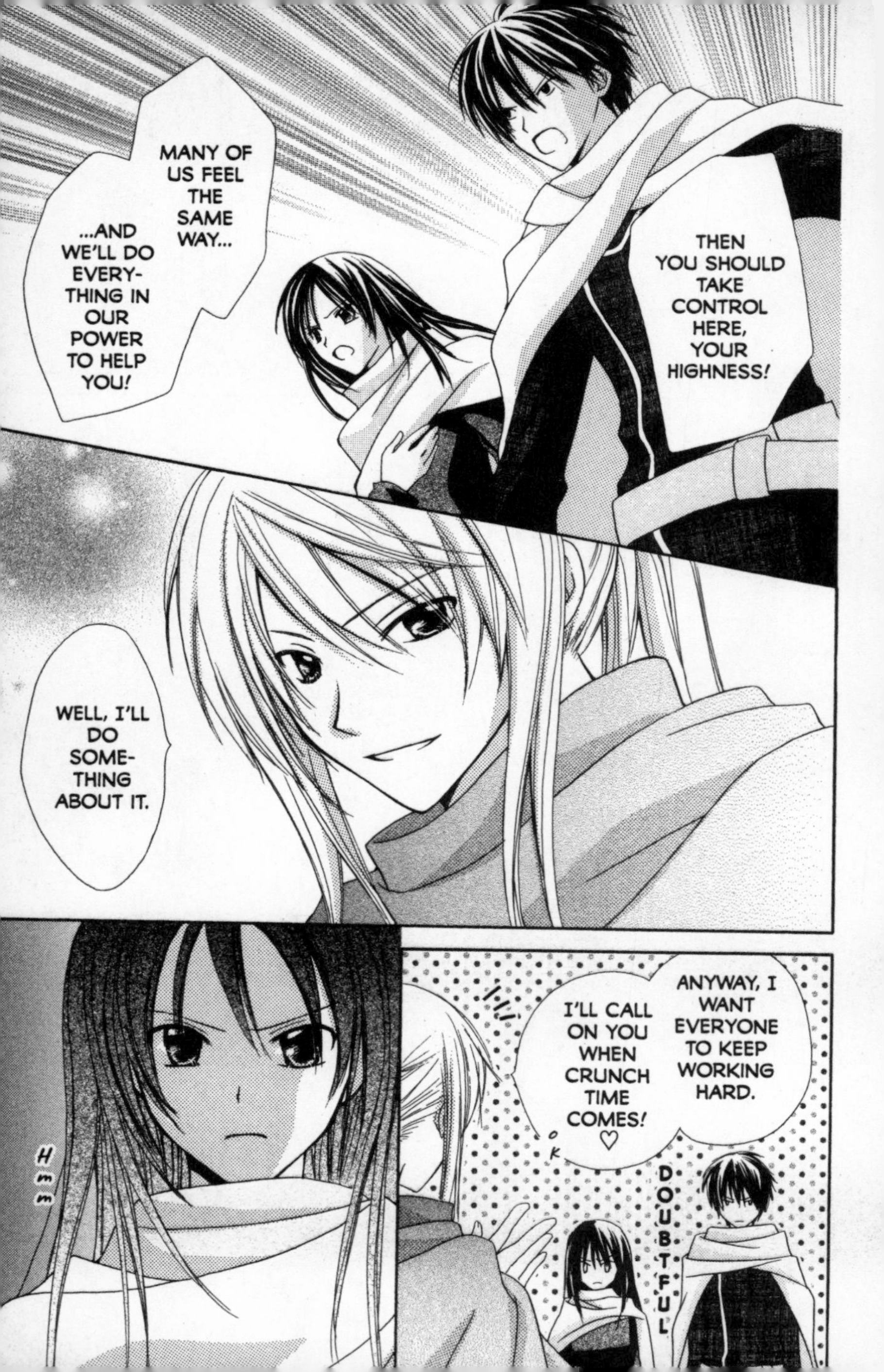
THEN YOU SHOULD TAKE CONTROL HERE, YOUR HIGHNESS!
MANY OF US FEEL THE SAME WAY...
...AND WE'LL DO EVERY-THING IN OUR POWER TO HELP YOU!
WELL, I'LL DO SOME-THING ABOUT IT.
ANYWAY, I WANT EVERYONE TO KEEP WORKING HARD.
I'LL CALL ON YOU WHEN CRUNCH TIME COMES! ♡
OK
DOUBTFUL
Hmm

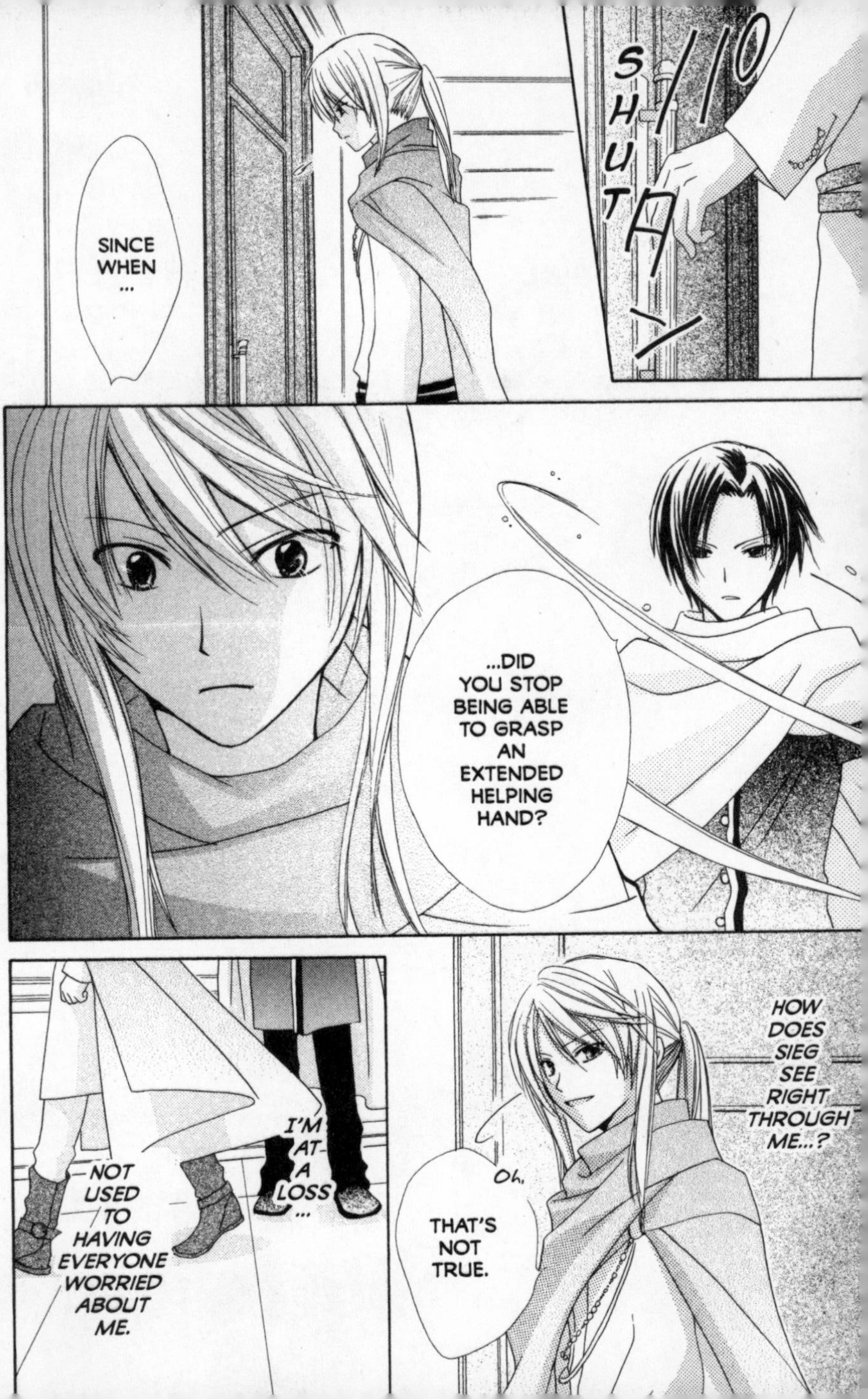
SHUT
SINCE WHEN ...
...DID YOU STOP BEING ABLE TO GRASP AN EXTENDED HELPING HAND?
HOW DOES SIEG SEE RIGHT THROUGH ME...?
Oh,
THAT'S NOT TRUE.
I'M AT A LOSS ...
NOT USED TO HAVING EVERYONE WORRIED ABOUT ME.

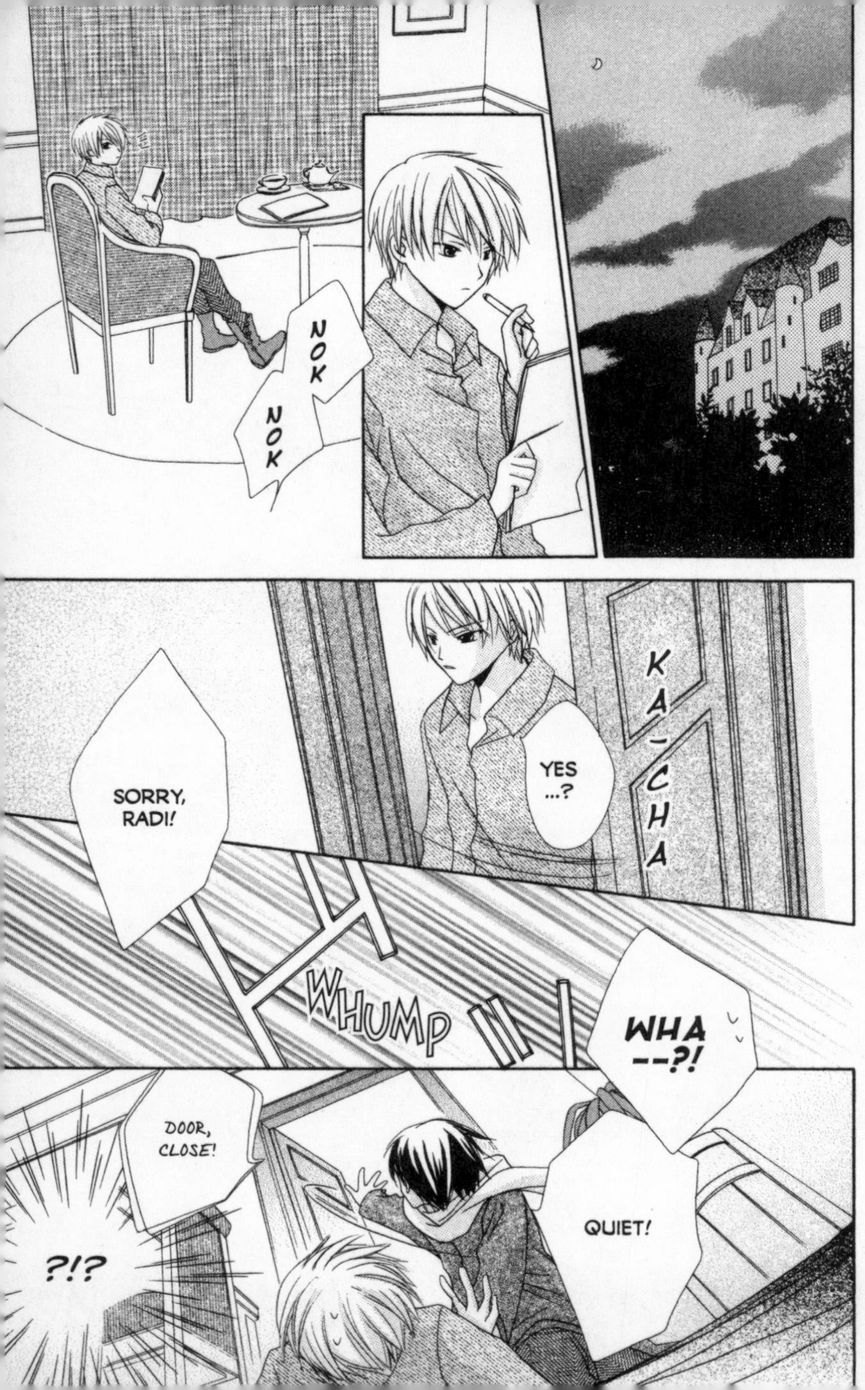
NOK NOK
KA-CHA
YES ...?
SORRY, RADI!
WHUMP
WHA --?!
QUIET!
DOOR, CLOSE!
?!?

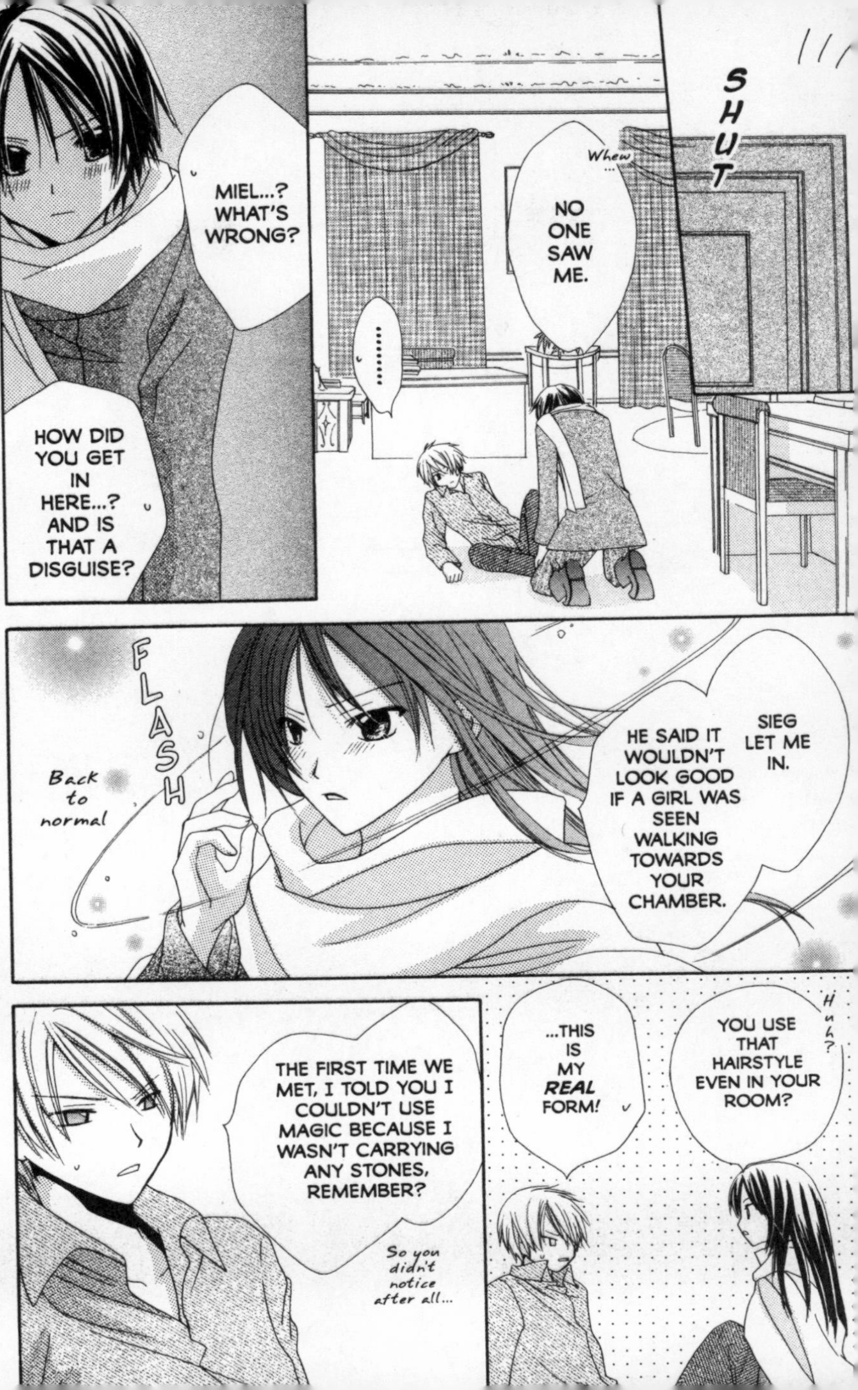
SHUT
Whew...
NO ONE SAW ME.
......
MIEL...? WHAT'S WRONG?
HOW DID YOU GET IN HERE...? AND IS THAT A DISGUISE?
SIEG LET ME IN.
HE SAID IT WOULDN'T LOOK GOOD IF A GIRL WAS SEEN WALKING TOWARDS YOUR CHAMBER.
FLASH
Back to normal
Huh?
YOU USE THAT HAIRSTYLE EVEN IN YOUR ROOM?
...THIS IS MY *REAL* FORM!
THE FIRST TIME WE MET, I TOLD YOU I COULDN'T USE MAGIC BECAUSE I WASN'T CARRYING ANY STONES, REMEMBER?
So you didn't notice after all...

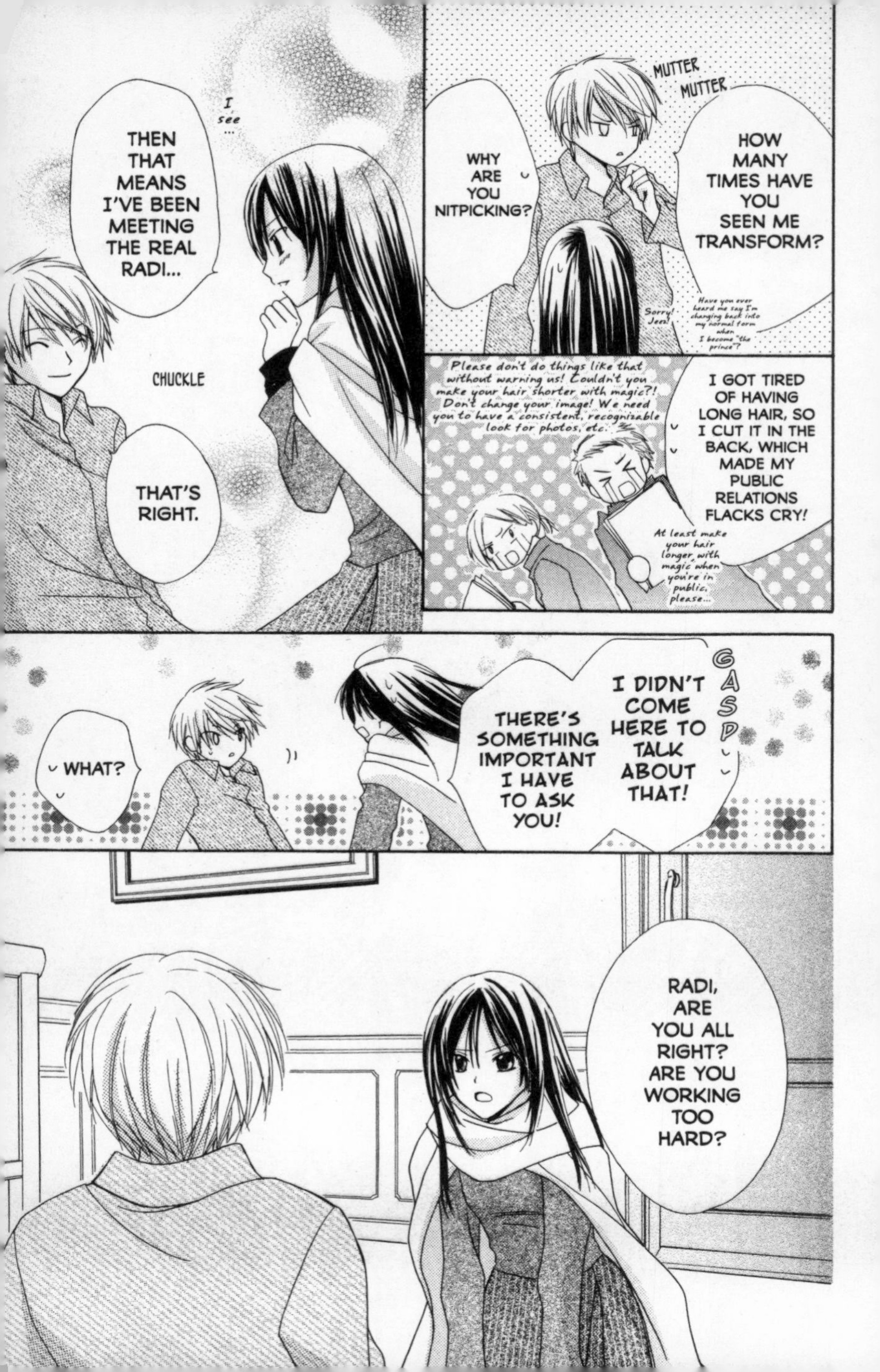
MUTTER MUTTER
HOW MANY TIMES HAVE YOU SEEN ME TRANSFORM?
Have you ever heard me say I'm changing back into my normal form when I become "the prince"?
WHY ARE YOU NITPICKING?
Sorry! Jees!
I GOT TIRED OF HAVING LONG HAIR, SO I CUT IT IN THE BACK, WHICH MADE MY PUBLIC RELATIONS FLACKS CRY!
At least make your hair longer with magic when you're in public, please...
Please don't do things like that without warning us! Couldn't you make your hair shorter with magic?! Don't change your image! We need you to have a consistent, recognizable look for photos, etc.
I see...
THEN THAT MEANS I'VE BEEN MEETING THE REAL RADI...
CHUCKLE
THAT'S RIGHT.
GASP
I DIDN'T COME HERE TO TALK ABOUT THAT!
THERE'S SOMETHING IMPORTANT I HAVE TO ASK YOU!
WHAT?
RADI, ARE YOU ALL RIGHT? ARE YOU WORKING TOO HARD?

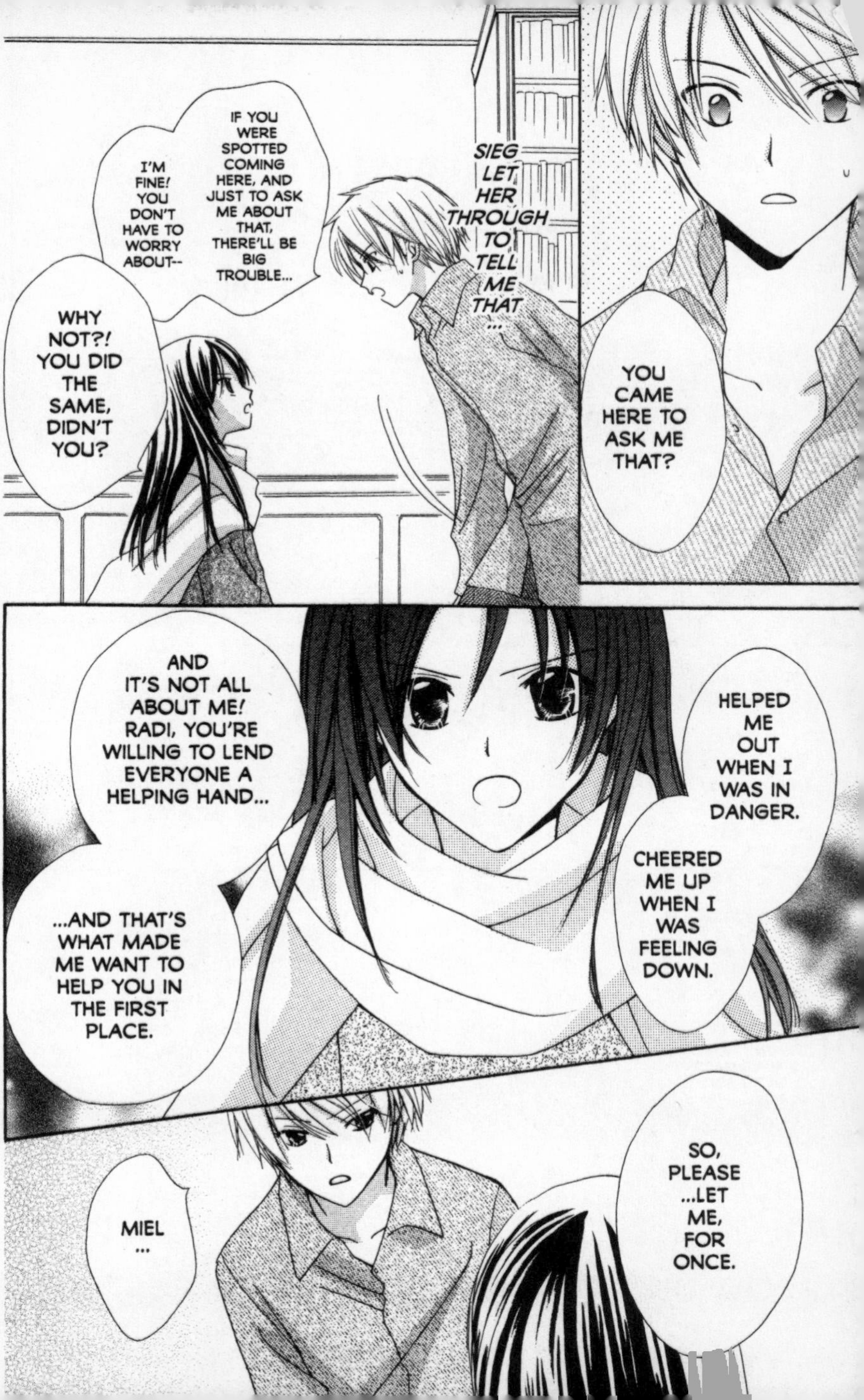
YOU CAME HERE TO ASK ME THAT?
SIEG LET HER THROUGH TO TELL ME THAT...
IF YOU WERE SPOTTED COMING HERE, AND JUST TO ASK ME ABOUT THAT, THERE'LL BE BIG TROUBLE...
I'M FINE! YOU DON'T HAVE TO WORRY ABOUT--
WHY NOT?! YOU DID THE SAME, DIDN'T YOU?
AND IT'S NOT ALL ABOUT ME! RADI, YOU'RE WILLING TO LEND EVERYONE A HELPING HAND...
HELPED ME OUT WHEN I WAS IN DANGER.
CHEERED ME UP WHEN I WAS FEELING DOWN.
...AND THAT'S WHAT MADE ME WANT TO HELP YOU IN THE FIRST PLACE.
SO, PLEASE ...LET ME, FOR ONCE.
MIEL ...

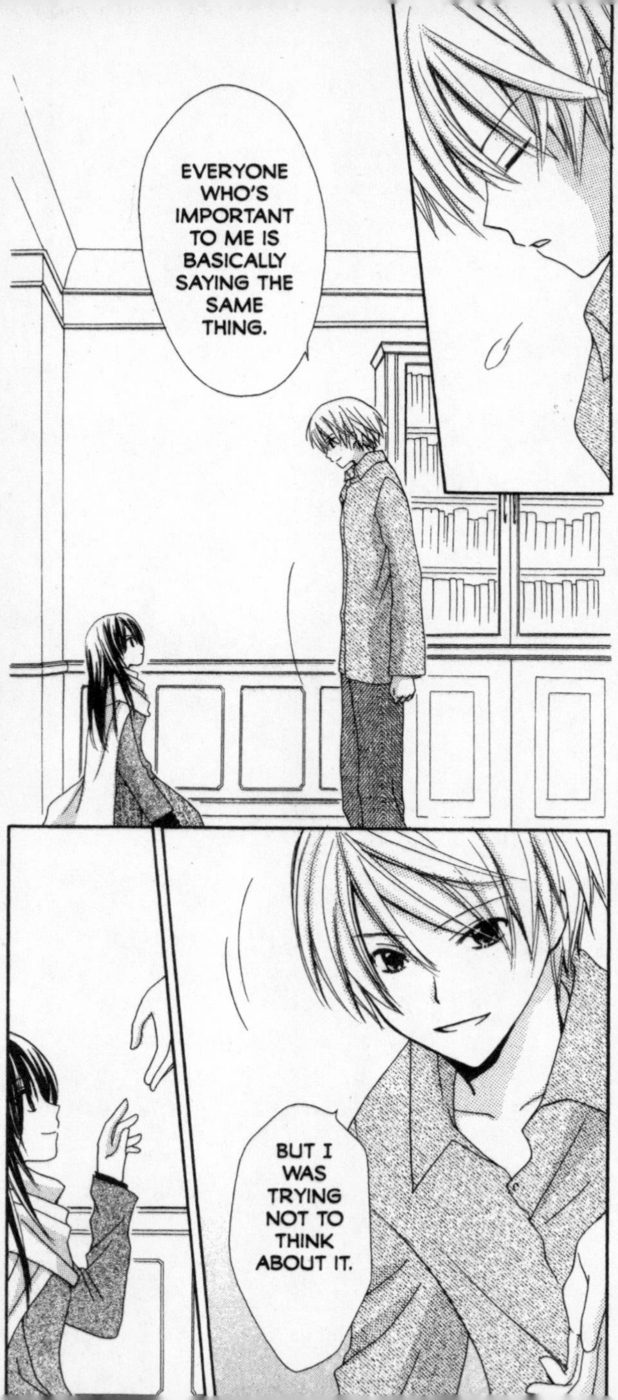
EVERYONE WHO'S IMPORTANT TO ME IS BASICALLY SAYING THE SAME THING.
BUT I WAS TRYING NOT TO THINK ABOUT IT.

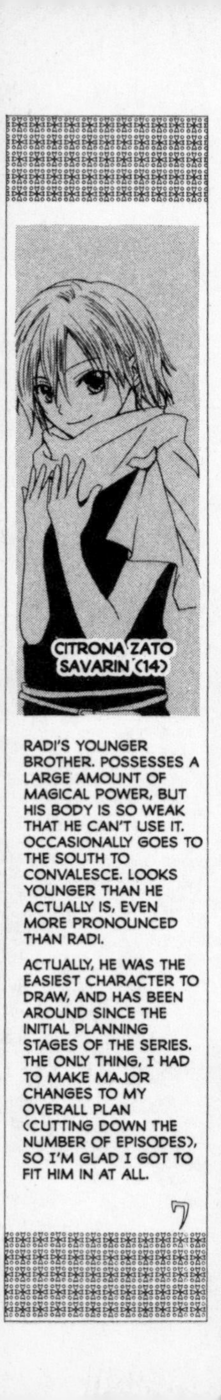
CITRONA ZATO SAVARIN (14)

RADI'S YOUNGER BROTHER. POSSESSES A LARGE AMOUNT OF MAGICAL POWER, BUT HIS BODY IS SO WEAK THAT HE CAN'T USE IT. OCCASIONALLY GOES TO THE SOUTH TO CONVALESCE. LOOKS YOUNGER THAN HE ACTUALLY IS, EVEN MORE PRONOUNCED THAN RADI.

ACTUALLY, HE WAS THE EASIEST CHARACTER TO DRAW, AND HAS BEEN AROUND SINCE THE INITIAL PLANNING STAGES OF THE SERIES. THE ONLY THING, I HAD TO MAKE MAJOR CHANGES TO MY OVERALL PLAN (CUTTING DOWN THE NUMBER OF EPISODES), SO I'M GLAD I GOT TO FIT HIM IN AT ALL.

7

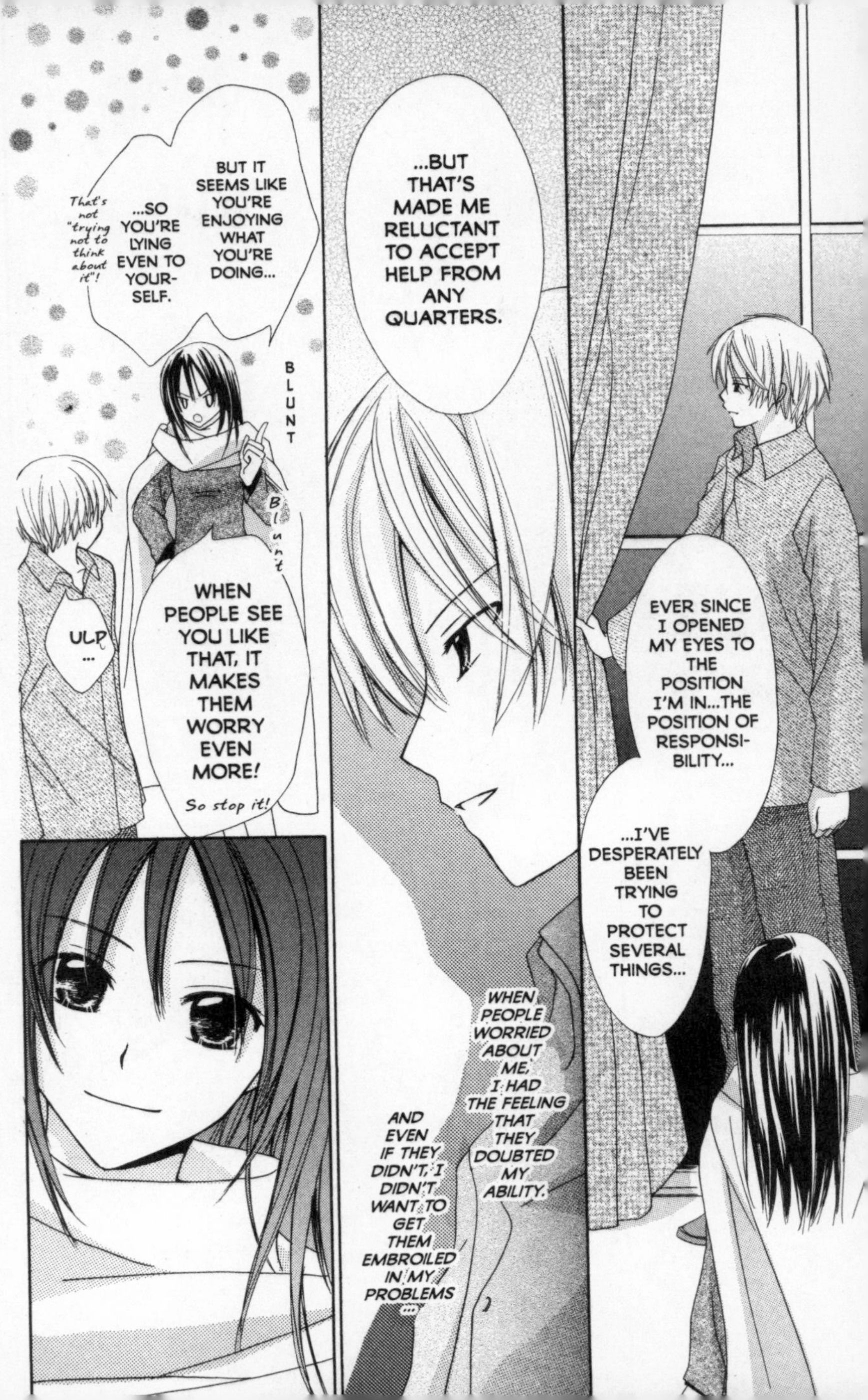
EVER SINCE I OPENED MY EYES TO THE POSITION I'M IN...THE POSITION OF RESPONSIBILITY...
...I'VE DESPERATELY BEEN TRYING TO PROTECT SEVERAL THINGS...
...BUT THAT'S MADE ME RELUCTANT TO ACCEPT HELP FROM ANY QUARTERS.
WHEN PEOPLE WORRIED ABOUT ME, I HAD THE FEELING THAT THEY DOUBTED MY ABILITY.
AND EVEN IF THEY DIDN'T, I DIDN'T WANT TO GET THEM EMBROILED IN MY PROBLEMS...
BUT IT SEEMS LIKE YOU'RE ENJOYING WHAT YOU'RE DOING...
...SO YOU'RE LYING EVEN TO YOURSELF.
That's not "trying not to think about it"!
BLUNT
Blunt
WHEN PEOPLE SEE YOU LIKE THAT, IT MAKES THEM WORRY EVEN MORE!
So stop it!
ULP...

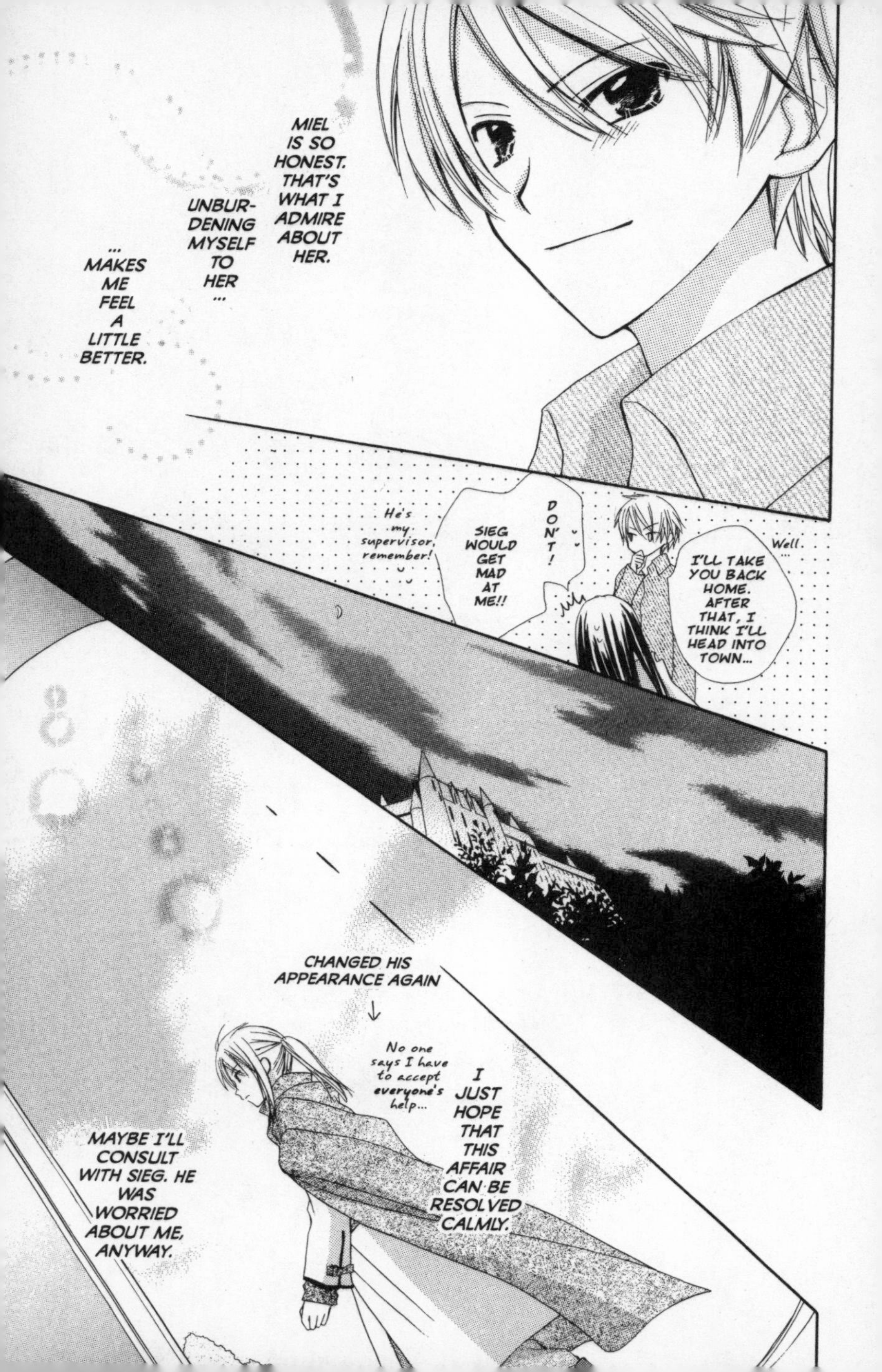
MIEL IS SO HONEST. THAT'S WHAT I ADMIRE ABOUT HER.
UNBURDENING MYSELF TO HER ...
... MAKES ME FEEL A LITTLE BETTER.
Well...
I'LL TAKE YOU BACK HOME. AFTER THAT, I THINK I'LL HEAD INTO TOWN...
DON'T!
SIEG WOULD GET MAD AT ME!!
He's my supervisor, remember!
CHANGED HIS APPEARANCE AGAIN
I JUST HOPE THAT THIS AFFAIR CAN BE RESOLVED CALMLY.
No one says I have to accept everyone's help...
MAYBE I'LL CONSULT WITH SIEG. HE WAS WORRIED ABOUT ME, ANYWAY.

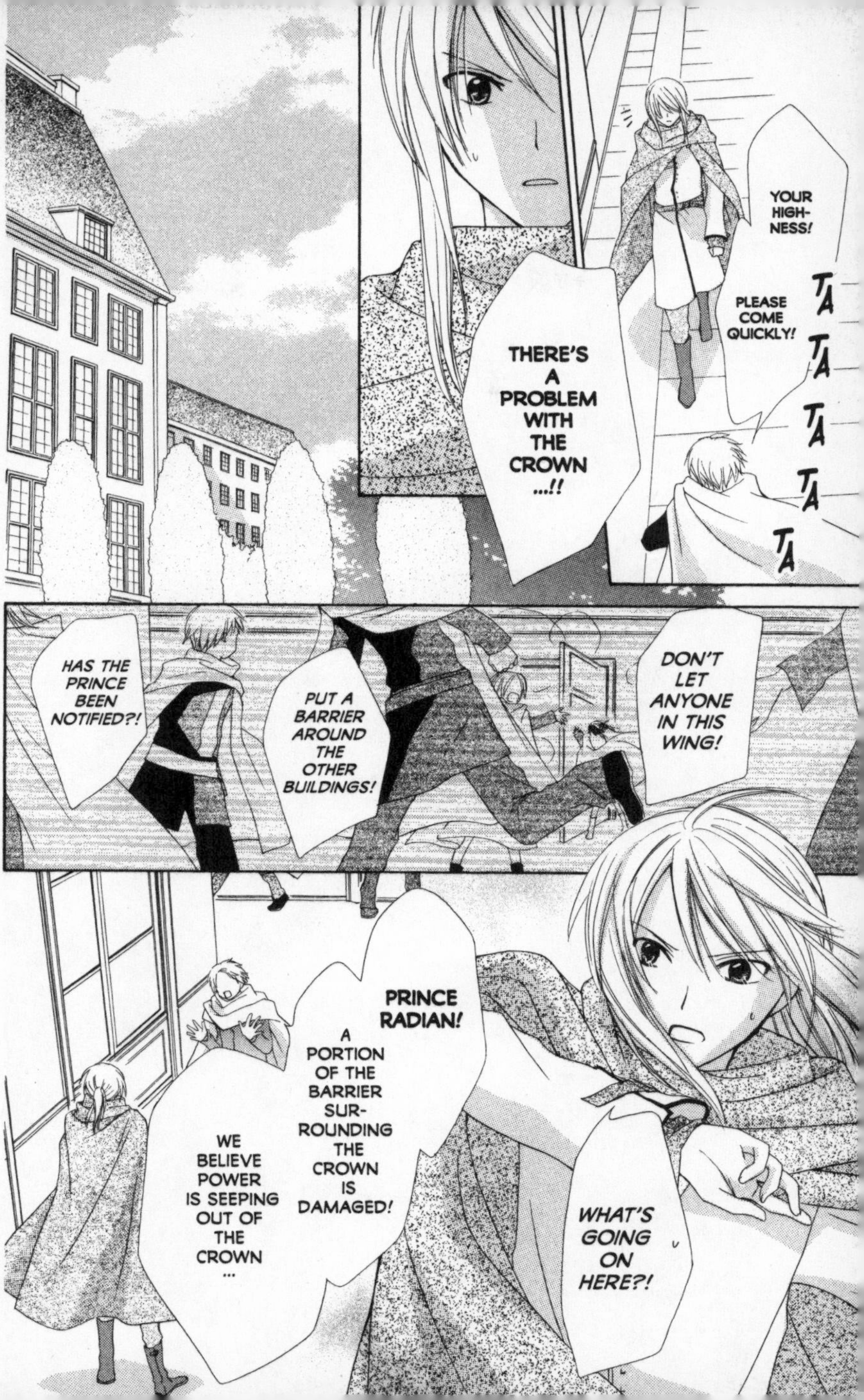
YOUR HIGH-NESS!
PLEASE COME QUICKLY!
TA TA TA TA TA
THERE'S A PROBLEM WITH THE CROWN ...!!
DON'T LET ANYONE IN THIS WING!
PUT A BARRIER AROUND THE OTHER BUILDINGS!
HAS THE PRINCE BEEN NOTIFIED?!
WHAT'S GOING ON HERE?!
PRINCE RADIAN!
A PORTION OF THE BARRIER SUR-ROUNDING THE CROWN IS DAMAGED!
WE BELIEVE POWER IS SEEPING OUT OF THE CROWN ...

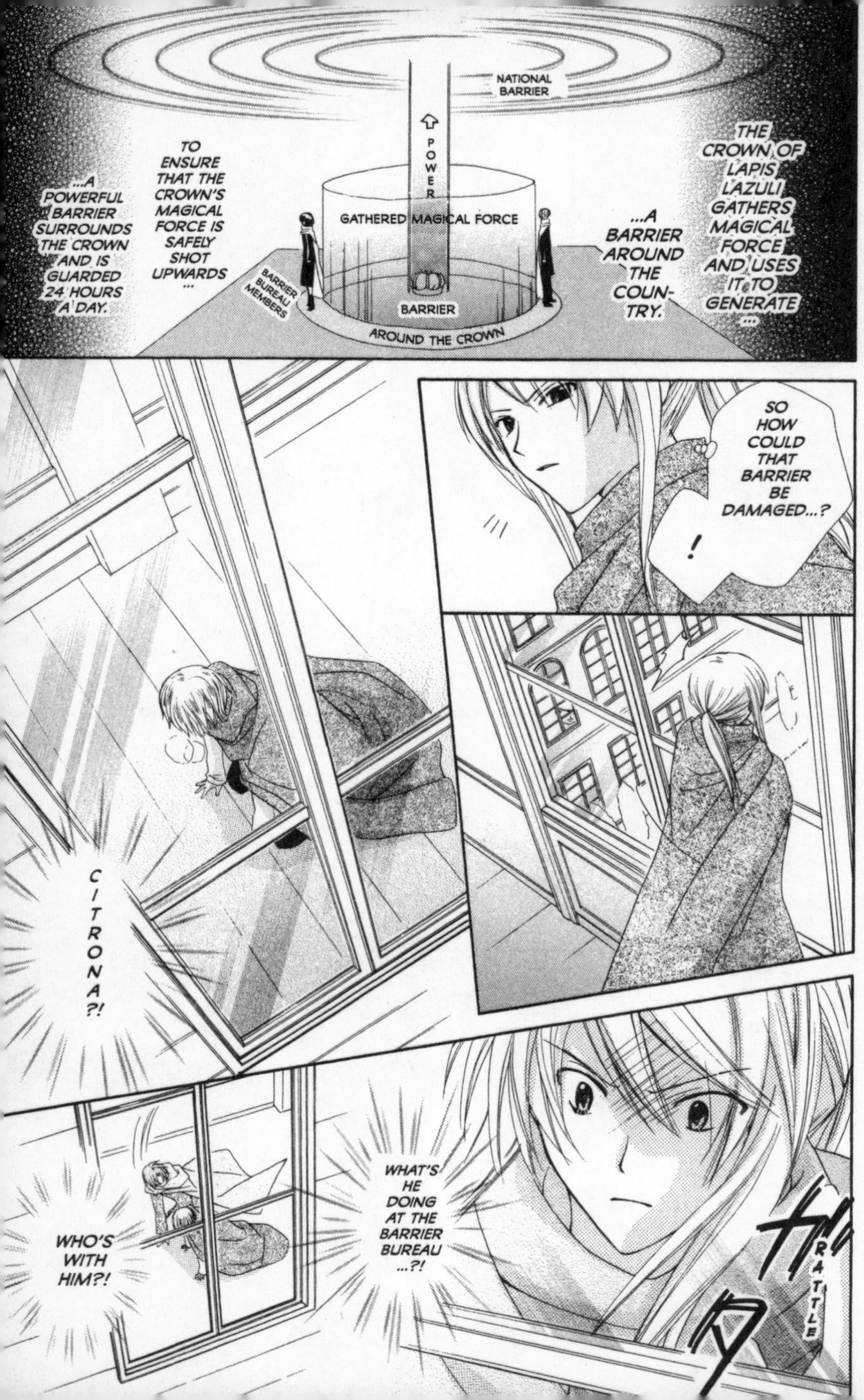
THE CROWN OF LAPIS LAZULI GATHERS MAGICAL FORCE AND USES IT TO GENERATE...
...A BARRIER AROUND THE COUNTRY.
NATIONAL BARRIER
POWER
GATHERED MAGICAL FORCE
BARRIER AROUND THE CROWN
BARRIER BUREAU MEMBERS
TO ENSURE THAT THE CROWN'S MAGICAL FORCE IS SAFELY SHOT UPWARDS...
...A POWERFUL BARRIER SURROUNDS THE CROWN AND IS GUARDED 24 HOURS A DAY.
SO HOW COULD THAT BARRIER BE DAMAGED...?
!
CITRONA?!
RATTLE
WHAT'S HE DOING AT THE BARRIER BUREAU...?!
WHO'S WITH HIM?!

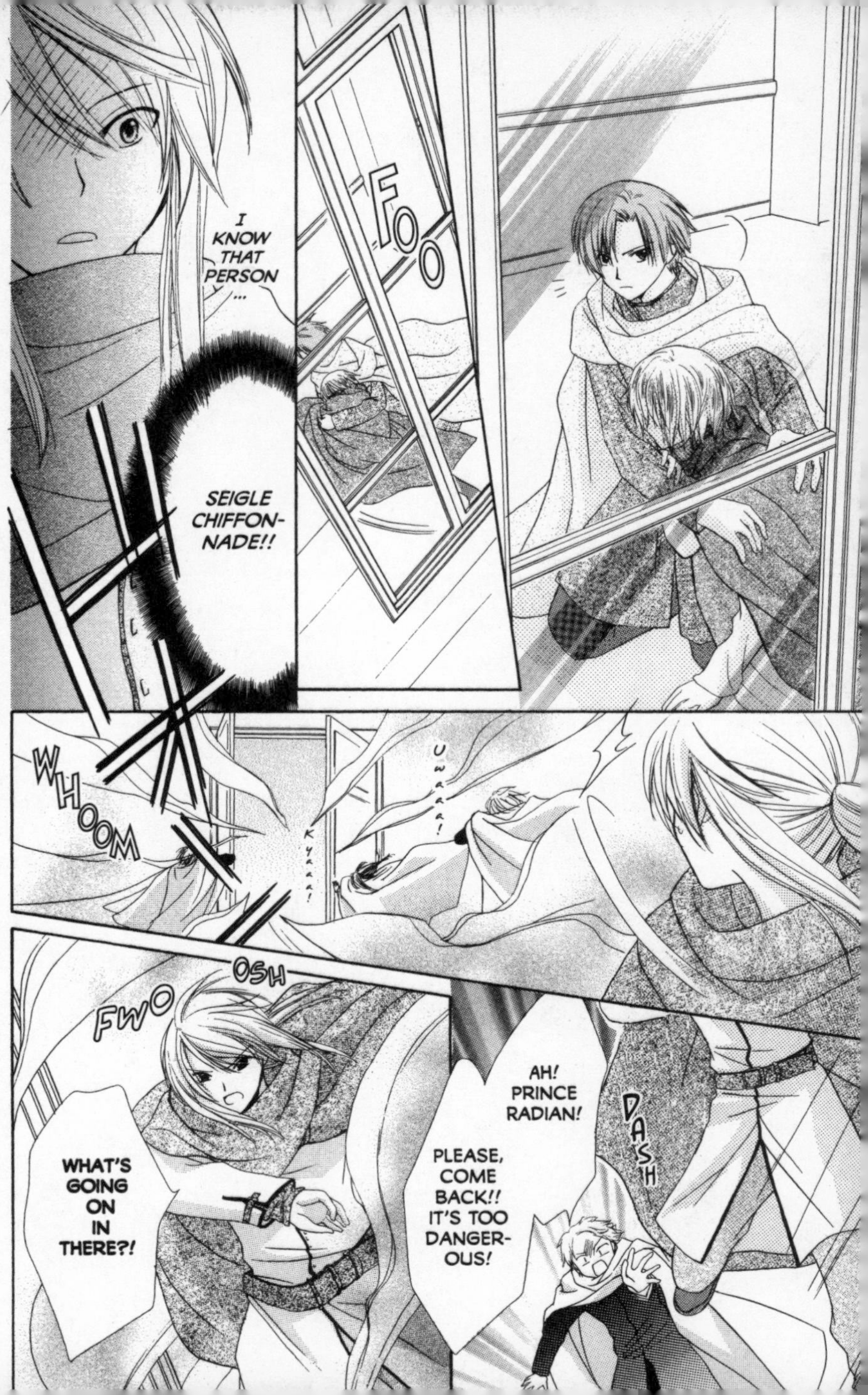
FOOO
I KNOW THAT PERSON ...
SEIGLE CHIFFON-NADE!!
Uwaaaa!
Kyaaaa!
WHOOM
DASH
AH! PRINCE RADIAN!
PLEASE, COME BACK!! IT'S TOO DANGER-OUS!
FWOOSH
WHAT'S GOING ON IN THERE?!

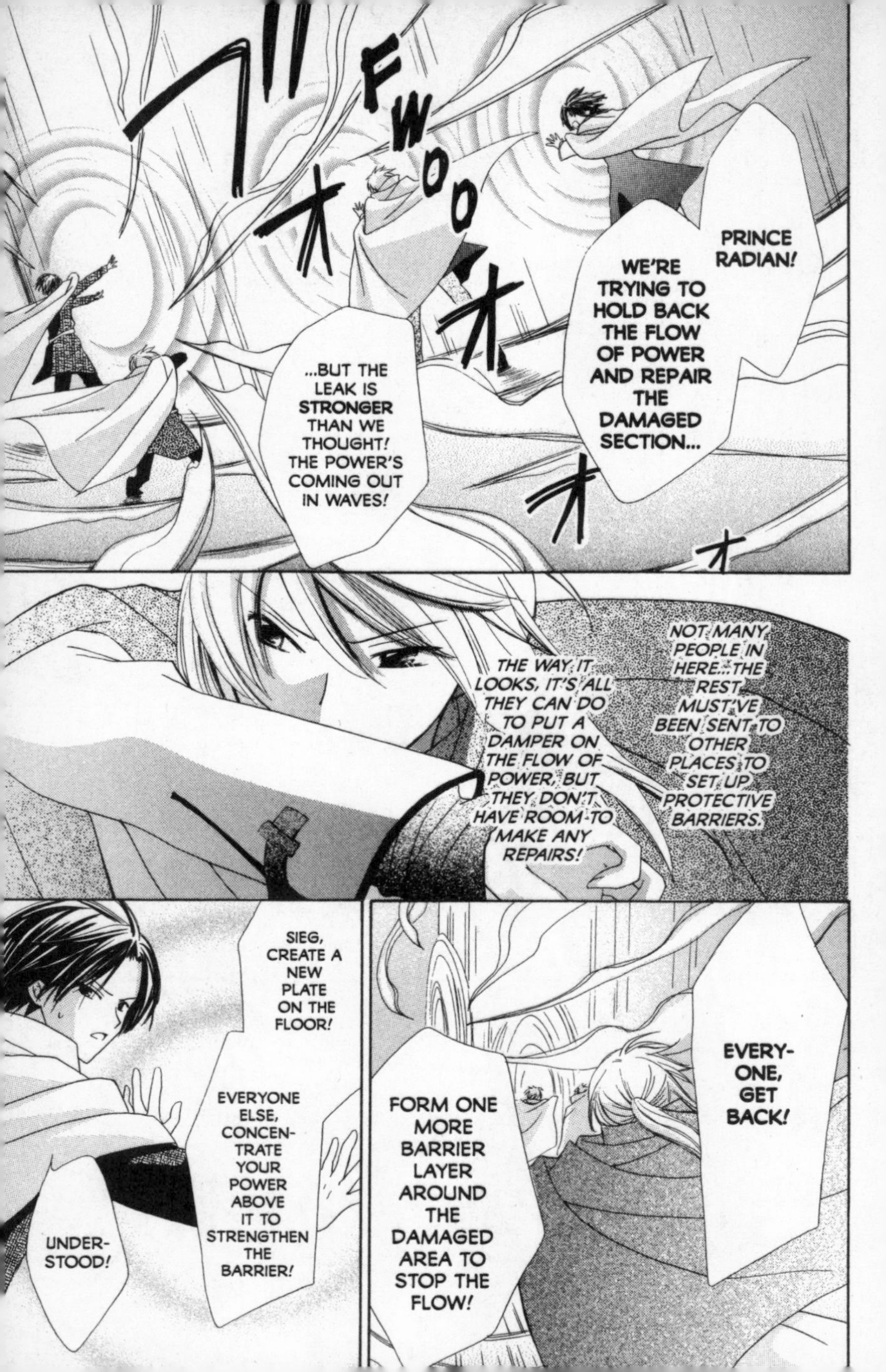
FWOOO
PRINCE RADIAN!
WE'RE TRYING TO HOLD BACK THE FLOW OF POWER AND REPAIR THE DAMAGED SECTION...
...BUT THE LEAK IS STRONGER THAN WE THOUGHT! THE POWER'S COMING OUT IN WAVES!
NOT MANY PEOPLE IN HERE... THE REST MUST'VE BEEN SENT TO OTHER PLACES TO SET UP PROTECTIVE BARRIERS.
THE WAY IT LOOKS, IT'S ALL THEY CAN DO TO PUT A DAMPER ON THE FLOW OF POWER, BUT THEY DON'T HAVE ROOM TO MAKE ANY REPAIRS!
EVERY-ONE, GET BACK!
FORM ONE MORE BARRIER LAYER AROUND THE DAMAGED AREA TO STOP THE FLOW!
SIEG, CREATE A NEW PLATE ON THE FLOOR!
EVERYONE ELSE, CONCEN-TRATE YOUR POWER ABOVE IT TO STRENGTHEN THE BARRIER!
UNDER-STOOD!

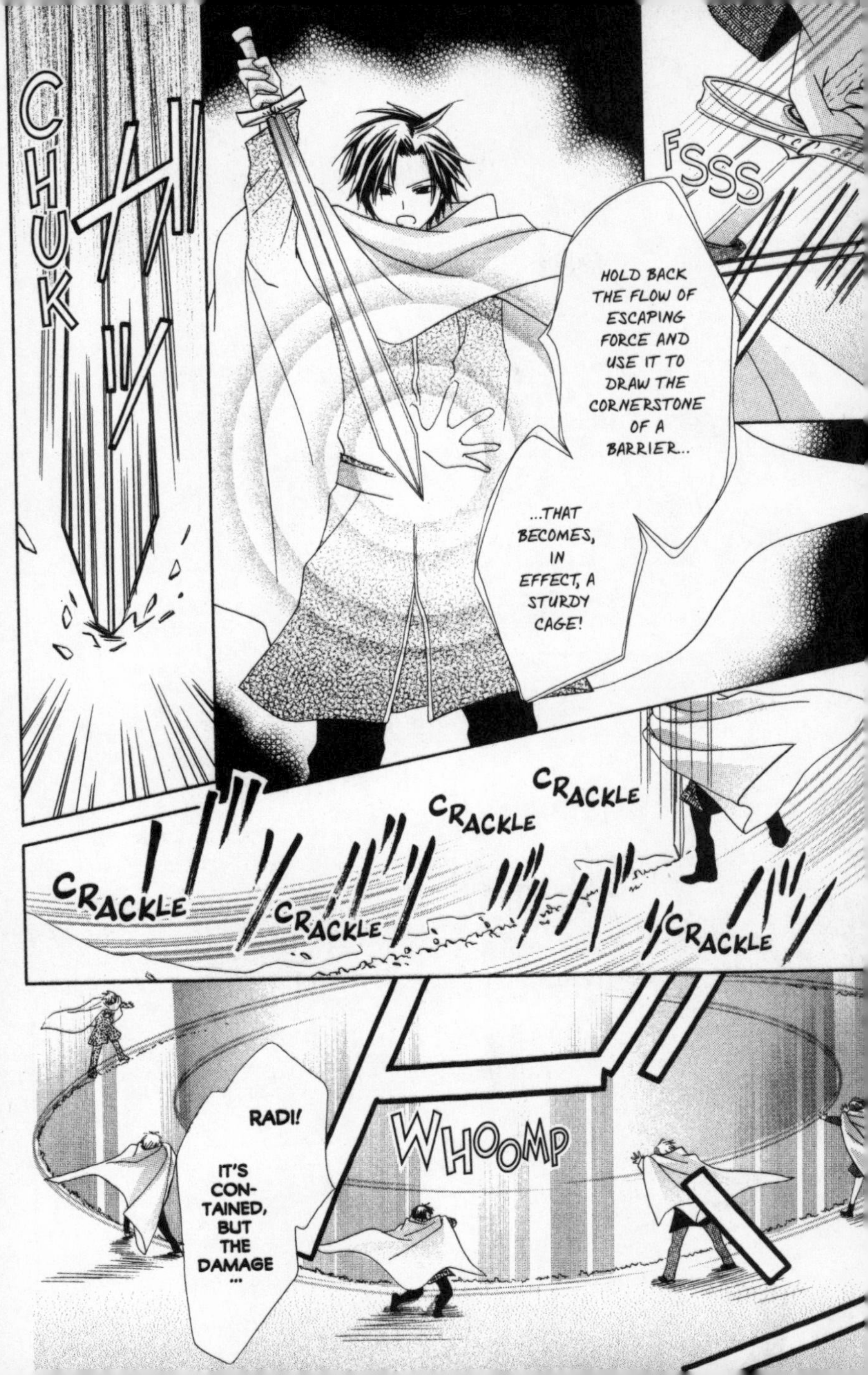
FSSS
HOLD BACK THE FLOW OF ESCAPING FORCE AND USE IT TO DRAW THE CORNERSTONE OF A BARRIER...
...THAT BECOMES, IN EFFECT, A STURDY CAGE!
CHUK
CRACKLE
CRACKLE
CRACKLE
CRACKLE
CRACKLE
WHOOMP
RADI!
IT'S CON-TAINED, BUT THE DAMAGE...

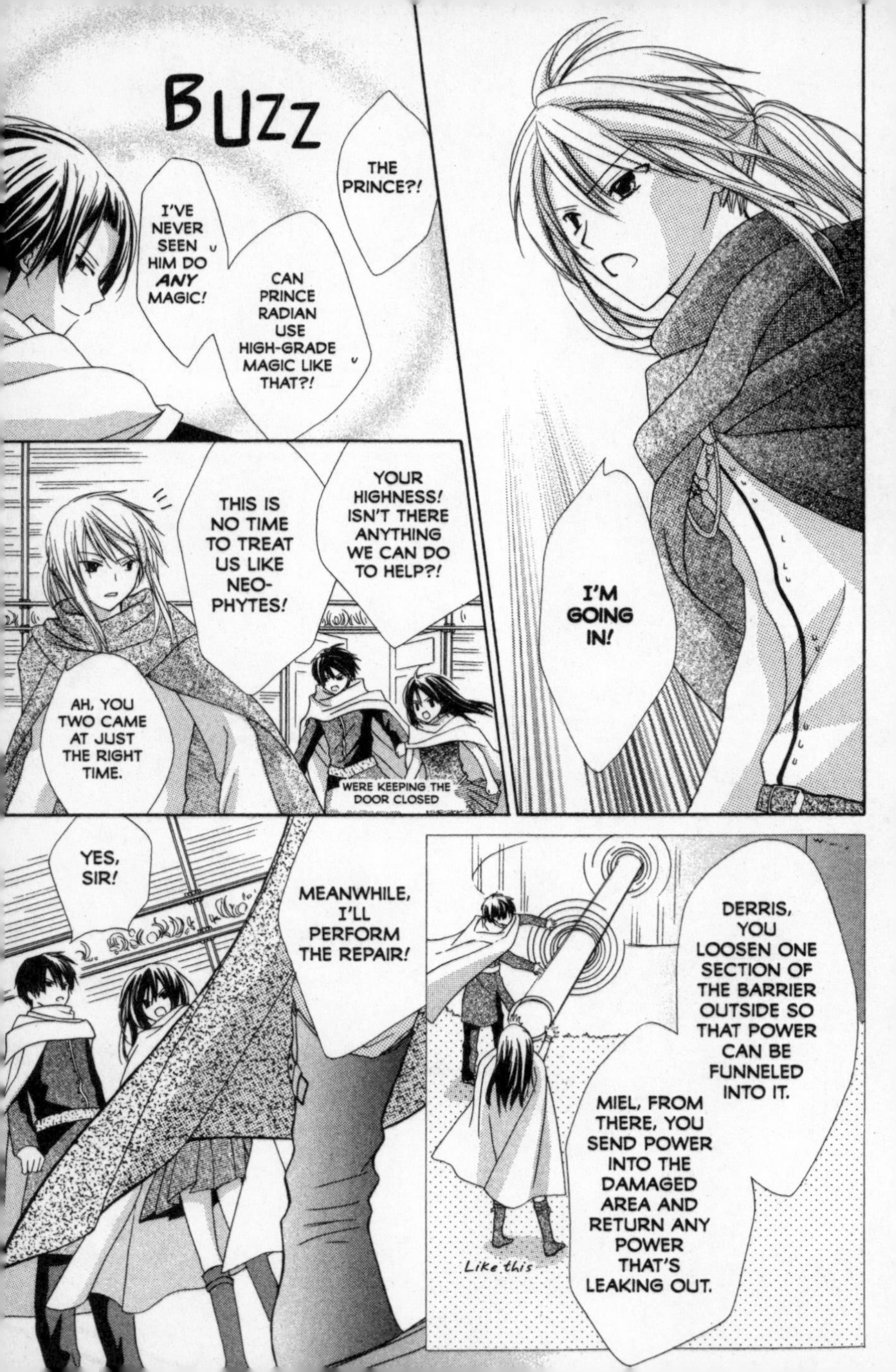
I'M GOING IN!
BUZZ
THE PRINCE?!
CAN PRINCE RADIAN USE HIGH-GRADE MAGIC LIKE THAT?!
I'VE NEVER SEEN HIM DO *ANY* MAGIC!
YOUR HIGHNESS! ISN'T THERE ANYTHING WE CAN DO TO HELP?!
THIS IS NO TIME TO TREAT US LIKE NEO-PHYTES!
AH, YOU TWO CAME AT JUST THE RIGHT TIME.
WERE KEEPING THE DOOR CLOSED
DERRIS, YOU LOOSEN ONE SECTION OF THE BARRIER OUTSIDE SO THAT POWER CAN BE FUNNELED INTO IT.
MIEL, FROM THERE, YOU SEND POWER INTO THE DAMAGED AREA AND RETURN ANY POWER THAT'S LEAKING OUT.
Like this
MEANWHILE, I'LL PERFORM THE REPAIR!
YES, SIR!

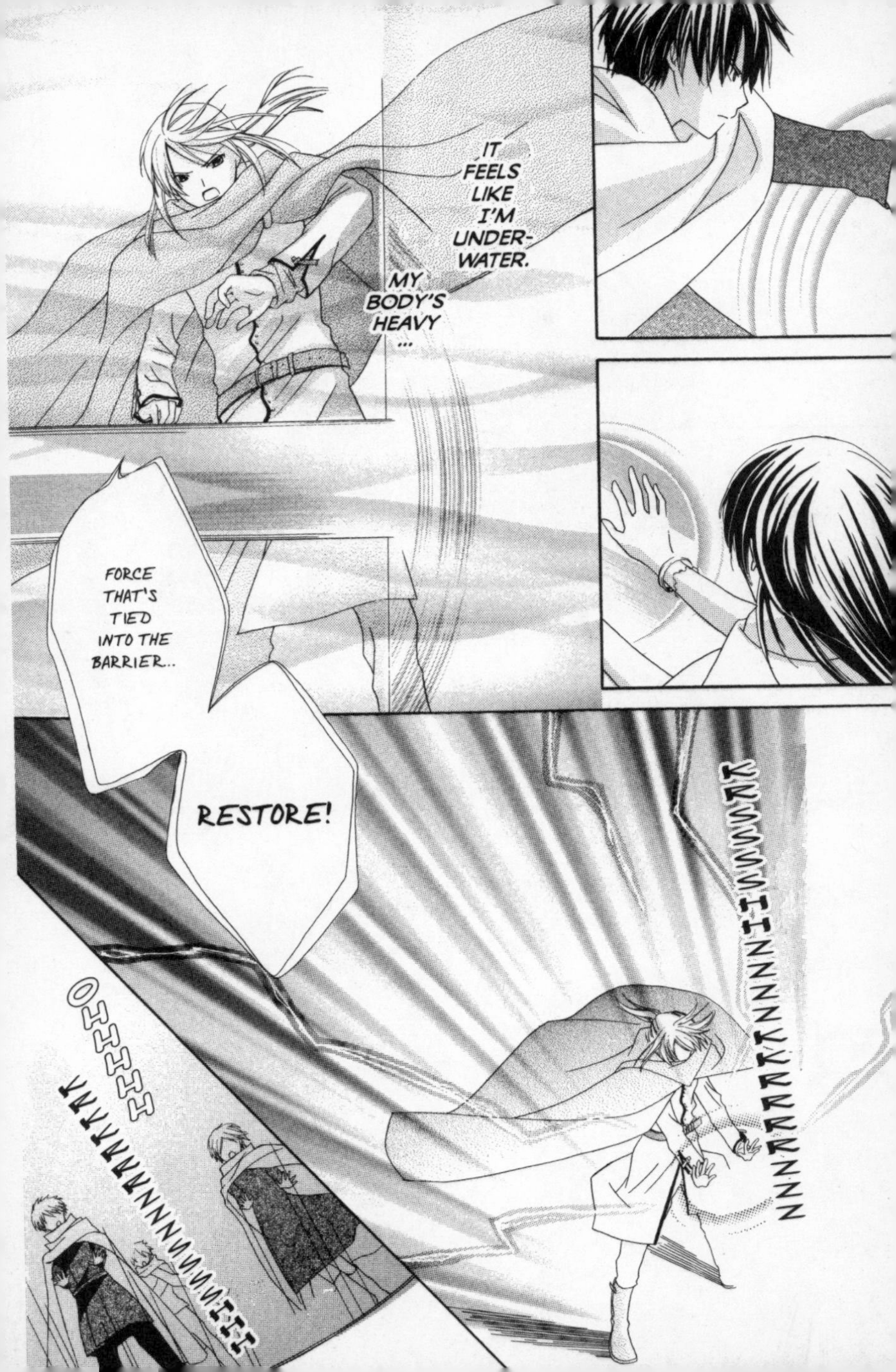
IT FEELS LIKE I'M UNDER-WATER.
MY BODY'S HEAVY...
FORCE THAT'S TIED INTO THE BARRIER...
RESTORE!
KRSSSSHHNNNNKKRRRRZZZZ
OHHHHH
KRKKRRRNNNNNNNNNNN!!!

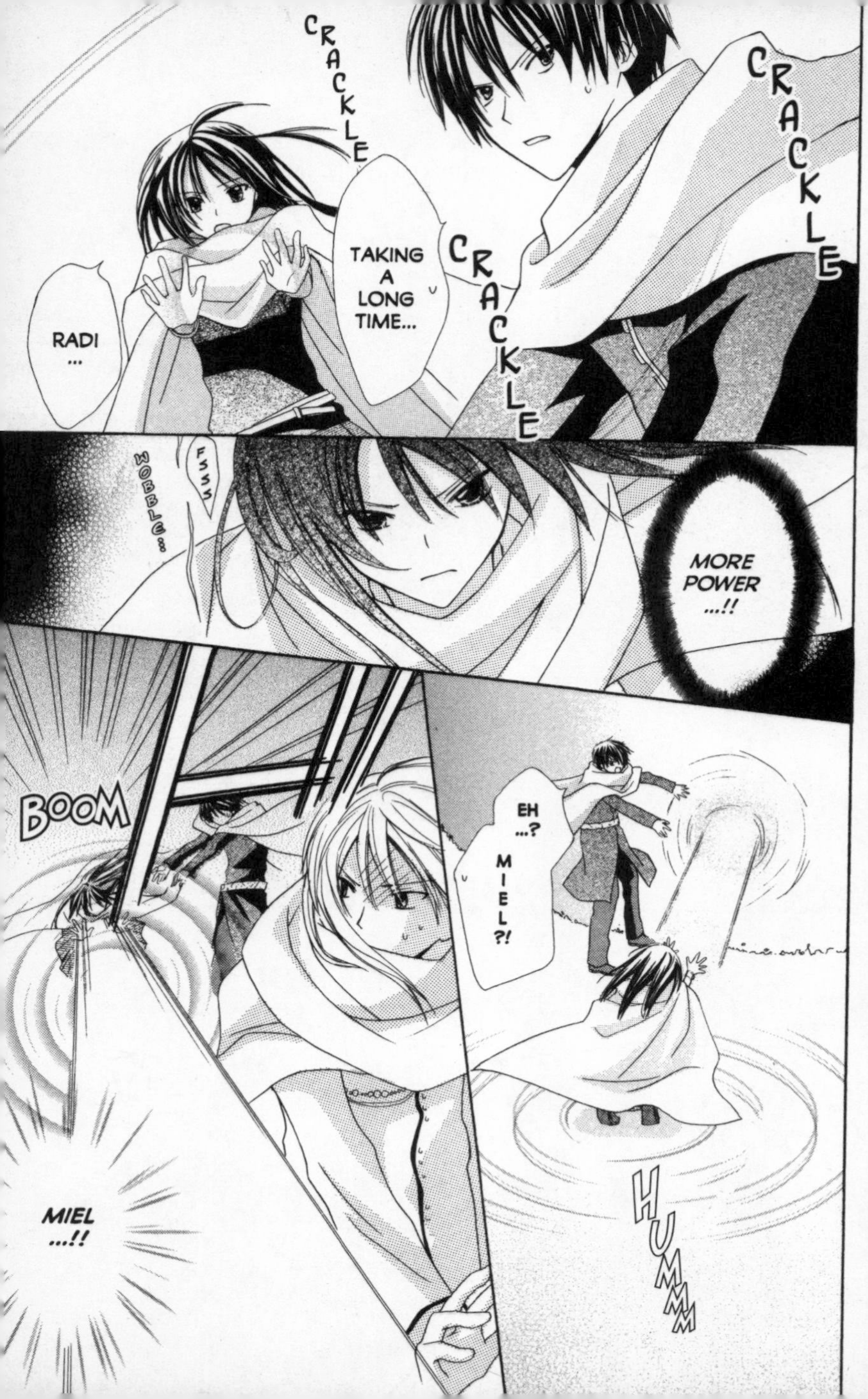
CRACKLE
CRACKLE
TAKING A LONG TIME...
CRACKLE
RADI ...
MORE POWER ...!!
FSSS
WOBBLE...
EH ...? MIEL?!
HUMMM
BOOM
MIEL ...!!

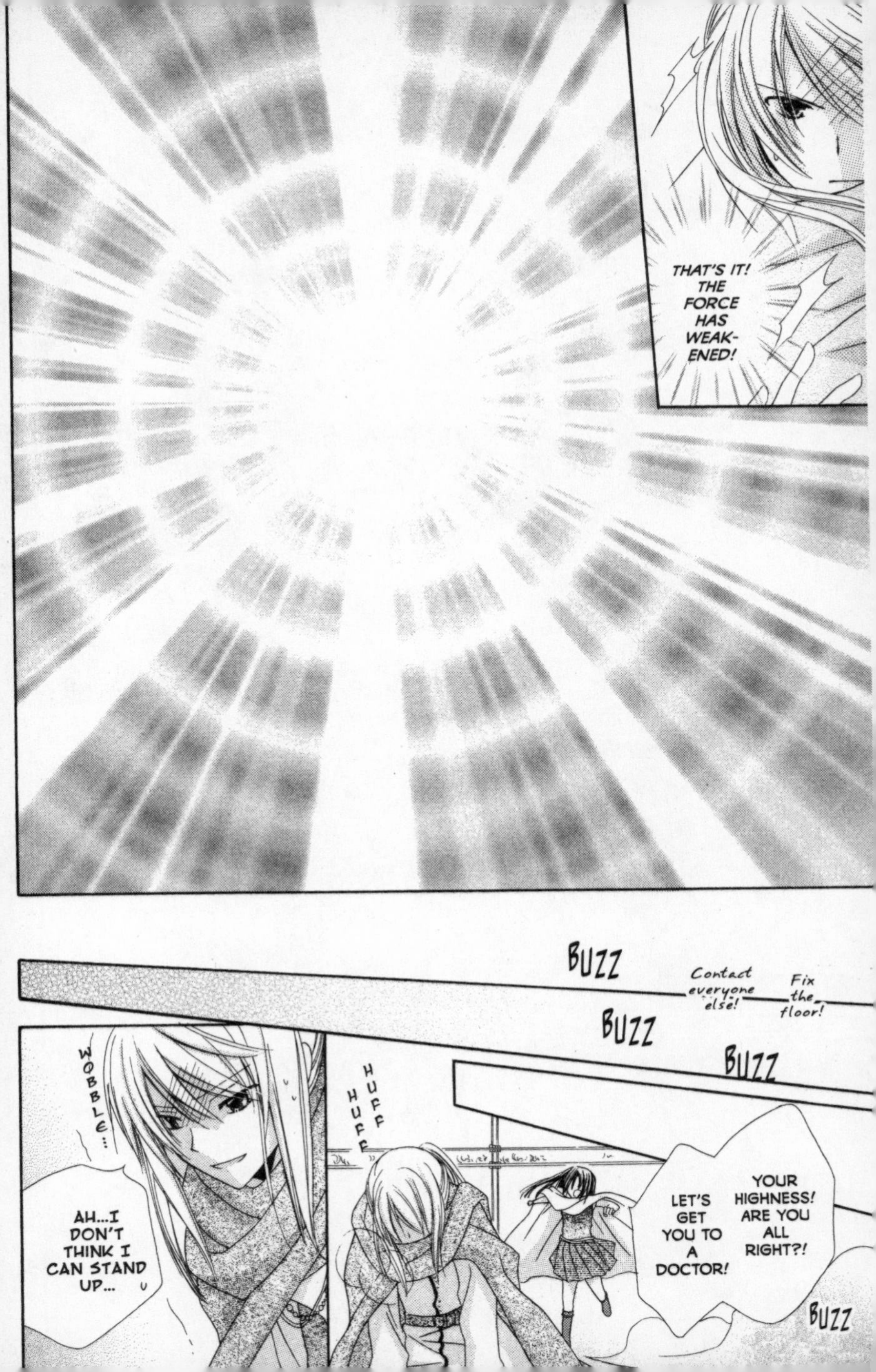
THAT'S IT! THE FORCE HAS WEAKENED!
BUZZ
Fix the floor!
Contact everyone else!
BUZZ
BUZZ
YOUR HIGHNESS! ARE YOU ALL RIGHT?!
LET'S GET YOU TO A DOCTOR!
HUFF HUFF
BUZZ
WOBBLE...
AH...I DON'T THINK I CAN STAND UP...

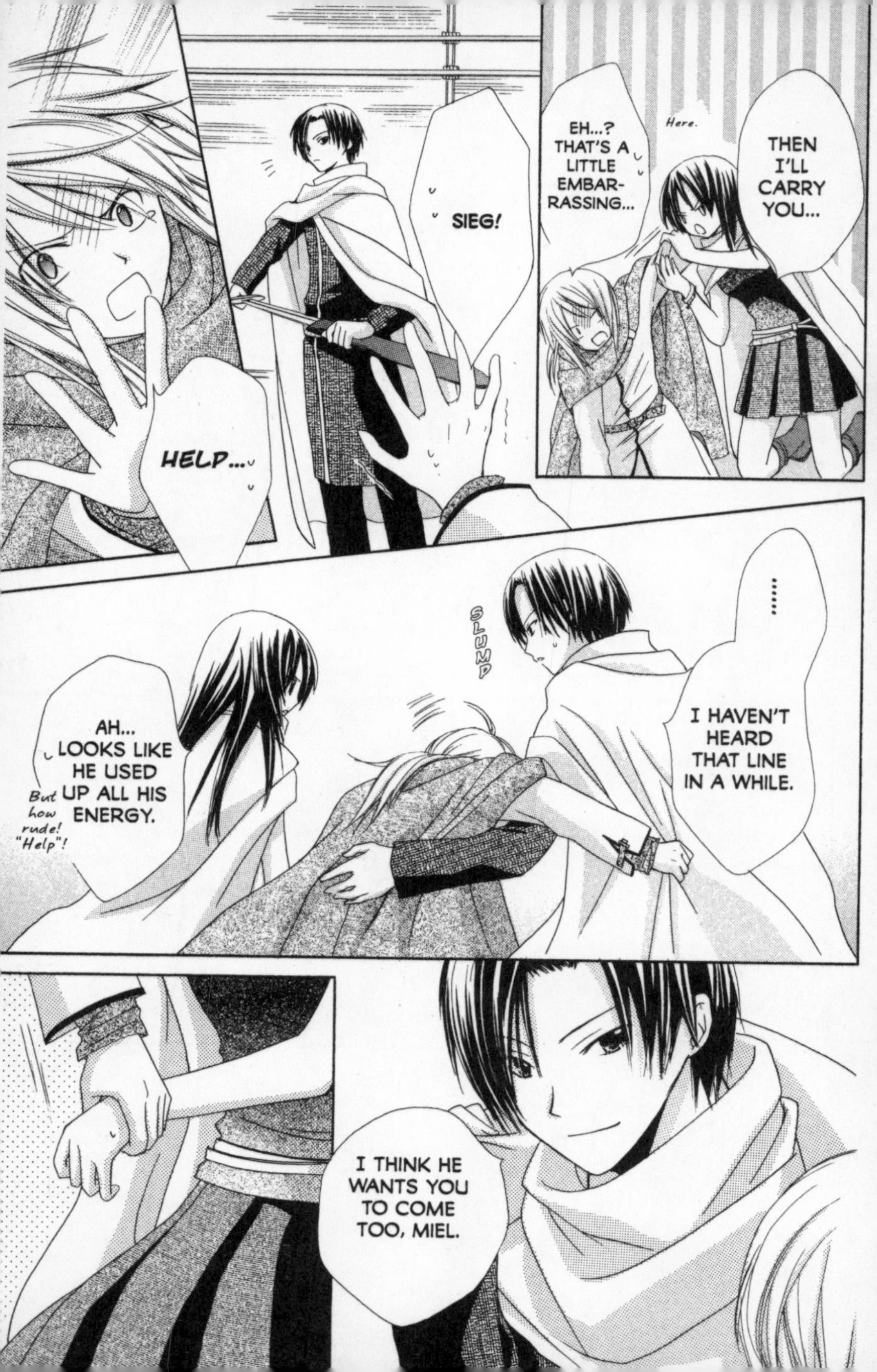
THEN I'LL CARRY YOU...
Here.
EH...? THAT'S A LITTLE EMBARRASSING...
SIEG!
HELP...
......
SLUMP
I HAVEN'T HEARD THAT LINE IN A WHILE.
AH... LOOKS LIKE HE USED UP ALL HIS ENERGY.
But how rude! "Help"!
I THINK HE WANTS YOU TO COME TOO, MIEL.

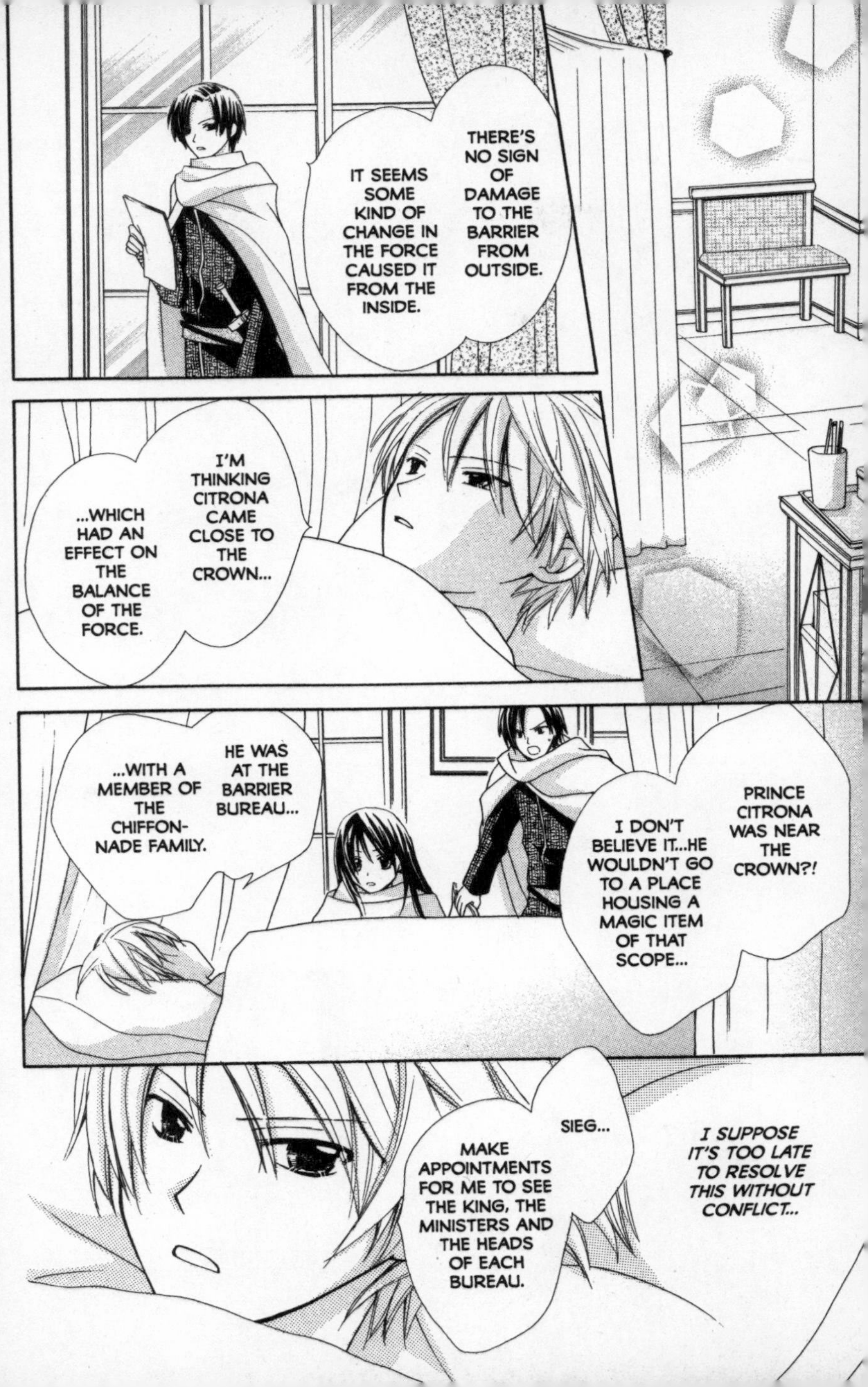
THERE'S NO SIGN OF DAMAGE TO THE BARRIER FROM OUTSIDE.
IT SEEMS SOME KIND OF CHANGE IN THE FORCE CAUSED IT FROM THE INSIDE.
I'M THINKING CITRONA CAME CLOSE TO THE CROWN...
...WHICH HAD AN EFFECT ON THE BALANCE OF THE FORCE.
PRINCE CITRONA WAS NEAR THE CROWN?!
I DON'T BELIEVE IT...HE WOULDN'T GO TO A PLACE HOUSING A MAGIC ITEM OF THAT SCOPE...
HE WAS AT THE BARRIER BUREAU...
...WITH A MEMBER OF THE CHIFFON-NADE FAMILY.
I SUPPOSE IT'S TOO LATE TO RESOLVE THIS WITHOUT CONFLICT...
SIEG...
MAKE APPOINTMENTS FOR ME TO SEE THE KING, THE MINISTERS AND THE HEADS OF EACH BUREAU.

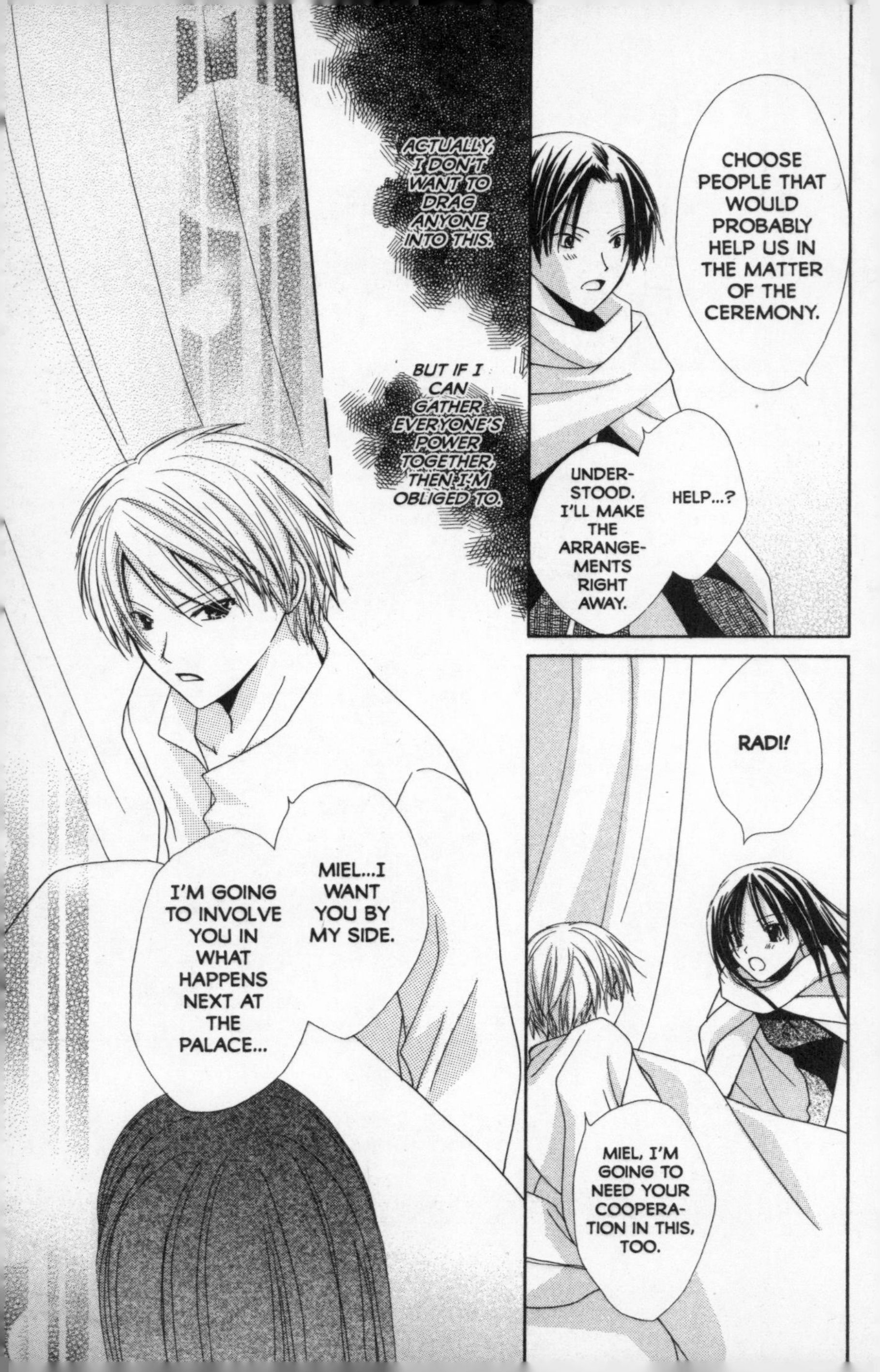
CHOOSE PEOPLE THAT WOULD PROBABLY HELP US IN THE MATTER OF THE CEREMONY.
HELP...?
UNDER-STOOD. I'LL MAKE THE ARRANGE-MENTS RIGHT AWAY.
RADI!
MIEL, I'M GOING TO NEED YOUR COOPERA-TION IN THIS, TOO.
ACTUALLY, I DON'T WANT TO DRAG ANYONE INTO THIS.
BUT IF I CAN GATHER EVERYONE'S POWER TOGETHER, THEN I'M OBLIGED TO.
MIEL...I WANT YOU BY MY SIDE.
I'M GOING TO INVOLVE YOU IN WHAT HAPPENS NEXT AT THE PALACE...

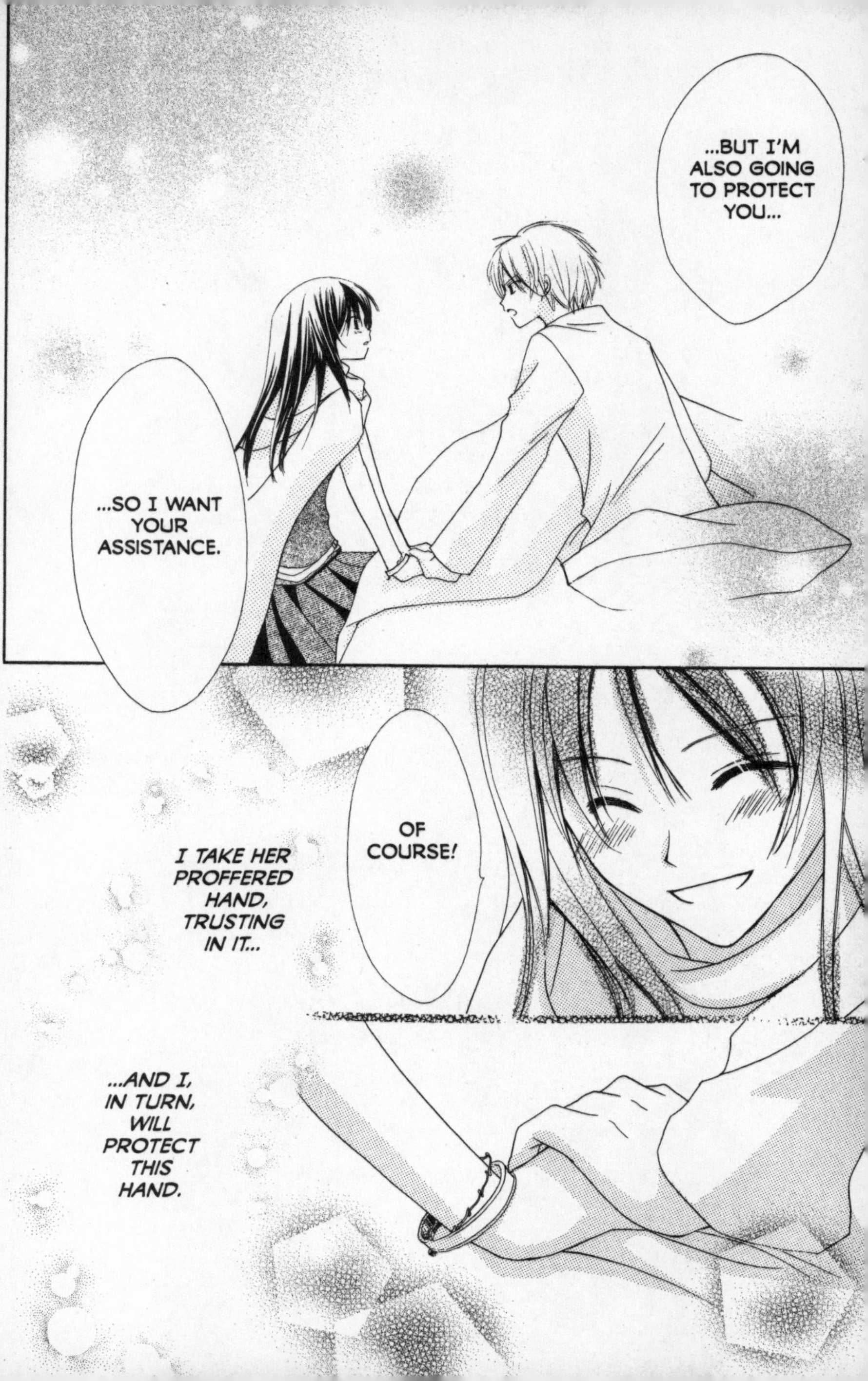
...BUT I'M ALSO GOING TO PROTECT YOU...
...SO I WANT YOUR ASSISTANCE.
OF COURSE!
I TAKE HER PROFFERED HAND, TRUSTING IN IT...
...AND I, IN TURN, WILL PROTECT THIS HAND.

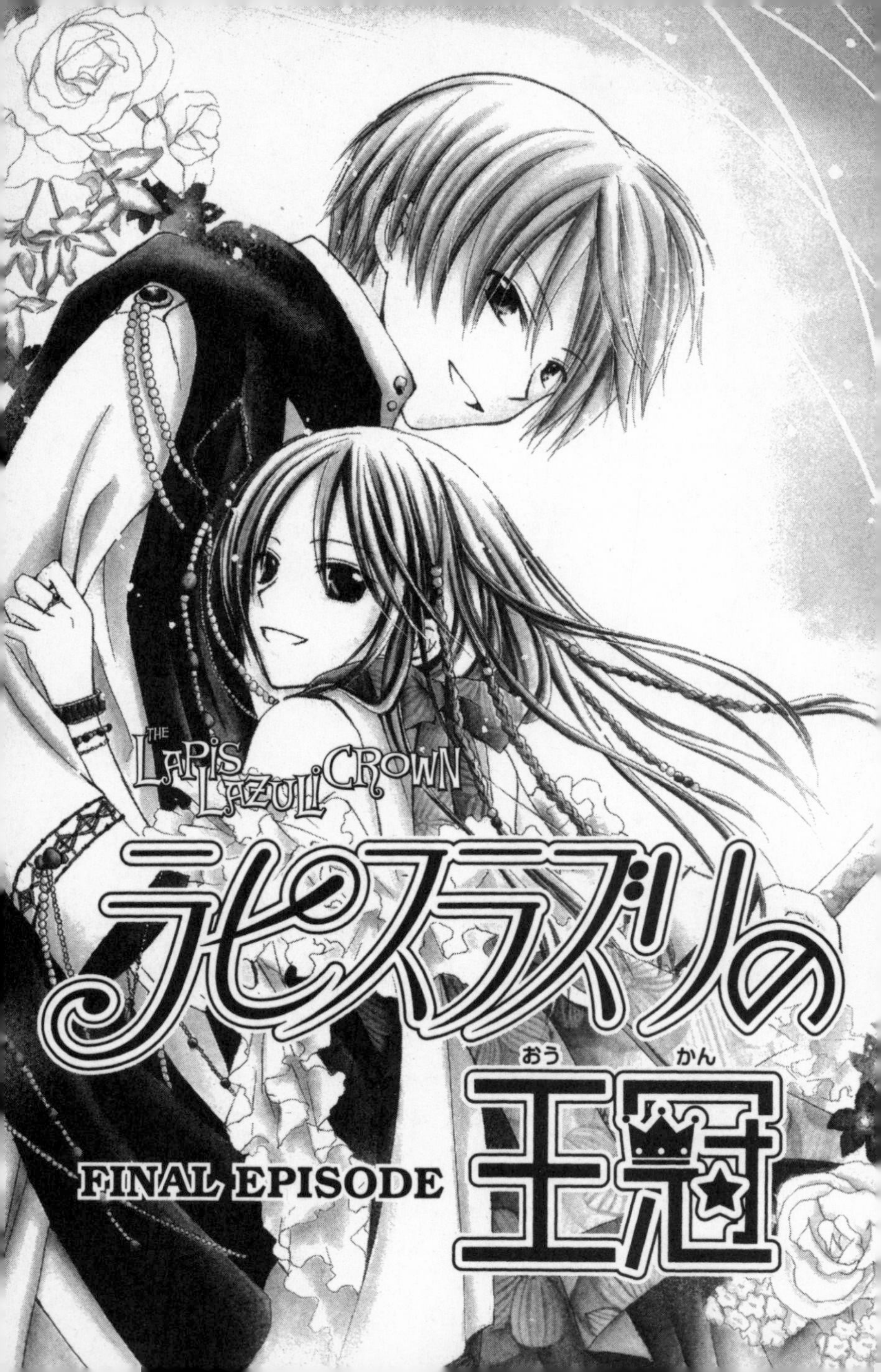
THE LAPIS LAZULI CROWN
ラピスラズリの王冠(おうかん)
FINAL EPISODE

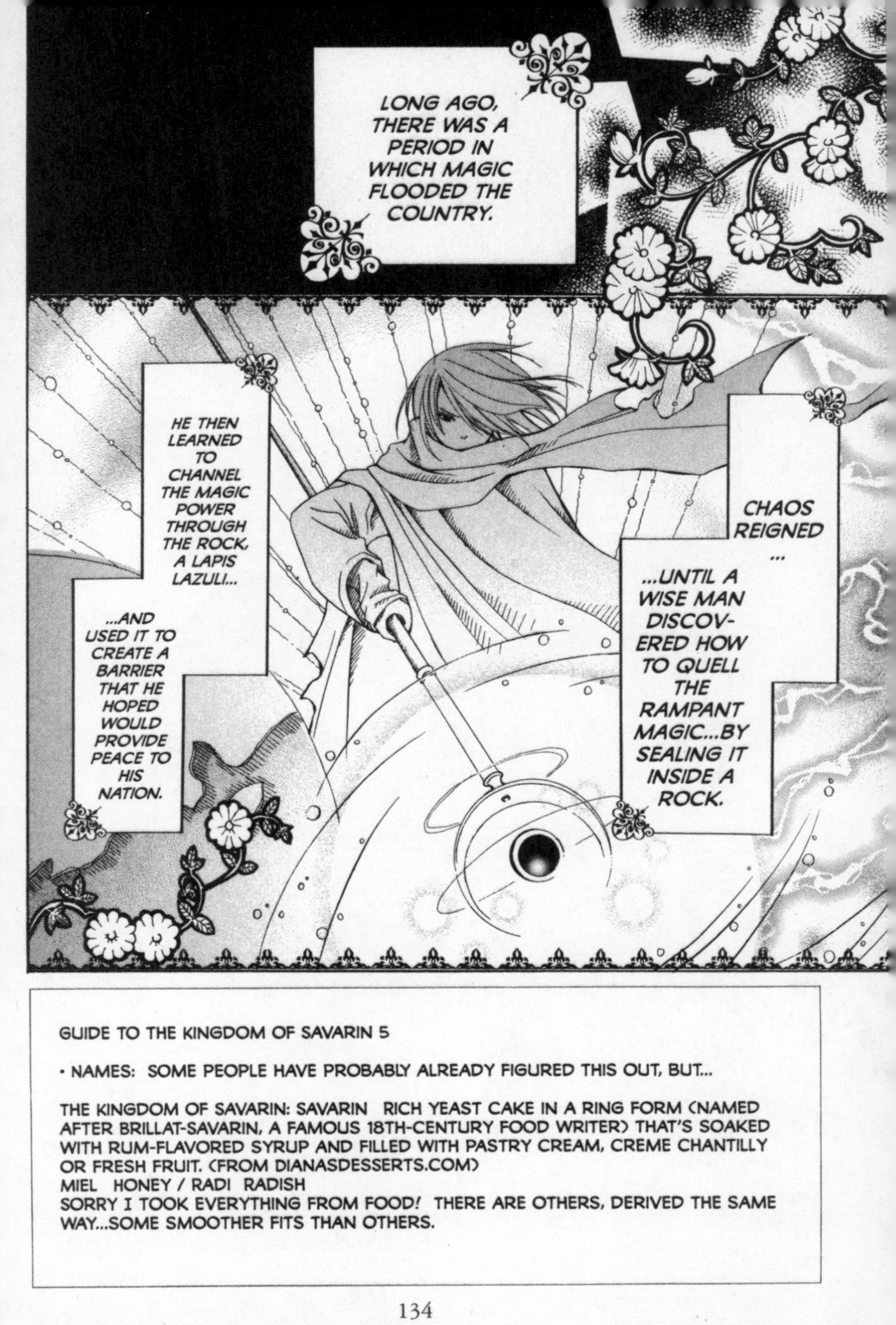
LONG AGO, THERE WAS A PERIOD IN WHICH MAGIC FLOODED THE COUNTRY.
CHAOS REIGNED ...
...UNTIL A WISE MAN DISCOV- ERED HOW TO QUELL THE RAMPANT MAGIC...BY SEALING IT INSIDE A ROCK.
HE THEN LEARNED TO CHANNEL THE MAGIC POWER THROUGH THE ROCK, A LAPIS LAZULI...
...AND USED IT TO CREATE A BARRIER THAT HE HOPED WOULD PROVIDE PEACE TO HIS NATION.

GUIDE TO THE KINGDOM OF SAVARIN 5

• NAMES: SOME PEOPLE HAVE PROBABLY ALREADY FIGURED THIS OUT, BUT...

THE KINGDOM OF SAVARIN: SAVARIN RICH YEAST CAKE IN A RING FORM (NAMED AFTER BRILLAT-SAVARIN, A FAMOUS 18TH-CENTURY FOOD WRITER) THAT'S SOAKED WITH RUM-FLAVORED SYRUP AND FILLED WITH PASTRY CREAM, CREME CHANTILLY OR FRESH FRUIT. (FROM DIANASDESSERTS.COM)
MIEL HONEY / RADI RADISH
SORRY I TOOK EVERYTHING FROM FOOD! THERE ARE OTHERS, DERIVED THE SAME WAY...SOME SMOOTHER FITS THAN OTHERS.

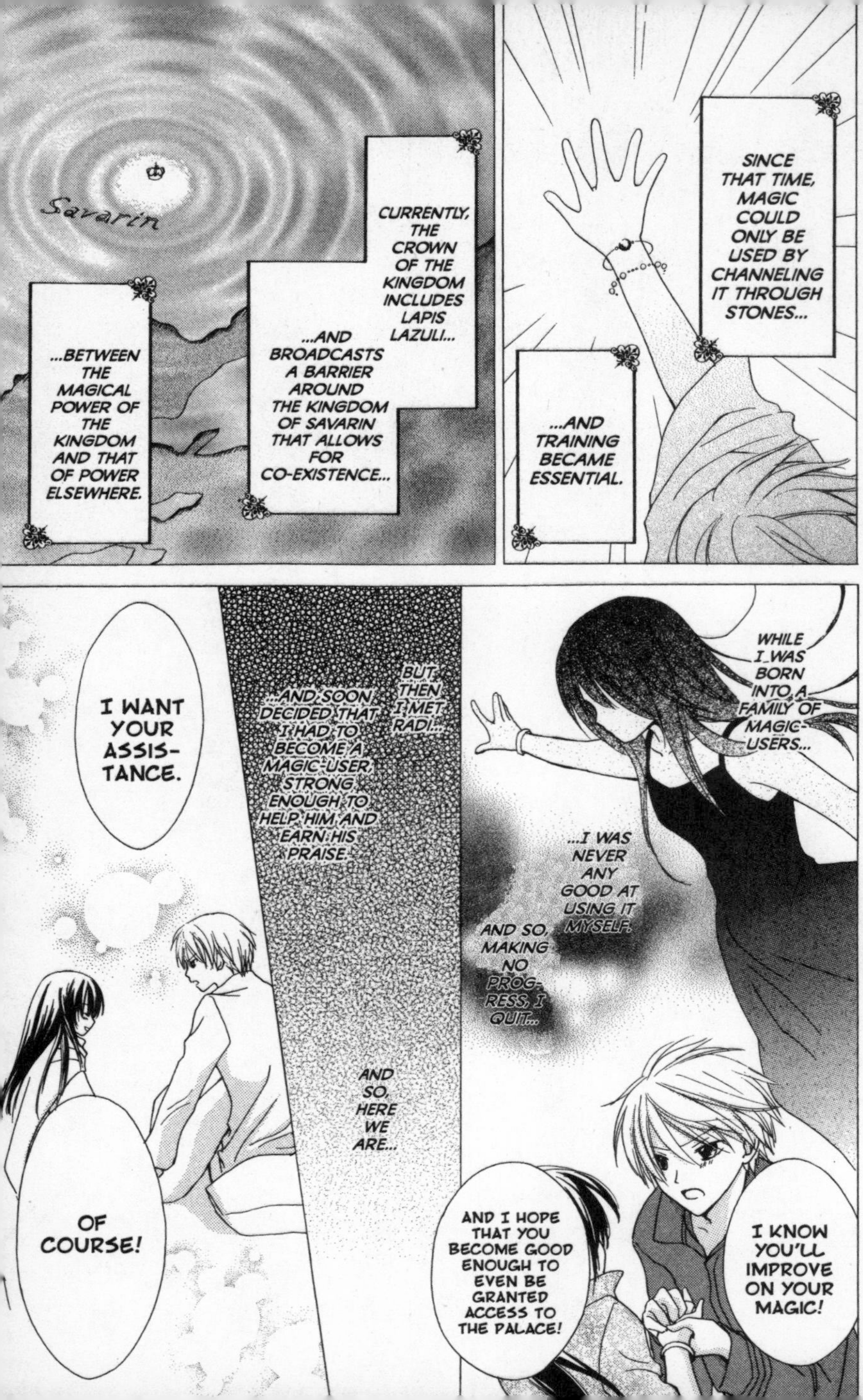
SINCE THAT TIME, MAGIC COULD ONLY BE USED BY CHANNELING IT THROUGH STONES...
...AND TRAINING BECAME ESSENTIAL.
Savarin
CURRENTLY, THE CROWN OF THE KINGDOM INCLUDES LAPIS LAZULI...
...AND BROADCASTS A BARRIER AROUND THE KINGDOM OF SAVARIN THAT ALLOWS FOR CO-EXISTENCE...
...BETWEEN THE MAGICAL POWER OF THE KINGDOM AND THAT OF POWER ELSEWHERE.
WHILE I WAS BORN INTO A FAMILY OF MAGIC-USERS...
...I WAS NEVER ANY GOOD AT USING IT MYSELF.
AND SO, MAKING NO PROG-RESS, I QUIT...
I KNOW YOU'LL IMPROVE ON YOUR MAGIC!
AND I HOPE THAT YOU BECOME GOOD ENOUGH TO EVEN BE GRANTED ACCESS TO THE PALACE!
BUT THEN I MET RADI...
...AND SOON DECIDED THAT I HAD TO BECOME A MAGIC-USER STRONG ENOUGH TO HELP HIM AND EARN HIS PRAISE.
AND SO, HERE WE ARE...
I WANT YOUR ASSIS-TANCE.
OF COURSE!

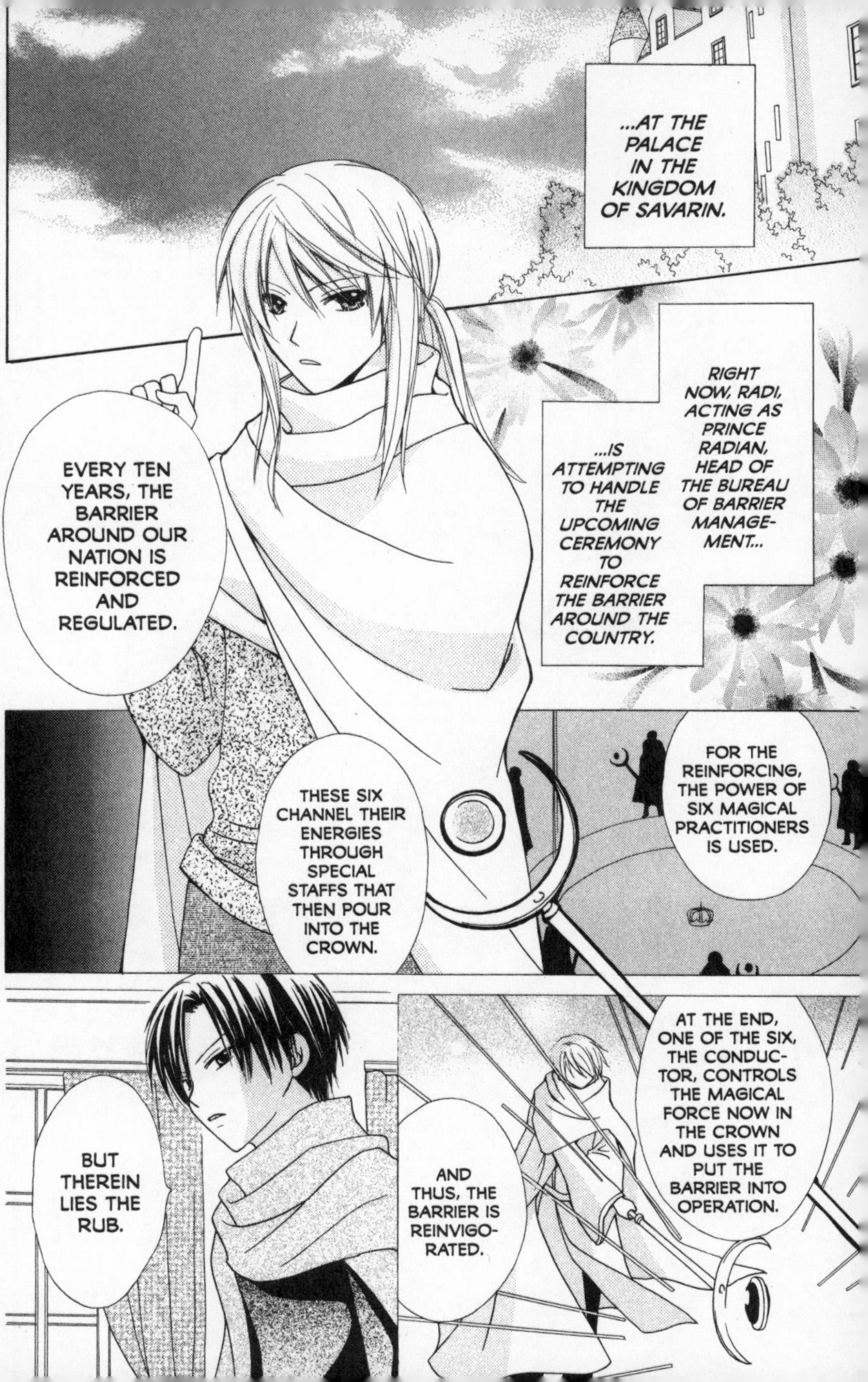
...AT THE PALACE IN THE KINGDOM OF SAVARIN.
RIGHT NOW, RADI, ACTING AS PRINCE RADIAN, HEAD OF THE BUREAU OF BARRIER MANAGE-MENT...
...IS ATTEMPTING TO HANDLE THE UPCOMING CEREMONY TO REINFORCE THE BARRIER AROUND THE COUNTRY.
EVERY TEN YEARS, THE BARRIER AROUND OUR NATION IS REINFORCED AND REGULATED.
FOR THE REINFORCING, THE POWER OF SIX MAGICAL PRACTITIONERS IS USED.
THESE SIX CHANNEL THEIR ENERGIES THROUGH SPECIAL STAFFS THAT THEN POUR INTO THE CROWN.
AT THE END, ONE OF THE SIX, THE CONDUC-TOR, CONTROLS THE MAGICAL FORCE NOW IN THE CROWN AND USES IT TO PUT THE BARRIER INTO OPERATION.
AND THUS, THE BARRIER IS REINVIGO-RATED.
BUT THEREIN LIES THE RUB.

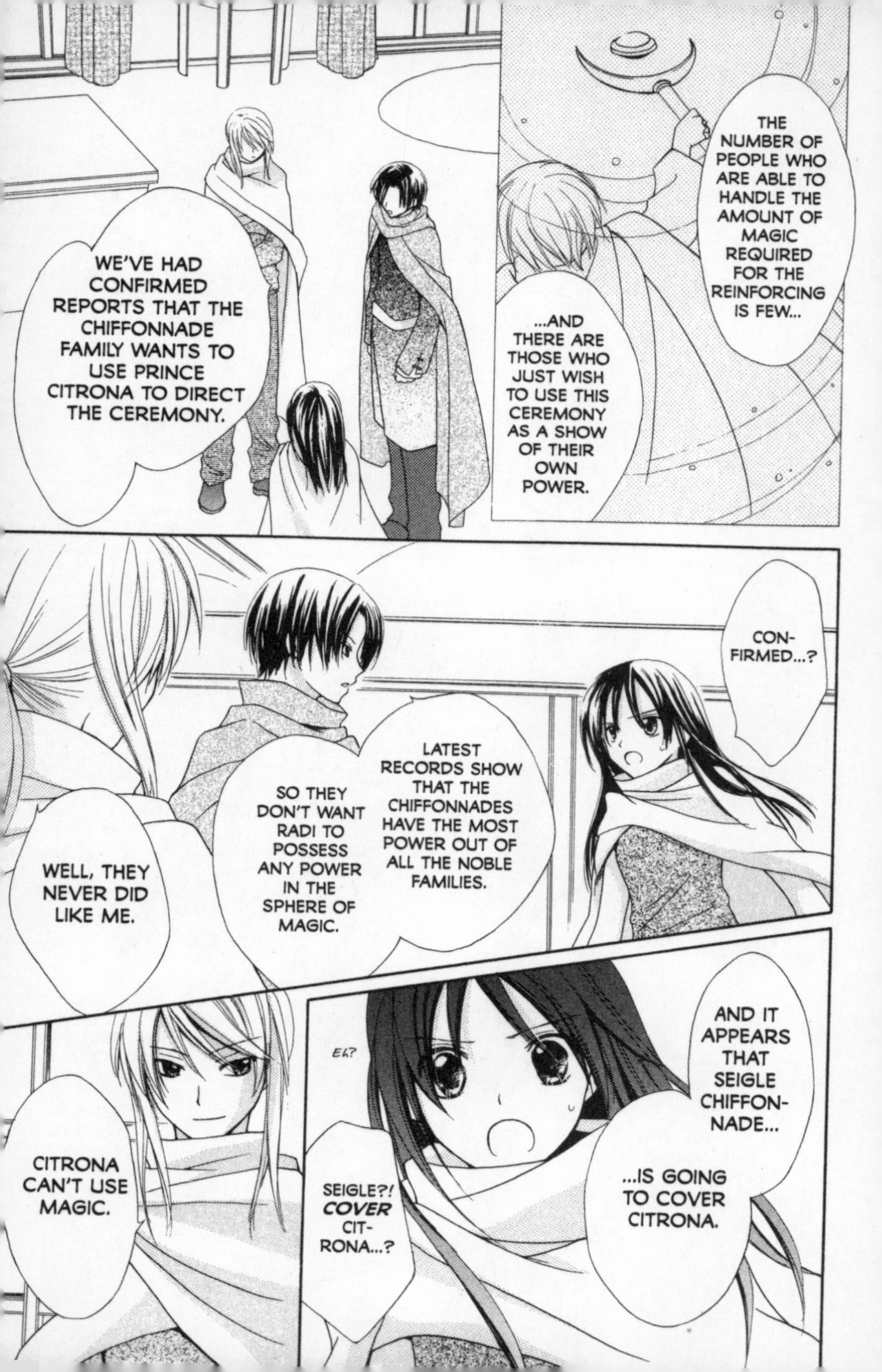
THE NUMBER OF PEOPLE WHO ARE ABLE TO HANDLE THE AMOUNT OF MAGIC REQUIRED FOR THE REINFORCING IS FEW...
...AND THERE ARE THOSE WHO JUST WISH TO USE THIS CEREMONY AS A SHOW OF THEIR OWN POWER.
WE'VE HAD CONFIRMED REPORTS THAT THE CHIFFONNADE FAMILY WANTS TO USE PRINCE CITRONA TO DIRECT THE CEREMONY.
CON-FIRMED...?
LATEST RECORDS SHOW THAT THE CHIFFONNADES HAVE THE MOST POWER OUT OF ALL THE NOBLE FAMILIES.
SO THEY DON'T WANT RADI TO POSSESS ANY POWER IN THE SPHERE OF MAGIC.
WELL, THEY NEVER DID LIKE ME.
AND IT APPEARS THAT SEIGLE CHIFFON-NADE...
Eh?
...IS GOING TO COVER CITRONA.
SEIGLE?! *COVER* CIT-RONA...?
CITRONA CAN'T USE MAGIC.

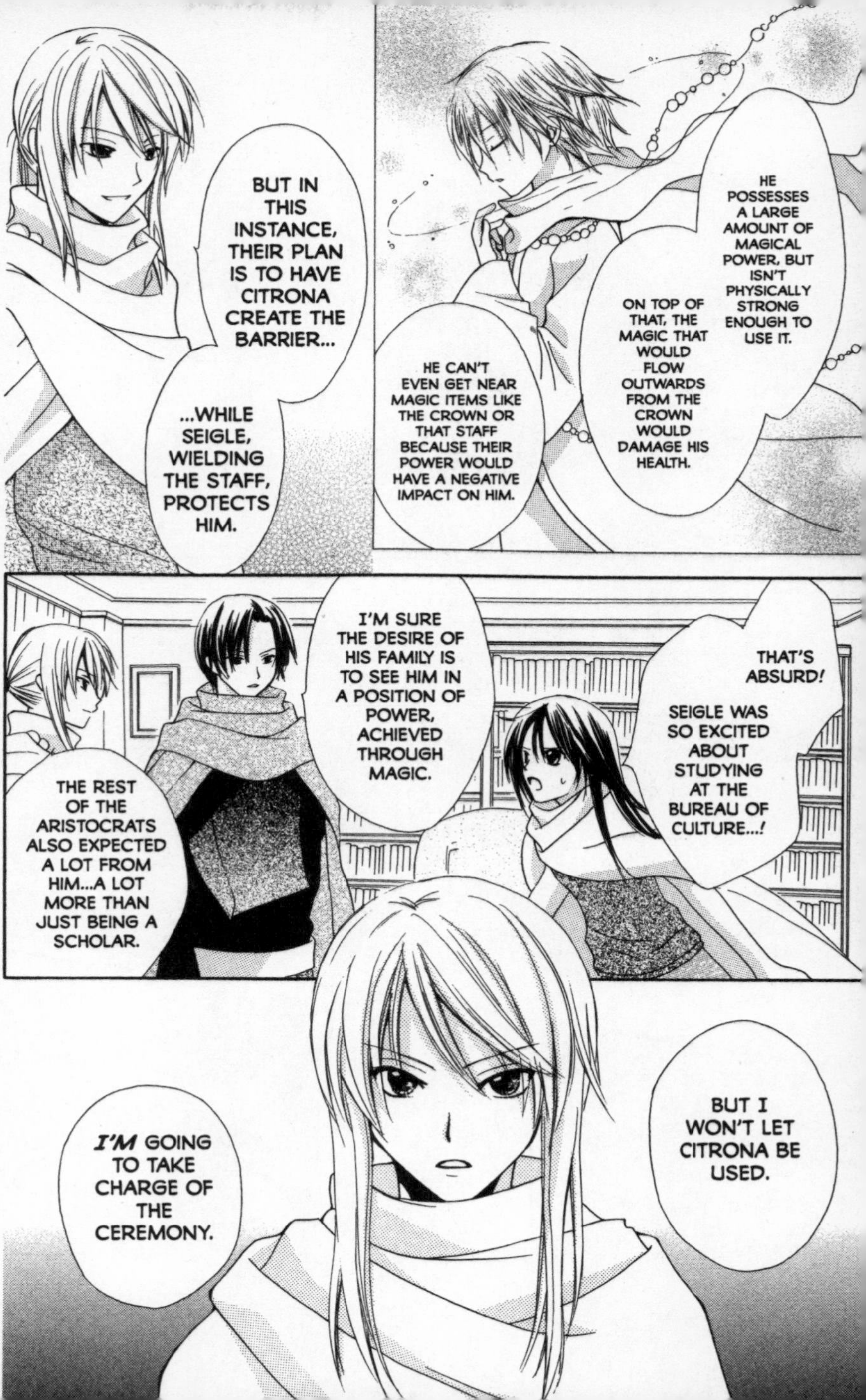
HE POSSESSES A LARGE AMOUNT OF MAGICAL POWER, BUT ISN'T PHYSICALLY STRONG ENOUGH TO USE IT.
ON TOP OF THAT, THE MAGIC THAT WOULD FLOW OUTWARDS FROM THE CROWN WOULD DAMAGE HIS HEALTH.
HE CAN'T EVEN GET NEAR MAGIC ITEMS LIKE THE CROWN OR THAT STAFF BECAUSE THEIR POWER WOULD HAVE A NEGATIVE IMPACT ON HIM.
BUT IN THIS INSTANCE, THEIR PLAN IS TO HAVE CITRONA CREATE THE BARRIER...
...WHILE SEIGLE, WIELDING THE STAFF, PROTECTS HIM.
THAT'S ABSURD!
SEIGLE WAS SO EXCITED ABOUT STUDYING AT THE BUREAU OF CULTURE...!
I'M SURE THE DESIRE OF HIS FAMILY IS TO SEE HIM IN A POSITION OF POWER, ACHIEVED THROUGH MAGIC.
THE REST OF THE ARISTOCRATS ALSO EXPECTED A LOT FROM HIM...A LOT MORE THAN JUST BEING A SCHOLAR.
BUT I WON'T LET CITRONA BE USED.
I'M GOING TO TAKE CHARGE OF THE CEREMONY.

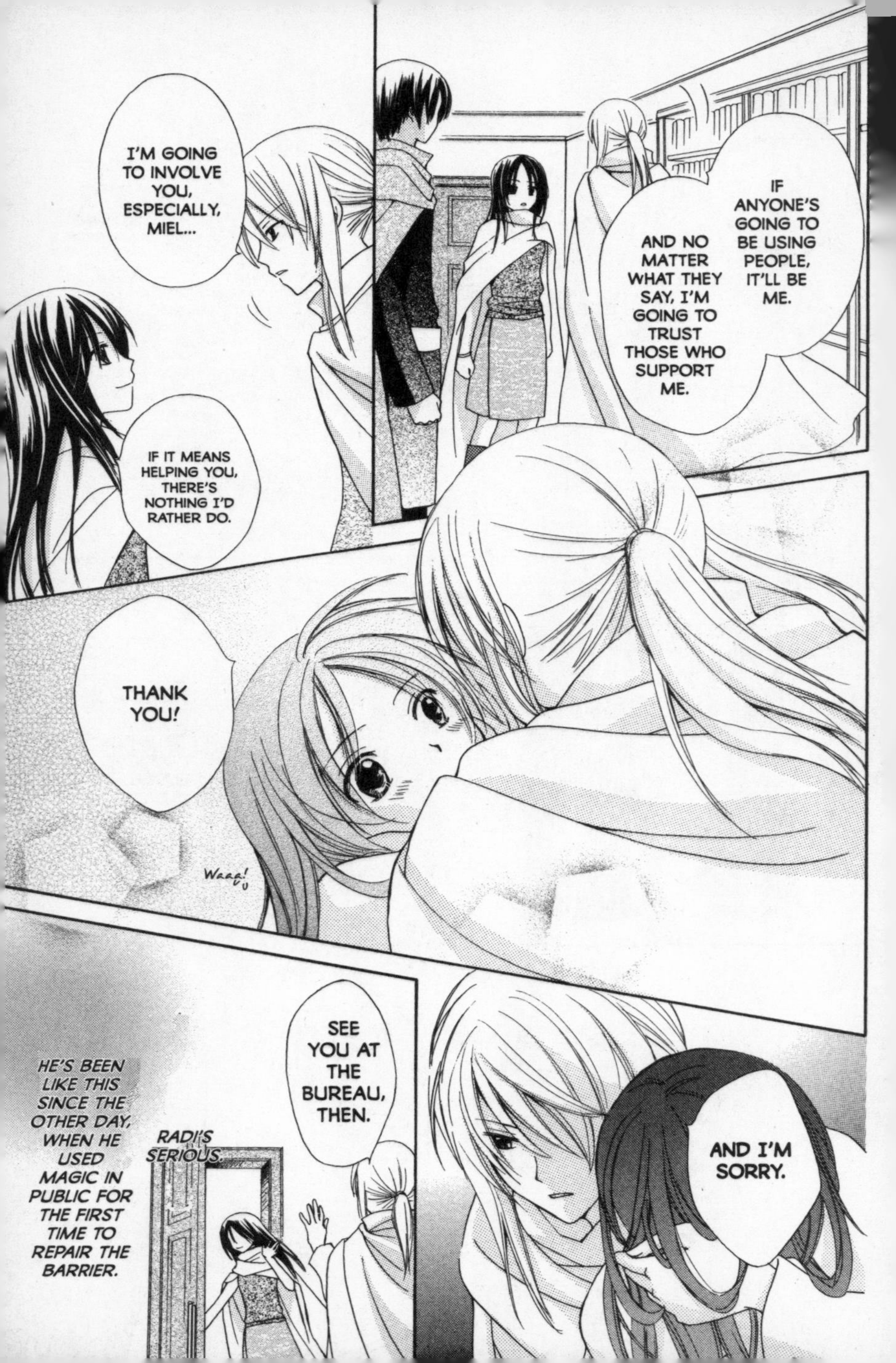
IF ANYONE'S GOING TO BE USING PEOPLE, IT'LL BE ME.
AND NO MATTER WHAT THEY SAY, I'M GOING TO TRUST THOSE WHO SUPPORT ME.
I'M GOING TO INVOLVE YOU, ESPECIALLY, MIEL...
IF IT MEANS HELPING YOU, THERE'S NOTHING I'D RATHER DO.
THANK YOU!
Waaa!
AND I'M SORRY.
SEE YOU AT THE BUREAU, THEN.
RADI'S SERIOUS.
HE'S BEEN LIKE THIS SINCE THE OTHER DAY, WHEN HE USED MAGIC IN PUBLIC FOR THE FIRST TIME TO REPAIR THE BARRIER.

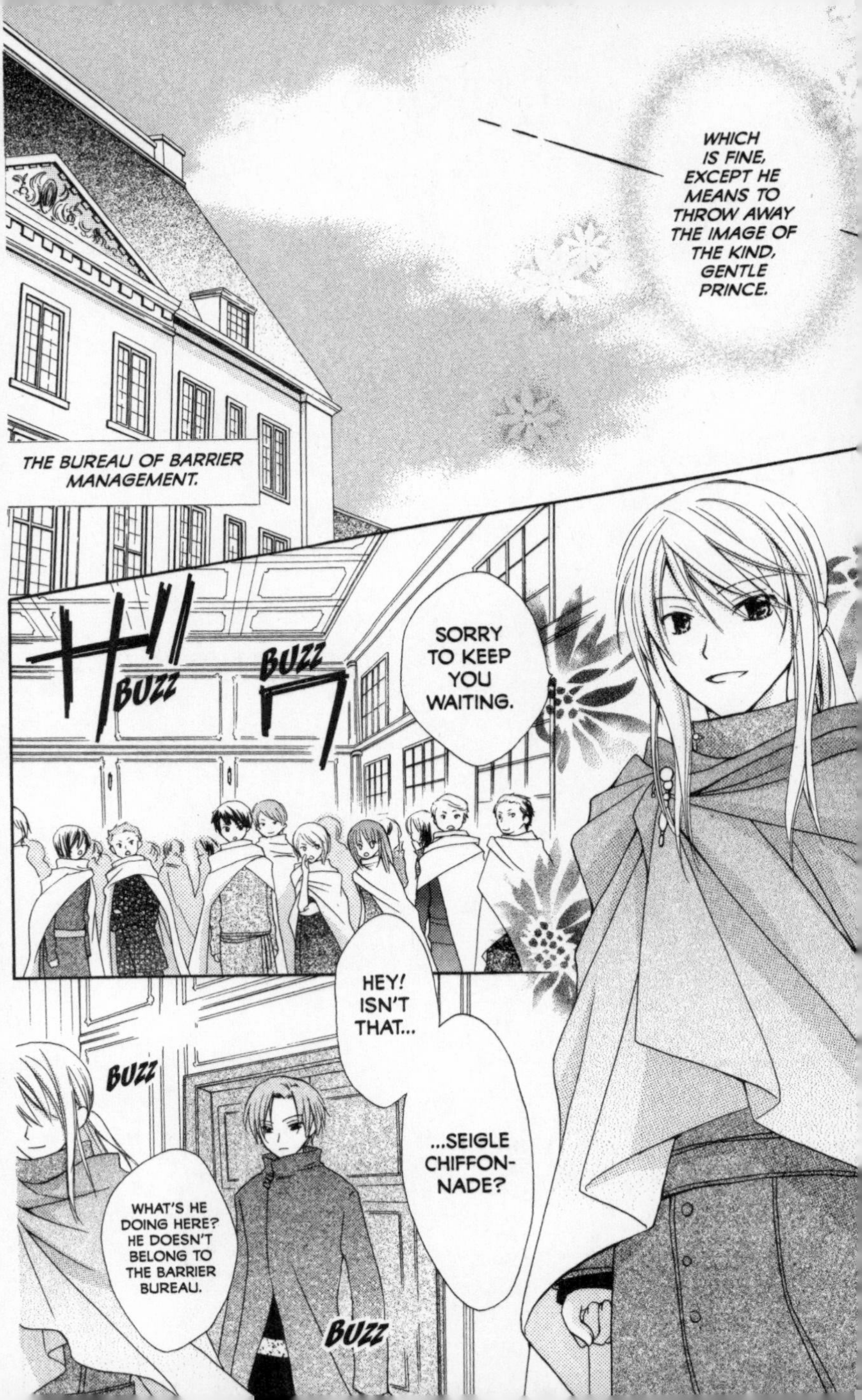
WHICH IS FINE, EXCEPT HE MEANS TO THROW AWAY THE IMAGE OF THE KIND, GENTLE PRINCE.
THE BUREAU OF BARRIER MANAGEMENT.
SORRY TO KEEP YOU WAITING.
BUZZ
BUZZ
HEY! ISN'T THAT...
...SEIGLE CHIFFON-NADE?
BUZZ
WHAT'S HE DOING HERE? HE DOESN'T BELONG TO THE BARRIER BUREAU.
BUZZ

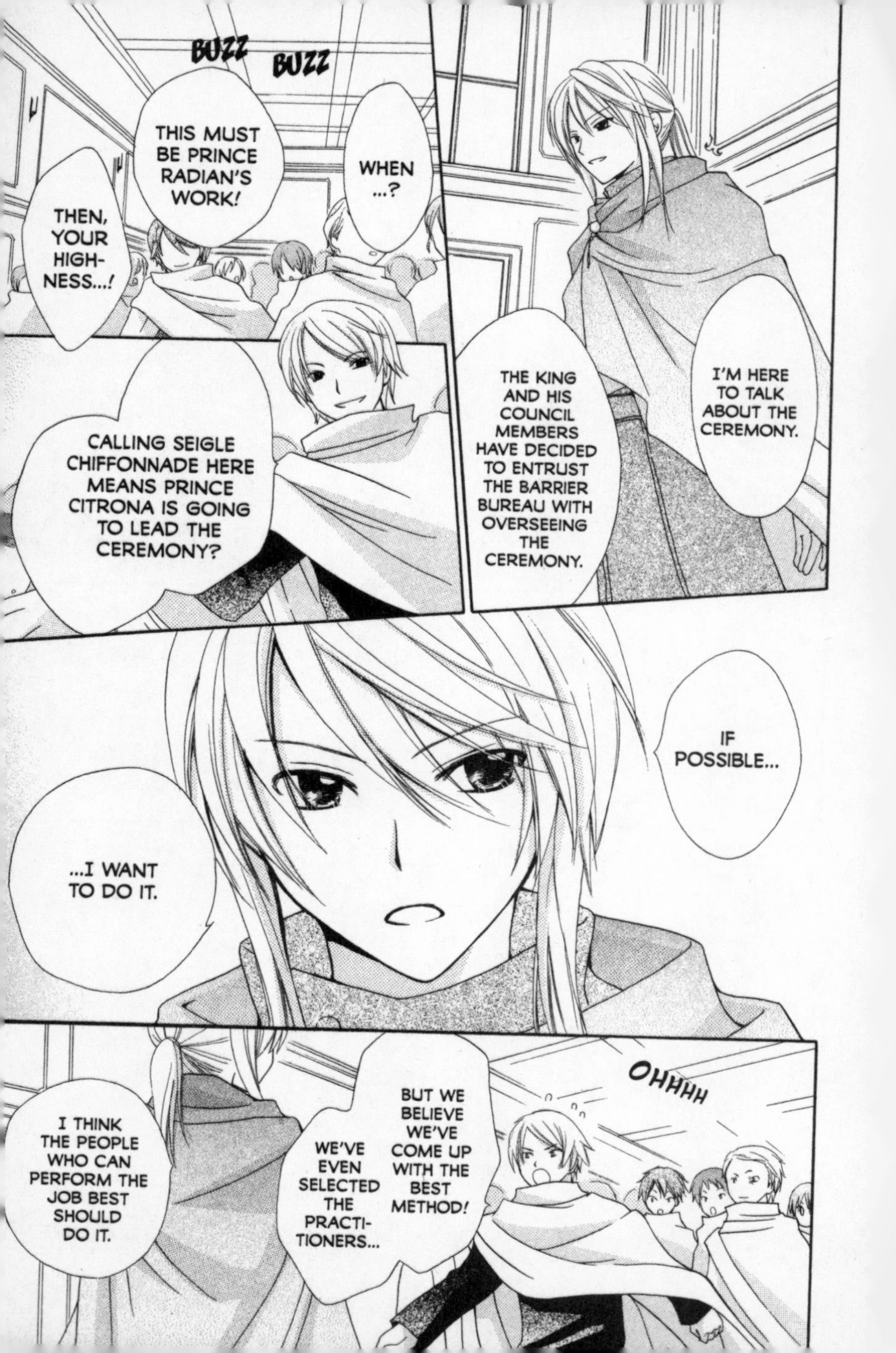

I'M HERE TO TALK ABOUT THE CEREMONY.
THE KING AND HIS COUNCIL MEMBERS HAVE DECIDED TO ENTRUST THE BARRIER BUREAU WITH OVERSEEING THE CEREMONY.
BUZZ
BUZZ
WHEN ...?
THIS MUST BE PRINCE RADIAN'S WORK!
THEN, YOUR HIGH-NESS...!
CALLING SEIGLE CHIFFONNADE HERE MEANS PRINCE CITRONA IS GOING TO LEAD THE CEREMONY?
IF POSSIBLE...
...I WANT TO DO IT.
OHHHH
BUT WE BELIEVE WE'VE COME UP WITH THE BEST METHOD!
WE'VE EVEN SELECTED THE PRACTI-TIONERS...
I THINK THE PEOPLE WHO CAN PERFORM THE JOB BEST SHOULD DO IT.

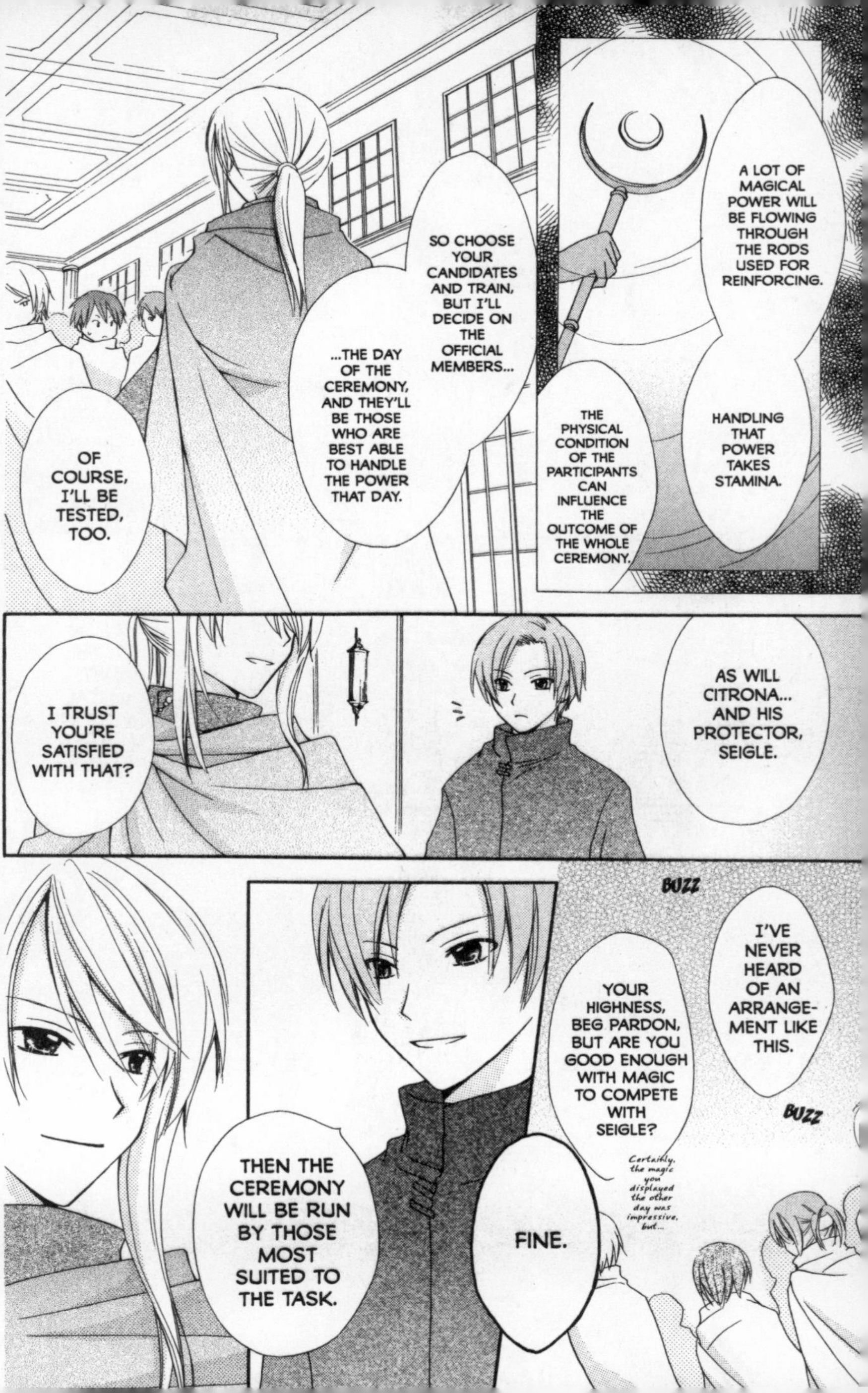
A LOT OF MAGICAL POWER WILL BE FLOWING THROUGH THE RODS USED FOR REINFORCING.
HANDLING THAT POWER TAKES STAMINA.
THE PHYSICAL CONDITION OF THE PARTICIPANTS CAN INFLUENCE THE OUTCOME OF THE WHOLE CEREMONY.
SO CHOOSE YOUR CANDIDATES AND TRAIN, BUT I'LL DECIDE ON THE OFFICIAL MEMBERS...
...THE DAY OF THE CEREMONY, AND THEY'LL BE THOSE WHO ARE BEST ABLE TO HANDLE THE POWER THAT DAY.
OF COURSE, I'LL BE TESTED, TOO.
AS WILL CITRONA... AND HIS PROTECTOR, SEIGLE.
I TRUST YOU'RE SATISFIED WITH THAT?
BUZZ
I'VE NEVER HEARD OF AN ARRANGE-MENT LIKE THIS.
YOUR HIGHNESS, BEG PARDON, BUT ARE YOU GOOD ENOUGH WITH MAGIC TO COMPETE WITH SEIGLE?
BUZZ
Certainly, the magic you displayed the other day was impressive, but...
FINE.
THEN THE CEREMONY WILL BE RUN BY THOSE MOST SUITED TO THE TASK.

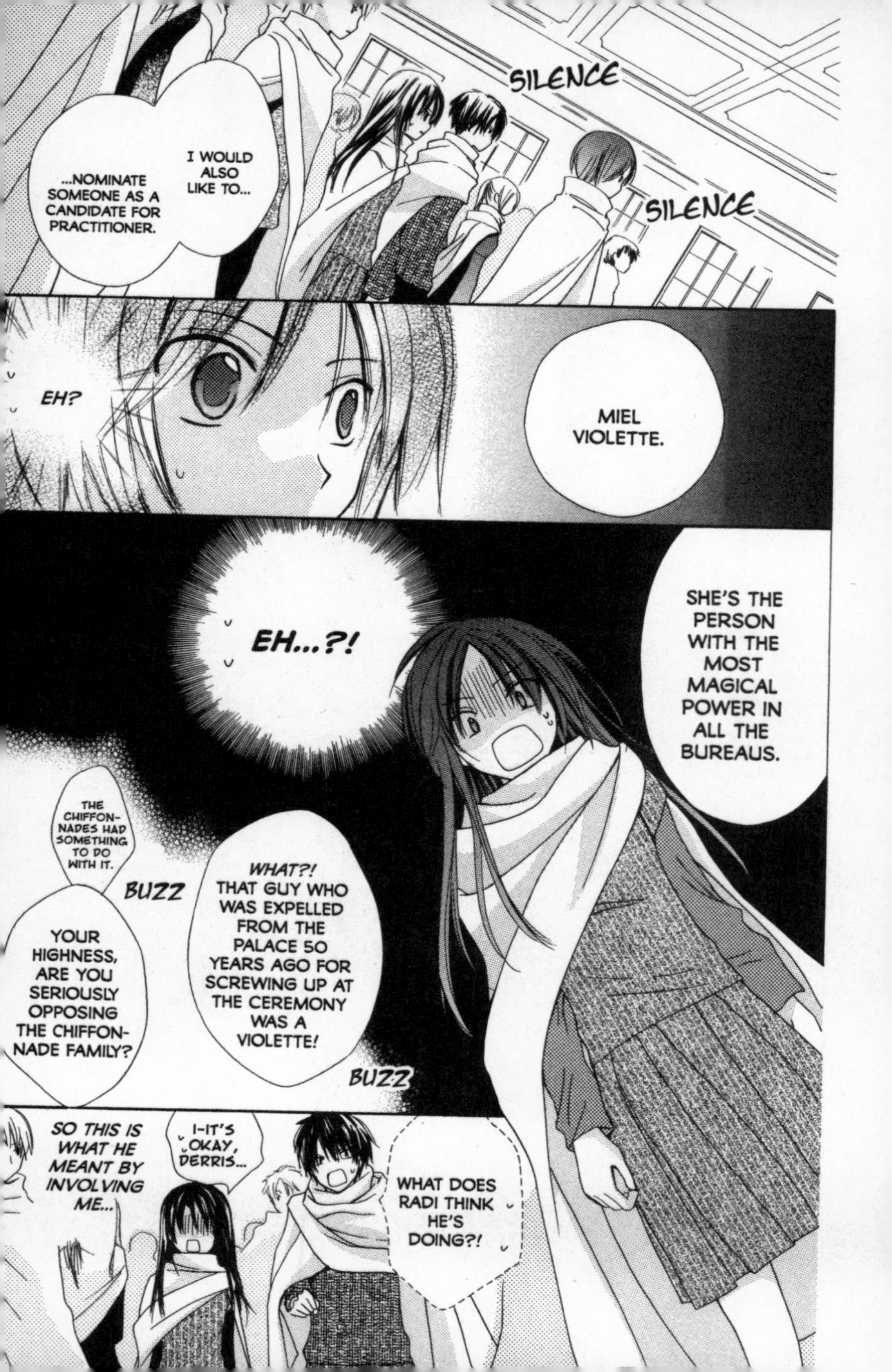
SILENCE
SILENCE
I WOULD ALSO LIKE TO...
...NOMINATE SOMEONE AS A CANDIDATE FOR PRACTITIONER.
MIEL VIOLETTE.
EH?
SHE'S THE PERSON WITH THE MOST MAGICAL POWER IN ALL THE BUREAUS.
EH...?!
WHAT?! THAT GUY WHO WAS EXPELLED FROM THE PALACE 50 YEARS AGO FOR SCREWING UP AT THE CEREMONY WAS A VIOLETTE!
BUZZ
THE CHIFFONNADES HAD SOMETHING TO DO WITH IT.
BUZZ
YOUR HIGHNESS, ARE YOU SERIOUSLY OPPOSING THE CHIFFONNADE FAMILY?
WHAT DOES RADI THINK HE'S DOING?!
I-IT'S OKAY, DERRIS...
SO THIS IS WHAT HE MEANT BY INVOLVING ME...

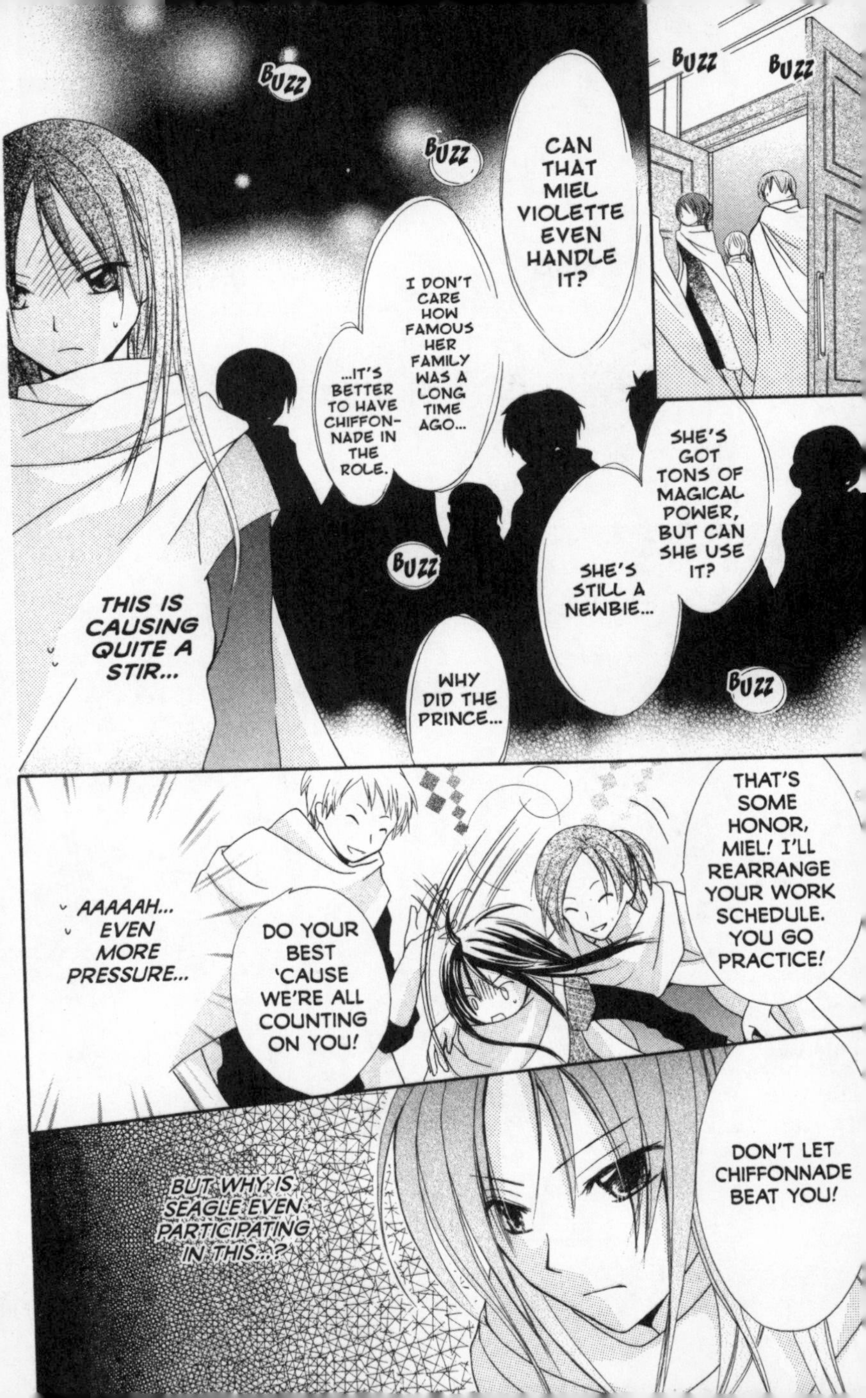
BUZZ
BUZZ
CAN THAT MIEL VIOLETTE EVEN HANDLE IT?
BUZZ
BUZZ
I DON'T CARE HOW FAMOUS HER FAMILY WAS A LONG TIME AGO...
...IT'S BETTER TO HAVE CHIFFONNADE IN THE ROLE.
SHE'S GOT TONS OF MAGICAL POWER, BUT CAN SHE USE IT?
SHE'S STILL A NEWBIE...
BUZZ
WHY DID THE PRINCE...
BUZZ
THIS IS CAUSING QUITE A STIR...
THAT'S SOME HONOR, MIEL! I'LL REARRANGE YOUR WORK SCHEDULE. YOU GO PRACTICE!
DO YOUR BEST 'CAUSE WE'RE ALL COUNTING ON YOU!
AAAAAH... EVEN MORE PRESSURE...
DON'T LET CHIFFONNADE BEAT YOU!
BUT WHY IS SEAGLE EVEN PARTICIPATING IN THIS...?

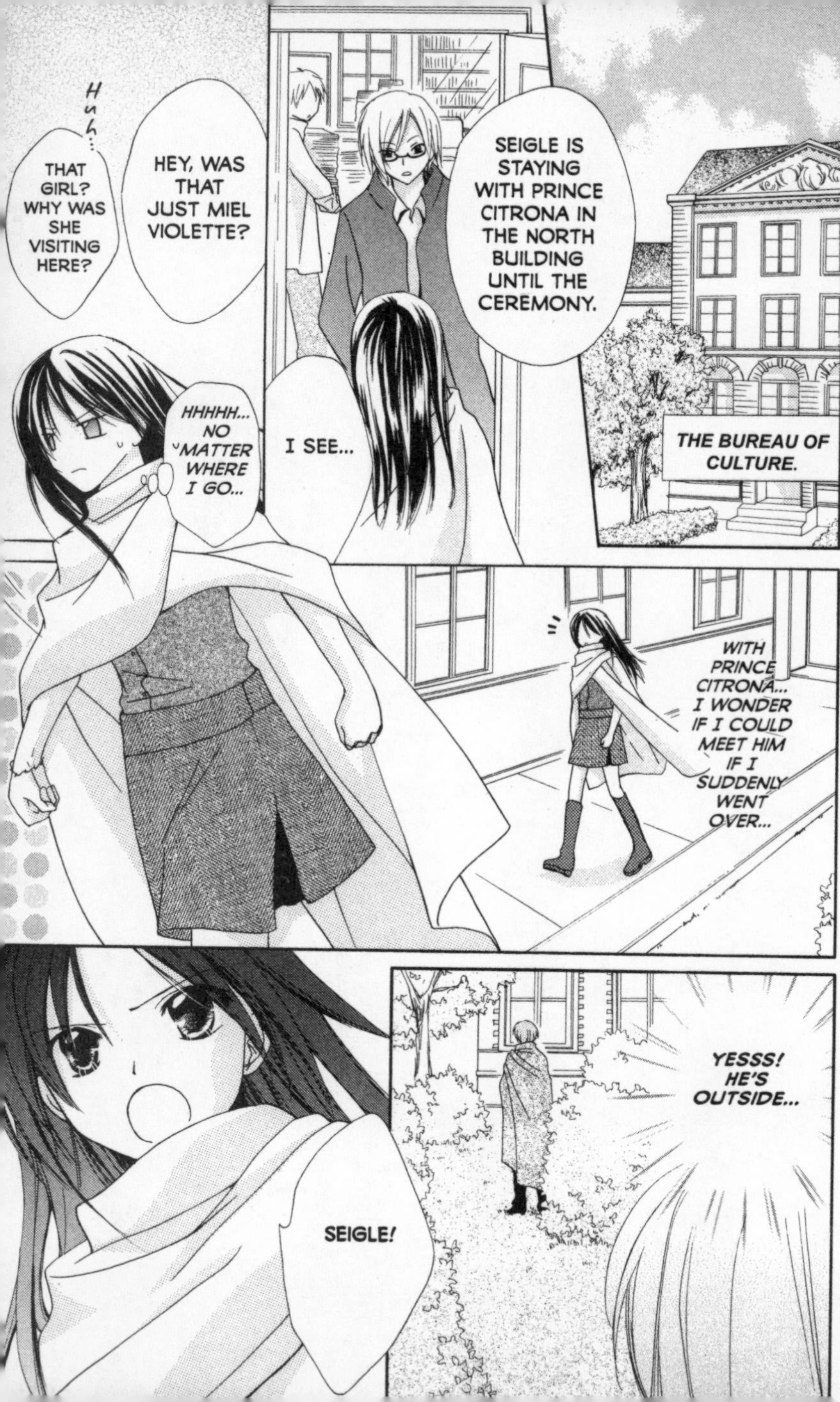
THE BUREAU OF CULTURE.
SEIGLE IS STAYING WITH PRINCE CITRONA IN THE NORTH BUILDING UNTIL THE CEREMONY.
I SEE...
HEY, WAS THAT JUST MIEL VIOLETTE?
Huh... THAT GIRL? WHY WAS SHE VISITING HERE?
HHHHH... NO MATTER WHERE I GO...
WITH PRINCE CITRONA... I WONDER IF I COULD MEET HIM IF I SUDDENLY WENT OVER...
YESSS! HE'S OUTSIDE...
SEIGLE!

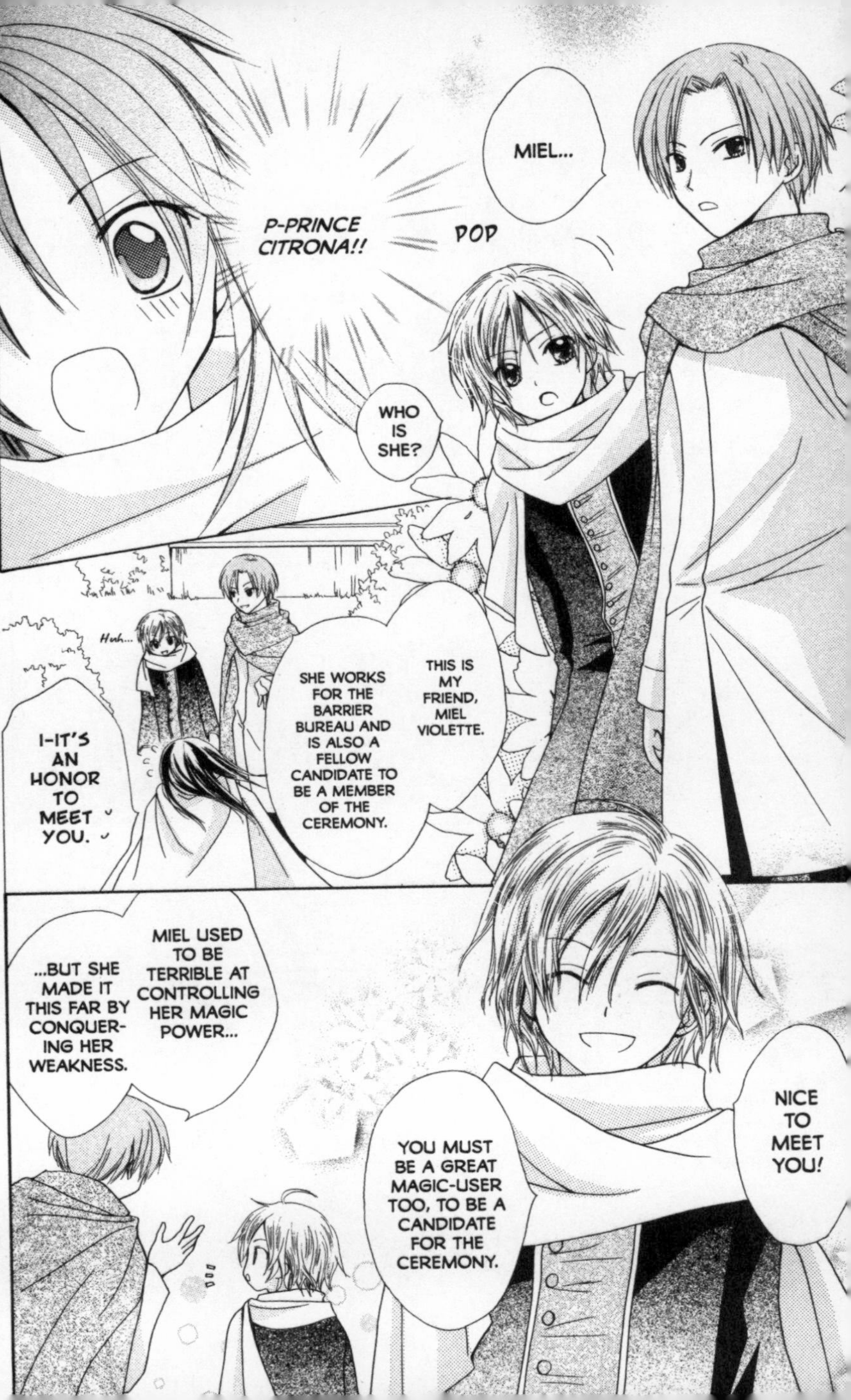
MIEL...
POP
P-PRINCE CITRONA!!
WHO IS SHE?
THIS IS MY FRIEND, MIEL VIOLETTE.
SHE WORKS FOR THE BARRIER BUREAU AND IS ALSO A FELLOW CANDIDATE TO BE A MEMBER OF THE CEREMONY.
Huh...
I-IT'S AN HONOR TO MEET YOU.
NICE TO MEET YOU!
YOU MUST BE A GREAT MAGIC-USER TOO, TO BE A CANDIDATE FOR THE CEREMONY.
MIEL USED TO BE TERRIBLE AT CONTROLLING HER MAGIC POWER...
...BUT SHE MADE IT THIS FAR BY CONQUERING HER WEAKNESS.

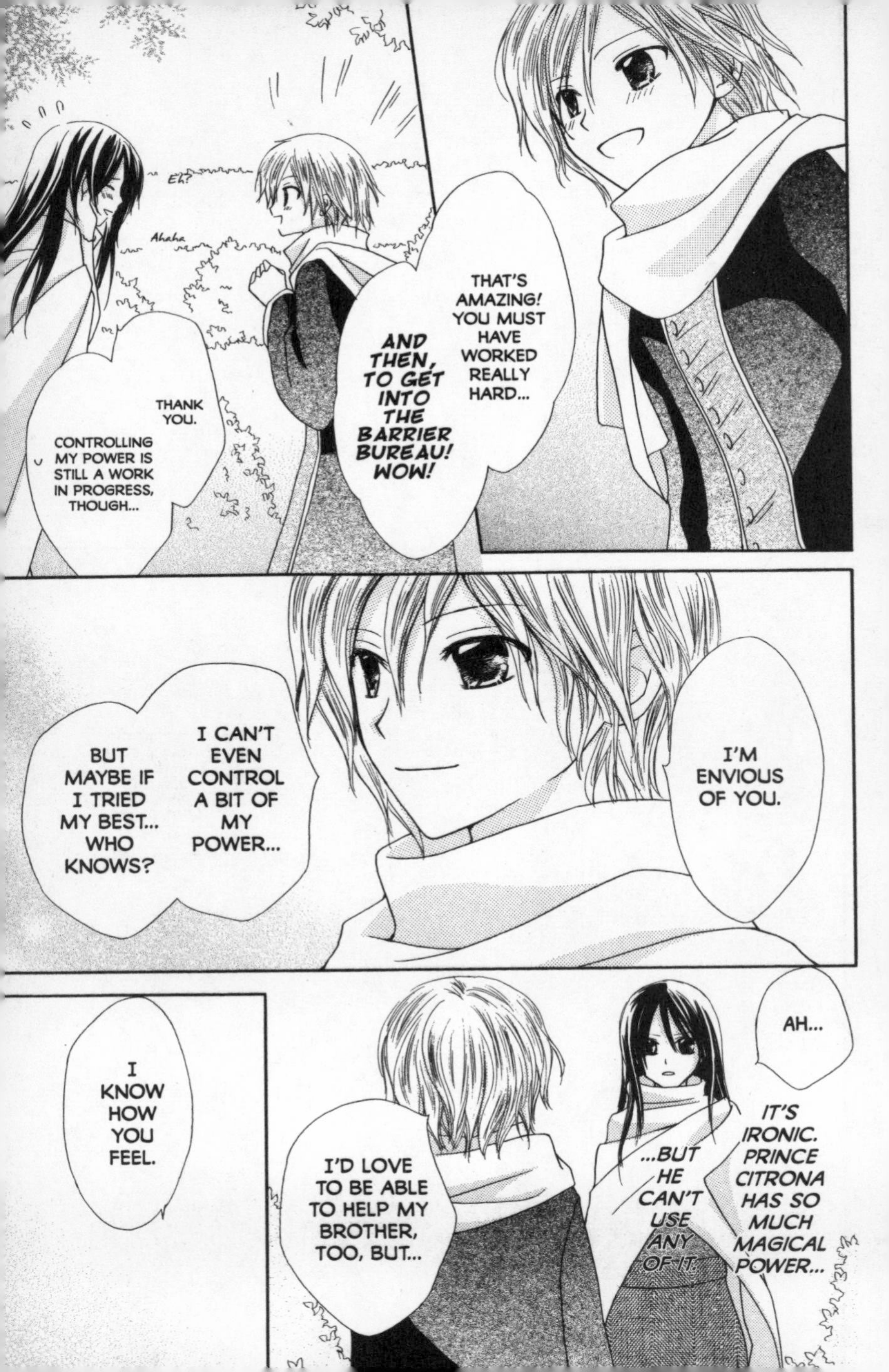
THAT'S AMAZING! YOU MUST HAVE WORKED REALLY HARD...
AND THEN, TO GET INTO THE BARRIER BUREAU! WOW!
Eh?
Ahaha
THANK YOU.
CONTROLLING MY POWER IS STILL A WORK IN PROGRESS, THOUGH...
I'M ENVIOUS OF YOU.
I CAN'T EVEN CONTROL A BIT OF MY POWER...
BUT MAYBE IF I TRIED MY BEST... WHO KNOWS?
AH...
IT'S IRONIC. PRINCE CITRONA HAS SO MUCH MAGICAL POWER...
...BUT HE CAN'T USE ANY OF IT.
I'D LOVE TO BE ABLE TO HELP MY BROTHER, TOO, BUT...
I KNOW HOW YOU FEEL.

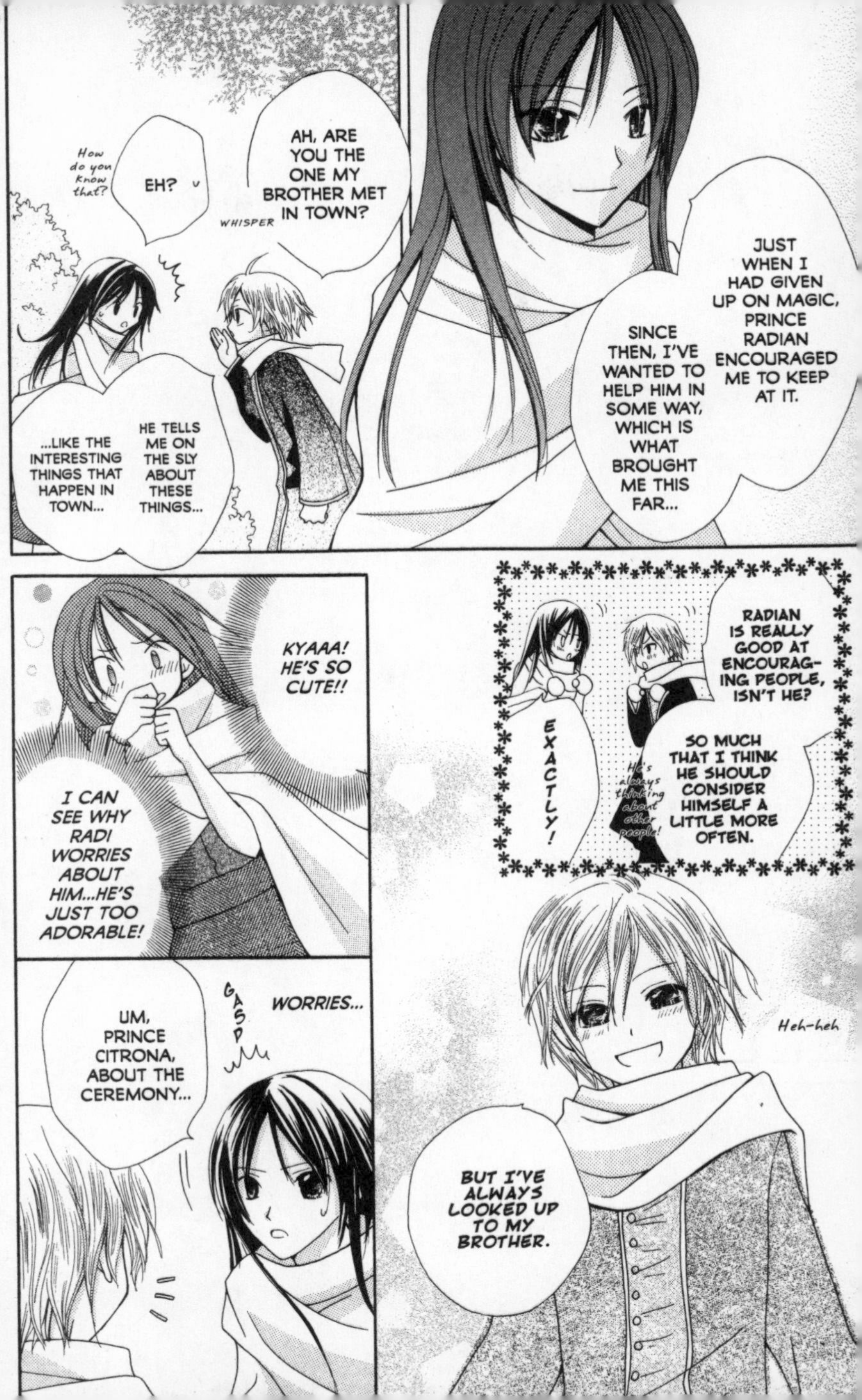
JUST WHEN I HAD GIVEN UP ON MAGIC, PRINCE RADIAN ENCOURAGED ME TO KEEP AT IT.
SINCE THEN, I'VE WANTED TO HELP HIM IN SOME WAY, WHICH IS WHAT BROUGHT ME THIS FAR...
AH, ARE YOU THE ONE MY BROTHER MET IN TOWN?
WHISPER
EH?
How do you know that?
HE TELLS ME ON THE SLY ABOUT THESE THINGS...
...LIKE THE INTERESTING THINGS THAT HAPPEN IN TOWN...
RADIAN IS REALLY GOOD AT ENCOURAG-ING PEOPLE, ISN'T HE?
EXACTLY!
SO MUCH THAT I THINK HE SHOULD CONSIDER HIMSELF A LITTLE MORE OFTEN.
He's always thinking about other people!
Heh-heh
BUT I'VE ALWAYS LOOKED UP TO MY BROTHER.
KYAAA! HE'S SO CUTE!!
I CAN SEE WHY RADI WORRIES ABOUT HIM...HE'S JUST TOO ADORABLE!
WORRIES...
GASP
UM, PRINCE CITRONA, ABOUT THE CEREMONY...

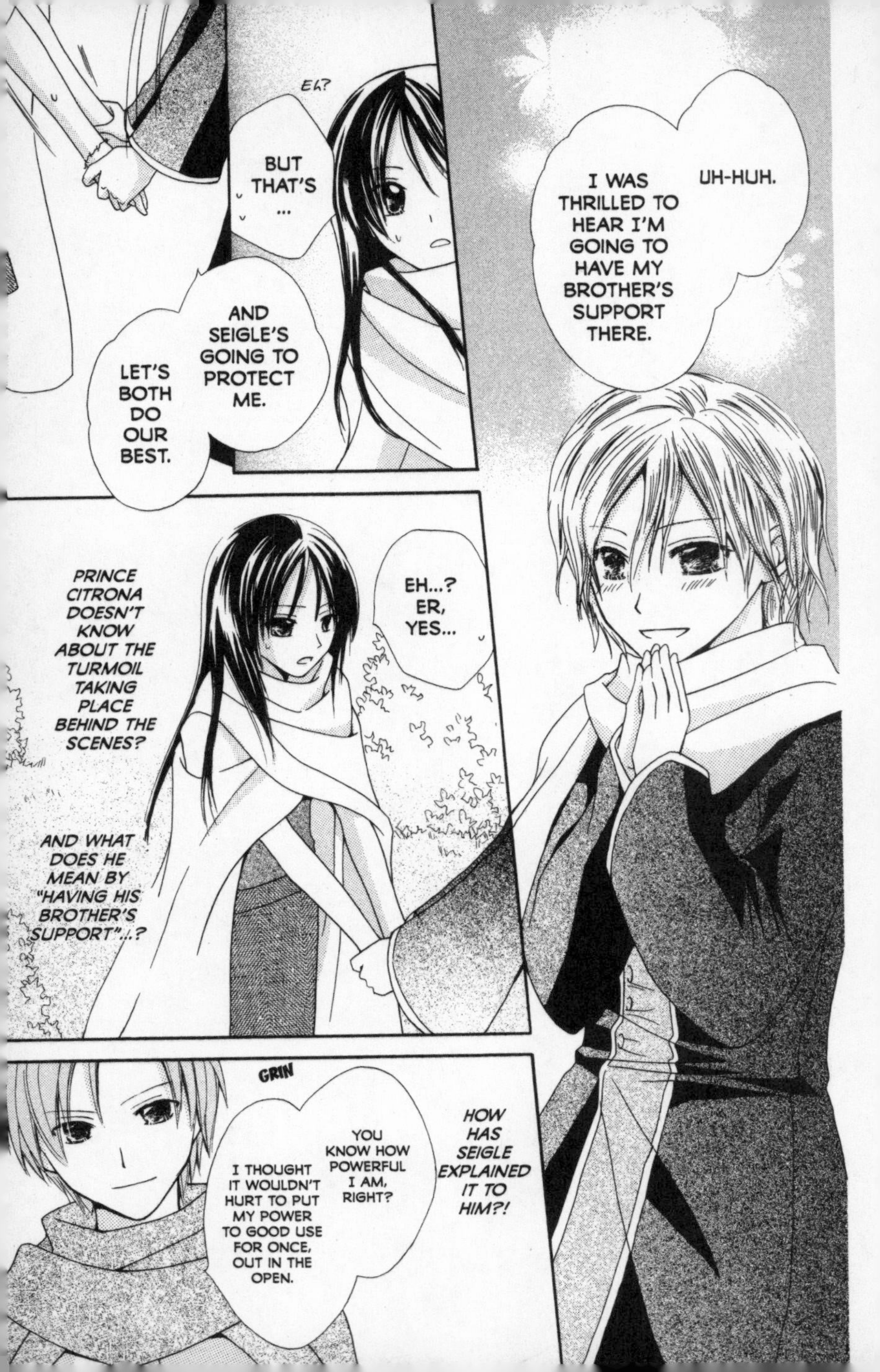
UH-HUH.
I WAS THRILLED TO HEAR I'M GOING TO HAVE MY BROTHER'S SUPPORT THERE.
EH?
BUT THAT'S ...
AND SEIGLE'S GOING TO PROTECT ME.
LET'S BOTH DO OUR BEST.
EH...? ER, YES...
PRINCE CITRONA DOESN'T KNOW ABOUT THE TURMOIL TAKING PLACE BEHIND THE SCENES?
AND WHAT DOES HE MEAN BY "HAVING HIS BROTHER'S SUPPORT"...?
HOW HAS SEIGLE EXPLAINED IT TO HIM?!
GRIN
YOU KNOW HOW POWERFUL I AM, RIGHT?
I THOUGHT IT WOULDN'T HURT TO PUT MY POWER TO GOOD USE FOR ONCE, OUT IN THE OPEN.

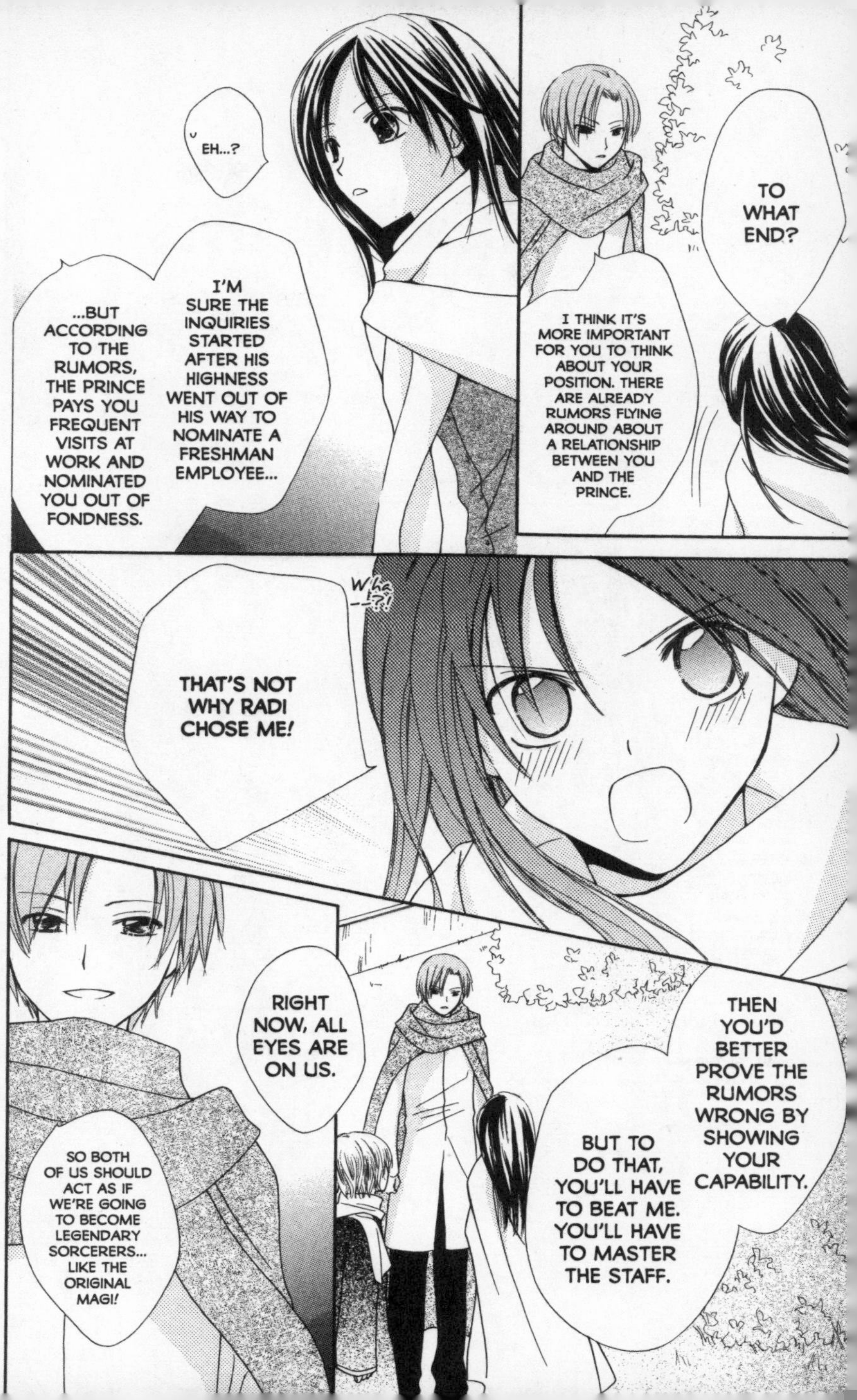
TO WHAT END?
I THINK IT'S MORE IMPORTANT FOR YOU TO THINK ABOUT YOUR POSITION. THERE ARE ALREADY RUMORS FLYING AROUND ABOUT A RELATIONSHIP BETWEEN YOU AND THE PRINCE.
EH...?
I'M SURE THE INQUIRIES STARTED AFTER HIS HIGHNESS WENT OUT OF HIS WAY TO NOMINATE A FRESHMAN EMPLOYEE...
...BUT ACCORDING TO THE RUMORS, THE PRINCE PAYS YOU FREQUENT VISITS AT WORK AND NOMINATED YOU OUT OF FONDNESS.
Wha--!?!
THAT'S NOT WHY RADI CHOSE ME!
THEN YOU'D BETTER PROVE THE RUMORS WRONG BY SHOWING YOUR CAPABILITY.
BUT TO DO THAT, YOU'LL HAVE TO BEAT ME. YOU'LL HAVE TO MASTER THE STAFF.
RIGHT NOW, ALL EYES ARE ON US.
SO BOTH OF US SHOULD ACT AS IF WE'RE GOING TO BECOME LEGENDARY SORCERERS... LIKE THE ORIGINAL MAGI!

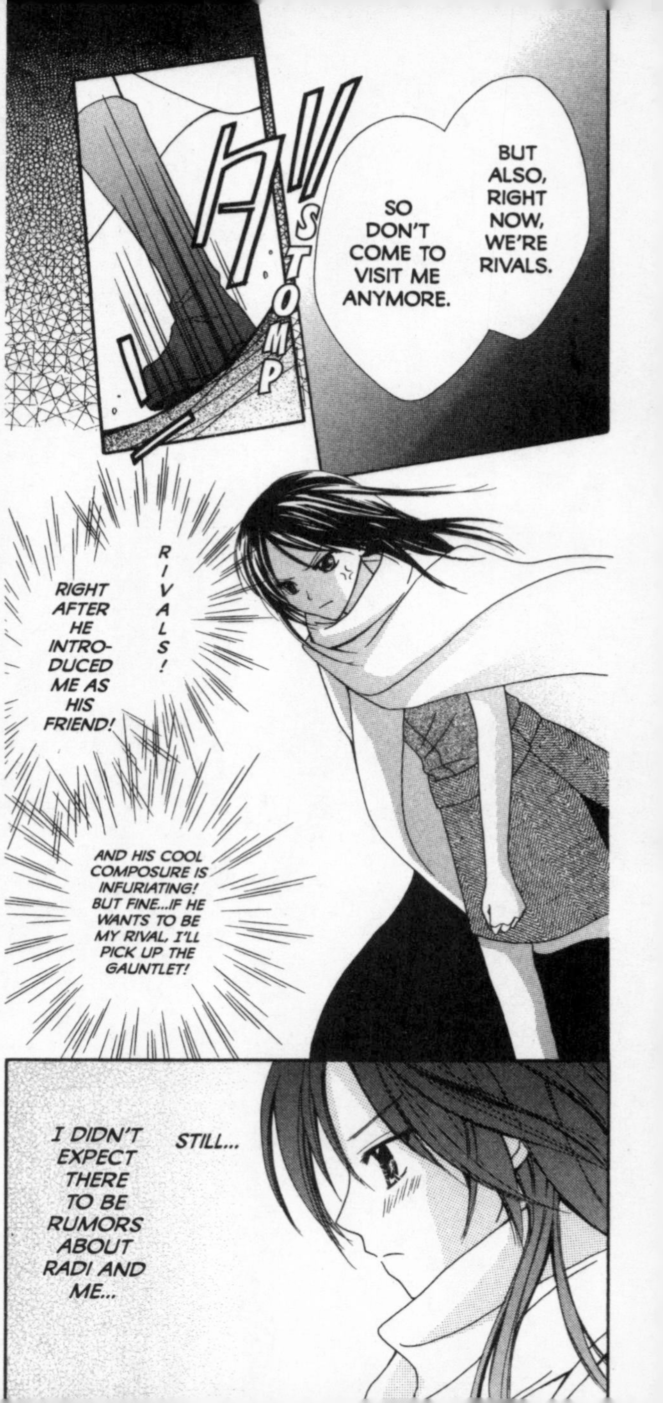
BUT ALSO, RIGHT NOW, WE'RE RIVALS.
SO DON'T COME TO VISIT ME ANYMORE.
STOMP
RIVALS!
RIGHT AFTER HE INTRODUCED ME AS HIS FRIEND!
AND HIS COOL COMPOSURE IS INFURIATING! BUT FINE...IF HE WANTS TO BE MY RIVAL, I'LL PICK UP THE GAUNTLET!
STILL...
I DIDN'T EXPECT THERE TO BE RUMORS ABOUT RADI AND ME...

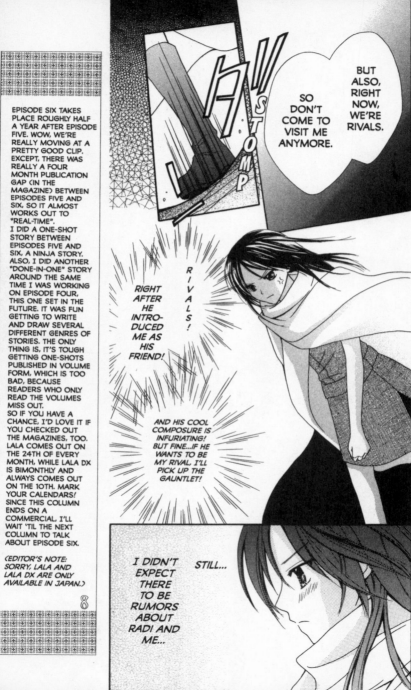

EPISODE SIX TAKES PLACE ROUGHLY HALF A YEAR AFTER EPISODE FIVE. WOW, WE'RE REALLY MOVING AT A PRETTY GOOD CLIP. EXCEPT, THERE WAS REALLY A FOUR MONTH PUBLICATION GAP (IN THE MAGAZINE) BETWEEN EPISODES FIVE AND SIX, SO IT ALMOST WORKS OUT TO "REAL-TIME".
I DID A ONE-SHOT STORY BETWEEN EPISODES FIVE AND SIX, A NINJA STORY. ALSO, I DID ANOTHER "DONE-IN-ONE" STORY AROUND THE SAME TIME I WAS WORKING ON EPISODE FOUR, THIS ONE SET IN THE FUTURE. IT WAS FUN GETTING TO WRITE AND DRAW SEVERAL DIFFERENT GENRES OF STORIES. THE ONLY THING IS, IT'S TOUGH GETTING ONE-SHOTS PUBLISHED IN VOLUME FORM, WHICH IS TOO BAD, BECAUSE READERS WHO ONLY READ THE VOLUMES MISS OUT.
SO IF YOU HAVE A CHANCE, I'D LOVE IT IF YOU CHECKED OUT THE MAGAZINES, TOO. LALA COMES OUT ON THE 24TH OF EVERY MONTH, WHILE LALA DX IS BIMONTHLY AND ALWAYS COMES OUT ON THE 10TH. MARK YOUR CALENDARS! SINCE THIS COLUMN ENDS ON A COMMERCIAL, I'LL WAIT 'TIL THE NEXT COLUMN TO TALK ABOUT EPISODE SIX.

(EDITOR'S NOTE: SORRY, LALA AND LALA DX ARE ONLY AVAILABLE IN JAPAN.)

8

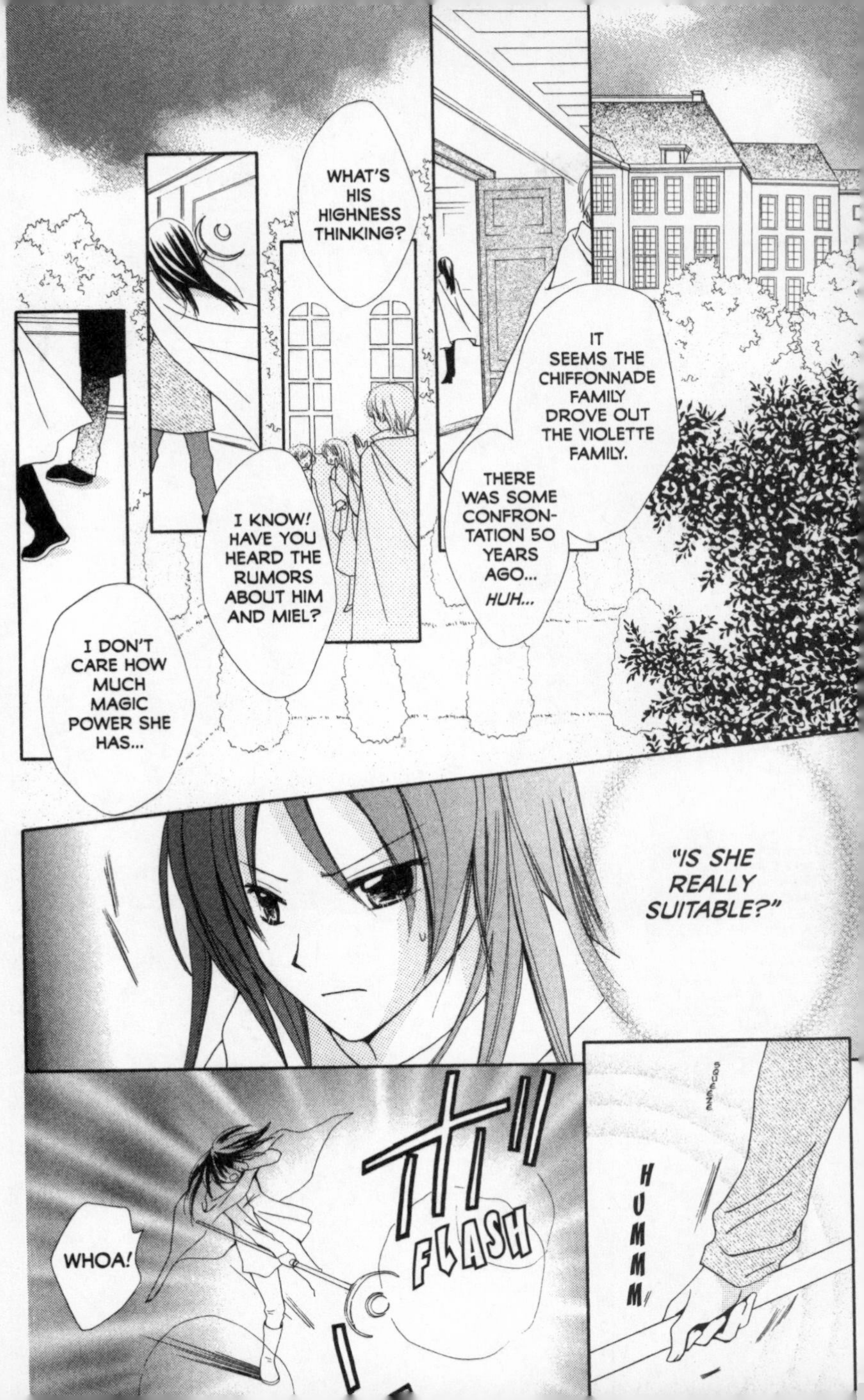
IT SEEMS THE CHIFFONNADE FAMILY DROVE OUT THE VIOLETTE FAMILY.
THERE WAS SOME CONFRON-TATION 50 YEARS AGO... *HUH...*
WHAT'S HIS HIGHNESS THINKING?
I KNOW! HAVE YOU HEARD THE RUMORS ABOUT HIM AND MIEL?
I DON'T CARE HOW MUCH MAGIC POWER SHE HAS...
"IS SHE REALLY SUITABLE?"
HUMMM
FLASH
WHOA!

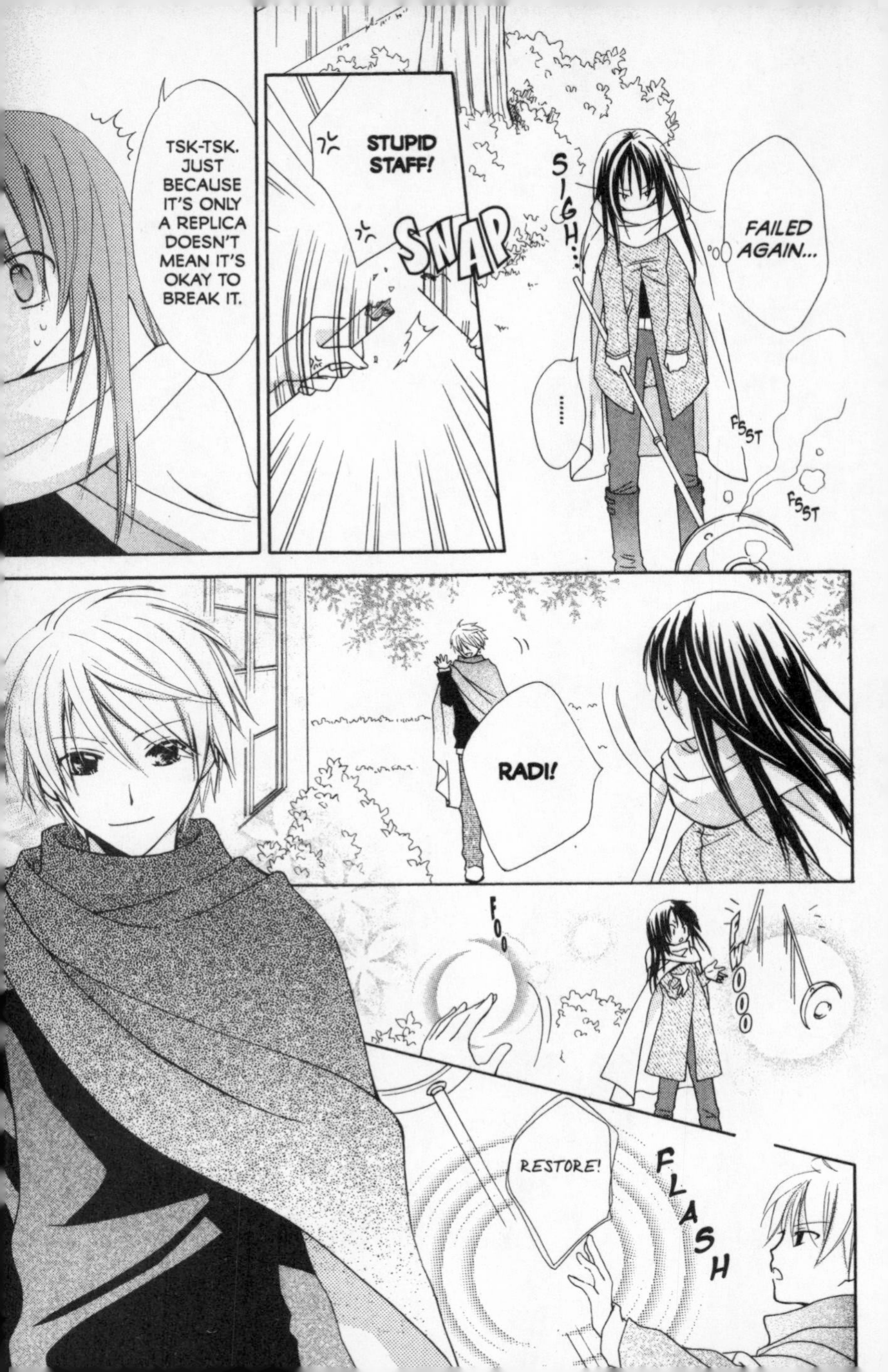
FAILED AGAIN...
SIGH...
......
FSST
FSST
STUPID STAFF!
SNAP
TSK-TSK. JUST BECAUSE IT'S ONLY A REPLICA DOESN'T MEAN IT'S OKAY TO BREAK IT.
RADI!
FOO
OOOO
RESTORE!
FLASH

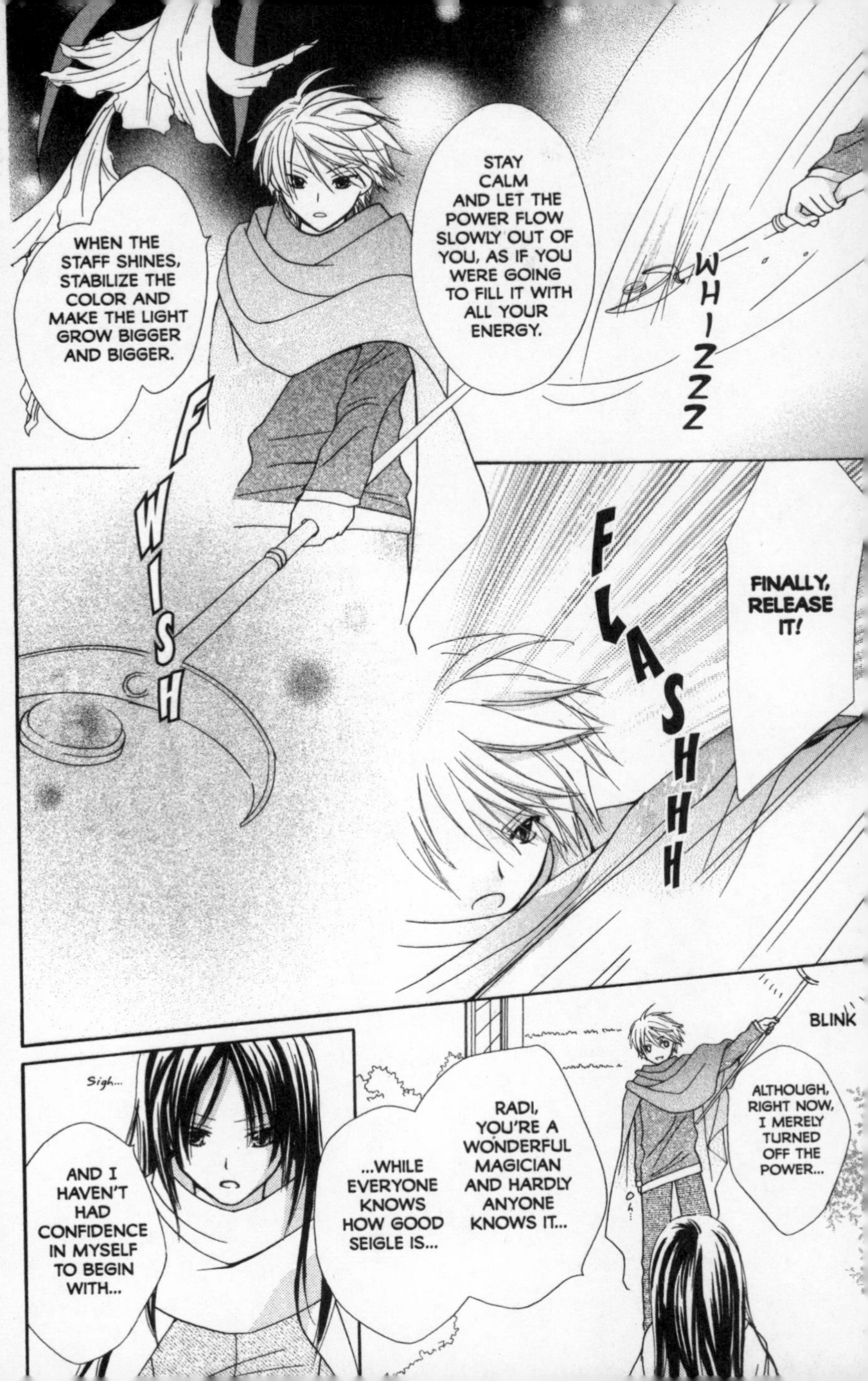
WHIZZZ
STAY CALM AND LET THE POWER FLOW SLOWLY OUT OF YOU, AS IF YOU WERE GOING TO FILL IT WITH ALL YOUR ENERGY.
WHEN THE STAFF SHINES, STABILIZE THE COLOR AND MAKE THE LIGHT GROW BIGGER AND BIGGER.
FWISH
FLASHHH
FINALLY, RELEASE IT!
BLINK
ALTHOUGH, RIGHT NOW, I MERELY TURNED OFF THE POWER...
Oh...
RADI, YOU'RE A WONDERFUL MAGICIAN AND HARDLY ANYONE KNOWS IT...
...WHILE EVERYONE KNOWS HOW GOOD SEIGLE IS...
Sigh...
AND I HAVEN'T HAD CONFIDENCE IN MYSELF TO BEGIN WITH...

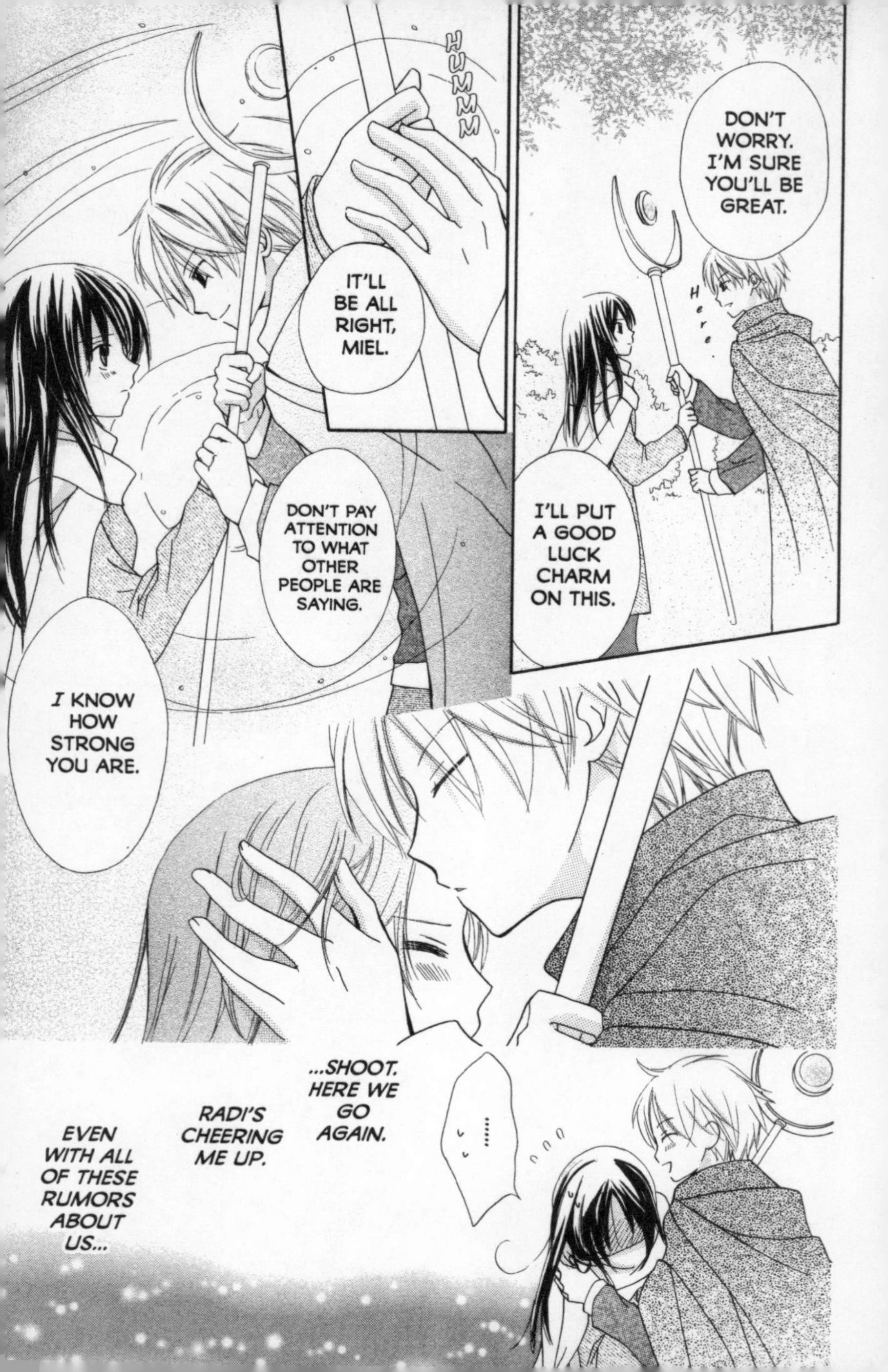
DON'T WORRY. I'M SURE YOU'LL BE GREAT.
Here
I'LL PUT A GOOD LUCK CHARM ON THIS.
HUMMM
IT'LL BE ALL RIGHT, MIEL.
DON'T PAY ATTENTION TO WHAT OTHER PEOPLE ARE SAYING.
I KNOW HOW STRONG YOU ARE.
......
...SHOOT. HERE WE GO AGAIN.
RADI'S CHEERING ME UP.
EVEN WITH ALL OF THESE RUMORS ABOUT US...

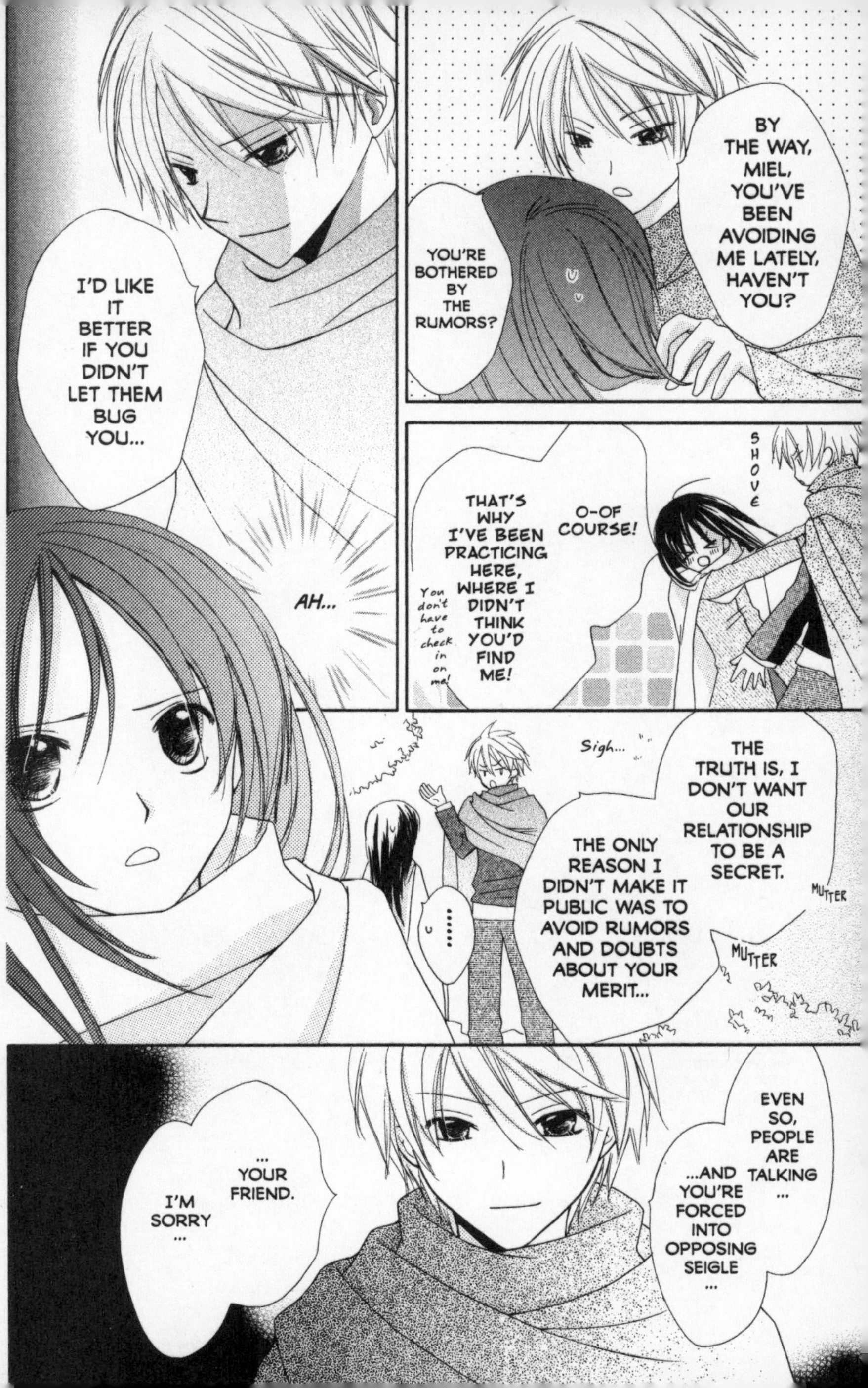
BY THE WAY, MIEL, YOU'VE BEEN AVOIDING ME LATELY, HAVEN'T YOU?
YOU'RE BOTHERED BY THE RUMORS?
SHOVE
O-OF COURSE!
THAT'S WHY I'VE BEEN PRACTICING HERE, WHERE I DIDN'T THINK YOU'D FIND ME!
You don't have to check in on me!
Sigh...
THE TRUTH IS, I DON'T WANT OUR RELATIONSHIP TO BE A SECRET.
MUTTER
THE ONLY REASON I DIDN'T MAKE IT PUBLIC WAS TO AVOID RUMORS AND DOUBTS ABOUT YOUR MERIT...
MUTTER
......
I'D LIKE IT BETTER IF YOU DIDN'T LET THEM BUG YOU...
AH...
EVEN SO, PEOPLE ARE TALKING...
...AND YOU'RE FORCED INTO OPPOSING SEIGLE...
... YOUR FRIEND.
I'M SORRY ...

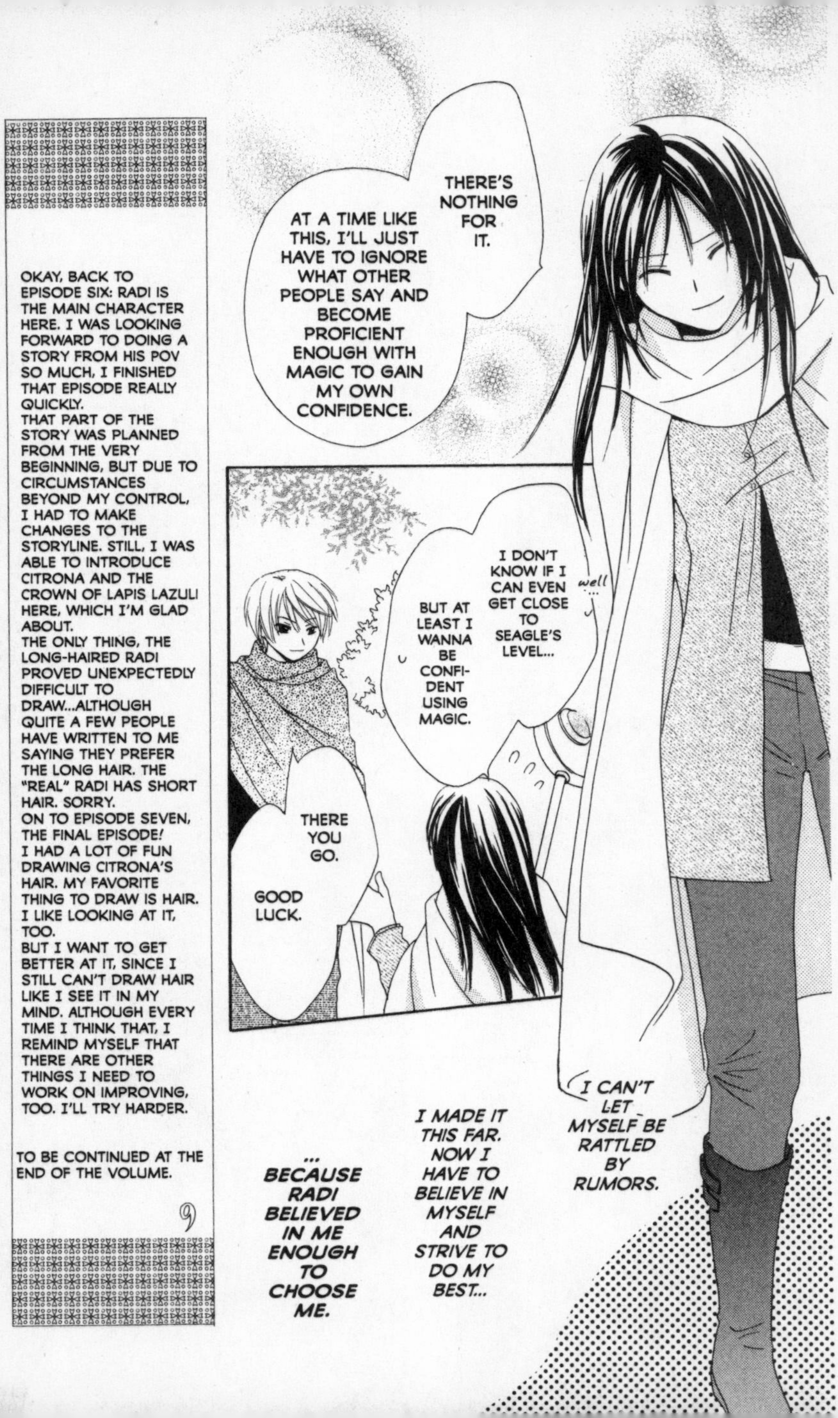
THERE'S NOTHING FOR IT.
AT A TIME LIKE THIS, I'LL JUST HAVE TO IGNORE WHAT OTHER PEOPLE SAY AND BECOME PROFICIENT ENOUGH WITH MAGIC TO GAIN MY OWN CONFIDENCE.
I DON'T KNOW IF I CAN EVEN GET CLOSE TO SEAGLE'S LEVEL...
well...
BUT AT LEAST I WANNA BE CONFIDENT USING MAGIC.
THERE YOU GO.
GOOD LUCK.
I CAN'T LET MYSELF BE RATTLED BY RUMORS.
I MADE IT THIS FAR. NOW I HAVE TO BELIEVE IN MYSELF AND STRIVE TO DO MY BEST...
...BECAUSE RADI BELIEVED IN ME ENOUGH TO CHOOSE ME.

OKAY, BACK TO EPISODE SIX: RADI IS THE MAIN CHARACTER HERE. I WAS LOOKING FORWARD TO DOING A STORY FROM HIS POV SO MUCH, I FINISHED THAT EPISODE REALLY QUICKLY.
THAT PART OF THE STORY WAS PLANNED FROM THE VERY BEGINNING, BUT DUE TO CIRCUMSTANCES BEYOND MY CONTROL, I HAD TO MAKE CHANGES TO THE STORYLINE. STILL, I WAS ABLE TO INTRODUCE CITRONA AND THE CROWN OF LAPIS LAZULI HERE, WHICH I'M GLAD ABOUT.
THE ONLY THING, THE LONG-HAIRED RADI PROVED UNEXPECTEDLY DIFFICULT TO DRAW...ALTHOUGH QUITE A FEW PEOPLE HAVE WRITTEN TO ME SAYING THEY PREFER THE LONG HAIR. THE "REAL" RADI HAS SHORT HAIR. SORRY.
ON TO EPISODE SEVEN, THE FINAL EPISODE!
I HAD A LOT OF FUN DRAWING CITRONA'S HAIR. MY FAVORITE THING TO DRAW IS HAIR. I LIKE LOOKING AT IT, TOO.
BUT I WANT TO GET BETTER AT IT, SINCE I STILL CAN'T DRAW HAIR LIKE I SEE IT IN MY MIND. ALTHOUGH EVERY TIME I THINK THAT, I REMIND MYSELF THAT THERE ARE OTHER THINGS I NEED TO WORK ON IMPROVING, TOO. I'LL TRY HARDER.

TO BE CONTINUED AT THE END OF THE VOLUME.

9

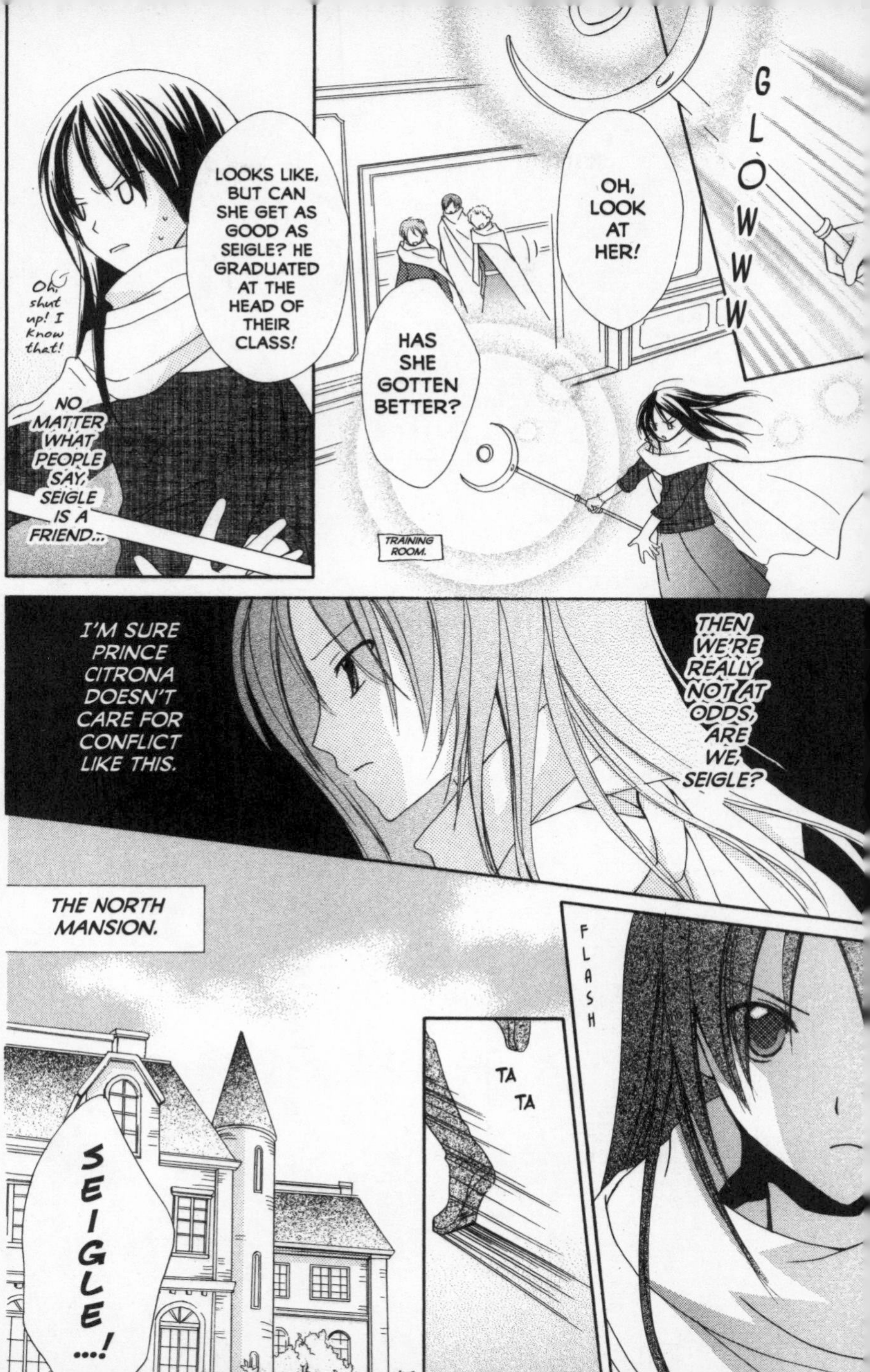
GLOWWW
OH, LOOK AT HER!
HAS SHE GOTTEN BETTER?
TRAINING ROOM.
LOOKS LIKE, BUT CAN SHE GET AS GOOD AS SEIGLE? HE GRADUATED AT THE HEAD OF THEIR CLASS!
Oh, shut up! I know that!
NO MATTER WHAT PEOPLE SAY, SEIGLE IS A FRIEND...
THEN WE'RE REALLY NOT AT ODDS, ARE WE, SEIGLE?
I'M SURE PRINCE CITRONA DOESN'T CARE FOR CONFLICT LIKE THIS.
FLASH
TA TA
THE NORTH MANSION.
SEIGLE...!

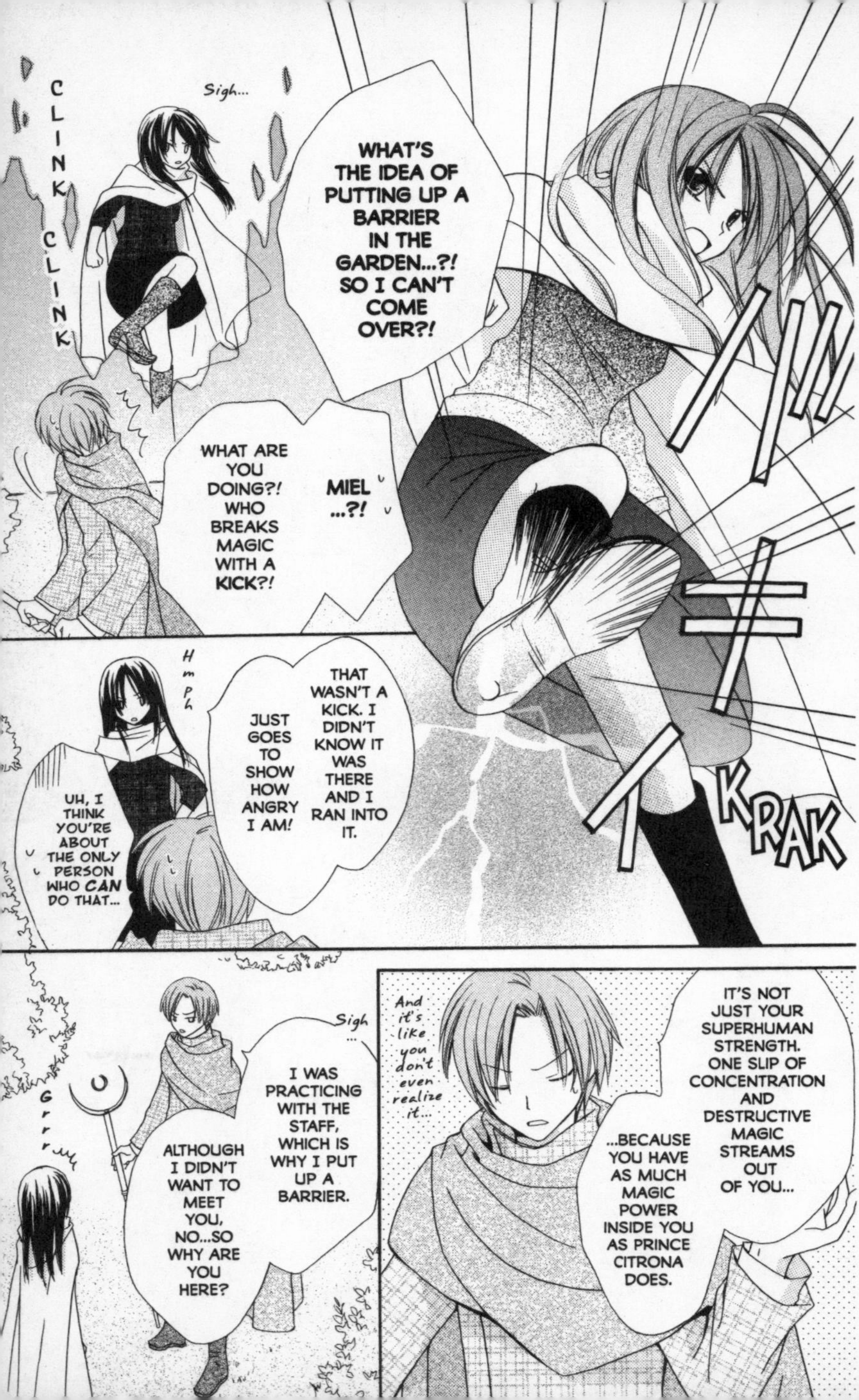
WHAT'S THE IDEA OF PUTTING UP A BARRIER IN THE GARDEN...?! SO I CAN'T COME OVER?!
KRAK
Sigh...
CLINK CLINK
MIEL ...?!
WHAT ARE YOU DOING?! WHO BREAKS MAGIC WITH A **KICK**?!
THAT WASN'T A KICK. I DIDN'T KNOW IT WAS THERE AND I RAN INTO IT.
JUST GOES TO SHOW HOW ANGRY I AM!
Hmph
UH, I THINK YOU'RE ABOUT THE ONLY PERSON WHO **CAN** DO THAT...
IT'S NOT JUST YOUR SUPERHUMAN STRENGTH. ONE SLIP OF CONCENTRATION AND DESTRUCTIVE MAGIC STREAMS OUT OF YOU...
...BECAUSE YOU HAVE AS MUCH MAGIC POWER INSIDE YOU AS PRINCE CITRONA DOES.
And it's like you don't even realize it...
Sigh...
I WAS PRACTICING WITH THE STAFF, WHICH IS WHY I PUT UP A BARRIER.
ALTHOUGH I DIDN'T WANT TO MEET YOU, NO...SO WHY ARE YOU HERE?
Grrr

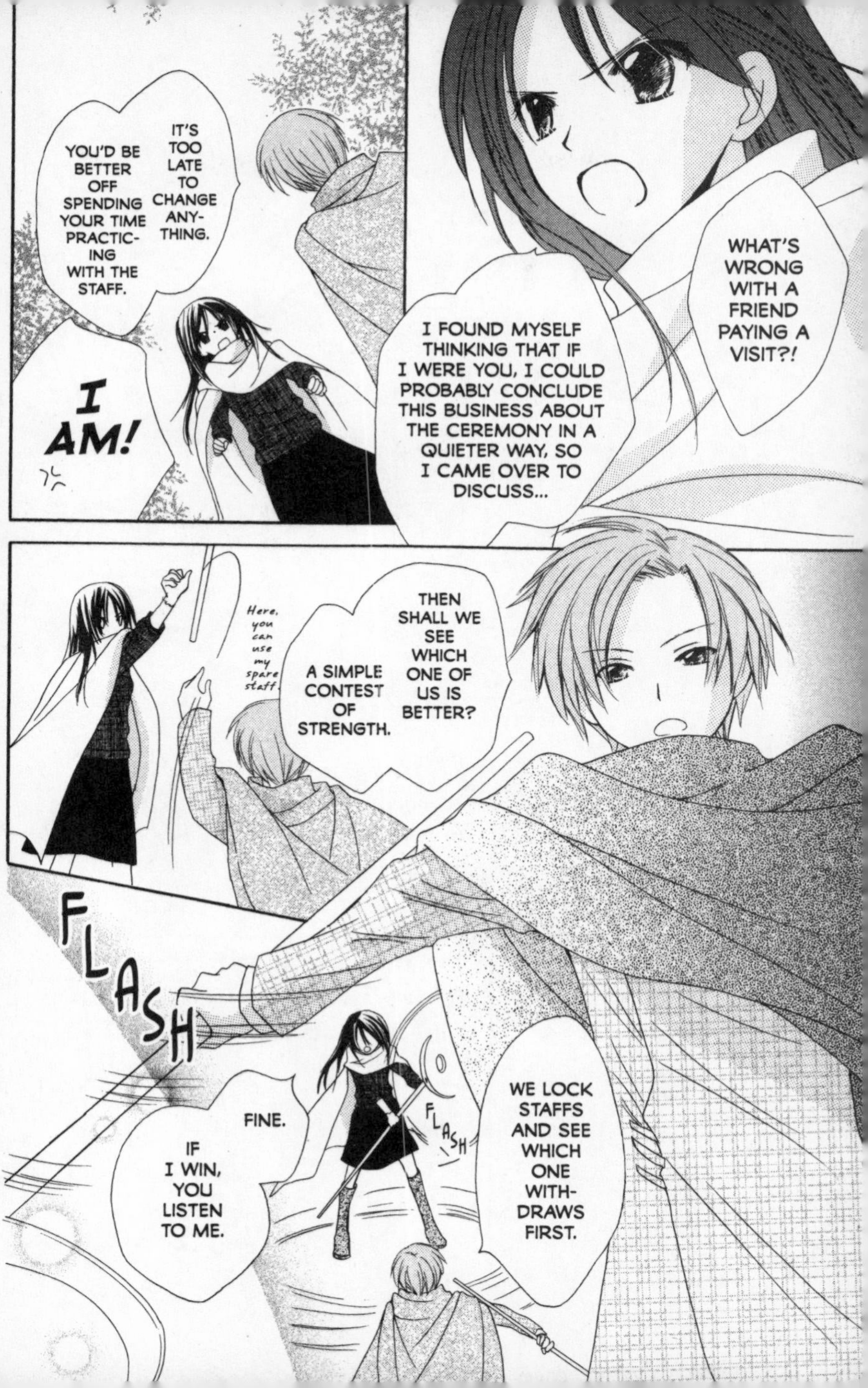
WHAT'S WRONG WITH A FRIEND PAYING A VISIT?!
I FOUND MYSELF THINKING THAT IF I WERE YOU, I COULD PROBABLY CONCLUDE THIS BUSINESS ABOUT THE CEREMONY IN A QUIETER WAY, SO I CAME OVER TO DISCUSS...
IT'S TOO LATE TO CHANGE ANY-THING.
YOU'D BE BETTER OFF SPENDING YOUR TIME PRACTIC-ING WITH THE STAFF.
I AM!
THEN SHALL WE SEE WHICH ONE OF US IS BETTER?
A SIMPLE CONTEST OF STRENGTH.
Here, you can use my spare staff.
FLASH
WE LOCK STAFFS AND SEE WHICH ONE WITH-DRAWS FIRST.
FLASH
FINE.
IF I WIN, YOU LISTEN TO ME.

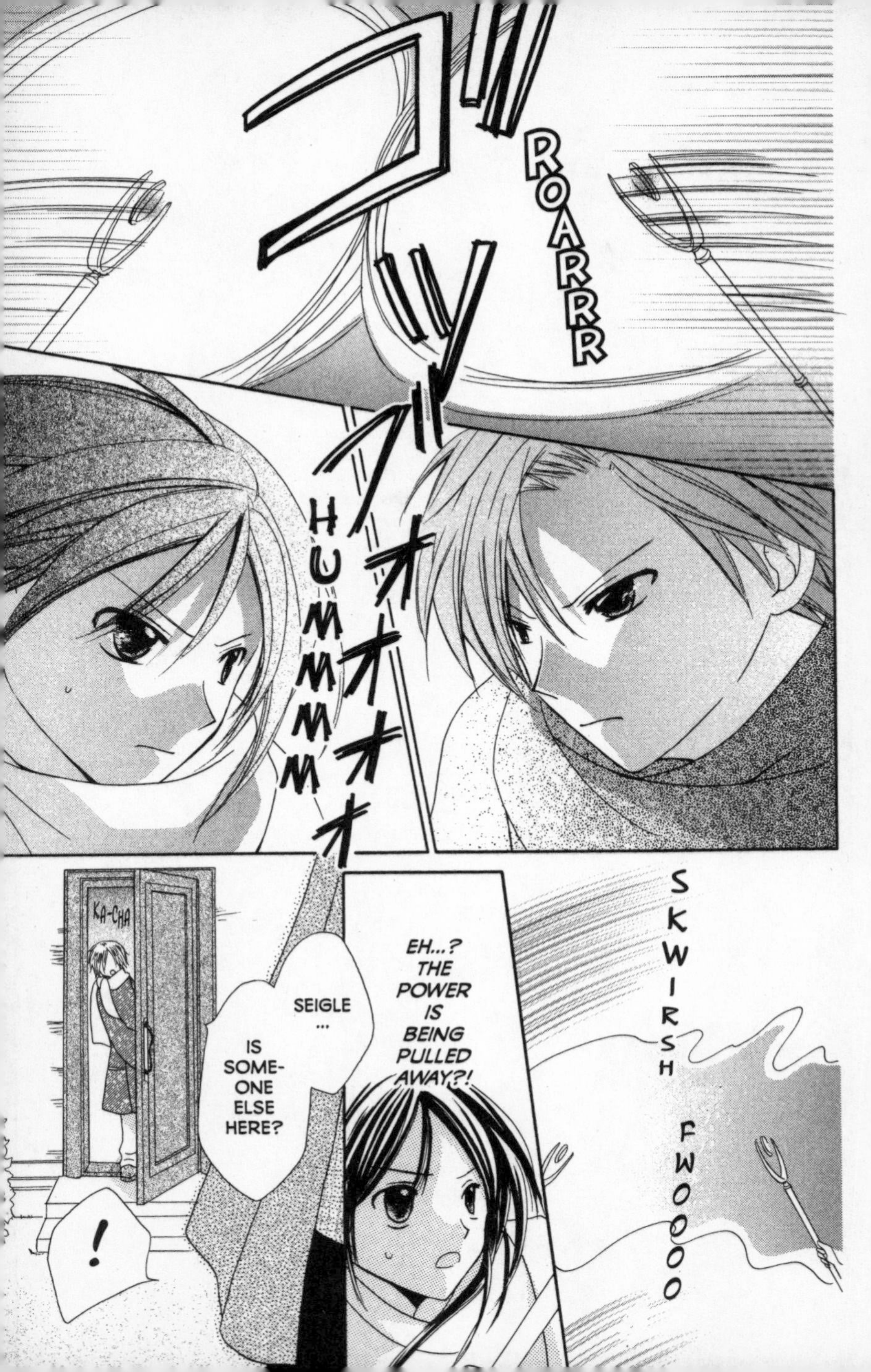
ROARRR
HUMMMMM
SKWIRSH
FWOOOOO
EH...? THE POWER IS BEING PULLED AWAY?!
SEIGLE ...
IS SOME-ONE ELSE HERE?
KA-CHA
!

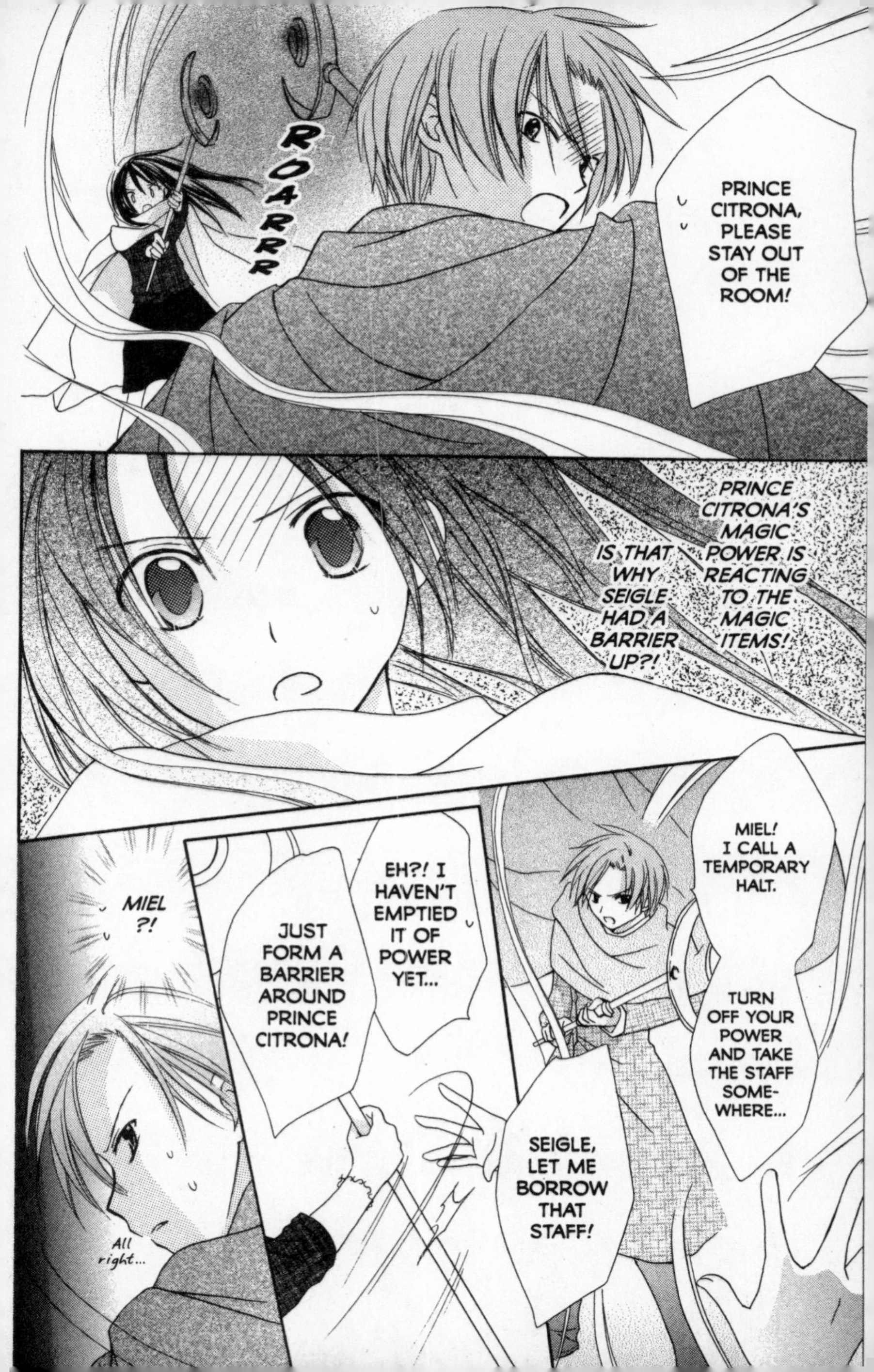
PRINCE CITRONA, PLEASE STAY OUT OF THE ROOM!
ROARRR
PRINCE CITRONA'S MAGIC POWER IS REACTING TO THE MAGIC ITEMS!
IS THAT WHY SEIGLE HAD A BARRIER UP?!
MIEL! I CALL A TEMPORARY HALT.
TURN OFF YOUR POWER AND TAKE THE STAFF SOME-WHERE...
SEIGLE, LET ME BORROW THAT STAFF!
EH?! I HAVEN'T EMPTIED IT OF POWER YET...
JUST FORM A BARRIER AROUND PRINCE CITRONA!
MIEL?!
All right...

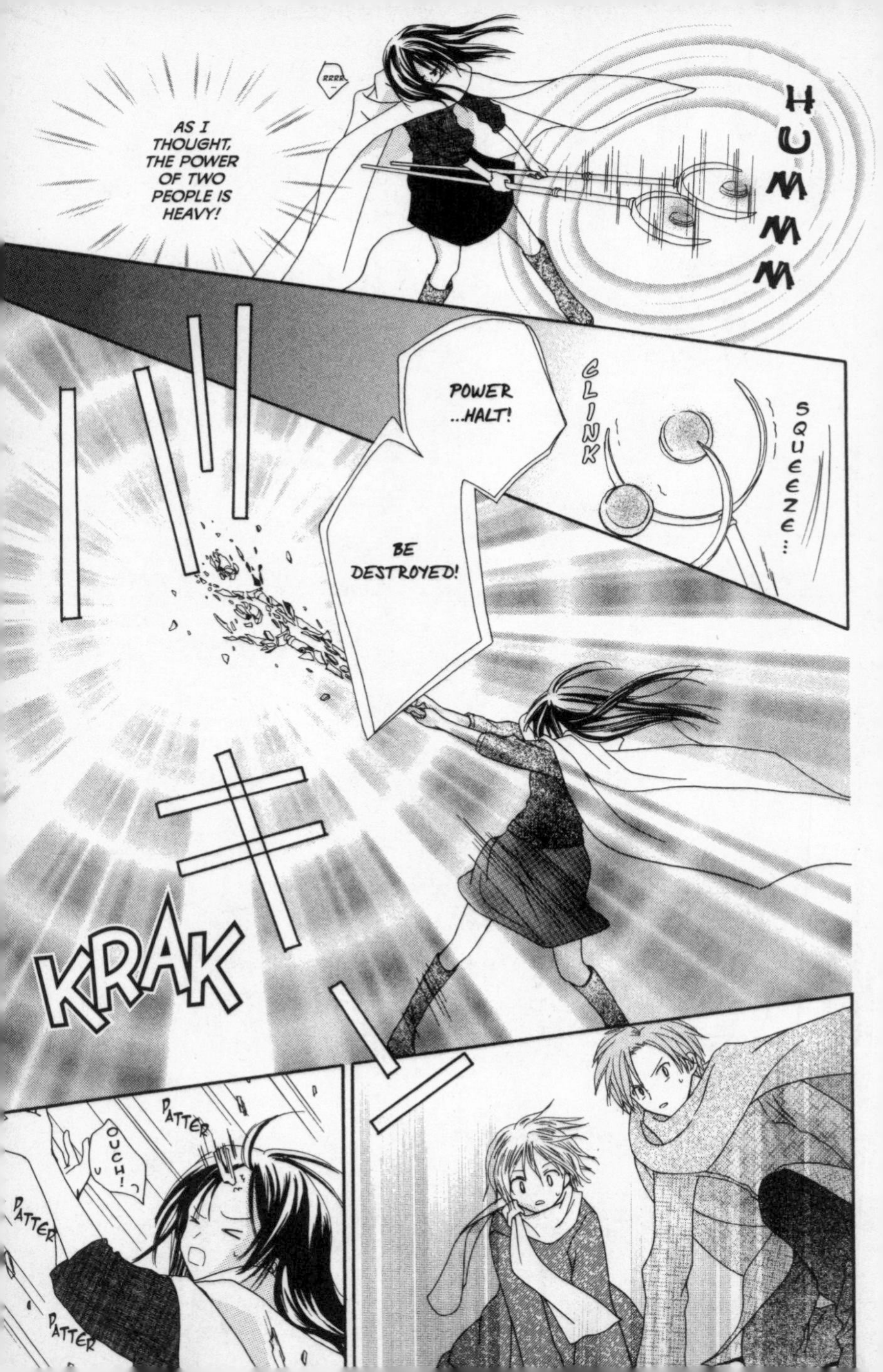
HUMMM
RRRR...
AS I THOUGHT, THE POWER OF TWO PEOPLE IS HEAVY!
SQUEEZE...
CLINK
POWER ...HALT!
BE DESTROYED!
KRAK
PATTER
OUCH!
PATTER
PATTER

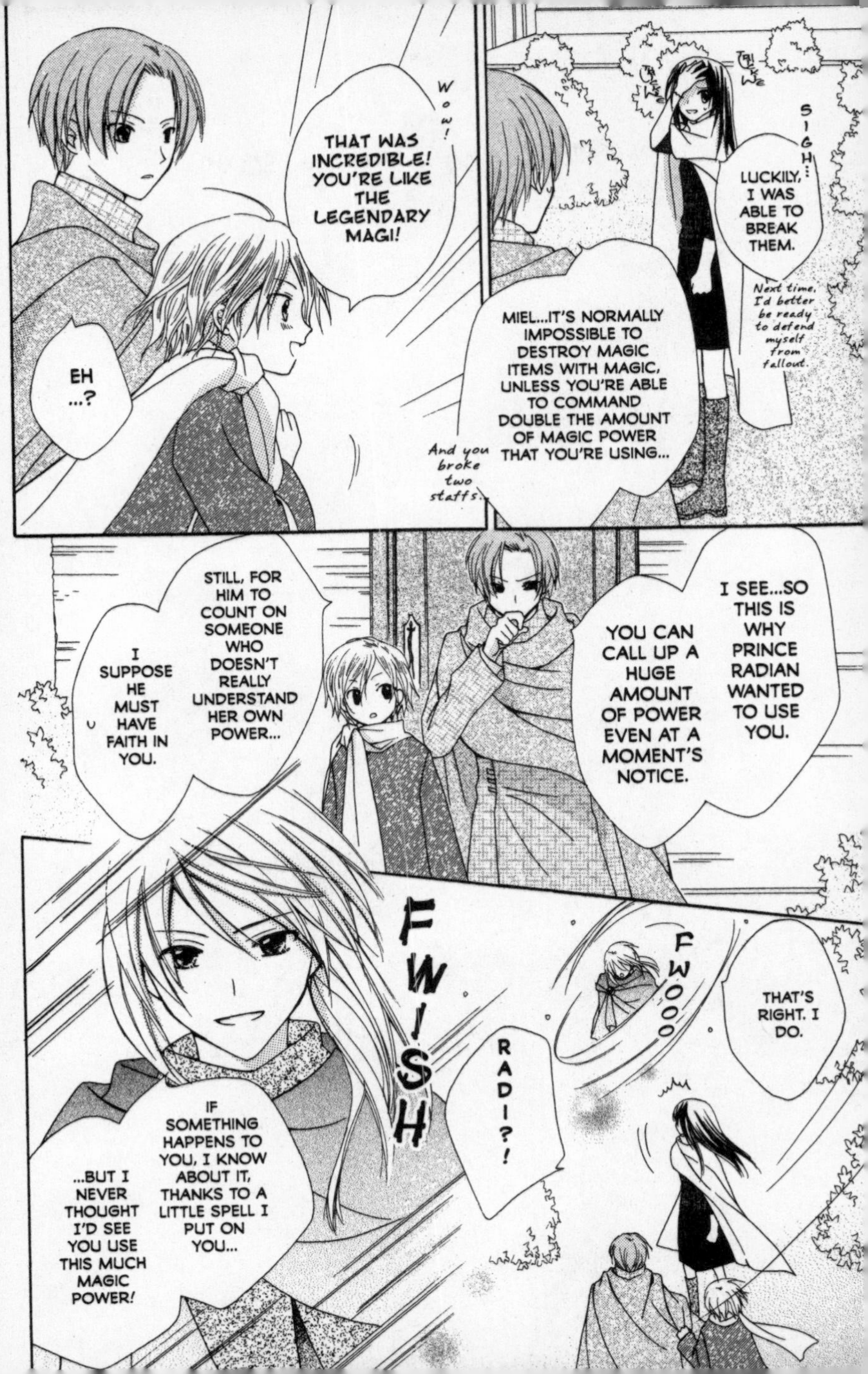
SIGH...
LUCKILY, I WAS ABLE TO BREAK THEM.
Next time, I'd better be ready to defend myself from fallout.
MIEL...IT'S NORMALLY IMPOSSIBLE TO DESTROY MAGIC ITEMS WITH MAGIC, UNLESS YOU'RE ABLE TO COMMAND DOUBLE THE AMOUNT OF MAGIC POWER THAT YOU'RE USING...
And you broke two staffs...
Wow!
THAT WAS INCREDIBLE! YOU'RE LIKE THE LEGENDARY MAGI!
EH ...?
I SEE...SO THIS IS WHY PRINCE RADIAN WANTED TO USE YOU.
YOU CAN CALL UP A HUGE AMOUNT OF POWER EVEN AT A MOMENT'S NOTICE.
STILL, FOR HIM TO COUNT ON SOMEONE WHO DOESN'T REALLY UNDERSTAND HER OWN POWER...
I SUPPOSE HE MUST HAVE FAITH IN YOU.
THAT'S RIGHT. I DO.
FWOOO
RADI?!
FWISH
IF SOMETHING HAPPENS TO YOU, I KNOW ABOUT IT, THANKS TO A LITTLE SPELL I PUT ON YOU...
...BUT I NEVER THOUGHT I'D SEE YOU USE THIS MUCH MAGIC POWER!

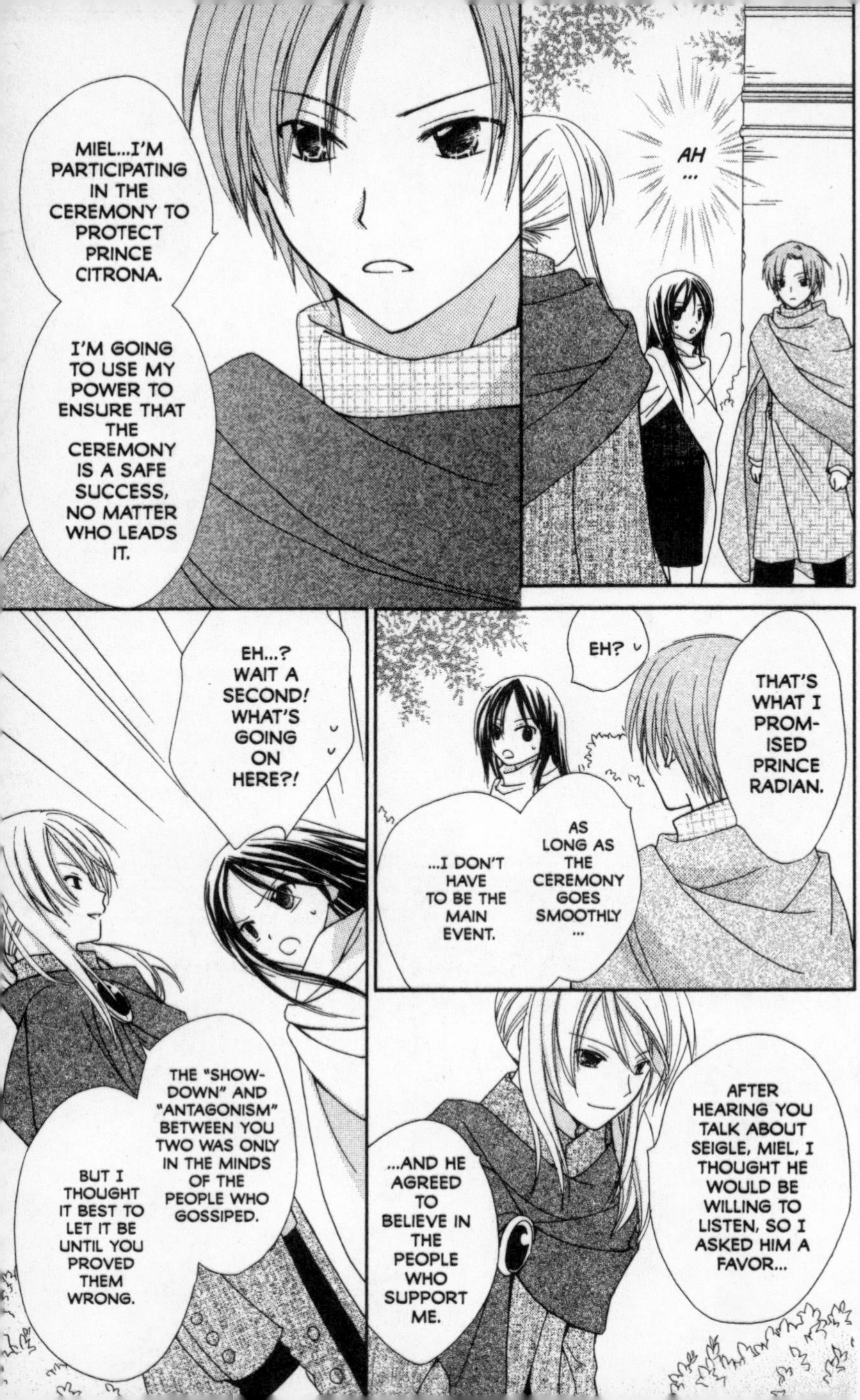
AH ...
MIEL...I'M PARTICIPATING IN THE CEREMONY TO PROTECT PRINCE CITRONA.
I'M GOING TO USE MY POWER TO ENSURE THAT THE CEREMONY IS A SAFE SUCCESS, NO MATTER WHO LEADS IT.
THAT'S WHAT I PROM-ISED PRINCE RADIAN.
EH?
AS LONG AS THE CEREMONY GOES SMOOTHLY ...
...I DON'T HAVE TO BE THE MAIN EVENT.
AFTER HEARING YOU TALK ABOUT SEIGLE, MIEL, I THOUGHT HE WOULD BE WILLING TO LISTEN, SO I ASKED HIM A FAVOR...
...AND HE AGREED TO BELIEVE IN THE PEOPLE WHO SUPPORT ME.
EH...? WAIT A SECOND! WHAT'S GOING ON HERE?!
THE "SHOW-DOWN" AND "ANTAGONISM" BETWEEN YOU TWO WAS ONLY IN THE MINDS OF THE PEOPLE WHO GOSSIPED.
BUT I THOUGHT IT BEST TO LET IT BE UNTIL YOU PROVED THEM WRONG.

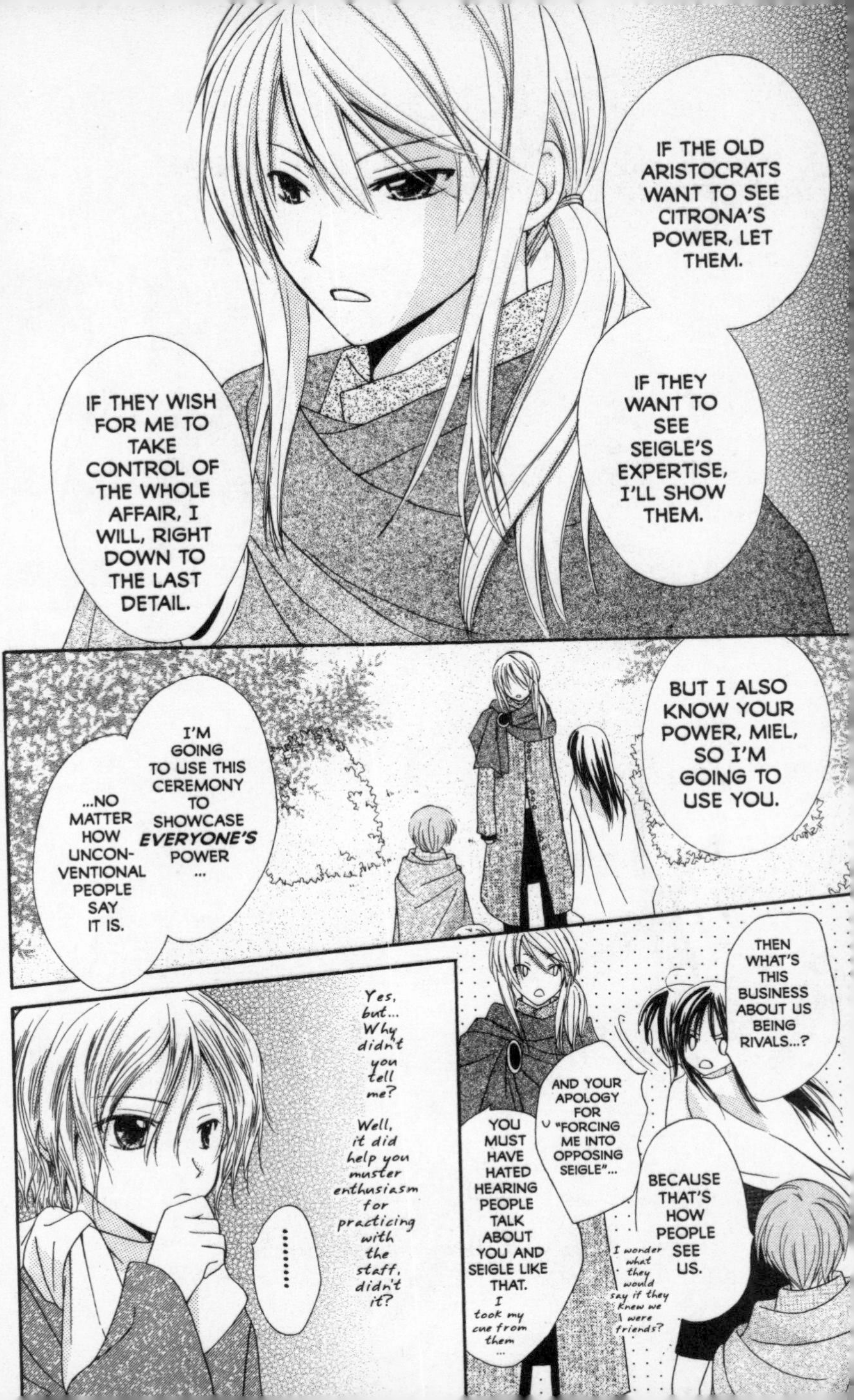
IF THE OLD ARISTOCRATS WANT TO SEE CITRONA'S POWER, LET THEM.
IF THEY WANT TO SEE SEIGLE'S EXPERTISE, I'LL SHOW THEM.
IF THEY WISH FOR ME TO TAKE CONTROL OF THE WHOLE AFFAIR, I WILL, RIGHT DOWN TO THE LAST DETAIL.
BUT I ALSO KNOW YOUR POWER, MIEL, SO I'M GOING TO USE YOU.
I'M GOING TO USE THIS CEREMONY TO SHOWCASE *EVERYONE'S* POWER ...
...NO MATTER HOW UNCON-VENTIONAL PEOPLE SAY IT IS.
THEN WHAT'S THIS BUSINESS ABOUT US BEING RIVALS...?
BECAUSE THAT'S HOW PEOPLE SEE US.
I wonder what they would say if they knew we were friends?
AND YOUR APOLOGY FOR "FORCING ME INTO OPPOSING SEIGLE"...
YOU MUST HAVE HATED HEARING PEOPLE TALK ABOUT YOU AND SEIGLE LIKE THAT.
I took my cue from them ...
Yes, but... Why didn't you tell me?
Well, it did help you muster enthusiasm for practicing with the staff, didn't it?
....

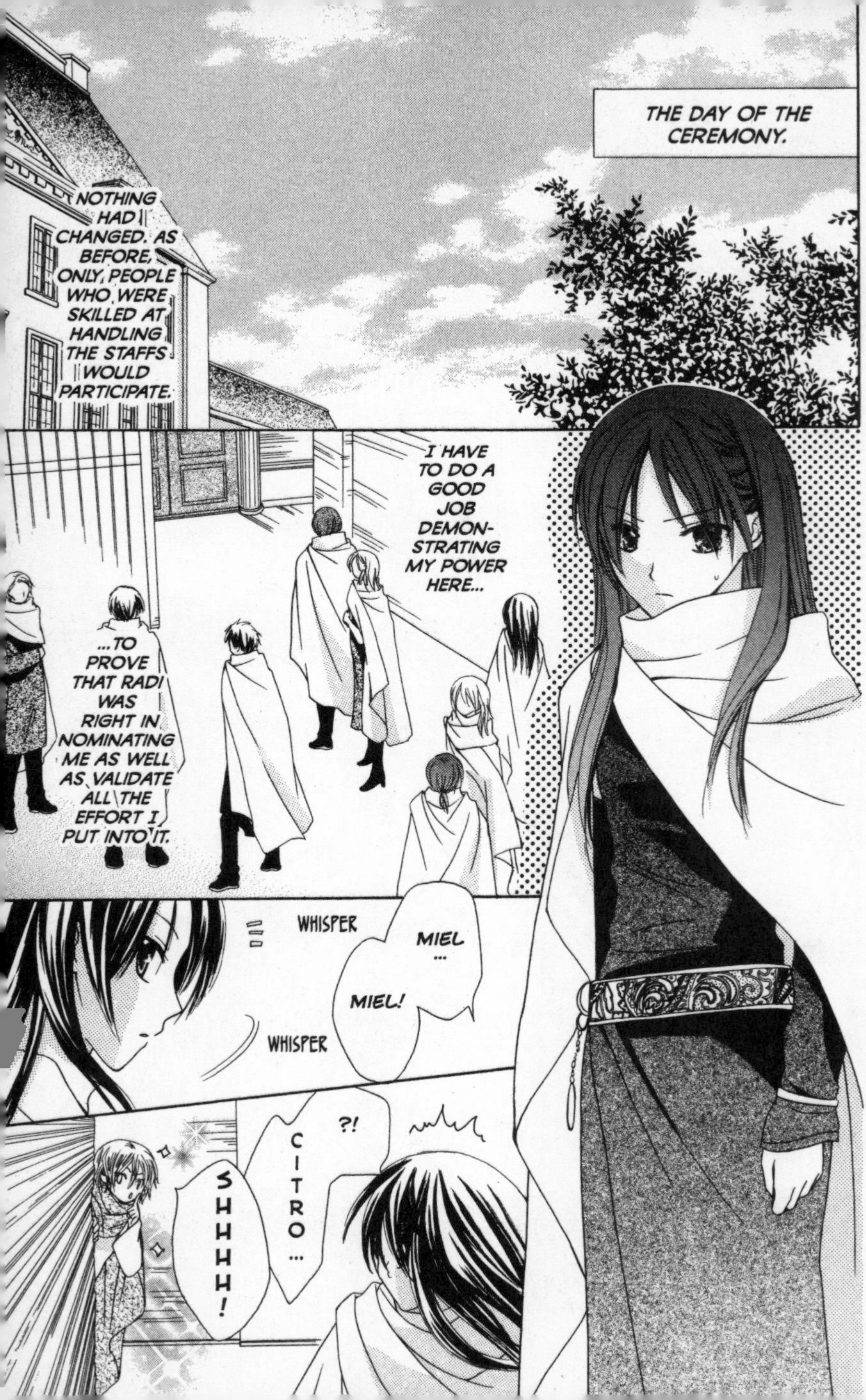
THE DAY OF THE CEREMONY.
NOTHING HAD CHANGED. AS BEFORE, ONLY PEOPLE WHO WERE SKILLED AT HANDLING THE STAFFS WOULD PARTICIPATE.
I HAVE TO DO A GOOD JOB DEMON-STRATING MY POWER HERE...
...TO PROVE THAT RADI WAS RIGHT IN NOMINATING ME AS WELL AS VALIDATE ALL THE EFFORT I PUT INTO IT.
WHISPER
MIEL...
MIEL!
WHISPER
?!
CITRO...
SHHHH!

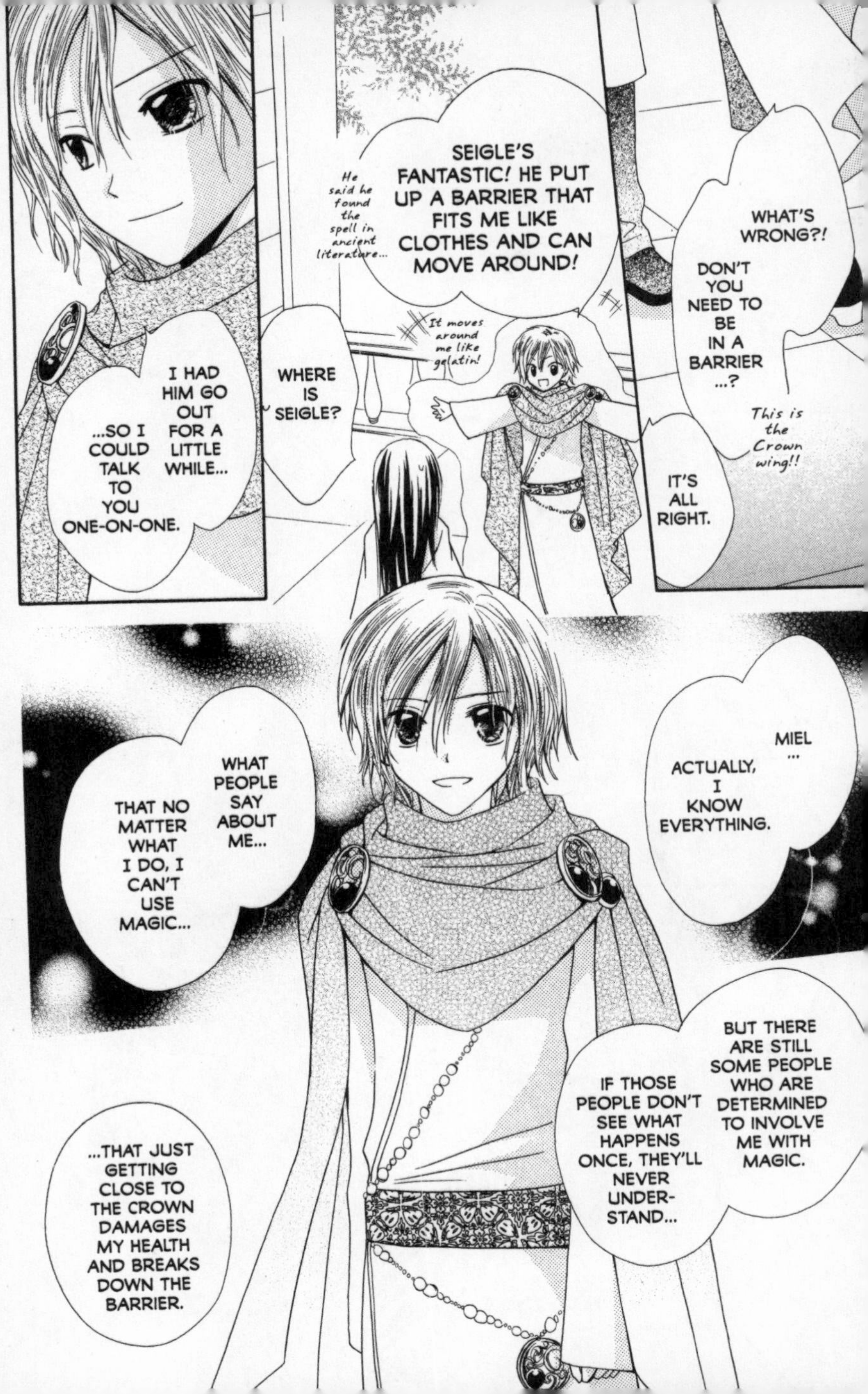
WHAT'S WRONG?!
DON'T YOU NEED TO BE IN A BARRIER ...?
This is the Crown wing!!
IT'S ALL RIGHT.
SEIGLE'S FANTASTIC! HE PUT UP A BARRIER THAT FITS ME LIKE CLOTHES AND CAN MOVE AROUND!
He said he found the spell in ancient literature...
It moves around me like gelatin!
WHERE IS SEIGLE?
I HAD HIM GO OUT FOR A LITTLE WHILE...
...SO I COULD TALK TO YOU ONE-ON-ONE.
MIEL ...
ACTUALLY, I KNOW EVERYTHING.
WHAT PEOPLE SAY ABOUT ME...
THAT NO MATTER WHAT I DO, I CAN'T USE MAGIC...
...THAT JUST GETTING CLOSE TO THE CROWN DAMAGES MY HEALTH AND BREAKS DOWN THE BARRIER.
BUT THERE ARE STILL SOME PEOPLE WHO ARE DETERMINED TO INVOLVE ME WITH MAGIC.
IF THOSE PEOPLE DON'T SEE WHAT HAPPENS ONCE, THEY'LL NEVER UNDER-STAND...

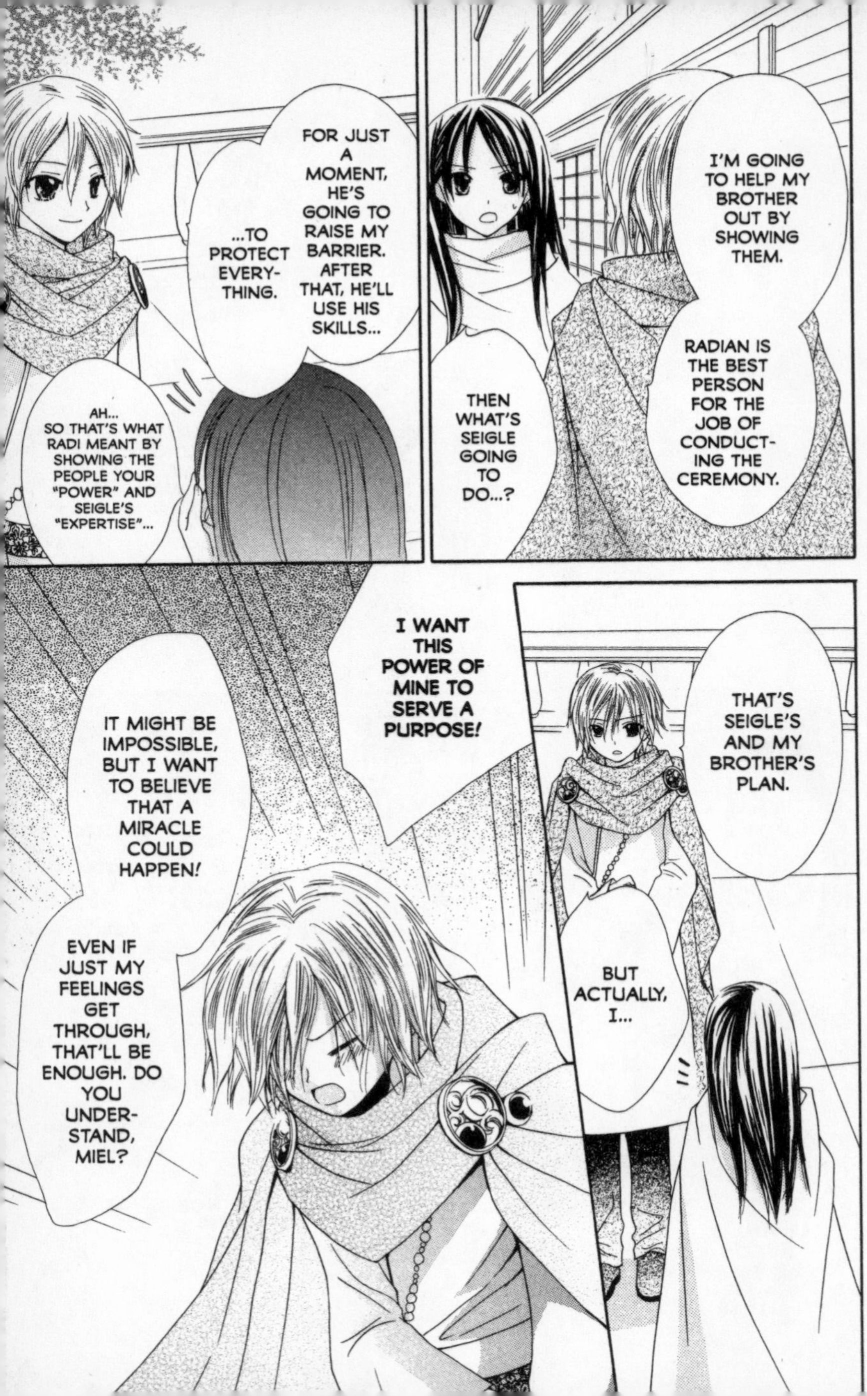
I'M GOING TO HELP MY BROTHER OUT BY SHOWING THEM.
RADIAN IS THE BEST PERSON FOR THE JOB OF CONDUCTING THE CEREMONY.
THEN WHAT'S SEIGLE GOING TO DO...?
FOR JUST A MOMENT, HE'S GOING TO RAISE MY BARRIER. AFTER THAT, HE'LL USE HIS SKILLS...
...TO PROTECT EVERYTHING.
AH... SO THAT'S WHAT RADI MEANT BY SHOWING THE PEOPLE YOUR "POWER" AND SEIGLE'S "EXPERTISE"...
THAT'S SEIGLE'S AND MY BROTHER'S PLAN.
BUT ACTUALLY, I...
I WANT THIS POWER OF MINE TO SERVE A PURPOSE!
IT MIGHT BE IMPOSSIBLE, BUT I WANT TO BELIEVE THAT A MIRACLE COULD HAPPEN!
EVEN IF JUST MY FEELINGS GET THROUGH, THAT'LL BE ENOUGH. DO YOU UNDERSTAND, MIEL?

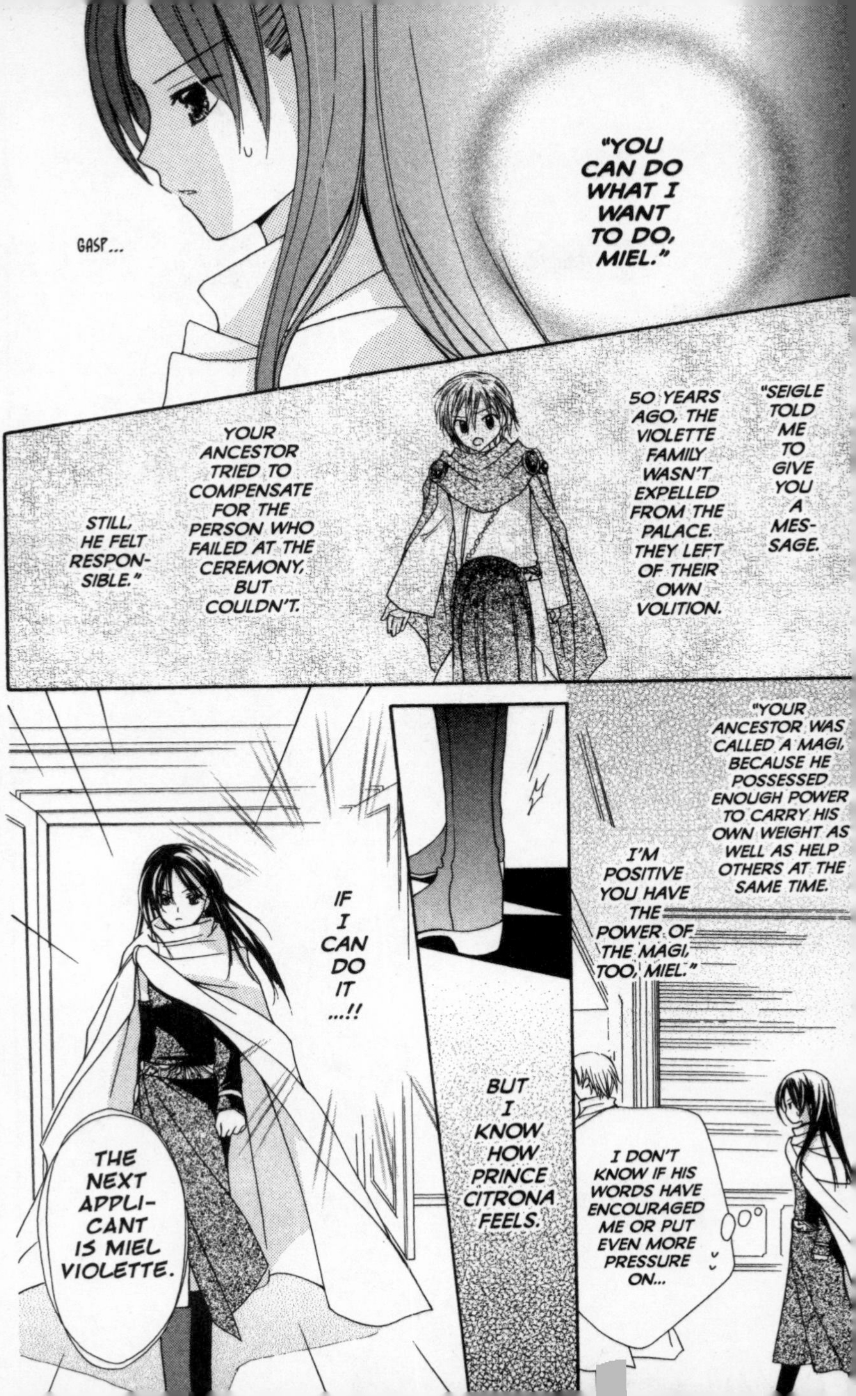

"YOU CAN DO WHAT I WANT TO DO, MIEL."
GASP...
"SEIGLE TOLD ME TO GIVE YOU A MES-SAGE.
50 YEARS AGO, THE VIOLETTE FAMILY WASN'T EXPELLED FROM THE PALACE. THEY LEFT OF THEIR OWN VOLITION.
YOUR ANCESTOR TRIED TO COMPENSATE FOR THE PERSON WHO FAILED AT THE CEREMONY, BUT COULDN'T.
STILL, HE FELT RESPON-SIBLE."
"YOUR ANCESTOR WAS CALLED A MAGI, BECAUSE HE POSSESSED ENOUGH POWER TO CARRY HIS OWN WEIGHT AS WELL AS HELP OTHERS AT THE SAME TIME.
I'M POSITIVE YOU HAVE THE POWER OF THE MAGI, TOO, MIEL."
I DON'T KNOW IF HIS WORDS HAVE ENCOURAGED ME OR PUT EVEN MORE PRESSURE ON...
BUT I KNOW HOW PRINCE CITRONA FEELS.
IF I CAN DO IT ...!!
THE NEXT APPLI-CANT IS MIEL VIOLETTE.

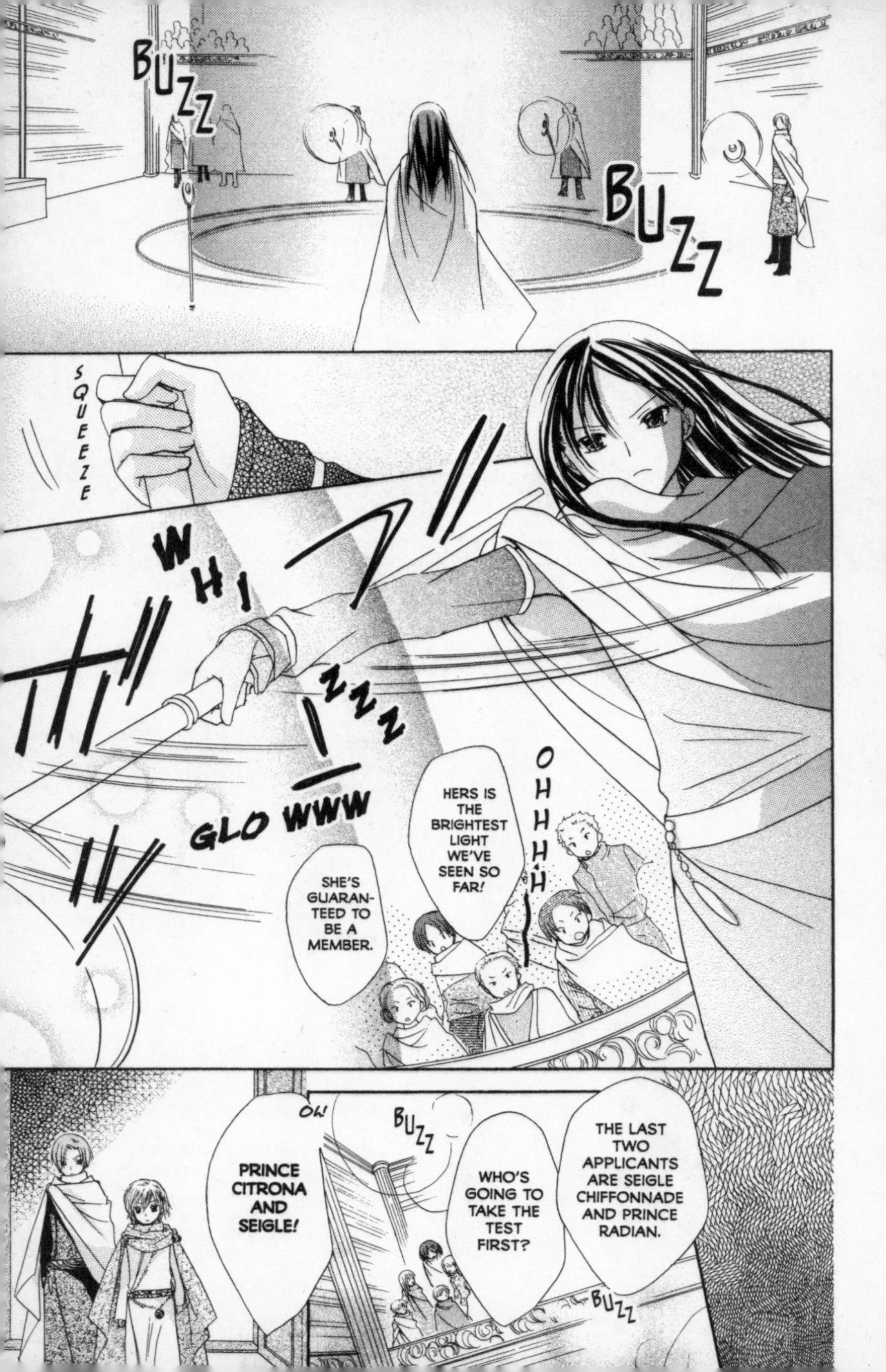
BUZZ
BUZZ
SQUEEZE
WHIZZZ
GLO WWW
OHHHH
HERS IS THE BRIGHTEST LIGHT WE'VE SEEN SO FAR!
SHE'S GUARAN-TEED TO BE A MEMBER.
THE LAST TWO APPLICANTS ARE SEIGLE CHIFFONNADE AND PRINCE RADIAN.
BUZZ
WHO'S GOING TO TAKE THE TEST FIRST?
BUZZ
OH!
PRINCE CITRONA AND SEIGLE!

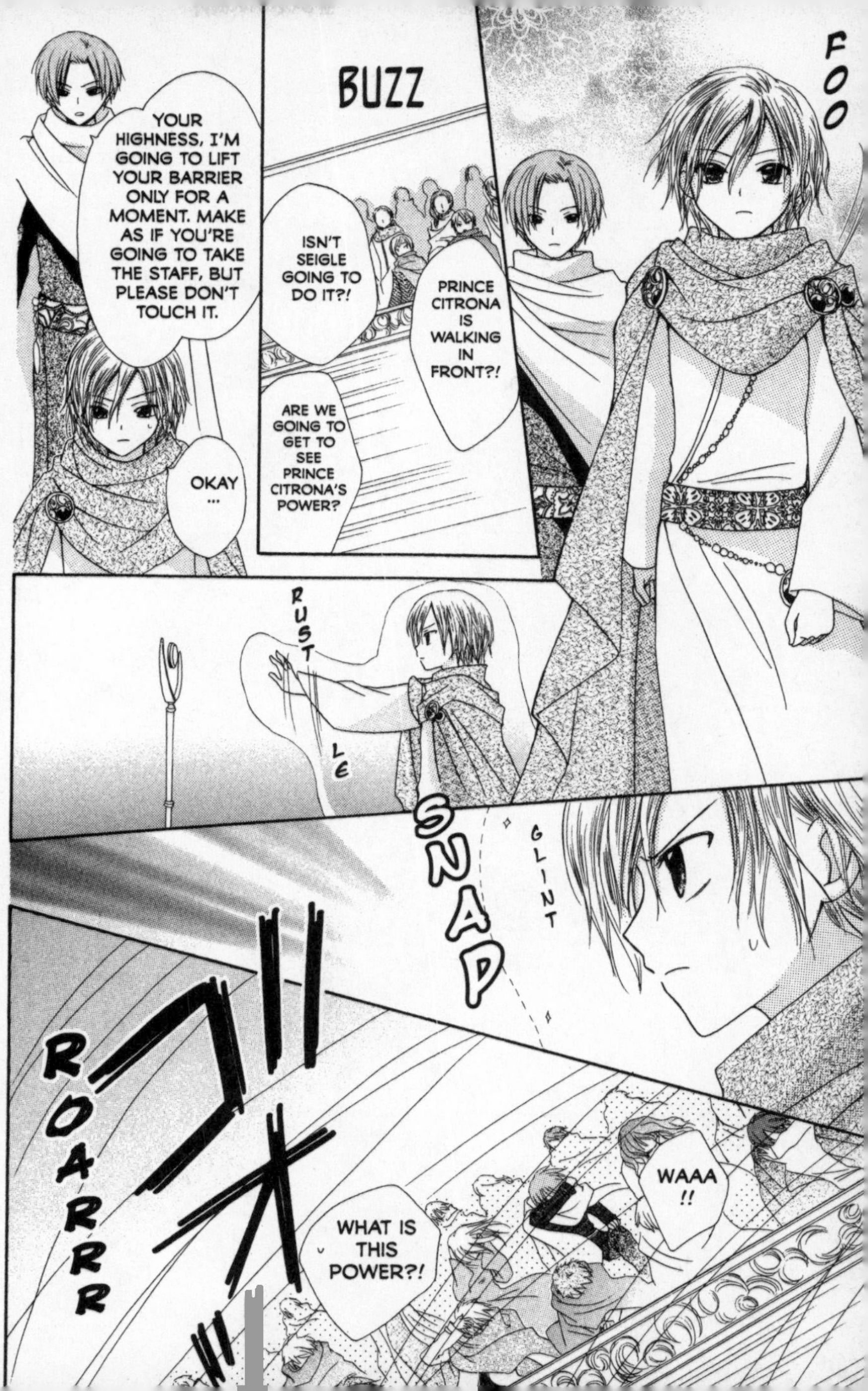
FOO
PRINCE CITRONA IS WALKING IN FRONT?!
BUZZ
ISN'T SEIGLE GOING TO DO IT?!
ARE WE GOING TO GET TO SEE PRINCE CITRONA'S POWER?
YOUR HIGHNESS, I'M GOING TO LIFT YOUR BARRIER ONLY FOR A MOMENT. MAKE AS IF YOU'RE GOING TO TAKE THE STAFF, BUT PLEASE DON'T TOUCH IT.
OKAY ...
RUST
LE
SNAP
GLINT
WAAA !!
WHAT IS THIS POWER?!
ROARRR

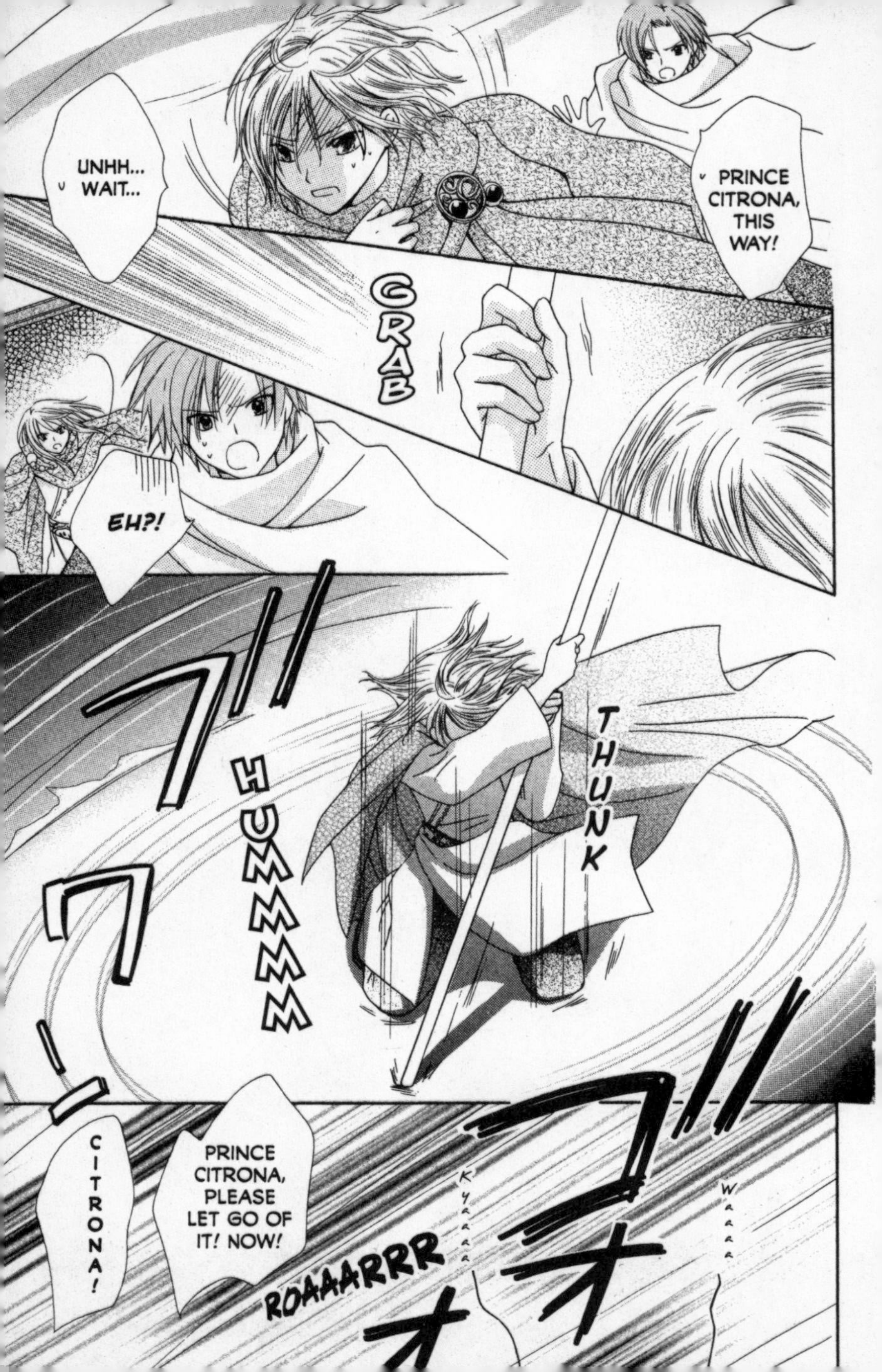
PRINCE CITRONA, THIS WAY!
UNHH... WAIT...
GRAB
EH?!
THUNK
HUMMMM
Waaaa
ROAAARRR
Kyaaaa
PRINCE CITRONA, PLEASE LET GO OF IT! NOW!
CITRONA!

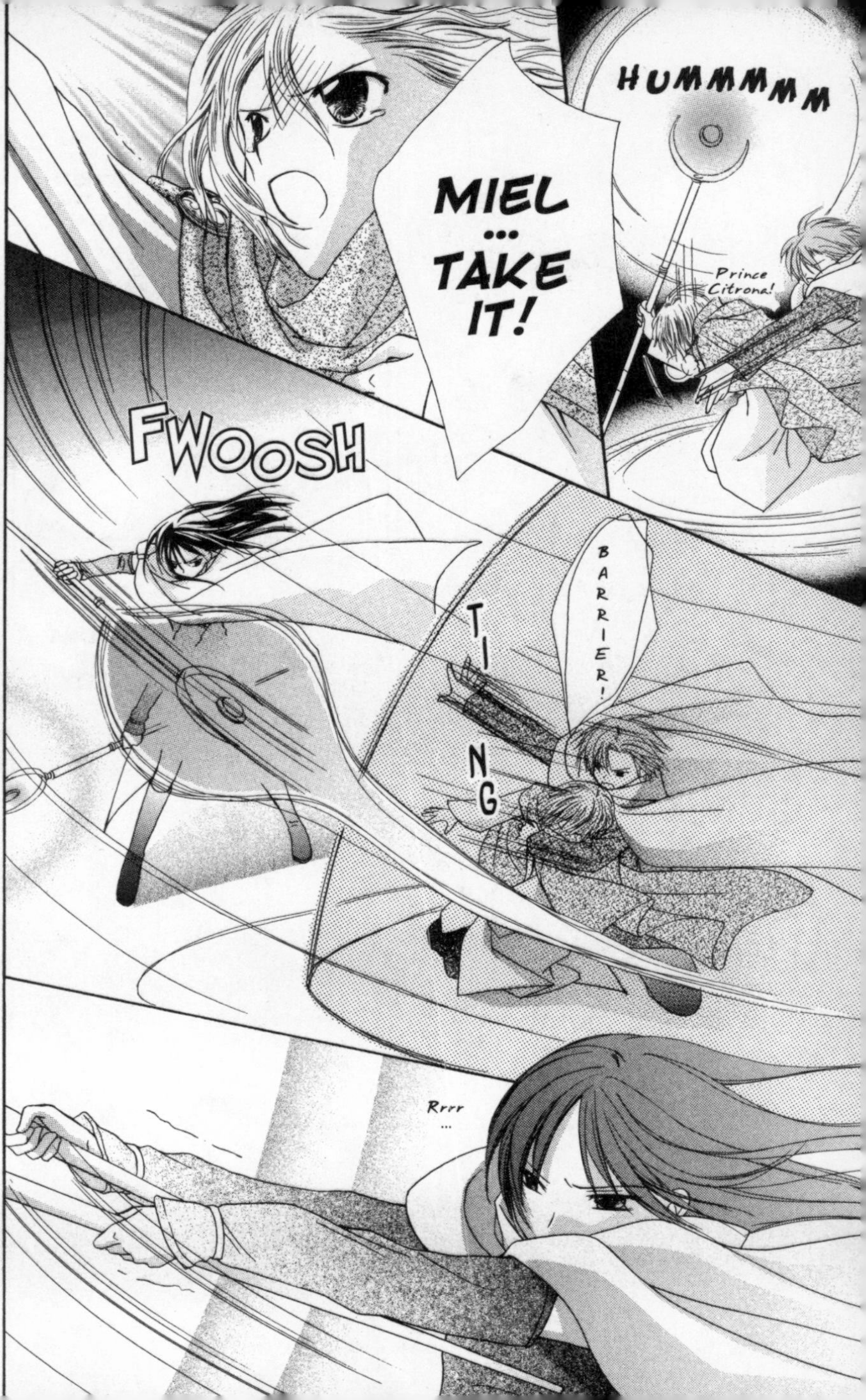
HUMMMMMM
Prince Citrona!
MIEL ... TAKE IT!
BARRIER!
TIING
FWOOSH
Rrrr ...

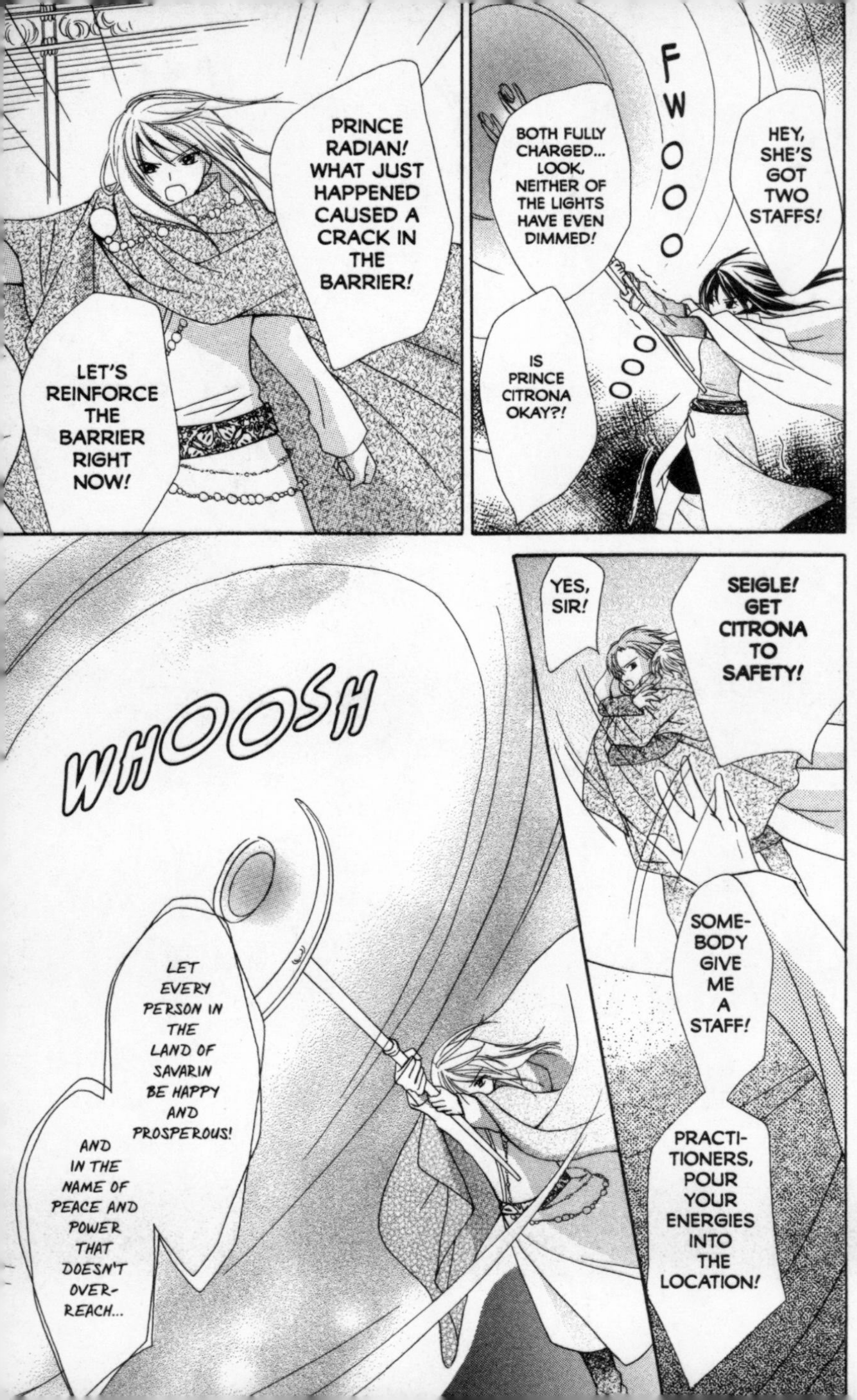
HEY, SHE'S GOT TWO STAFFS!
FWOOOOOOO
BOTH FULLY CHARGED... LOOK, NEITHER OF THE LIGHTS HAVE EVEN DIMMED!
IS PRINCE CITRONA OKAY?!
PRINCE RADIAN! WHAT JUST HAPPENED CAUSED A CRACK IN THE BARRIER!
LET'S REINFORCE THE BARRIER RIGHT NOW!
SEIGLE! GET CITRONA TO SAFETY!
YES, SIR!
SOME-BODY GIVE ME A STAFF!
PRACTI-TIONERS, POUR YOUR ENERGIES INTO THE LOCATION!
WHOOSH
LET EVERY PERSON IN THE LAND OF SAVARIN BE HAPPY AND PROSPEROUS!
AND IN THE NAME OF PEACE AND POWER THAT DOESN'T OVER-REACH...

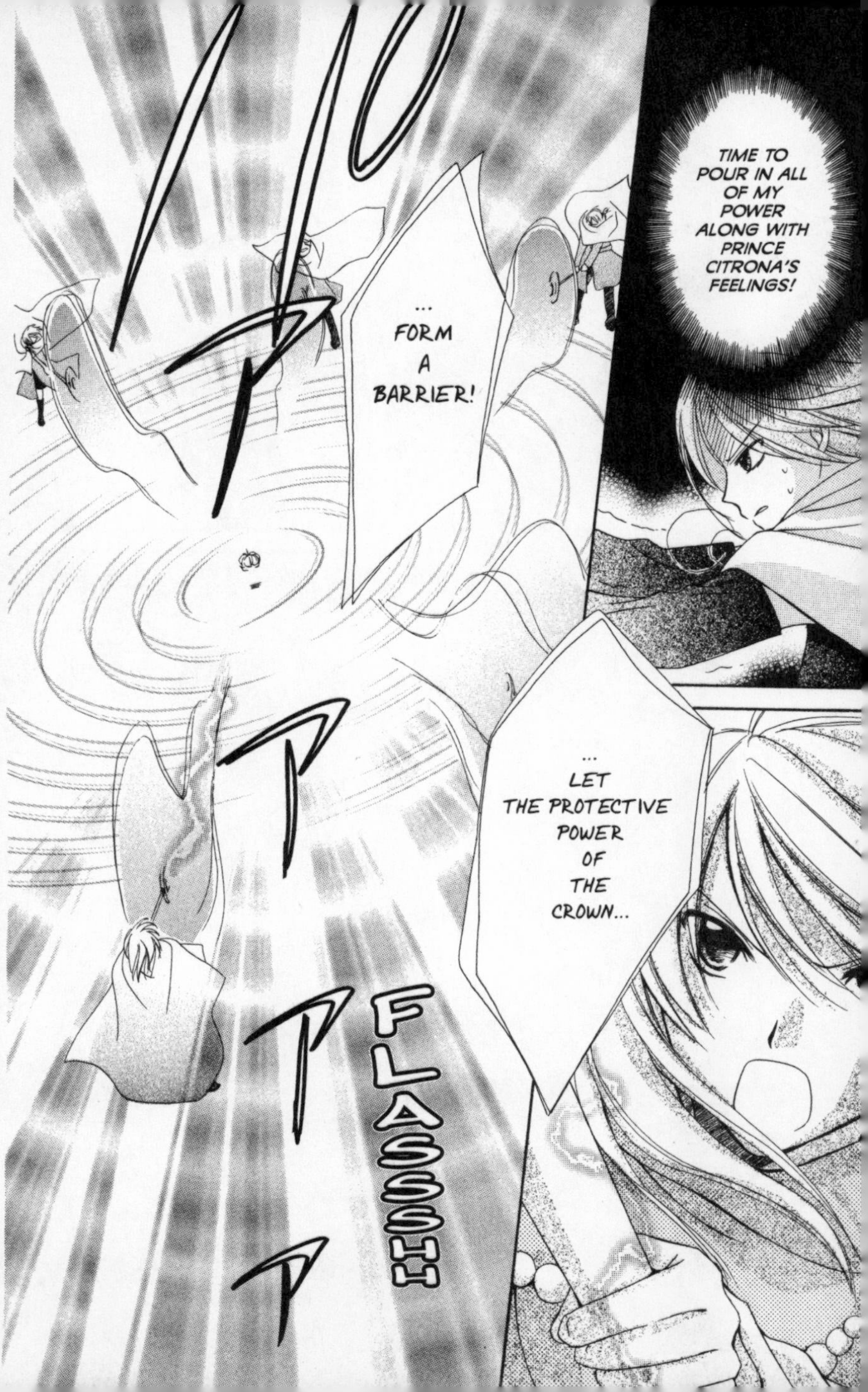
TIME TO POUR IN ALL OF MY POWER ALONG WITH PRINCE CITRONA'S FEELINGS!
... LET THE PROTECTIVE POWER OF THE CROWN...
... FORM A BARRIER!
FLASSHH

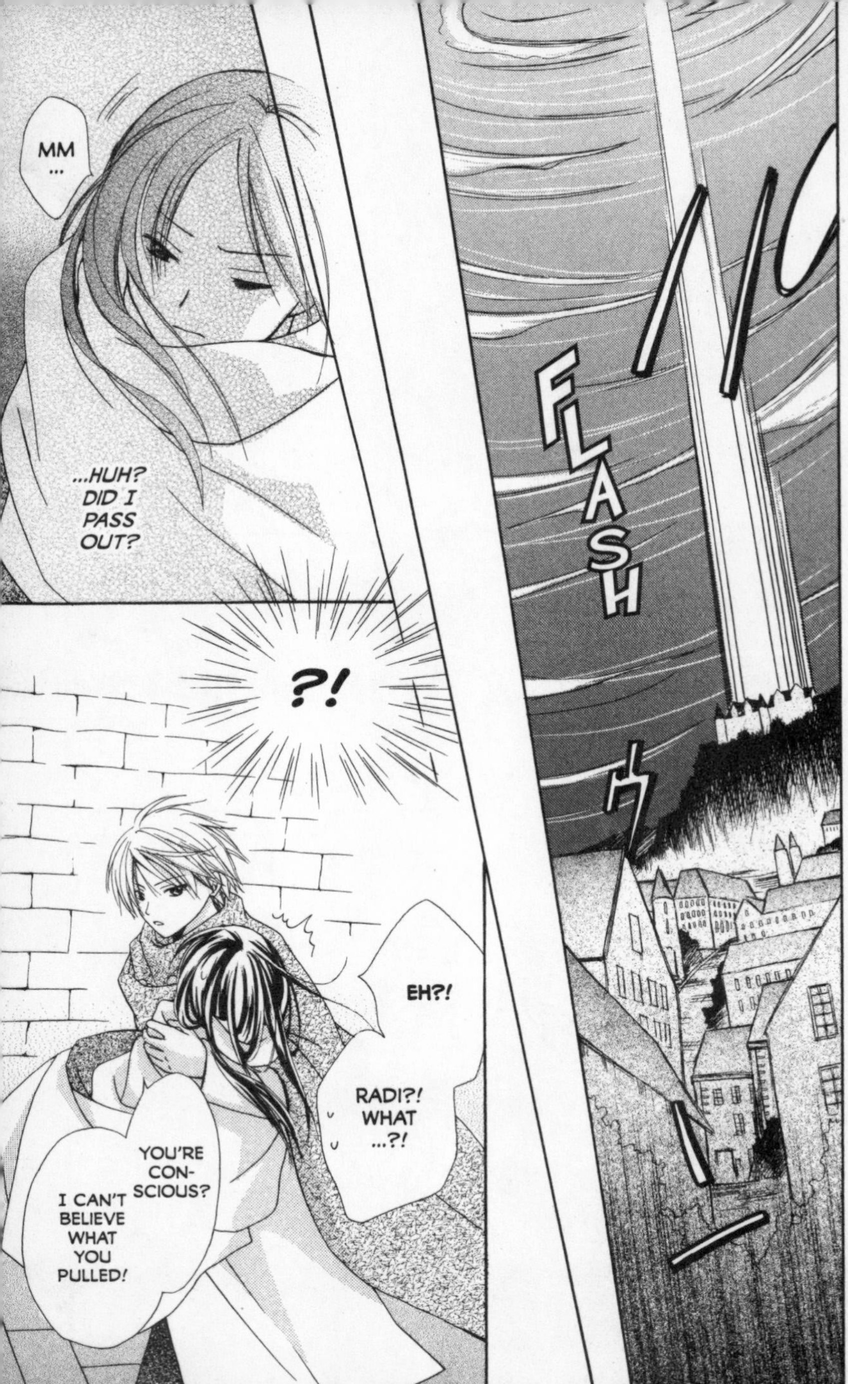
FLASH
MM ...
...HUH? DID I PASS OUT?
?!
EH?!
RADI?! WHAT ...?!
YOU'RE CON-SCIOUS?
I CAN'T BELIEVE WHAT YOU PULLED!

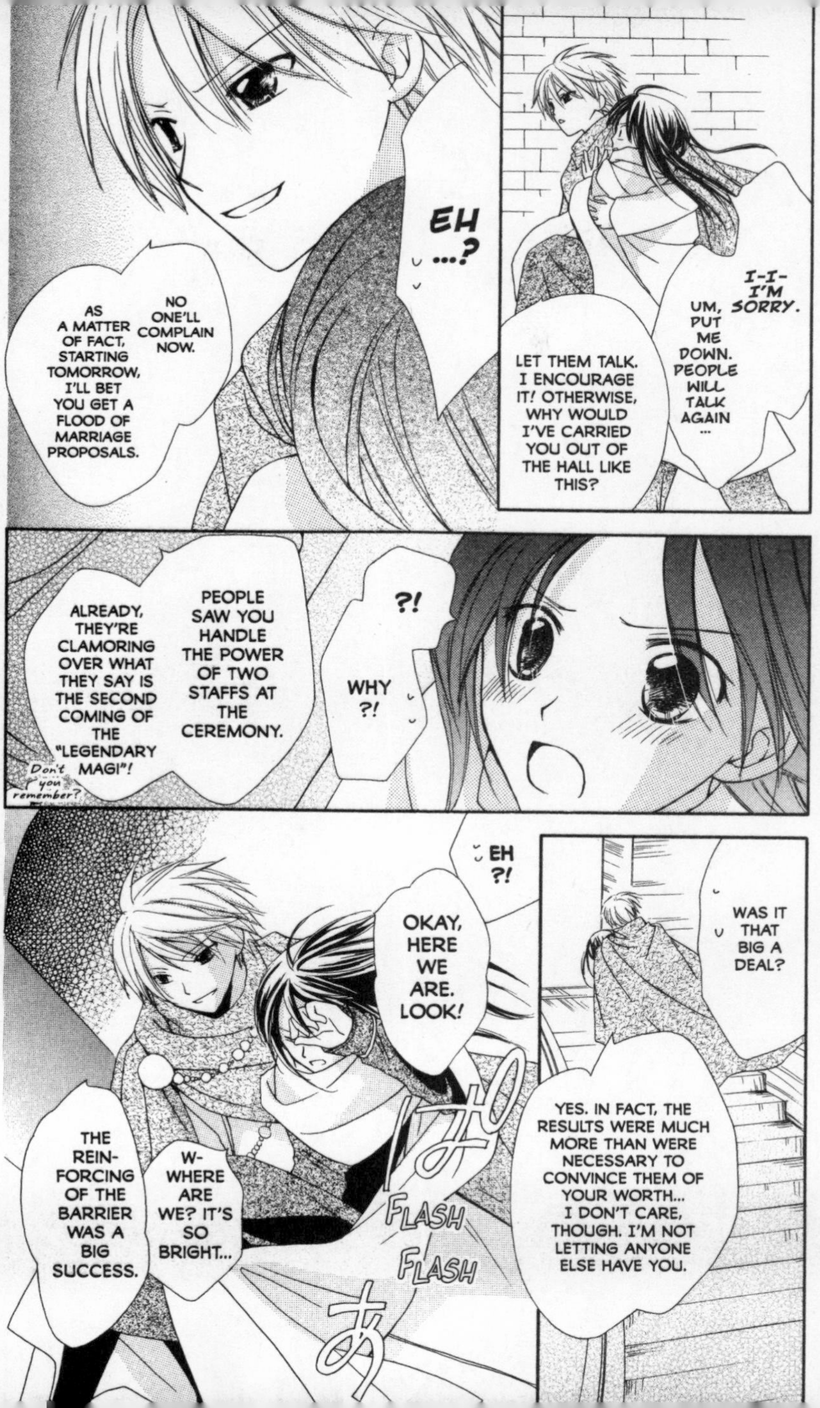
I-I-I'M SORRY.
UM, PUT ME DOWN. PEOPLE WILL TALK AGAIN ...
LET THEM TALK. I ENCOURAGE IT! OTHERWISE, WHY WOULD I'VE CARRIED YOU OUT OF THE HALL LIKE THIS?
EH ...?
NO ONE'LL COMPLAIN NOW.
AS A MATTER OF FACT, STARTING TOMORROW, I'LL BET YOU GET A FLOOD OF MARRIAGE PROPOSALS.
?!
WHY ?!
PEOPLE SAW YOU HANDLE THE POWER OF TWO STAFFS AT THE CEREMONY.
ALREADY, THEY'RE CLAMORING OVER WHAT THEY SAY IS THE SECOND COMING OF THE "LEGENDARY MAGI"!
Don't you remember?
WAS IT THAT BIG A DEAL?
YES. IN FACT, THE RESULTS WERE MUCH MORE THAN WERE NECESSARY TO CONVINCE THEM OF YOUR WORTH... I DON'T CARE, THOUGH. I'M NOT LETTING ANYONE ELSE HAVE YOU.
EH ?!
OKAY, HERE WE ARE. LOOK!
W-WHERE ARE WE? IT'S SO BRIGHT...
THE REIN-FORCING OF THE BARRIER WAS A BIG SUCCESS.
FLASH
FLASH

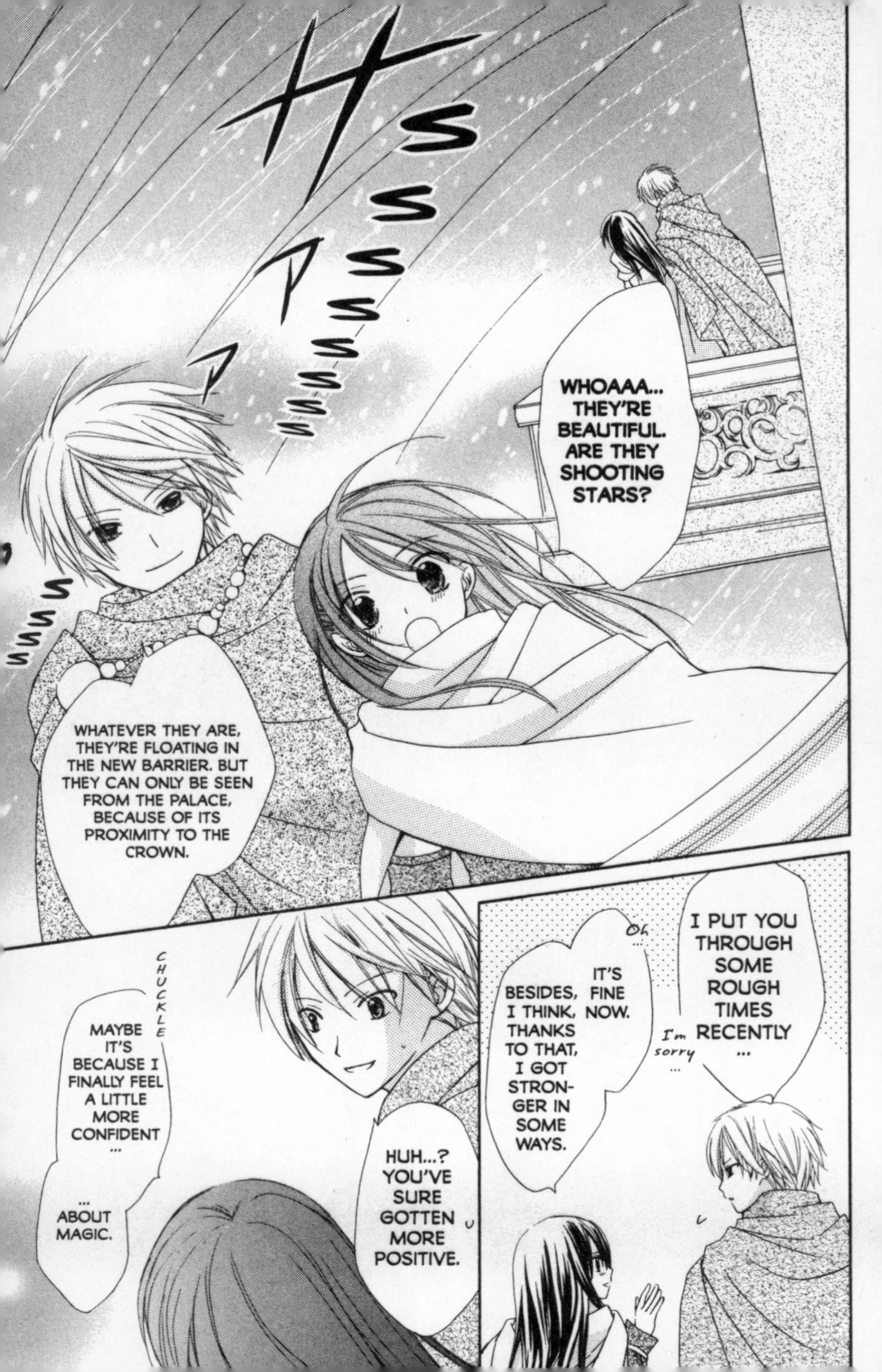
HSSSSSSS
SSSS
WHOAAA... THEY'RE BEAUTIFUL. ARE THEY SHOOTING STARS?
WHATEVER THEY ARE, THEY'RE FLOATING IN THE NEW BARRIER. BUT THEY CAN ONLY BE SEEN FROM THE PALACE, BECAUSE OF ITS PROXIMITY TO THE CROWN.
I PUT YOU THROUGH SOME ROUGH TIMES RECENTLY ...
I'm sorry ...
Oh ...
IT'S FINE NOW.
BESIDES, I THINK, THANKS TO THAT, I GOT STRONGER IN SOME WAYS.
HUH...? YOU'VE SURE GOTTEN MORE POSITIVE.
CHUCKLE
MAYBE IT'S BECAUSE I FINALLY FEEL A LITTLE MORE CONFIDENT ...
... ABOUT MAGIC.

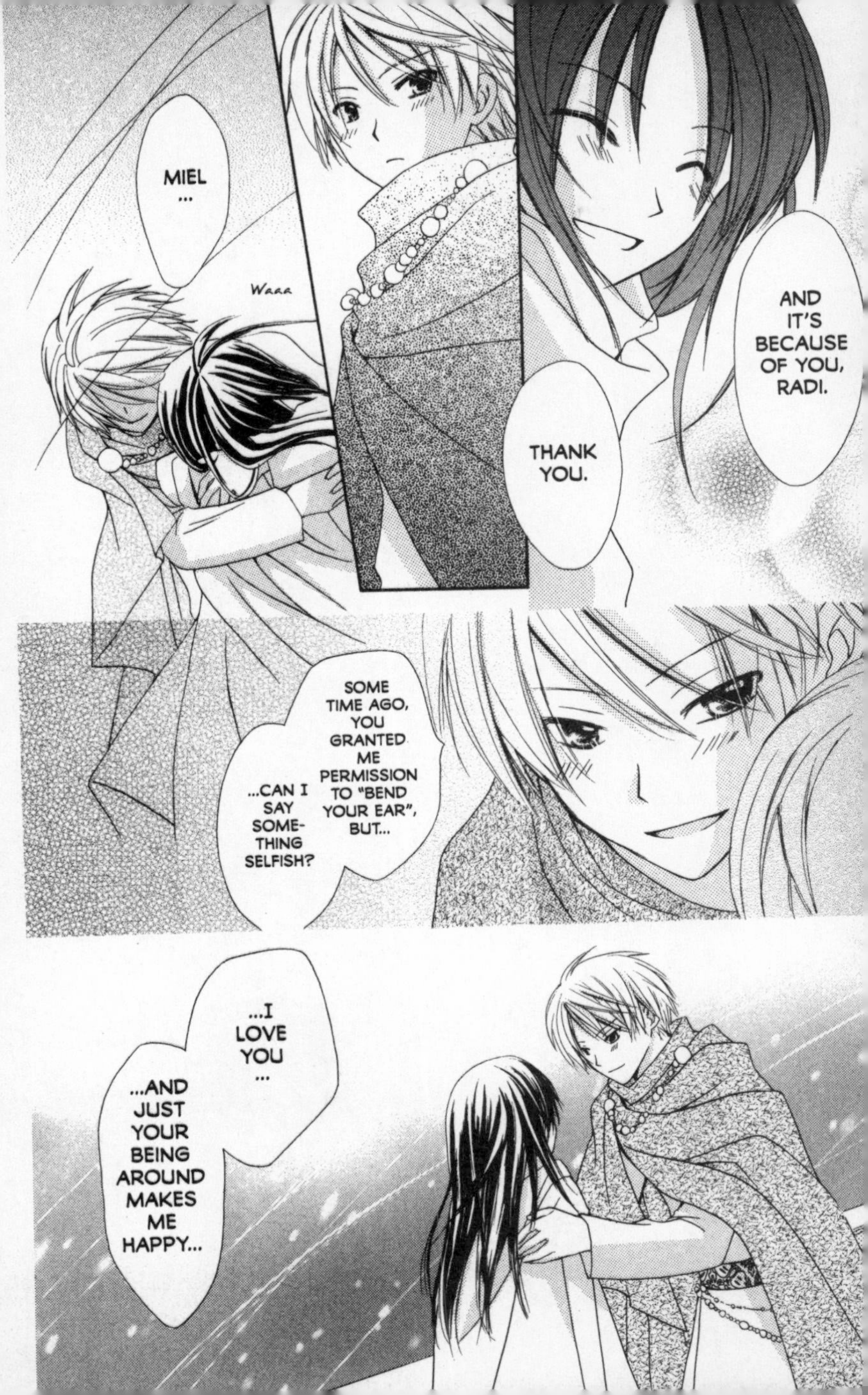
AND IT'S BECAUSE OF YOU, RADI.
THANK YOU.
MIEL ...
Waaa
SOME TIME AGO, YOU GRANTED ME PERMISSION TO "BEND YOUR EAR", BUT...
...CAN I SAY SOME-THING SELFISH?
...I LOVE YOU ...
...AND JUST YOUR BEING AROUND MAKES ME HAPPY...

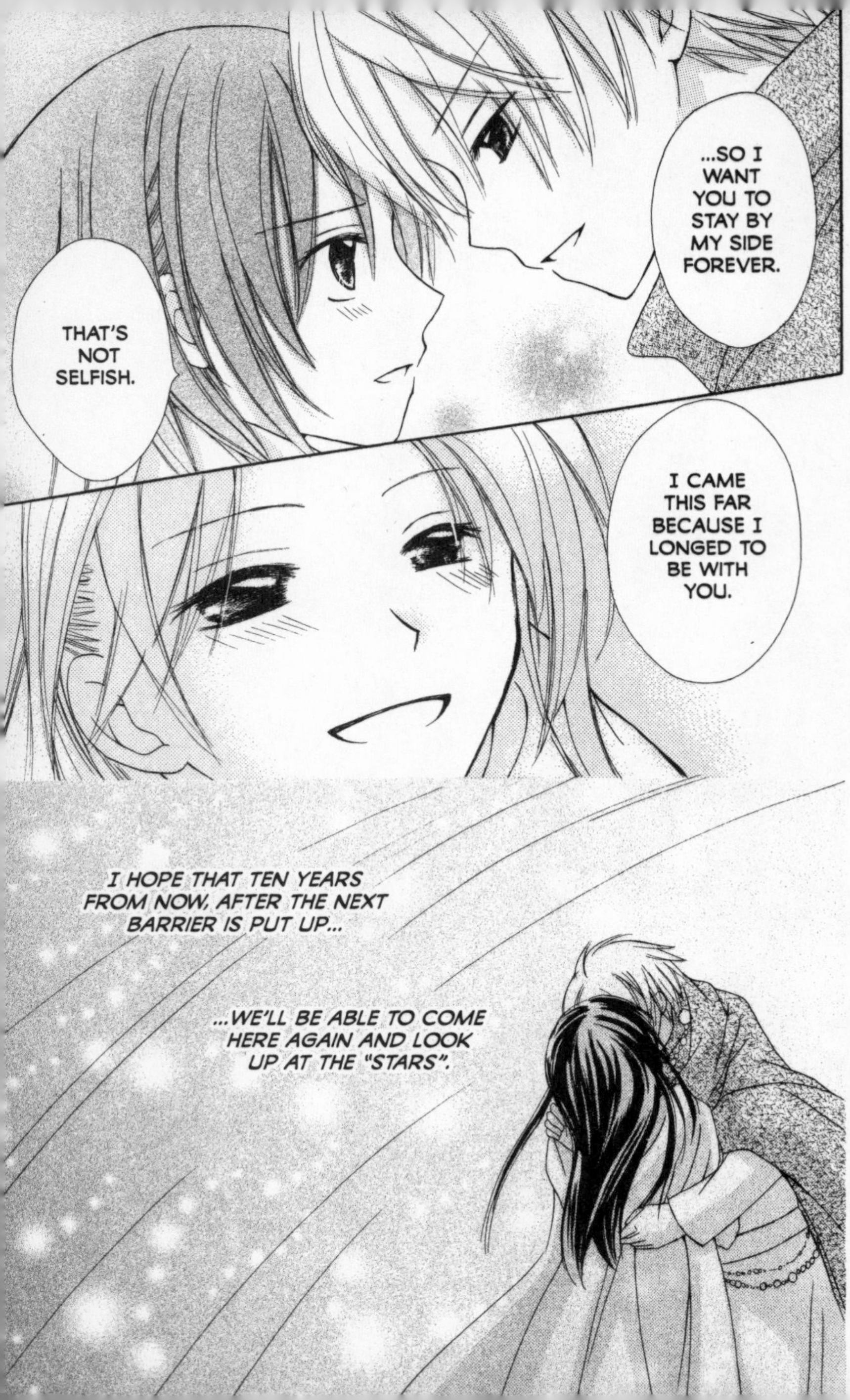
...SO I WANT YOU TO STAY BY MY SIDE FOREVER.
THAT'S NOT SELFISH.
I CAME THIS FAR BECAUSE I LONGED TO BE WITH YOU.
I HOPE THAT TEN YEARS FROM NOW, AFTER THE NEXT BARRIER IS PUT UP...
...WE'LL BE ABLE TO COME HERE AGAIN AND LOOK UP AT THE "STARS".

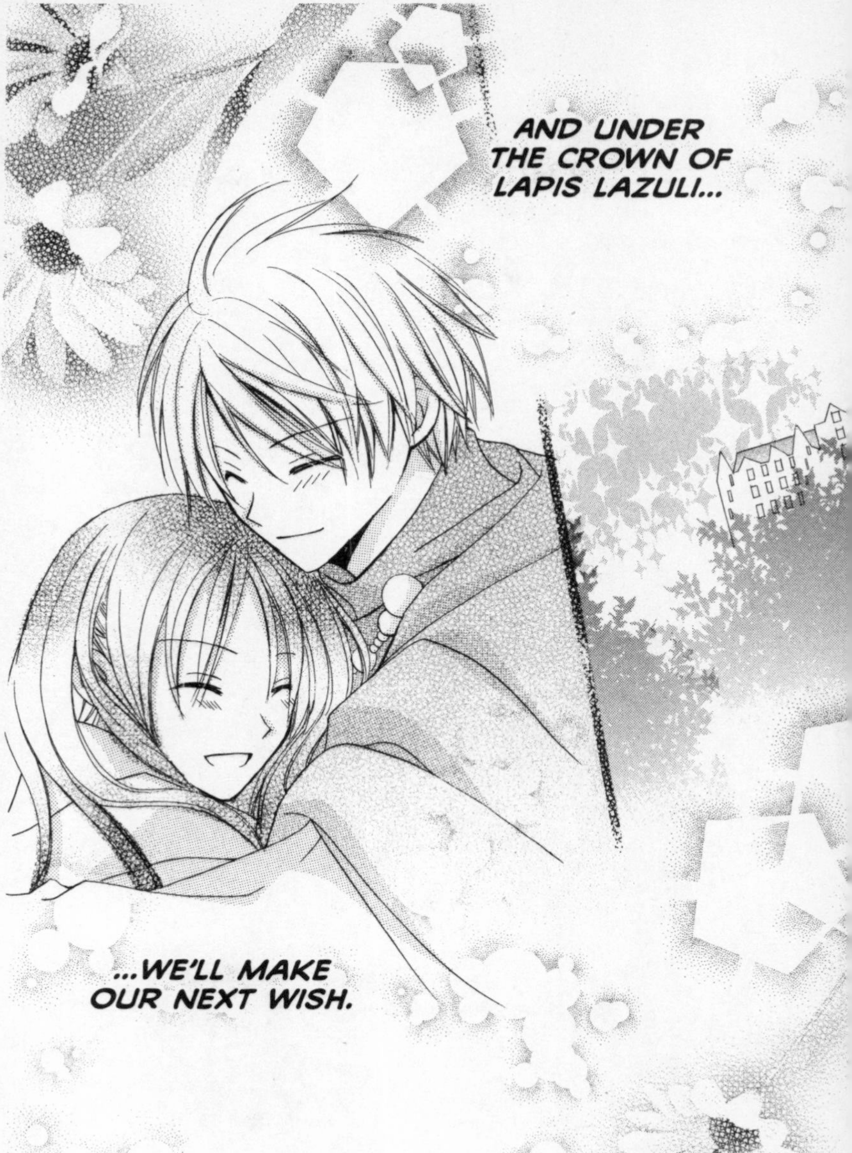
AND UNDER THE CROWN OF LAPIS LAZULI...
...WE'LL MAKE OUR NEXT WISH.

THE CROWN OF LAPIS LAZULI [2] / THE END

Natsuna kawase

THIS IS THE END-OF-VOLUME AFTERWORD.

THANK YOU FOR READING TO THE VERY END.
THIS IS THE FINAL VOLUME OF "THE LAPIS LAZULI CROWN".

EVENTS KIND OF RAN DOUBLE TIME IN THIS SECOND VOLUME, BUT I HOPE YOU ENJOYED IT.

THERE ARE SOME PLACES IN THE FINAL EPISODE WHERE I WISH I HAD A FEW MORE PAGES, BUT AT LEAST I GOT TO FINISH MY STORY WITHIN THE ALLOTTED PAGE COUNT. THE SCENES THAT DIDN'T MAKE IT IN FEATURED OTHER CHARACTERS, BUT TO SORT OF MAKE UP FOR THAT, I WROTE AND DREW A FEW "SINGLE PANELS" TO SHOW WHERE I WAS GOING WITH THOSE "LOST SCENES". I'LL LET YOUR IMAGINATION FILL IN THE REST. HOPE YOU LIKE IT.

AGAIN, I'D LOVE TO HEAR YOUR THOUGHTS ABOUT THIS SERIES. IF YOU WANT TO SHARE, SEND ME A MISSIVE TO:

NATSUNA KAWASE
C/O CMX
888 PROSPECT STREET SUITE 240
LA JOLLA, CA 92104

THE PICTURE BELOW SHOWS RADI (14) AND CITRONA (10) ENGROSSED IN A HANDICRAFT.

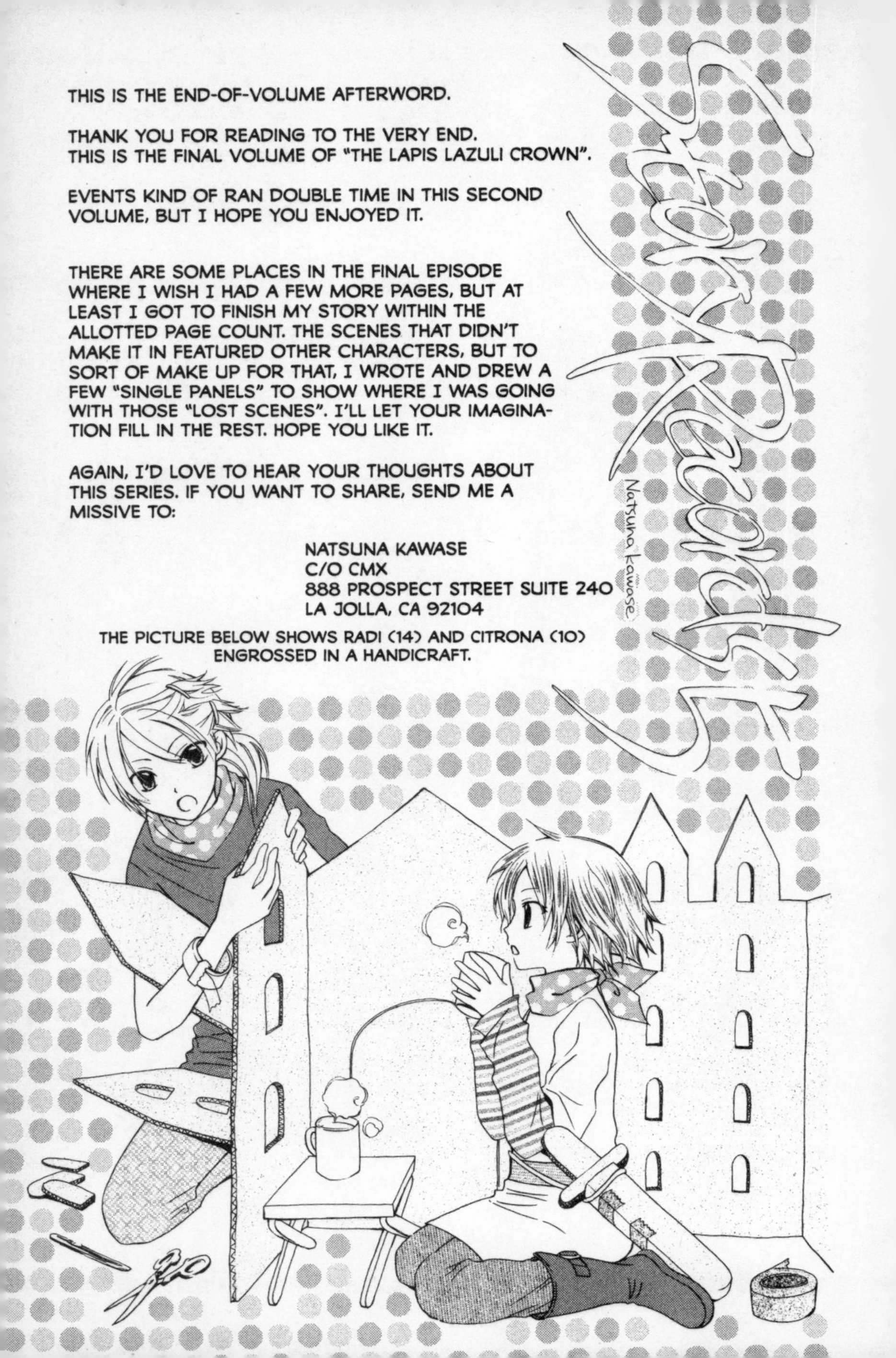

"RENEE, WHAT COURSE ARE YOU GOING TO TAKE? IF YOU'RE AIMING TO BE AN ADVANCED MAGIC-USER, YOU'D BETTER START STUDYING NOW. I'LL TUTOR YOU AND YOU CAN PAY ME FOR IT ONCE YOU BECOME SUCCESSFUL."

"DON'T SUBMIT TO SARA'S GREED. YOU CAN BECOME A MAGIC-USER AT THE PALACE WITHOUT THE ADVANCED QUALIFICATION."

"TRUE, BUT I TUTORED YOU AND YOU ENDED UP AT THE PALACE, MIEL."

"...I WANT TO BECOME A MAGIC TEACHER TO CHILDREN. I THINK I'M GOING TO HELP MOTHER WITH HER CRAM SCHOOL. DON'T WORRY ABOUT ME, YOU TWO..."

(WATCHING THEM STAND OUT IN EVERYTHING THEY DO HAS CONVINCED ME THAT "NORMAL" IS THE WAY TO GO...)

"I'VE GOTTEN STRONGER. MAYBE I'LL BE ABLE TO GO TO TOWN WITH YOU, EVENTUALLY, RADIAN."

"YOU COULD EVEN GO NOW! WE'LL JUST HAVE SEIGLE PUT A BARRIER AROUND YOU FIRST. I KNOW! NEXT TIME, WE'LL ALL GO! WE CAN SNEAK OUT OF THE PALACE AND I'LL GIVE YOU A TOUR OF THE TOWN!"

"REALLY? YAYYY! ♡"

"I'M SURE YOU TWO THINK YOU'LL GET MY COOPERATION, BUT IF IT'S BOTH OF YOU TOGETHER, YOU CAN FORGET THE SECRECY. IT'LL BE IMPOSSIBLE."

"IN THAT CASE, SIEG WILL GET PERMISSION FOR US." "I CAN'T WAIT!"

AS CITRONA GROWS, HE GETS A LITTLE PHYSICALLY STRONGER.

"Y'KNOW, I LIKE STRONG-WILLED GIRLS."

"WELL, ROSETTE'S OFF LIMITS!...HEY, HOW'D YOU KNOW SHE'S STRONG-WILLED?"

"WHAT DO YOU WANT, AN APOLOGY FOR MY PERSONALITY?!"

"I OFTEN GO TO THE BUREAU OF MEDICAL CARE, WHERE SHE TREATS ME FOR INJURIES."

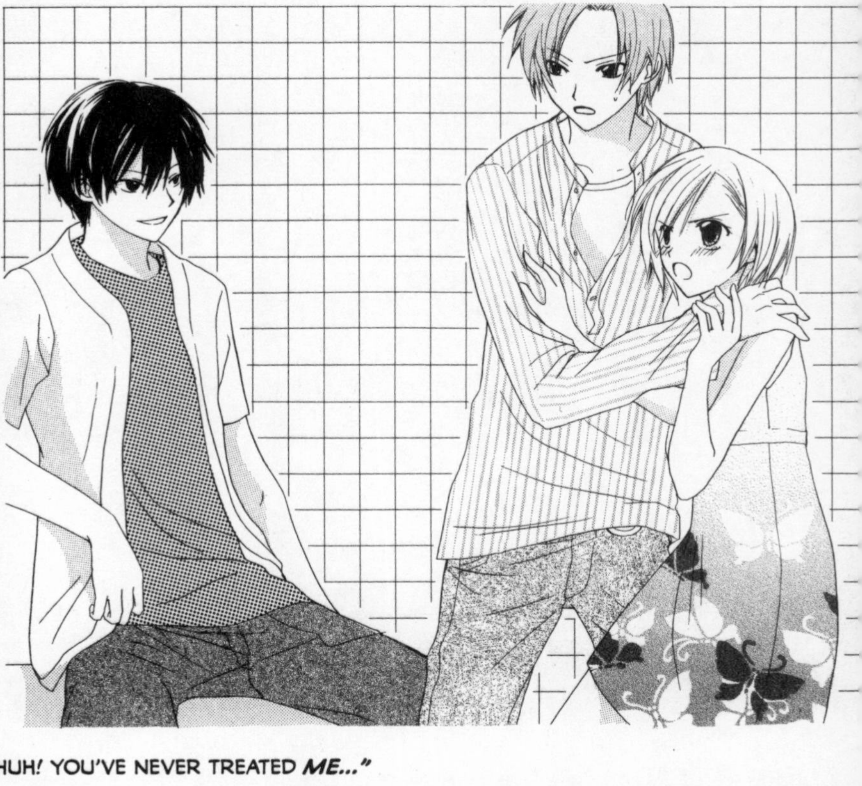

"HUH! YOU'VE NEVER TREATED ***ME...***"

"YOU NEVER GET HURT, SEIGLE. AND IF YOU DID, YOU COULD HEAL YOURSELF, RIGHT?"

ROSETTE'S AT THE BUREAU OF MEDICAL CARE. SEIGLE IS GOING TO TAKE THE TEST TO BECOME AN ADVANCED LEVEL MAGIC-USER. MAYBE DERRIS WILL GET MORE POPULAR WITH THE LADIES AS HE GETS OLDER.

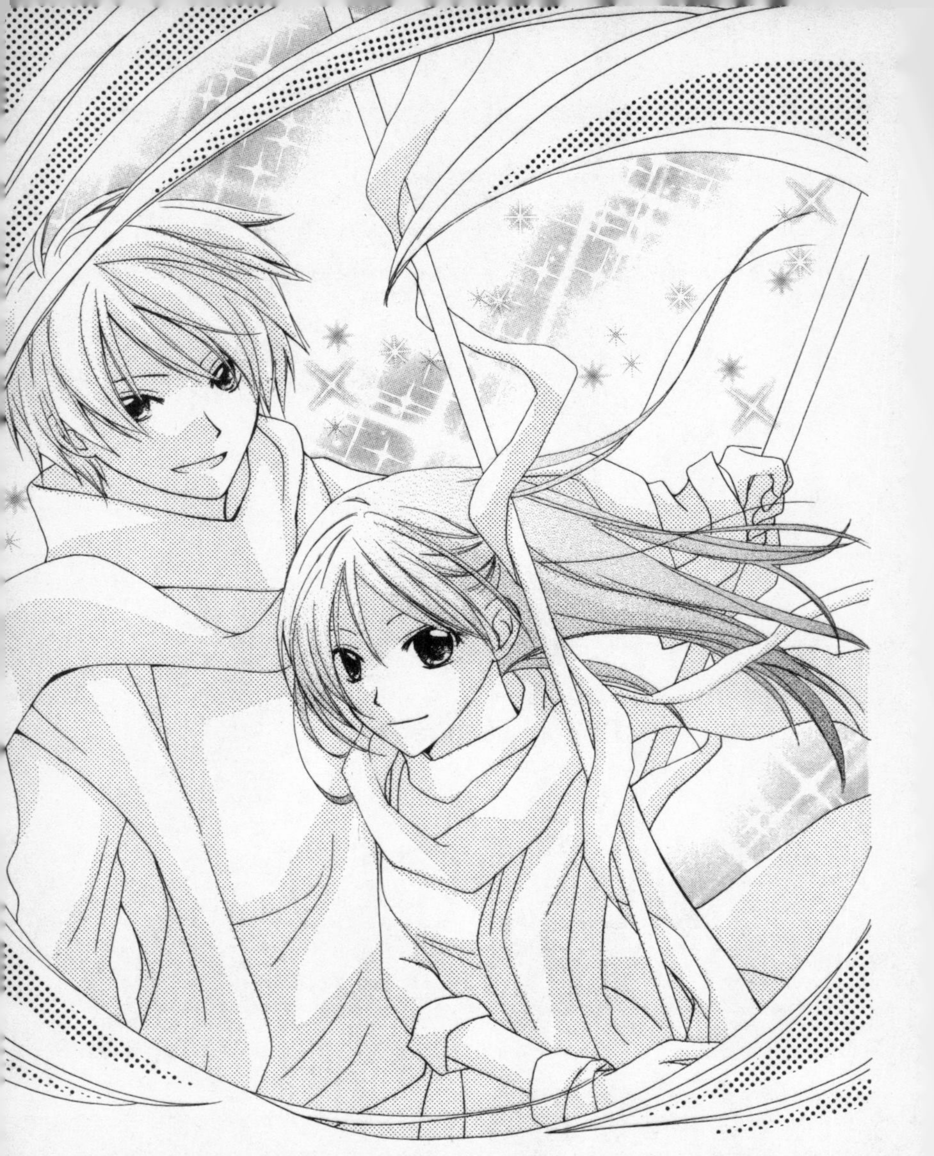

I DID A LOT OF PLANNING FOR THIS SERIES AND BY THE END, I HAD AN OVERFLOWING FILE OF MEMOS. I WASN'T ABLE TO USE EVERYTHING, BUT I HAD A GOOD TIME WRITING AND DRAWING "CROWN". I HOPE ALL OF YOU WHO READ THESE VOLUMES ALSO ENJOYED VISITING THIS WORLD. FROM HERE ON OUT, I'M GOING TO KEEP TRYING TO MAKE EVEN MORE INTERESTING STORIES. I'LL DO MY BEST, SO PLEASE KEEP READING.
FINALLY, I'D LIKE TO THANK MY EDITOR, EVERYONE WHO HAD ANYTHING TO DO WITH THIS SERIES (YURIN, ASAMIN, YOU'RE ALWAYS A HUGE HELP!), AND ALL OF YOU READERS.

THANK YOU VERY MUCH!! NATSUNA KAWASE

STORY RECORDS 5 / THE END